FOR REFERENCE

The Greenwood Encyclopedia of Clothing through World History

The Greenwood Encyclopedia of Clothing through World History

Volume 3
1801 to the Present

Edited by Jill Condra

GREENWOOD PRESS
Westport, Connecticut • London

Library of Congress Cataloging-in-Publication Data

The Greenwood encyclopedia of clothing through world history / edited by Jill Condra.
   p. cm.
  Includes bibliographical references and index.
  ISBN 978-0-313-33662-1 ((set) : alk. paper) — ISBN 978-0-313-33663-8
((vol 1) : alk. paper) — ISBN 978-0-313-33664-5 ((vol 2) : alk. paper) — ISBN
978-0-313-33665-2 ((vol 3) : alk. paper)
  1. Clothing and dress—History—Encyclopedias. I. Condra, Jill, 1968-
GT507.G74 2008
391.009—dc22   2007030705

British Library Cataloguing in Publication Data is available.

Library of Congress Catalog Card Number: 2007030705
ISBN: 978-0-313-33662-1 (set)
      978-0-313-33663-8 (vol. 1)
      978-0-313-33664-5 (vol. 2)
      978-0-313-33665-2 (vol. 3)

First published in 2008

Greenwood Press, 88 Post Road West, Westport, CT 06881
An imprint of Greenwood Publishing Group, Inc.
www.greenwood.com

Printed in the United States of America

The paper used in this book complies with the
Permanent Paper Standard issued by the National
Information Standards Organization (Z39.48-1984).

10 9 8 7 6 5 4 3 2 1

Contents

Preface

The history of clothing and world history go closely in hand, and to trace the evolution of clothing is to trace events that occurred in times and places long ago. Within the context of world events, clothing is a vital piece of material culture that can help to understand what has happened in the past and how it has affected our present. The way in which people dressed throughout time has always indicated, to a great extent, who they are. It also has been an indicator of where they come from, their lot in life, their wealth or poverty, or their occupation. Starting at the cradle of civilization, the following chapters and those in the other volumes trace the evolution of dress from prehistoric times through the classical eras of Rome and Greece to the Middle Ages and onward to the most recent times.

The study of clothing was once solely the provenance of the art historian, interested from the perspective of the paintings and sculptures they studied to understand what the subjects of the art were wearing. This process helped to authenticate and date the art but was not a study unto itself. It wasn't until the last half of the twentieth century that costume/clothing/dress history has become a subject of interest for its own sake. Still closely related to the study of art history, those who study costume have evolved in their own discipline from producing "hemline histories" to developing material culture models, based on anthropology and other methods, to put the clothing they find and study into context.

While a hemline history might look solely at the costumes and their minute details, tracing the evolution of a feature, such as the length of a hemline, to its most recent incarnation, little else about history is included. These original studies of dress were often seen by self-described "serious" historians as elitist and merely the domain of the connoisseurs, implying that although it may be interesting to look at fashion, it was not exactly important in the face of more rigorous study of military, political, or religious histories, for example. Clothing, and especially fashion, is often seen as frivolous and not the domain of the serious academic, and the original costume historians faced this criticism continually.

In light of this criticism, and as interest in tracing the evolution of clothing became more popular, things began to change. It became obvious that neither costume nor the other aspects of history can be studied in isolation and still provide a full picture and true understanding of history. Tracing the roots of clothing styles by looking at the geography, social setting, political situation, religious affiliation, technological development, pop culture (especially from the 1920s onward), and so forth gives the context from which to look at what people wore and perhaps sheds better light on the reasons they chose to wear the clothes they did. It can also do the reverse and shed light on why certain other social, political, or economic events occurred. Trade, for example, has always been heavily influenced by fashion demands around the world, and many a country has its roots in the trade of textiles used for fashion purposes (e.g., demand in Europe for the fashionable beaver hat allowed for exploration, trade, and development in the newly established colonies of Canada and the establishment of the Hudson Bay Company).

The original clothing histories that concentrated specifically on the clothes themselves remain a gold mine for modern costume and clothing historians and provide a wealth of detailed information about the garments, showing how they were worn and how they were constructed, often showing patterns and details of the textiles that allow students of costume to see every aspect of the garments. Much in the way of general social history can be gleaned from these sources, and taken together with the kind of studies such as the one in this series, a very thorough picture of clothing and world history can be achieved.

PROBLEMS WITH COSTUME EVIDENCE

As many of the authors in these volumes suggest, depending on the era, the sources of evidence to study dress are sometime difficult to interpret and trust as absolute. Unless there is an actual garment, or set of garments, other kinds of evidence must be used to look at the costumes people wore. These sources might include cave drawings, sculptures of the early Greeks and Romans, wall paintings in tombs, hieroglyphics from ancient Egypt, literature, journals, legends, oral histories, paintings of the seventeenth century, or photographs of the twentieth century.

The problem with any of these sources is that the are inherently biased, taken only from the perspective of the painter, photographer, or writer, who is free to embellish or gloss over aspects of the actual situation as he or she feels is fit. Painting a portrait in the eighteenth century, an artist may have been asked to omit a certain less-than-flattering feature of the subject, thus altering the evidence for future study, while presumably pleasing the person who was paying him. It is impossible to know for sure what is true in a depiction of a costume and what is idealized, but nevertheless the evidence is crucial, and the process of gathering as much detail as possible will allow the student of history to piece together a fairly accurate picture of the real thing.

Taking the evidence and backing it up with other sources of historical record only adds to the relative certainty of the claims made about the clothing people wore. Tracing the influences from one set of evidence to the next gives a clearer picture of the whole. The best source of evidence, of course, is the actual garment itself. But, unfortunately, given the organic nature of textiles used until relatively recent times, there are few very early garments surviving intact. As one progresses through time from the early prehistoric period, more and more pieces survive, and these account for the increased amount of information available for the past four centuries or so. Before that, there is little actual material culture left to study. We are fortunate enough to occasionally find the odd textile piece that has been preserved by luck in the dry deserts of Egypt, and there have been the chance discoveries of perfectly preserved "bog people" whose entire person is still intact, clothes and all (even the food they ate just before they died can be determined!). The problem, though, is that as soon as the textiles are exposed to oxygen and humidity, the process of decay begins immediately.

In later time periods, the luscious garments were used and reused, then sold secondhand to poorer people who wore the garments until they were threadbare and then used them for other purposes. As a result, very few extant pieces survive from before the late sixteenth and seventeenth centuries. For the student of these and later centuries, there are many surviving garments. Yet even these only tell part of the story. This is due to the fact that the extant pieces are usually only the most important garments worn by the wealthiest and most privileged in a society. It is very rare indeed to find a museum well stocked with peasant tunics and aprons. What does survive, and what is so alluring for those of us who adore textiles of any kind, are the beautiful and luxurious gowns, sumptuous skirts, and coats with over-the-top decorations. Often these garments were worn by royalty or courtiers in the great courts of Versailles or Florence in the romantic and exquisite Renaissance. These garments do not, however, represent what everyday people wore in their jobs and occupations. To embark on a study of peasant dress would be a short journey with so little available.

The existing gowns and men's suits, though not showing all facets of society, do represent the most fashionable of the time and are a good representation of the affluence that was shown on the backs of the aristocracy. Their garments were worn as symbols of who they were, where they were stationed in life and society, and to what class of people they belonged. Competition was blatant, and both men and women tried their best, in many eras, to outdo each other in their show of status through their clothing.

It is with all this in mind that costume historians undertake the study of clothing and fashion changes over time. As with any kind of history, the evidence provides only partial information, and so it is even more important to combine all aspects of history, in an interdisciplinary manner, to provide the context for the most accurate picture to be analyzed. Looking at social history alongside the clothing evidence, imperfect as it may seem, gives an excellent taste of the past.

GETTING DRESSED

What people wear on their bodies depends not only on the physical conditions in which they live but also on the availability of resources, the amount of money they have, and their associations within their communities. Clothing is the most personal of effects and can tell more about a person and the life he or she leads than any other kind of material history. The clothing artifact is precious for historians and anthropologists who study materials of the past. While an ancient piece of pottery or an eighteenth-century chair is valuable to the archaeologist, it indicates only a certain amount about the people who used it. It may inform about the materials available and the technology and design sense of the maker, but not about his size, habits, or personal preferences. On the other hand, clothing can tell a great deal about the individuals who wore the clothes, and as such is very valuable to study.

People wear clothes for a number of reasons, including protection from the environment, identification, status, comfort, sexual allurement, beauty, and a myriad of others. It is a recurring theme from chapter to chapter in these volumes that, in all the times and places throughout history, people appear to have dressed for the same reasons as we still do today. How those ideals manifested themselves is what differs from period to period and place to place. For example, what is now considered attractive or a symbol of great status would certainly not have been read the same way in the Renaissance or ancient Egypt—though there are similarities. Precious stones were and remain valuable and show a certain something about the wearer, namely, that they can afford such items. However, the extremely casual nature of clothing in today's society would have been unheard of in times gone by and would have seemed not only unflattering to the human form but also immoral.

Dress has been indelibly linked to manner and morals for centuries, and this is just some of the information clothes can communicate. The functions of dress have varied in detail over the centuries, but have remained clear identifiers of the people, place, and time of its wearing.

SCOPE OF THE VOLUMES

There are many terms used in the study of clothing, and they are often used interchangeably to mean what people wore. However, there are some very subtle differences, and it is worth identifying these differences at the outset of this study of clothing in world history. To talk about *clothing* means to talk about the garments people wore, to be sure, but it also encompasses other parts of the decoration and covering of the human form. In this set of volumes, the textiles used for clothing is a great focus, as are the changes seen over time, but there are also frequent glimpses of the other elements that went into personal adornment. Jewelry, headwear, shoes, bags or purses, and other accessories that are held, draped, tied, and attached to the body all affect the clothing of the wearer and the look it achieves. This study undertakes to look at all these things within the parameters of both high-fashion, and where possible, peasant clothing.

Dress is a term applied, like *clothing*, more generally to the entire outfit or trend in styles worn by people through the ages. *Costume* implies, increasingly it seems recently, theatrical and special-occasion or fancy dress—things not worn as a norm—but the term is also still used to identify the garments and accessories generally. *Adornment* is another term that identifies objects worn to enhance and dress the body.

These terms are all used as a way of talking about the same or similar things, but depending on the country or culture in question, different terms seem to be more common than others. For example, museums in the United Kingdom tend to have "costume collections," but "dress" is often used in discussion about the garments themselves. For the purposes of this book, all these terms are used purposefully to denote the wearing of garments, both of the wealthy and not-so-wealthy, as well as accessories, cosmetics, hairstyles, and anything to do with how people looked in history.

To make the study as complete and true to the title as possible, historical divisions have been identified into chapters grouped together in the three volumes. All three attempt to cover the important political, social, economic, technological, and cultural history of the times. Introductions to each chapter deal with the major events of the time and place. Each chapter then delves into the clothing people wore and ties the events to the choices people made in their dress.

Early history is covered in volume 1, looking at clothing from prehistoric times to the end of the Middle Ages and Byzantine eras, roughly to 1500. In this volume, discussions focus on several cultures from around the Western world, including Egypt, Greece, Rome, Persia, and the northern portions of continental Europe. Volume 2 follows clothing history from the sixteenth century through 1800 and looks at clothing in Europe, North America, Latin America, Japan, Korea, India, and China. This volume opens with the postrevolutionary period in Europe at the start of the nineteenth century and covers the history and dress of people throughout the increasingly small world, examining aspects of dress from most regions of the world where there is historical record.

This set of volumes, however, does not claim to cover all of history in all of the world throughout time. This would be an impossible undertaking, so it is with care that the geographical and time divisions have been chosen, as they represent a good sample of the events that were occurring around the world and how these events affected the ways people clothed themselves. Commonalities are evident if close attention is paid to the details within each chapter. For example, rituals surrounding moving from childhood to adulthood are roughly similar in all places and times and usually involve a change in dress style, often accompanied by a ceremony to mark the occasion. Dressing for status and identification is another common theme, as is the idea that children through time and to the present, with few exceptions, have dressed in a strikingly similar manner to their parents after babyhood.

Clothing in every culture and time period is used for ceremonial purposes and carries great meaning and symbolism. Coronation gowns and liturgical attire are painstakingly designed and made, and each element might represent some important idea associated with the monarchy or priesthood. In some eras where religion is of utmost importance to the development of culture, religious garb is studied, but this is not necessarily an important part of clothing in all places or in all time periods and so is not discussed in other chapters at all. It is impractical in a work of this huge scope to look at the same aspects of dress throughout. Instead, the time, events, and place dictate the differences in subheadings to most appropriately fit the subject matter. So, during the Byzantine era, religious garb is studied, but once the late twentieth century is covered, religious clothing is no longer emphasized.

Military dress can be a study unto itself, and there are many books and websites devoted to the evolution of armor and military uniforms. In this book, armor is described, for example, in terms of the Renaissance, when it was commonly worn by people; it is also noteworthy as a useful piece of durable material culture, because much has survived where many contemporaneous textile artifacts have long decayed. Military uniforms are revisited in the twentieth century in the context of the two world wars and the effect this look had on regular clothing of nonmilitary men, women, and children.

Looking at different places during the same time period will reveal a certain sameness in the clothing people wore. There was often one prevailing style, with deviations in detail from place to place. When explorers were off discovering new places in the name of their European homelands, they often brought their own distinct styles and textiles, which were traded with the locals, hence creating a merging of styles all over the world. The interchange of goods, especially textile goods, helped to shape the shared fashion choices among many people far away from each other, resulting in features that were often the same or very similar. People in Latin America, for example, in many time periods wore styles very similar to—and with certain aspects exactly the same as—those in France; in the middle of the twentieth century, women in Buenos Aires were seen in the highest of high fashions from the French runways. Cultural highlights might distinguish certain aspects and interpretations of the *haute couture* fashions, but they were also decidedly the same in many respects.

What this book is not is a look at the folk costumes of the countries and times within the scope. While there is the occasional mention of folk dress—the Scottish kilt, for example—there is little discussion of folk attire. That facet of study needs its own series of books with a concrete plan to study all the costumes in cultures, historical and more recent throughout time.

HOW TO USE THIS BOOK

These volumes have been written by some of the best writers in the area of costume studies, who are often specialists in one area or era in clothing history and have spent a good deal of their lives dedicated to the study of clothing history.

In this look at history and clothing, the abbreviations BC (Before Christ) and AD (Anno Domini) have been replaced with the newer parlance of BCE (Before the Common Era) and CE (Common Era).

At the beginning of each chapter, a timeline allows a quick reference to what occurred, both in terms of general history and developments in the areas of clothing and textiles, in the relevant geographical areas. Some of the timelines are more complicated and indicate a greater amount of available information, while others simply outline some of the key world and textile-related events.

Following the timelines are the introductions to the general histories of time and place. These vary according to what happened in the specific period and location and are reflections of economics, political structure and events, monarchies, exploration, technological developments, governments, social pressures and concerns, religion, military history, and international affairs. All of these are meant to provide the reader with the context needed to understand the clothing section that follows.

The portion of each chapter directly related to clothing begins with a general introduction to the themes in dress of the age and place. Then dress is looked at in terms of gender, with men's and women's clothing separately discussed. The important items of clothing are mostly defined within the text, but words that are specific to clothing history and may not be commonly known are also contained in a glossary at the end of each volume. Each chapter is illustrated with images that reflect what is described—paintings, decorations, or photographs of the actual clothing, depending on the time period. While some images are placed within the text, many more are contained in the color inserts in the center of the volumes. Children's clothing is covered in a necessarily smaller section at the end of each chapter, owing to the fact that there is often little information pertaining to the children, especially in very early times, and also that children often dressed in the same or similar styles to their parents. Most chapters also contain a number of highlighted boxes with curious or intriguing information about a certain aspect of the history.

At then end of each chapter, there is a list of recommended books for further study, along with a few websites that will help with further research on the topic and time period. These resources are followed by a list of suggestions (by no means exhaustive) of films, documentaries, or television shows that do a good job of depicting the costume history of the time and place in question. There are markedly more such films available for more recent or modern history, of course. The lists vary in terms of the dates they were made and the countries, but all are English-language movies or programs.

TEXTILE TERMS FROM FIBERS TO FABRIC AND CLOTHING

In order to understand some of what is contained in these books it is important to start this process with some of the basic textile and clothing terms needed to read and comprehend the information. Following is a list of the key terms:

Textile: A general term applied to fibers, yarns, and fabrics; anything to do with the production of these things is part of the textile complex.

Fabric: The piece of cloth used to construct garments and other soft goods. It can be a knit, woven, or nonwoven fabric.

Knit fabric: A fabric produced by one continuous yarn interlooping with one or more yarns. It is stretchy and was not commonly used before the seventeenth century.

Woven fabric: A fabric made through the process of weaving on a loom. Looms have been used in different forms since the beginning of time. Weaving is a process whereby a *warp* thread—the lengthwise thread running vertically on the loom—is alternately interwoven with the *weft* threads that run horizontally, creating a pattern. These threads sit at 90° angles to one another and can be made into all kinds of patterns and designs. Woven fabrics were made as early as the discovery of fibers.

Yarns: Threads that are spun (twisted) from loose fibers cultivated in a range of ways. The spun yarn can be further twisted with other yarns to create *plied yarns* of greater bulk and strength. Yarns can be made from natural fiber or manufactured fibers, or a combination of these.

Fibers: The base substance of yarn. These can be *staple length* (shorter) or *filament length* (longer) and are generally twisted to make the yarn used to make fabric. Fibers can be either natural or manufactured.

Natural fibers: Fibers that are either *cellulosic* and come from plants, such as cotton or linen, or *protein*-based and come from animals or insects, such as wool and silk. Except for silk fiber, natural fibers are *staple* (short) length and are twisted into yarns. Silk, a natural filament yarn, is extruded from the silkworm in one continuous strand.

Manufactured fibers: Fibers made from chemicals extruded through a spinerette into long continuous filaments, which can be cut into staple lengths if desired. These include nylon, polyester, and spandex, to name just a few.

Dyes: Textiles are dyed in many different colors and have been for hundreds of years. They can be dyed with natural or synthetic dyes now, but historically dyes were found in nature and applied to natural fibers. Often maintaining color on textiles was a problem, and *mordants* became a necessary part of the dyeing process. Dyes are generally from an organic source, that is, plant or animal matter. Historical sources of natural dyes include berries, insects, flowers, and other naturally occurring substances. Dyes, which are much smaller molecules than pigments, do not adhere to the surface of a fiber or textile material but rather bond with the fiber chemically and color the fibers throughout. Dyes allow fibers, yarns, or whole textiles to be colored at any time during the textile production process. Since their application is so versatile, different effects can be created.

Pigments: When prints were introduced, a different kind of coloring agent than dye was needed. Pastes or pigments are applied to textiles for printing patterns. The color sits on top of the fibers rather than being absorbed into the core of the fiber. Inorganic pigments must be applied, much as paint would be applied, to the textile or fabric as a whole piece, while fibers or yarns are not generally colored with pigments. A modern example of a pigment application would be stamping (direct) or stenciling (indirect), but the principle remains the same.

The Nineteenth Century

Sara M. Harvey

TIMELINE

1804	Napoleon Bonaparte emperor of France; Empress Josephine, his wife, is a great fashion icon
	Frenchman Joseph Marie Jacquard invents an attachment for the loom allowing intricate figured designs, named after him, that are still called Jacquard weaves
1815	Battle of Waterloo in France
1812	The War of 1812 between Britain and United States
1813	Jane Austen's *Pride and Prejudice* published in England
1818	American retailer Brooks Brothers provides mass consumption suits for men
1820	King George installed as King of England
1830	King Louis Philippe installed as King of France
1837	England's Queen Victoria begins her reign
	French brand Hermès starts selling leather goods including luggage and bags
1845	Elias Howe patents the sewing machine
	Workday limited to twelve hours for children in Britain
1848	Karl Marx and Friedrich Engels issue *Communist Manifesto*; in France, the Second French Republic is proclaimed
1851	London's Great Exhibition introduces many new textile innovations at the Crystal Palace
1858	Charles Worth, the first couturier, opens fashion house in Paris
1859	Darwin publishes *Origin of the Species*
1861–1865	American Civil War
1863	Slavery officially ends in the United States
1865	Abraham Lincoln assassinated
1870–1871	Franco-Prussian War resulting in Napoleon III's surrender and abdication; France falls into civil war
1871	Otto von Bismarck is chancellor of Germany
1874	William Morris heads the British Arts and Crafts Movement
1889	Paris hosts *La Grande Exposition Universelle* with the Eiffel Tower as one of the attractions
1890	The development of the Art Nouveau style
1892	*Vogue* magazine launched
1898	Spanish-American War

HISTORY

At the opening of the nineteenth century, two of the most influential countries were rebuilding themselves from the chaos of revolution. The United States won its independence from England in 1776 and France overthrew its monarchy in 1789. In England, a series of unpopular kings made the monarchy unpopular throughout Great Britain and the British Empire; but in 1837 Victoria I ascended to the throne and ruled for sixty-four years. This stability of government in England was a great boon in the midst of the political and social upheaval that would continue throughout the century. Like her predecessor Elizabeth I, this queen would also become so iconic as to lend her name as the major descriptor of the greater part of the century known as the Victorian Age.

England at the start of the century was in poor shape; it had lost the American colonies and by 1810 King George III had become so incapacitated by porphyria[1] that he was removed from rule and his son took over as prince regent. George III is still the longest reigning king in British history. This period in England is known as the "Regency Period" and spans the years 1811–1820, when George III finally died and his son was officially crowned King George IV. The young prince regent was known for his taste and style and was colloquially known as "the first Gentleman of Europe." The Regency period was also a time for great literature. Jane Austen was writing during this time and her novels *Sense and Sensibility, Pride and Prejudice,* and *Emma* continue to be enduring classics. Modern writers strive to emulate her style and there is a subgenre of romance novels known as "Regency Romances" that are placed during this time period.

Although he had been remarkably well loved as regent, George IV was a very unpopular king. His marriage to Queen Caroline was rocky, and the couple only produced one child, a daughter, Princess Charlotte. Tragically, Charlotte and her son both died during his birth in 1817 and left the monarchy with no legitimate heirs. George IV was forced by his ministers to agree to the Catholic emancipation in 1829, which allowed Catholics to sit in Parliament. This often overshadows his other, more popular achievements, such as creating England's first professional police department at Scotland Yard, and his ambitious building projects like the Royal Pavilion at Brighton and the renovations of Windsor Castle and Buckingham Palace. He died in seclusion at age sixty-seven and his brother, William IV, succeeded him in 1830.

William IV had been a sailor and never thought he would be king. He was sixty-two when he took the throne and entirely unprepared for the duties of a monarch. He had been living with his mistress of many years before he was forced into a political marriage in 1818 to Princess Adelaide of Saxe-Meiningen. Unfortunately, none of their children survived past infancy and the succession remained in crisis. Although William IV was not a strong ruler, he did enact several parliamentary reforms that curtailed many electoral abuses of power. This allowed for political power to be shared more effectively between the old wealthy boroughs and the new and burgeoning industrialized cities of England. When William IV died in 1837, his niece Victoria had just reached the age of majority and found herself next in line for the throne.

Victoria I was the only child of Edward, Duke of Kent, who was the fourth son of George III. She was well educated and an accomplished writer and artist. Under Victoria's rule, England established an empire that encompassed a third of the globe and it was said that "the sun never set on the English Empire." She was crowned Queen of the United Kingdom of Great Britain and Ireland in 1837 and then Empress of India in 1876. She was one of the first "constitutional monarchs" of England and wielded considerably less direct political power than her predecessors but commanded terrific influence. She was married to Prince Albert who was of the Saxe-Couberg and Gotha family and was also her first cousin. Because she was queen, it was her duty to propose to him, which she did in 1839. They were married in 1840. Between 1840 and 1857, Queen Victoria and Prince Albert had nine children, all of whom lived to adulthood and were married into other royal and noble households. Victoria and Albert were great patrons of the arts and founded many museums and academies, and also hosted many national exhibitions. When Albert died in 1861, at age forty-two, the queen was devastated. He had been her husband, her companion and dearest friend, and also her most trusted adviser. Victoria sank into a deep depression and remained in mourning for the rest of her life. This triggered the Victorian obsession with death and the complicated mourning rituals for which this era is well known. Victoria did not resume her full royal duties until the end of the 1860s, and even then it was with little of the vigor she had displayed in years past. But she remained involved in all aspects of government until her death in 1901. She is still the longest-ruling monarch in the history of England and she became the symbol for the English Empire and was much beloved by her people. Although there were seven attempts on her life, she never let it dampen her spirits or her attitude toward her subjects. Victoria's death ended the reign of the House of Hanover over England.

Although the Victorian age was one of expansion and invention, there was a darker side to it as well. Victoria was against giving women the right to vote, although she did allow that any person who was worth at least £10 a year could vote. British women were outraged that their monarch, a fellow female, could have say in the governing policies of their country but they could not. She also continued a love-hate relationship with Ireland throughout her life. Victoria loved Ireland and its people, but her Minister to Ireland, Lord John Russell, exacerbated the Irish Potato Famine,[2] also known as the Great Hunger, and is blamed for the very high number of deaths by being too slow to send aid to the starving country. England was still demanding shipments of grain and livestock from Ireland while the Irish people died by the hundreds of starvation and illness. Contemporary scholars have commented that "God sent the blight, but the English made the famine."[3] Queen Victoria's popularity never rebounded in Ireland after the start of the famine in 1845, and her last visit to Ireland in 1900 spurred revolutionaries into the actions that would lay the foundations of the Irish Republican Army and the fight to be free of English rule.

Industrialization also took a heavy toll on England. Although the rise of the factory system gave more people greater access to quality goods at lower prices, it came at a great cost. Workers flocked to cities from rural areas and the population boom greatly taxed the infrastructure and led to poor sanitation, overcrowding, and squalid living conditions. Although these issues were present in other industrialized areas of the world, London's urban slums were forever immortalized by authors such as Charles Dickens.

When Victoria died in 1901, England was a vastly different place than it had been at the beginning of the century. The monarchy was valued and revered, not only nationally, but around the world. England held an esteemed place in the worlds of art, literature, and trade. The nineteenth century in England also saw the rise of the middle class, and by the middle of the century there was a sense of peace and prosperity that would remain steady through the beginning of World War I at the start of the twentieth century.

France also had its fair share of dramatic changes in government. At the dawning of the nineteenth century, the post-Revolution Directoire, an executive council of five men, was straining to maintain control over the country. Napoleon Bonaparte, then a young and ambitious Corsican, had worked his way up from second lieutenant in the French Army to the rank of major general. He was a military genius and his leadership brought French victory over the Austrians in Italy in 1796–1797 and the British and the Turks in Egypt in 1798–1799. He was seen as a great hero by nearly everyone in France, so there was little opposition when he and his co-conspirators staged a coup d'etat in 1799 that named him First Consul. By 1804, he had gathered enough power and influence that he crowned himself Emperor of France. Among Napoleon's first duties were the reorganization of the government into an efficient entity and sweeping reforms of the French educational system. Napoleon was a charismatic leader and his Imperial court was the center of style. His wife, the Empress Josephine, was a woman of elegance and refinement, but sadly she was barren. While she had two children from a previous marriage, she was never able to produce an heir with Napoleon and agreed to a divorce in early 1810. They remained on amicable terms until her death in 1814. Napoleon remarried in March of that year and his new empress, Archduchess Maria Louise, gave birth to a son and heir in 1811.

While empress, Josephine supported her husband's desire for modest and feminine dress that was made from French textiles. Napoleon stimulated the French garment industry by severely restricting such popular items as cotton muslin and elaborately patterned cashmere shawls from India. While Josephine's passion for shawls drove her to continue to import hers without her husband's knowledge, she certainly did her part to keep the French textile and garment industry running in high gear. An inventory of her wardrobe taken in 1809 showed that she possessed 666 winter dresses, 230 summer dresses, and 60 cashmere shawls.[4] Napoleon also had an extensive wardrobe as befitted his station. In 1811, his order for the coming year's clothing included 9 coats of various styles, 48 pairs of breeches, 48 white waistcoats, 48 flannel vests, 4 dozen shirts, 4 dozen handkerchiefs, 2 dozen cravats, 1 dozen black collars, 2 dozen pairs of silk stockings, 2 dozen pairs of socks, 4 hats, 24 pairs of shoes, and 6 pairs of boots.[5]

Although Napoleon's empire would stretch across nearly all of Europe, it would be fairly short-lived. In 1812, Napoleon marched on Moscow and tried to depose the Russian tsar; but the onset of winter forced him to retreat and he was beset by the Russian forces which were far more used to the climate than the French. Prior to this devastating battle, the Napoleonic Wars had been largely successful and Napoleon controlled large portions of continental Europe from Spain and Italy to the edges of the Ottoman Empire (present-day Turkey) and Russia. French confidence in Napoleon's rule was well eroded by the loss of life, and in 1814 Napoleon abdicated the throne and fled to the Island of Elba. Empress Maria Louise served as regent during Napoleon's absences, and when he abdicated, she fled home to Austria and never saw her husband again. Napoleon only remained on Elba for one year, escaping back into France, and back into power, in 1815. This second part of Napoleon's rule is referred to as *les Cent Jours,* the One Hundred Days. The coalition of nations seeking to stop Napoleon's hegemony was ultimately successful and brought about Napoleon's final defeat at Waterloo, Belgium, in 1815. After Waterloo, Napoleon I was exiled to the island of St. Helena where he would remain until his death in 1821. On each occurrence of abdication and exile, Napoleon abdicated in favor of his young son Napoleon François Joseph Charles, known as Napoleon II even though he never officially ruled France in any real capacity. He was taken back with his mother to Vienna, Austria, when she fled France, and he was raised there with the title Duke of Reichstadt. He died in Vienna of tuberculosis in 1832.

In July 1815, the European coalition forces swept into France and restored the Bourbon monarchy. Louis XVIII, brother to the ill-fated Louis XVI, became king. With the return of the Bourbon monarchy, the interest in revival styles became popular and costume balls were commonplace at court. Louis XVIII was succeeded by his brother Charles X in 1824. Charles was a poor ruler and sought to restore absolute rule to France in place of the constitutional monarchy that Louis XVIII had formed. In July of 1830, a three-day revolution ousted Charles X from the throne. The revolutionaries were, once more, comprised of working-class men, journalists, and students. Like their predecessors, they also showed their allegiance to their cause by their dress, rejecting fashionable dress and wearing clothes more suited to laborers instead of stiff collars and wrapped cravats. The Parisians did not approve of Charles' successor, his grandson, and instead offered the crown to Louis Philippe, the Duke of Orleans. Louis Philippe was from another branch of the Bourbon family and his father, although an aristocrat, had been a supporter of the French Revolution.

Louis-Philippe became the last king of France in 1830, but his reign was marked by a great deal of unrest as he proved to be as conservative and uncooperative as the previous king. At first he was commonly referred to as the "Citizen King" and he took the title of King of the French rather than the previous style of King of France. In February 1848, he acquiesced to the revolutionaries and abdicated the throne in favor of his grandson, Philippe. He then fled to England with his wife and lived there until his death in 1850 when his body was returned to France and buried in the family tomb.

With the 1848 rebellion came a desire to abolish the monarchy entirely and France ushered in the age of the Second Republic and elected Louis-Napoleon Bonaparte president. Louis-Napoleon was the son of Napoleon's brother Louis, and Josephine's daughter, Hortense. Like his uncle, this Napoleon also rose quickly to power and secured himself the title of emperor, becoming Napoleon III. The Second Republic became the Second Empire in 1852. During the Second Empire, France once more assumed a place of leadership on the world stage. The Tuileries Palace became the center of French Imperial social life and the beautiful and gracious Empress Eugenie presided over a fashionable court. Although Eugenie's wardrobe for court occasions was lavish, her everyday dress was actually quite simple, and she had little interest in fashion and allowed herself to be dressed for state functions by her couturier, Charles Frederick Worth, an Englishman living and working in Paris.

The Second Empire was a glamorous and prosperous time, but again, like his uncle, Napoleon III's downfall came with war. Although the French were successful in dealing with uprisings in colonial Algeria and the Crimean Wars, the Austro-Prussian War in 1866 was problematic. Napoleon III could not bring himself to ally with Austria even though Prussia's victory would spell disaster for France's power in Europe. With Prussia's defeat of Austria, they came after France next, beginning the Franco-Prussian War. After the French army was defeated by the Prussians in 1870, Napoleon III abdicated the Imperial throne and fled to England with his wife and their son. He died there in 1873. His son was killed fighting for the British in South Africa in 1879. Eugenie, however, lived until 1920. They are all buried in the monastery that Eugenie founded in Hampshire, England.

The Third Republic was forged in a bloody civil war in the spring of 1871 known as the Commune. This Third Republic of France would last through 1940.

The United States became a major player on the world's political stage during the nineteenth century. In 1800, the United States was comprised of only sixteen states, all east of the Mississippi River. Early in the century, there was a strong expansionist movement that continued until 1860, with the start of the American Civil War. The Louisiana Purchase was made in 1803 and it added approximately 828,000 square miles (530 million acres) to the United States' territory. This area, comprising all of modern-day Arkansas, Missouri, Iowa, Oklahoma, Kansas, Nebraska, and Louisiana, and portions of present-day Minnesota, North Dakota, South Dakota, New Mexico, Texas, Montana, Wyoming, Colorado, was bought from the French at a price of $.03 per acre for a total of about $15 million. Thomas Jefferson braved much opposition to make the purchase, which he considered to be tactically necessary to keep the Port of New Orleans in American control and away from any possible interference from France and Spain. Americans were encouraged to push westward across the Mississippi, and to help facilitate this, Meriwether Lewis and William Clark departed for their Corps of Discovery journey up the Missouri River on August 31, 1803. Theirs was the first known party to lead an overland expedition to the Pacific coast and back. The Corps of Discovery expedition lasted from 1803–1806.

During the first decade of the nineteenth century, Thomas Jefferson was the president of the United States. He was born in 1743 in Virginia, the third of eight children. He was taught to read and write in English, French, and Latin. When his father died in 1757, he inherited five thousand acres of land that would eventually become his home, Monticello. Jefferson was the first governor of Virginia, the first secretary of state of the United States, the second vice president of the United States, and the third president of the United States. He is best known for being the principal author of the Declaration of Independence. He was a supporter of states' rights and the separation of church and state. When he left the office of the presidency in 1809, he began work on starting a university that would become the University of Virginia, which opened in 1819 and began classes in 1825. The university library was renowned, and Jefferson would often invite the students, faculty, and staff to his home. Jefferson died on July 4, 1826.

Although the country was hardly a generation out from the Revolutionary War, the United States and England went to war again in the War of 1812. James Madison, who had served as Jefferson's secretary of state, was president. England was also fighting France during this time, and with its forces split, it was much easier for the United States to gain the upper hand. The war was officially ended in 1814 with the Treaty of Ghent. The treaty was ratified by the Americans in February of 1815, but not before the Battle of New Orleans in January where General Andrew Jackson led the American forces to a decisive victory over the British. When news of peace finally arrived on February 13, 1815, the British troops retreated from the United States and sailed back home to England.

James Madison was the nation's fourth president. He was born in Virginia in 1751 and his presidency soon found itself in turbulent times. But with the American success after the War of 1812, a new sense of nationalism revitalized the country and Madison capitalized on its success. He was best known as a contributor to the *Federalist Papers* and compiling the list of constitutional amendments that came to be known as the Bill of Rights. He was also married to Dorothea Dandrige Payne, who went by the nickname "Dolley." Dolley Madison was America's first First Lady and was instrumental in defining the role of the president's wife as an adviser and ceremonial figure. For all intents and purposes, she was Jefferson's First Lady since he was a widower, but she had the privilege to serve as First Lady in her own right when her husband was elected president in 1809. Unfortunately, in the years after his presidency, Madison suffered from poor health and financial hardship. He died in 1836, the last living signatory of the U.S. Constitution.

James Monroe followed James Madison as president of the United States. He was America's fifth president and served from 1817–1825; Monroe was responsible for many noteworthy achievements. He oversaw the acquisition of Florida from the Spanish in 1819, the Missouri Compromise of 1820, and the Monroe Doctrine of 1823. The Missouri Compromise allowed Missouri to remain a slave state, although the other states in the Louisiana Territory would be barred from owning slaves. The idea was to keep a balance of states that allowed slavery and those that did not. When Alabama applied for admission into the Union, its slave-state status was equalized by admitting Maine, a free state. The Monroe Doctrine was seen as a defining moment in early American foreign policy. It proclaimed that Europe could no longer colonize North or South America nor interfere in any way with the independent nations of the Americas. It also stated that the United States would remain neutral in any and all conflicts between European countries, as well as conflicts between the countries and their colonies, unless such actions took place in the Americas.

John Quincy Adams became the sixth president of the United States. He was the son of John Adams, the country's second president, and he won the election in a very unconventional manner. There were five candidates running for president in 1824: John Quincy Adams, Andrew Jackson, Henry Clay, William H. Crawford, and John C. Calhoun. When Crawford suffered a stroke and dropped from the race, there was no longer a clear leader, and after both the popular and electoral votes were counted, none of the candidates could claim a majority, although Jackson claimed to have had the most votes. The decision then went to the House of Representative who dropped Clay from the running and put the remaining three men on a new ballot. Clay then threw his support behind Adams who had been listed first on the ballot. When Adams won the election, he made Clay his secretary of state, which drew many complaints, especially from Andrew Jackson. When Adams was sworn in, he took his oath of office not on a Bible, but on a book of laws. Adams had a considerable amount of trouble with Congress as they were deeply split over the 1824 election. Because of Andrew Jackson, who was a Tennessee senator at the time, and his followers, Adams had a difficult time coming to political agreements with the Congress. With the congressional elections of 1827, Adams had almost no support whatsoever in Congress. When Andrew Jackson won the election of 1828, Adams did not attend his inauguration. Adams's strength was in his foreign policy. He had been a major contributor to the Monroe Doctrine and also forged treaties with many European nations. He was well regarded as a great diplomat by the rest of the world. After leaving the office of the president, Adams served as a congressman for seventeen years, until his death in 1848.

Andrew Jackson became the nation's seventh president, serving from 1829–1837. Jackson was born in South Carolina in 1767 and fought in the Revolutionary War. He moved to Tennessee in 1787 and became a lawyer as well as one of Tennessee's first congressmen. He also served as a senator, Tennessee's attorney general, and a renowned military leader. He cultivated a reputation for being tough and went by the nickname "Old Hickory." Besides the scandal of the 1824 election, Jackson was also known for his brutal handling of the removal of Native Americans. He signed the Indian Removal Act in 1830 and it allowed the president to negotiate the resettlement of native tribes outside of U.S. borders in land farther west. Jackson did not advocate the forcible removal of native populations, but his policies were often interpreted to involve force. His greatest challenge in this arena was with the Cherokee Nation. In 1832, the Supreme Court had ruled that the state of Georgia could not enforce its laws upon the Cherokee tribal lands. Jackson used this issue to negotiate a removal of Cherokee from the area, enticing them with land elsewhere that would not be under any state's jurisdiction. A small faction of Cherokee negotiated the Treaty of New Echota, but the majority of the tribe opposed it. Although thousands of Cherokee signed a petition to protest the treaty, they were ignored and in 1838 federal troops were sent in to forcibly remove the last Cherokee holdouts. Although it was Martin Van Buren who enforced the treaty so brutally resulting in the "Trail of Tears," a march through the South and into Oklahoma where thousands of Cherokee perished, the creation of such a volatile situation is viewed as Jackson's responsibility. Jackson was a man used to getting his own way, and he was often at odds with both his supporters and detractors. In 1835, Jackson was the first president to have an attempt on his life.

When Martin Van Buren came to office in 1848, he found the country in fine shape financially and economically but had the "Indian problem" to contend with. He had been both vice president and secretary of state to Andrew Jackson and his nickname was "Old Kinderhook." And like Jackson, Van Buren's wife died before he was elected and never served as First Lady. Unlike Jackson, Van Buren's presidency was characterized by economic problems and weak foreign policy. He was not elected to a second term.

Following Martin Van Buren as president of the United States was William Henry Harrison, the ninth president of the United States. Harrison had been the first governor of the Indiana Territory and was a general in the battle of Tippecanoe, where he earned the nickname of "Old Tippecanoe." A popular campaign slogan for Harrison and his vice president, John Tyler, was "Tippecanoe and Tyler, too!"[6] Harrison took office at the age of sixty-eight and was, at that point, the oldest man to become president. He also became the first president to die in office. His presidency was the briefest in the history of the office—thirty days.

John Tyler, the vice president, took over the office after Harrison died. He was the first vice president to take over for a president who had died, an action that would become the official process of succession codified by the Twenty-fifth Amendment in 1967. Tyler's greatest achievement in office was the annexation of the Republic of Texas in 1845. Texas had won its independence from Mexico in 1837 and existed as a sovereign nation within North America for nine years. But Mexico viewed the annexation of Texas as a declaration of war and broke off diplomatic relations. The Mexican-American War was begun the following year, in 1846.

The Mexican-American War became the responsibility of the nation's eleventh president, James K. Polk. Polk was a democrat from Tennessee and he was a strong believer of Manifest Destiny, adding a vast geographic area to the United States that dwarfed the size of the Louisiana Purchase. He secured the land that contains present-day Oregon, Washington, and Idaho, and ended the Mexican-American War in 1848 with the Treaty of Guadalupe Hidalgo, which granted the United States the current states of California, Nevada, and Utah, as well as large areas of what is now Colorado, Wyoming, New Mexico, and Arizona for the price of $15 million dollars. By the end of his term, Polk had acquired just about all of what is now the contiguous forty-eight states. He also oversaw the opening of the U.S. Naval Academy in 1845, the issuing of America's first postage stamps in 1847, and the groundbreaking for the Washington Monument in 1848. Polk also signed into law the legislation allowing for the founding and construction of the Smithsonian Institute in 1846. James Smithson, a British scientist, left a bequest to the United States in 1835 for the creation of an establishment to increase knowledge. After eight years of deliberation, Congress decided on a museum system that would be a public and private partnership and the crenellated main Institute building was completed in 1855. During Polk's term in office gold was discovered in California. This added to the already feverish desire to move westward to the Pacific Ocean, and by 1849, the Gold Rush had begun.

Although he was a popular leader, Polk was the first president to retire after only one term and not seek reelection. He died shortly thereafter. His successor to the presidency was Zachary Taylor. Taylor was a military veteran and went by the nickname "Old Rough and Ready." He was the first president ever elected who had never held a public office. He had been a Southern slaveholder but did not want the incoming territories to be slave states. He was eager for New Mexico and California to achieve statehood. California had been a sovereign republic, like Texas had been, for about one month in 1846, at the start of the Mexican-American War. When California was annexed to the United States, the former republic government expressed a great interest in being accepted to the Union as soon as possible. California bypassed the territory stage and applied to the Union as a free state in 1849; it was granted statehood in 1850. Taylor died suddenly and unexpectedly in mid-1850 of gastroenteritis only sixteen months into his term and was succeeded by his vice president, Millard Fillmore.

Fillmore was never elected president; he finished out Taylor's term and failed to get his party's nomination in both the 1852 and 1856 elections. But what Fillmore was able to accomplish was the Compromise of 1850, which sought once again to balance the free and slave states as new territories were being created in the western part of the country. Taylor had been against such a compromise, feeling very strongly that slavery should not be allowed in the new territories. But Fillmore felt that a compromise was necessary to preserve the integrity of the Union. The Fugitive Slave Act was also passed in 1850 and it declared that slaves had to be returned to their rightful owners, even if they had escaped to a free state. The original law had been in existence since 1793, but it was rarely enforced. Additionally, individual state laws often removed that state's responsibility to return escaped and runaway slaves. The Fugitive Slave Act of 1850 made the northern free states complicit in slavery by requiring them to return any slaves that escaped to their areas. This did two things: first, it made the abolitionists reconsider their plans and instead route runaway slaves up to Canada, and second, it ramped up the tensions between the free and abolitionist North and the slaveholding South, and made the breakdown of the Union that led to the Civil War almost inevitable. Fillmore also managed to split his own political party, the Whigs, into northern and southern factions. He also upheld American neutrality in Europe by staying out of the failed Hungarian revolution, but he did seek to open up trade with Japan and sent Commodore Matthew Perry to the island nation. Fillmore served his three-year term without a vice president. Fillmore's splitting of the Whigs led to their eventual collapse and he was the last president of the United States to have been a Whig and to have been neither a republican nor a democrat. Although most of the Whigs went into the Republican Party, Fillmore opted to stay with smaller political groups that better reflected his beliefs.

In 1853, Franklin Pierce took office. He was the first president born in the nineteenth century and the fourteenth person to hold the office. He was a Northerner but was often ridiculed for having Southern sympathies. He was handsome and charming and the youngest president ever to be elected at age forty-eight. Two months before he took office, Pierce and his wife and only living child were involved in a train accident. Pierce and his wife watched with horror as their last son was crushed to death. This greatly affected Pierce as he took office, and it drove his wife into a deep depression. She was very shy and deeply religious and did not participate as First Lady. He is one of the few presidents to have not sworn his oath of office on a Bible; instead, he affirmed it on a book of laws, just as Thomas Jefferson had. Pierce specifically chose his cabinet to include a wide selection of people of different backgrounds and beliefs. His cabinet was, to date, the only one that remained unchanged throughout the entire four-year term of a president. Pierce's major legacy was the Kansas-Nebraska Act of 1854, which essentially repealed the Missouri Compromise of 1820 and reopened the heated debate over slavery in the west. The Kansas-Nebraska act created two territories—one on each side of the 40th parallel—and allowed each of them to choose to allow slavery or not. The Missouri Compromise had banned slavery north of latitude 36° 30'. Both proslavery and antislavery groups poured into Kansas, attempting to secure it as a state that supported their own views. This guerrilla warfare is known as Bleeding Kansas and presaged the Civil War by bringing the latent hostilities about slavery and states rights out into open warfare. This turmoil would come as a surprise to Pierce who thought that giving the territories the right to choose their status would appease the disparate groups. But the two sides played out in the microcosm of the Kansas Territory with the antislavery groups forming the Topeka Constitutional Convention and the proslavery groups forming the Territorial Legislature. The Topeka Constitutional Convention was made up of members elected by the people actually living in Kansas, whereas the Territorial Legislature was elected by those who had come to Kansas from Missouri, the neighboring slave state. Pierce decided to take a larger role in fashioning the government of the Kansas Territory and sent federal troops into Topeka in 1855 to put a stop to the ratifying of the Topeka Constitution, declaring the convention a rebel group. This angered both antislavery groups and those concerned with state's rights. When the convention attempted to rally and apply for admittance to the Union as a free state, more federal troops were sent in.

Pierce was out of office before the Kansas issue was even settled. He was, and still is to date, the only elected president ever to fail to be nominated by his party for reelection for a second term. James Buchanan succeeded him in 1857 and held the office of president until 1861. He was the only U.S. president to date that never married. And he is consistently ranked as one of America's worst presidents, right along with Pierce and Harrison. Buchanan was a supporter of the rights of slave owners and sympathized with their desire to open up Cuba to plantations and slavery. He agreed with the Dred Scott Decision of 1857, which ruled that no one of African descent could ever be a U.S. citizen, slave or free. It also ruled that although Scott had resided in free states and been allowed to legally marry, usually forbidden to slaves, he and his family were still to be considered under the ownership of the Emerson Family. At first, the decision was made by a lower court that Scott and his family were indeed free, but the decision was overturned by the Supreme Court and Buchanan supported it. The Dred Scott case also stated that Congress had no authority to prohibit slavery in the territories. The political turbulence in the Kansas territory was still a top priority to the federal government. In 1857, the Lecompton Constitution, a proslavery document, was accepted by Buchanan but not ratified by the state. Enough antislavery groups boycotted the vote, and the Constitution could not get a majority vote. The Lecompton Constitution was eventually abandoned. Ultimately, Kansas was admitted to the Union under the Wyandotte Constitution as a free state in 1861. But this did nothing to quell the debate between free states and slave states. The congressional floor often erupted with arguments between the two groups; these opposing sides reflected the geographic background of the delegates: northerners and southerners. In addition to slavery, several other issues brought them at odds. During the national convention in Charleston, South Carolina, there was no consensus concerning the next presidential nominee and many of the southern delegates walked out on the convention. Stephen Douglas was ultimately nominated by the Democratic Party. Abraham Lincoln was the Republican nominee and although his name appeared on no southern ballots, he would go on to win the presidency in 1861. The delegates who had left the convention grouped together to form the Confederate States of America in 1861. They were all southern states in primarily cotton-growing areas. South Carolina was the leader of this group, and it took with it seven other states: Mississippi, Florida, Alabama, Georgia, Louisiana, and Texas. Buchanan declared the secession illegal but also felt that he had no legal right to stop them. The Confederate States armed forts and prepared for a battle; they refused to compromise. On the ninth of January, 1861, the federal government sent a civilian ship, *Star of the West,* to deliver supplies and troops to Fort Sumter, a stronghold the government refused to give up. The ship was fired upon by the Confederates as it returned to New York. These were the first shots of the Civil War, but Buchanan made no move to do a thing about it, leaving it all to the next president, Abraham Lincoln.

Abraham Lincoln was the nation's sixteenth president and an outspoken opponent of slavery. He was the first Republican president and he won through the support of the North alone, defeating popular democrat Stephen Douglas and two other candidates. Lincoln was not even on the ballot in nine states. Lincoln was in a very difficult position, which he handled with great delicacy and aplomb, although there were many outspoken groups that tried to rally against him to no avail. Like Buchanan, he refused to acknowledge the Confederacy as an entity separate from the United States and even addressed this issue in his first inaugural address. Lincoln tried to soothe the Confederates and keep the border states from joining in by supporting the proposed Corwin Amendment that would allow slavery to remain legal in states where it was already permitted. But the Confederates were committed to forming their own sovereign country by that point and ignored the amendment, which did not pass the remaining legislature. But Lincoln was opposed to the Crittenden Compromise, which would allow for the permanent existence of slavery and stated that no future law could be proposed by Congress to repeal slavery in the designated slave-South—which was south of the 36°30' line as decreed by the Missouri Compromise of 1850. This compromise was summarily rejected by Congress in 1861 that saw no compromise whatsoever in giving the Confederacy everything that it wanted. At the time Lincoln took office, the Confederacy was no longer willing to reconcile with the Union.

Lincoln was just as unwilling to engage the Confederates militarily as Buchanan had been, but he was willing to take that step if the Confederates were to attack any Union operation. This happened in April of 1861 when Confederates in South Carolina fired on the *Star of the West* at Fort Sumter and captured the Union troops stationed there. Lincoln then called on the state governors to send troops to protect the capital, reclaim taken forts, and protect the Union. Even though the Southern states had seceded, he still believed in the idea of the Union unbroken. Virginia was not willing to send troops to battle against a fellow state, and when the federal government insisted, Virginia joined the Confederate States along with North Carolina, Tennessee, and Arkansas. The remaining slave sates of Missouri, Kentucky, Maryland, and Delaware did not secede and Lincoln promised that there would be no interference concerning slavery in their states. Rump governments that supported the Confederacy were formed in these states, but the Union forces captured and detained the leaders when they were found. Lincoln made it very clear that the war was being fought to preserve the Union and not to abolish slavery. But the Emancipation Proclamation was put into effect on September 1862, serving to erode the structure of the South by destroying its ability to maintain the agrarian lifestyle that sustained their economy. Abolitionists were very critical of Lincoln for taking too much time to press for emancipation and not making it the first priority in the war against the South.

Other domestic issues were still in need of presidential attention during the war. Lincoln was responsible for signing into law the Homestead Act of 1862, which allowed vast tracts of land in the western territories to be purchased at very low prices and the Morrill Land-Grant Colleges Act also of 1862, which provided government grants for agricultural universities in each state. Lincoln also approved grants for the construction of the Transcontinental Railway and for the National Bank. By the end of his first term in 1864, the Union had won key victories at Gettysburg, Vicksburg, and Chattanooga, but the war was beginning to get bogged down in a stalemate thanks to the military skill of the Confederate general Robert E. Lee. Lincoln promoted Ulysses S. Grant to the post of general of Union forces and supported his victory by any means necessary, even though it came at the high cost of many Union casualties. During Lincoln's reelection campaign, he chose Andrew Johnson, a Tennessee Democrat, as his running mate to appeal to Union supporters in the Confederate states. There was a great fear that he would be defeated, and he made a pledge that regardless of the outcome of the election, he would continue to fight the war and bring the Union back together into one peaceful nation. Lincoln gave his famous Gettysburg Address on November 19, 1963, at the dedication of the Soldiers' National Cemetery in Gettysburg, Pennsylvania, about four months after a decisive Union victory at Gettysburg. Although the speech lasted only two minutes and the exact wording has been lost to history, it remains one of the most iconic and legendary presidential addresses in not only the United States, but of the world. Lincoln was reelected in 1864.

The year 1864 was also a turning point in the Civil War. General William Tecumseh Sherman made his famous march to the sea in September of that year, burning Atlanta, Georgia, nearly to the ground and forging on to Savannah. The port of Savannah was captured on December 22, 1864, and the city was spared Sherman's wrath by plying the general with money, guns, and cotton. Although Sherman's scorched-earth tactics have been historically reviled by the people of Georgia, and Atlanta in particular, his military might during that historic march crippled the Confederacy and brought about a much swifter end to the war. Early in the war, Lincoln was very concerned about the rebuilding of the South and had begun to lay plans for the Reconstruction. He was moderate in his views and did not seek to further alienate the South but truly bring the country back together as one prosperous nation as he has promised all along. He faced a great deal of opposition from many in Congress who sought to further punish the South for its rebellion after the war was won. Lincoln put Andrew Johnson in power as the governor of Tennessee after that state fell to Union forces in December 1864 and proposed a plan that would allow Louisiana back into the Union if 10 percent of its voters would agree to it. Radicals in Congress saw this as being far too lenient and passed their own versions of Reconstruction in 1864 with the Wade-Davis Bill. It barred any officer of the

Confederacy from ever voting or holding office and would not allow states to return to the Union until 50 percent of the population swore an "Ironclad Oath" that they had never taken up arms against the Union or willfully supported the Confederacy in any way. Since the majority of the population in the Confederate states was unable to swear such an oath, it would have left those states in political limbo. The Wade-Davis Bill was vetoed by Lincoln and never took effect. When asked what he had planned for the rebels after the defeat of the Confederacy, Lincoln was quoted as saying, "Let 'em up easy."[7]

Unfortunately for the South, Lincoln was assassinated in April 1865, just one month after his reelection. During the play *Our American Cousin* at Ford's Theatre in Washington, DC, actor and Confederate spy John Wilkes Booth sneaked into Lincoln's box and shot him point-blank in the back of the head. Booth then leapt to the stage, breaking his leg, and was said to have shouted, *"Sic semper tyrannis!"* ("Thus always to tyrants!")[8] Lincoln was moved across the street where doctors attended him. He never regained consciousness and was pronounced dead at 7:10 A.M. on the morning following the shooting, April 15, 1865. His body was taken to the White House where he became the first president to lie in state.

Upon Lincoln's death, Vice President Andrew Johnson became the seventeenth president of the United States. He was eager to continue Lincoln's plan to a conciliatory Southern Reconstruction but often vetoed civil rights bills. This made him extremely unpopular with the Congress and a target for congressional radicals who were gaining more support and more control of the government. He was the first president to be impeached; the proceedings began in 1868, but he was acquitted by a single vote. Had his impeachment stood, then a precedent would have been set that it was acceptable to have a president removed for purely political purposes. But Johnson's lasting legacy was the purchase of Alaska from the Russians in 1867. It would prove to be a boon to the United States when gold was discovered there in 1880 and oil in 1968.

Ulysses S. Grant, the erstwhile general of the Union forces, was elected president in 1869 and held office until 1877, serving two full terms. While Johnson was in office, Grant had a strained relationship with him; they were at odds over the treatment of the South and the course of Reconstruction. Grant presided over the last half of the Reconstruction process and did not quite share the lenient views of Lincoln or Johnson, but he was steadfast that there should be an army presence in the South to ensure the rights of freed slaves and he granted amnesty to Confederate leaders. He dealt harshly with the violent Ku Klux Klan and was devoted to protecting not only black Southerners, but pro-Unionists that were being persecuted. Grant was also accused of being an antisemite, but this was an allegation he vehemently denied. His management of financial and economic issues lost the support of not only the Congress but the general public. Financial panics and depressions were common in the 1870s as a struggling South tried to rebound from the impact of the Civil War, and worker strikes were common. Although the railroad business was booming, it was unreliable and many companies went bankrupt. The New York Stock Exchange was closed for ten days in 1873. The financial crisis finally worked itself out about 1879. Grant's greatest legacy is considered to be the establishment of Yosemite National Park in March 1872.

Rutherford B. Hayes followed Grant in one of the nation's most disputed presidential elections in 1876. Samuel J. Tilden had 184 of the electoral votes

versus Hayes's 165, with 20 votes left uncounted. The states in contention were
Florida, South Carolina, and Louisiana. Oregon was also an issue as one of the
electors had to be removed and replaced because he was an elected official. After a long and bitter dispute, the votes were ultimately awarded to Hayes and he
won the presidency. Historians believe that a deal may have been struck that
would help to end Reconstruction and take federal troops out of the South in
exchange for putting a Republican in office. It came to be called the Compromise of 1877 and it had the unfortunate consequence of the eventual loss of
the voting rights of the freed slaves and other African Americans. Hayes was
sworn in as the nineteenth president of the United States in a private ceremony,
in fear that the defeated Tilden's supporters would attempt to sabotage the
event. This ceremony was held on March 3, 1877. Hayes was publicly sworn in
the following Monday, March 5, 1877. Hayes was responsible for the poor handling of the rail workers' strike in 1877. He sent in federal troops to seize control of the volatile situation, and the troops fired on the striking workers.
Eventually, peace was maintained, but Hayes lost a great deal of popular support that he would never be able to win back. But a noteworthy piece of legislation he signed was a bill in 1879 that allowed female attorneys to argue cases in
front of the Supreme Court.

James A. Garfield took office in 1881 and became the first president to be
elected from the House of Representatives. He also became the second president to be assassinated and had the second shortest term in office at six months
and fifteen days. He was shot twice by Charles Julius Guiteau, a disgruntled
man who had not been awarded a post in the government for which he had
applied: the post of U.S. consul in Paris, for which he was not even remotely
qualified. He also was known to be a religious fanatic and mentally ill. Although
the bullet wounds themselves were not mortal, Garfield eventually died of heart
failure after a long battle with several massive internal infections caused by
unsanitary hospital conditions. Guiteau was found guilty of causing the president's death, although it was argued at the time that the substandard medical
care truly caused his demise. Guiteau was hanged for the offense in Washington, DC, on June 20, 1882.

Chester A. Arthur, who had been Garfield's vice president, became the twenty-
first president in 1881. He served a term until 1885. Although Guiteau, who
assassinated Garfield, made mention of Arthur's name at the time of the attack,
Arthur knew nothing about it and had no role in planning the shooting. He was
a cautious man and wary of the factions within the Republican Party. He was also
often melancholy as his beloved wife Nell had died not long before his election,
and he mourned her all his days. He never had anyone else step in as First Lady,
asking only that his sister Mary assist him in caring for his young daughter and
assume a few social duties. His implication in the shooting of Garfield also drove
Arthur into seclusion for over two and a half months until Garfield died and
Arthur had to officially succeed him as president. Arthur was determined to make
the best of his situation and devoted himself to civil service reform, which he
achieved with the Pendleton Act of 1883. He also passed the nation's first general
federal immigration law. Although Arthur sought to be elected in his own right,
he did not win the Republican nomination. He died shortly after leaving office of
a brain hemorrhage in 1886. He was known to be a fashionable man and dressed
the part of the president, always looking elegant and professional.

Grover Cleveland was elected to be the twenty-second president in 1885. He was also elected to be the twenty-fourth president in 1893, making him the only U.S. president to date that has served two nonconsecutive terms. He was also the first Democrat elected since Buchanan in 1856. He was known to be a man of the people who believed in honesty and morals and stood against corruption and imperialism. He pressed for the Gold Standard but alienated those who supported the Silver Standard. He ended the Pullman Strike in 1894, but not in a manner that appeased the striking railroad unions. He was against women's suffrage, saying in a 1905 article in *The Ladies' Home Journal*, "Sensible and responsible women do not want to vote. The relative positions to be assumed by men and women in the working out of our civilization were assigned long ago by a higher intelligence."[9] During Cleveland's second term, Utah was admitted to the Union in 1896.

After Cleveland's first term, Benjamin Harrison was president, serving as the nation's twenty-third president. Harrison was the grandson of William Henry Harrison, the ninth president, who had died in office after only one month. He was a Republican and was best known for his federal spending, said to have reached one billion dollars. Harrison received far less of the popular vote than Cleveland but managed to win the election with the electoral votes alone. Although he was not terribly popular by the end of his term, he was nominated by the Republican Party but defeated by Cleveland who ran again and was elected again in 1893.

William McKinley was the last president elected in the nineteenth century. He took office in 1897 and served until 1901. He revolutionized campaigning with new advertising styles that are still used in modern elections. He was successful in annexing Guam, Puerto Rico, the Philippines, and Hawaii. McKinley easily won his reelection bid in 1900, but was assassinated in Buffalo, New York, in 1901 by Leon Frank Czolgosz. As with Garfield, the initial gunshot wound itself was not fatal, but gangrene set in and McKinley succumbed to it eight days after he was shot. McKinley had been speaking at the Pan-American Exposition and although hi-tech equipment such as electric lights and an X-ray machine were being displayed, none of these things were used to help treat his wounds. Like Guiteau, Czolgosz was found guilty of murder even though he did not directly cause the president's death. He was electrocuted in Auburn Prison in Auburn, New York, on October 29, 1901.

The late nineteenth century was also a time of great romanticism surrounding the American West. Cities like Deadwood, South Dakota; Dodge City, Kansas; and Tombstone, Arizona were the sites of many historic and fictionalized accounts. Fort Dodge, Kansas, was founded in 1864, and Dodge City was established several years later in 1872. It was one of the first frontier towns to grab the public's imagination. The original "Boot Hill" cemetery was thought to have been founded in Dodge City and used until 1878. Deadwood, South Dakota, was a gunslinger town where Wild Bill Hickok and Calamity Jane both lived. Hickok was killed there in 1876 during a poker game. The hand he held contained a pair of aces and a pair of eights and is still known as the "dead man's hand." But one of the most iconic cities of the Old West was Tombstone, Arizona, site of the infamous Gunfight at the O.K. Corral in 1881. Thirty shots were fired in thirty seconds between Wyatt Earp, Virgil Earp, Morgan Earp, and Doc Holliday and Billy Claiborne, Frank McLaury, Tom McLaury,

Billy Clanton, and Ike Clanton. Both McLaurys and Billy Clanton were killed. It is one of the most recurrent scenes in media set in the Western genre.

Aside from cities, a few people made names for themselves. Jesse James and his brother Frank had once been pro-Confederate guerillas in Missouri, but the Civil War had left them and many others destitute. They committed their first bank robbery in 1866 and by 1868 had joined Cole Younger in forming the James–Younger Gang. They fancied themselves Robin Hood types who had been driven to a life of crime by a corrupt and unjust government. Newspapers around the country carried Jesse James's essays and letters, and he became quite a folk hero. Jesse James was finally killed in 1882 while adjusting a picture hanging on the wall of his safehouse. Although rumors abounded that he had in fact survived, no evidence has ever been produced to corroborate them.

Billy the Kid was another outlaw turned folk hero. He surfaced during the Lincoln County Cattle Wars in Lincoln, New Mexico. His aliases included Henry McCarty, Henry Antrim, and William H. Bonney. He was originally part of a quasilegal vigilante group known as the Regulators, hired by John Tunstill, a Lincoln cattle rancher. When Tunstill was killed, the gang vowed revenge and were deputized in order to avenge his murder. He was promised amnesty by the new New Mexico governor Lew Wallace in 1879 for testifying about the events that lead up to the Lincoln County Cattle Wars. The Kid was supposed to be put under token arrest until the trial, but it all turned out to be a ruse in order to capture him. He escaped with the help of his posse of former Tunstill Regulators, known to the Kid as his "pals." Billy the Kid was said to have killed twenty-one people, one for every year of his life, but that number has never been substantiated. Supposedly he was killed by Sheriff Pat Garrett on July 14, 1881, in Fort Sumner. Some sources, including Garrett's wife, say that the Kid was not killed that night and that a double was used to help him escape.

Buffalo Bill Cody was one of the few Old West legends that did not come to a nefarious end. William Cody had been a Pony Express courier, a Union Army scout during the Civil War, a guide for homesteaders heading across the frontier, and one of America's premier showmen. He saw the value of the myth of the American West and created the Buffalo Bill Wild West Show to showcase it. By the end of the nineteenth century, Buffalo Bill was one of the world's most recognizable celebrities, and his Wild West Show had played all over the world, most notably at Queen Victoria's Diamond Jubilee celebration in 1887. More than just an entertainer, Buffalo Bill sought to capture and preserve the essence of the American West, a world that was drastically changing with expansion and development. He was also a strong supporter of the rights of Native Americans and women and spoke out against overhunting the bison. Buffalo Bill founded the town of Cody, Wyoming, in 1896, not far from the gates of Yellowstone National Park. Buffalo Bill died of kidney failure in 1917, but his legacy as one of the best-known heroes of the American West lives on.

The nineteenth century was a time of great change and challenge across the United States, Europe, and the world. The mode of dress changed just as quickly, shifting with the times to reflect the social statements of the day. Advances in printing, photography, and communication made these changes available to a large number of people in a small amount of time. With this historical background, a clearer picture of the dress of this century can be formed.

TRADE AND ITS INFLUENCE ON FASHION

Trade in the nineteenth century was just as important as it had been in previous eras, but now countries like England and France had dedicated colonies and port cities in India, China, and various island nations. Cotton from India was still a very important commodity in Europe. The Empire fashion for ladies in France in the early part of the century called for yards of fine, white muslin. Silk had never lost its appeal or prominence and imports of Chinese and other Asian silks were still very high, especially as secure sea routes allowed for much faster and safer transportation to Europe. But soon, domestic replicas were being produced and demand for foreign goods dropped off. This was helped by many European governments attempting to restrict imports and bolster their own industries and economies. A richly patterned wool shawl was the accessory of choice for the well-dressed Empire woman. Napoleon's wife Josephine had a collection of sixty shawls and there was a mania for them in France as well as in England and throughout Europe. These shawls, called *shāls,* had originated as a part of men's wardrobe in Kashmir, a northern province of the Indian subcontinent.[10] The fiber came from the soft undercoat of the Kashmir goat, known by the Anglicized name of *cashmere,* and was woven into luxuriously soft shawls with traditional motifs. It is not known exactly when these shawls first came to Europe, but by the opening of the nineteenth century they were all the rage and the demand far exceeded the supply. The shawls were originally made by hand on small looms in the Kashmir area and featured designs of *būtās,* traditional motifs of flowering plants[11] and *boteh,* images representing the stylized shoots of the date palm.[12] But as Indian production could not keep up with European demand, domestic weavers in Europe began to create imitations. The largest of these imitation shawl operations was in Paisley, Scotland. Using the Jacquard loom and local fibers, the Scottish mills in Paisley began to produce great quantities of shawls. As the shawls were being created in Europe, they were also being assimilated. Slowly, the traditional motifs from India began to change and take on characteristics indicative of the art and decorative tastes of Europe. The stylized shoots and flowers had changed shape, looking more like a teardrop or pinecone. This motif became so closely linked with the Scottish weaving mills that they began to be known as "paisley shawls" after the name of the town in which they were made. Soon after, any shawl, regardless of origin, was referred to as "paisley" if it was decorated with that motif.[13] By the late nineteenth century, the paisley design was so popular and in such demand that Indian manufacturers were creating it specifically for export.

In 1830, fanciful hairstyles based very loosely on Chinese styles of hairdressing were very popular. They were referred to as *à la Chinoise* and showed that China was still a major source of trade and an influence on fashion. *Chinoiserie* had been a popular mode for decorative arts and fashion throughout the seventeenth and eighteenth centuries. But China would suddenly be forced from the spotlight of public interest when Japan opened its ports to Western trade in the middle of the century. China, Russia, Europe, and the United States had all been vying for the opportunity to engage Japan in trade. Japan's isolation was also cause for concern among seafaring countries that neighbored Japanese waters.

In July of 1853, Commodore Matthew Perry sailed into Tokyo Bay with a small American naval force and dropped anchor. Perry carried a letter from President Millard Fillmore requesting that Japanese ports be opened to trade and welcoming of ships requesting aid and supplies. Perry also mentioned that if the Japanese government was not obliged to cooperate, a larger American fleet would be following. The Japanese government was shocked at the size of this small contingent of American ships and opened two ports to them. The Japanese also signed treaties and trade agreements with England, Russia, and the Netherlands. Trade soon flourished between Japan and the West. Collectors prized Japanese objets d'arte such as lacquerware, porcelain, glass, paintings, prints, and textiles.

It was in textiles that Japan would excel. In 1860, there was a silkworm blight in Europe that created a demand for imports of silk, silkworms, and silkworm eggs. Japan also developed mechanized reeling methods that were far more efficient than the hand-reeling techniques of Europe and China. Japan was able to produce a superior silk thread that was more uniform in weight and thickness. As a result, Japan captured a large portion of the world silk market. They also eagerly adopted large-scale, Western manufacturing procedures and by the combination of a better product being produced at a faster rate, Japan was able to nearly monopolize the textile industry by the end of the nineteenth century. In 1875, A. L. Liberty opened a shop in London specifically dedicated to the import and sale of Japanese goods. His selection included fashion and decorative textiles, embroideries, carpets, porcelain, lacquerware, and a variety of purely decorative objects and curiosities. Later, Liberty would focus on textiles only, becoming one of the premier silk importers and distributors in Europe.

Fine and decorative arts, as well as fashion, were profoundly impacted by the sudden influx of Japanese styles. The Aesthetic, Arts and Crafts, and Art Nouveau artistic movements can all trace commonalities to Japanese stylistic influences. As with most types of cultural exchange, ideas are often the most valuable commodity involved in trade.

TEXTILES

The two most popular and important textiles in the nineteenth century were cotton and silk. Both of these textiles were considered luxury goods as they were not indigenous to Europe and had to be imported from the East. Early in the nineteenth century, cotton muslin gowns were in fashion, but when Napoleon became Emperor in 1804 he cut off importation of cotton from India, which was under English rule. He also ordered all silk and cotton that had been bought from England to be burned and turned his attentions to the French silk mills of Lyons. The French silk industry had been successful throughout the seventeenth and eighteenth centuries but had been abandoned after the French Revolution. Napoleon's plan would reinvigorate the French economy by producing a luxury good that could be exported, would employ many of the out-of-work artisans that had returned to Paris after The Terror, and return France to its once high standing in the world of arts and crafts. He commissioned the silk mills not only for dress fabric for the ladies of his court, but for upholsteries, bedclothes, and wall coverings for his palaces. The aristocratic and wealthy women of Paris, having disposed of all foreign textiles, were all but forced to buy new fabric for dresses from Lyons.

Beyond the soft draping white silk used in Empire gowns, the Lyons silk mills produced other weaves and colors. Soon France was producing and exporting fine silk velvets, brocades, moirés, satins, and damask across Europe and into the United States. By the winter of 1808, the Lyons silk industry had recovered to its pre-Revolution height of success. They also ran a successful dye works and produced silks in rich colors popular for the period. Bold shades of red were favored, as well as various brown tones, lilac, emerald, and pale green.

The great success of the French silk industry was due, in large part, to another Frenchman, Joseph Marie Jacquard (1752–1834). Jacquard had been employed as a straw hat maker and then as a silk weaver. In 1801, he found a way to improve the punch-card method of Jacques de Vaucanson's loom that had been devised in 1745. Jacquard used pasteboard cards punched with holes. Each hole corresponded to a part of the intended woven design. In 1801, he created his first prototype loom that wove a pattern into the fabric based on the punches in the cards. Each punched hole in the card corresponded to a hook that would either be raised or lowered. The hooks were attached to the warp yarns and then attached to harnesses. The punches in the cards told the harnesses to go up or down, and could control one, a few, or many hooks that would manipulate the warp threads. The complex design is based simply on whether the weft yarn crosses over, or under, the warp at any given intersection. Jacquard's punch-card controlled loom made it very easy to orchestrate which warps were raised so that the weft could pass beneath and which warps were lowered so the weft could go over the top. Before punch-cards, looms that were used to create brocades and other patterned and figures fabrics had to be manipulated by hand. These were known as draw-looms because each warp had to be drawn up or down individually. This type of loom was capable of very intricate weaves, but it was so time-consuming and labor intensive that the fabric it produced was extremely expensive. Although the Jacquard loom can take days to thread and set up, once the weaving process is begun, it is very efficient. The punch-card method of Vaucanson allowed for the creation of very simple patterns, such as stripes or checks. Jacquard saw that the simple technology could be perfected to create very complex woven patterns. The Jacquard loom was perfected by 1805 and put into regular use at the Lyons silk mills.

Napoleon also offered his patronage to the Manufacture des Gobelins, an esteemed tapestry workshop run by a French family of textile crafters and dyers. He ordered a large-scale tapestry replica of his coronation portrait in 1808. The tapestry was so popular that versions of it printed on cotton were made and sold all over France and much of Europe. These printed textiles were the work of the German artisan Christophe-Philippe Oberkampf. He had come to the town of Jouy-en-Josas outside of Versailles and set up a textile printing facility in 1759. His toile de Jouy (cloth from the town of Jouy-en-Josas, or alternatively, cloth of joy), was a huge success. It featured pastoral or historical scenes printed by an engraved copper roller. The scenes were monochrome but very detailed. The usual colors for his printing were black, red, or green on a ground of white. Toile de Jouy, known simply as toile, remains a popular design style for printed fabric.

With the return of prosperity and stability in France came the return of shopping for pleasure. There were thousands of dressmakers and tailors of all price ranges in Paris, all clamoring for the patronage of a courtier. Dressing for occasions and shopping for whimsy had not been indulged since before the revolution and fashionable ladies were eager to return to their old routines of visiting the dressmaker and the milliner and outfitting themselves in clothes at the height of style.

While France was reinventing their silk industry at the opening of the nineteenth century, England was enjoying a monopoly on cotton. England had colonized India in the seventeenth century and opened up lucrative cotton trading with them through the British East India Company. Over the following two hundred years, the English had instituted industrialization and the factory system to increase production of export goods. Attempts at growing cotton in England had failed and the soil and climate of India was far more suited to the crop. The English also utilized native labor in the tedious tasks of collecting and cleaning the cotton bolls and preparing them for the spinning and weaving process. In some cases, the cotton remained in India where it was made into traditional textiles such as palampore bed coverings, fabric for men's banyan robes, and other exotic textiles. There was still an appetite for Indian items made and decorated in the traditional way, but most of the cotton harvest was picked and cleaned in India, then sent in bulk to England to be processed into yarn and woven.

The prevailing fashions of the time called for cotton garments, especially softly draped printed cottons. In reaction to Napoleon's ban on textile imports from England, the English but a ban on textiles imported from France. That left the English people no other recourse but to outfit themselves in English cotton. England's cotton industry enjoyed great success as it spun and wove enough cotton yardage to clothe the country. Although white muslin would remain the most popular, colored cottons began to come into vogue, especially among married and older women. Cotton was easy to dye and rich shades could be produced—popular colors included reds and blues. Fabrics printed with stripes and small, repeating patterns were frequently worn.

A cotton fabric that had a small, repeated print was known as calico. Originally, calico was just a low quality or poorly processed cotton fabric, but frequently those were the ones chosen to be printed to cover any flaws and to make them marketable. These fabrics primarily came from Calicut, India, and were called chaliyans by the natives. Calico fabrics were very popualr during this time period in England as Regency dress moved into a more colorful period. They were also a favorite textiles in the United States. During the westward expansion of the 1830s–1850s, pioneer women regualrly wore calico dresses. When quilting first became popular in the 1850s, calico became a staple fabric for crafters. Calico remains extremely popular as quilting material to this day.

When Napoleon was removed from power in 1814, France and England began trading with one another again. The French were able to enjoy fine English cottons and the English marveled at the richness of French silks. In the later years of the Empire/Regency period, the simple, draped silhouette was expanding towards the large proportions it would achieve in the 1820s. This called for a collaboration of textiles: stiffer silks with more body for the gowns, and cotton for the starched petticoats worn beneath them. England and France helped to keep each other's textile industries busy.

The American textile industry of the early part of the nineteenth century was limited to home-based craft. Villages would often get together to share the tasks of spinning and weaving for the whole population. It was not until Francis Cabot Lowell visited England's cotton mills in 1810 that this all began to change. He was the son of a wealthy and prominent family from Boston and he was looking to turn a sleepy river town in Massachusetts into America's first cotton mill. He founded the Boston Manufacturing Company there in 1813 and the small village soon grew into the bustling mill town of Lowell, named after the mill's founder. The Lowell mill was the first of its kind in the United States; it could convert raw cotton into a finished textile all in the same building. Lowell brought back plans and machinery from England and improved them for use in his own mill, making his operation more efficient and progressive than any other mill.

The United States was becoming a player in the cotton industry. Cotton plants, the source of the fiber, flourished in the warmer climate of the southeastern regions and Americans engineered clever ways, such as the cotton gin, to maximize efficiency in the harvesting. Soon many textile mills were opening in New England and the area was on its way to becoming the textiles leader of the United States. The cotton supplied to these mills came mostly through Charleston, South Carolina, and it became the wealthiest city in the South. Sadly, this wealth came at the expense of human life as it helped to propagate the slave trade.

Through the middle of the nineteenth century, the United States became a major exporter of cotton products. The long-staple fiber variety of cotton that flourished in America produced a superior product to the short-staple fiber varieties of India. American cotton could also be sold at a lower price because they did not have to transport the raw cotton halfway across the world to be processed. The United States exported finished cotton textiles, greige goods, and raw long-staple cotton. As the demand for American cotton increased, more port towns blossomed along the eastern seaboard from Georgia to Massachusetts.

One of the most iconic and enduring uses of cotton was denim. Pants made out of the blue warp-faced twill became popular as work clothes for miners in California during the Gold Rush of the late 1840s and 1850s. Levi Strauss had originally brought canvas with him to California from New York to sell at his dry goods store. But when the miners wanted better pants, he found a new use for the yardage. When he ran out of canvas, he looked into other fabric such as cotton jean and the wool-blend serge de Nimes. They both were well known to be sturdy and colorfast, although serge de Nimes was the stronger of the two fabrics. It seems the Strauss took the weaving technique of the serges de Nimes, using two different thread types for the warp and weft but made them out of cotton like jean. Serge de Nimes had traditionally always been blue, but jean was usually brown or natural colored. The indigo blue was by far the most popular and has been the signature color of denim ever since. It was, and still is, woven with a strong, high-twist blue cotton warp and a thicker, lower-twist white cotton weft. Strauss went on to create a profitable business selling his denim "waist overalls." They remain to be one of the world's most popular garment for men, women, and children and an enduring symbol of the United States.

But the cotton industry had its darker side. While the North decried the reprehensible use of slavery in cotton growing in the South, the Northerners were practicing another form of enforced labors on the production side. As mills grew larger and needed more workers, they aggressively recruited women and children from impoverished and rural areas. Women and children were preferred for mill work because of their small hands. The "Lowell system" recruited teenage girls and put them up in dormitories that included their clothing, room, and board. The girls were subject to strict rules and curfews, including mandatory attendance at the town's local church. After room and board, most girls saved what little wages they were given to send back home to their families. Others spent theirs on the latest fashions and frivolities, although they had no opportunities to wear them. Work days were long and the work was tiring and often dangerous. Although the girls were well fed and housed, they had no freedom to come and go as they pleased. Nor were they allowed to quit their jobs if they grew tired of them or take extra days off. Sick days were taken out of the week's wages and if a girl was ill for any length of time, she could quickly end up owing the company money.

In the 1820s, there were several strikes of female mill workers and seamstresses in New York and New Hampshire. The demands of the workers were never met, but it began to put the plight of textile workers into the social consciousness. Most girls did not complain about their long hours and low pay. They knew if they made too much of a fuss that they would be fired and replaced. Even though the work was difficult, there were always those willing to take it, especially during the 1830s and 1840s when economic depressions created an employment crisis. Trainloads of farm girls from the Midwest came just about every week, seeking their fortunes in the big cities. Many of them would not live to see their homes again.

After the opening of the Erie Canal in 1825, goods and people were far easier to transport between the Midwest and the East Coast. New York City rose to prominence as America's fashion center with its ready-to-wear market. Originally focused on men's wear, New York City became the home of major retailers like Brooks Brothers and Macy's.

The United States was also a major exporter of beaver pelt. Beaver was the preferred fiber for fine felt hats. The market for high-quality beaver drove trappers from the United States and Canada into thick, unexplored woods in search of their quarry. In Canada, fur was traded through the Hudson Bay Company. American fur trading was primarily handled by the American Fur Company opened in 1808 by John Jacob Astor. Although mink, sable, and fox were also trapped and traded, the money was in beaver. The Astors became one of New York City's, and the country's, wealthiest and most influential families.

The nineteenth century was a time of great invention and innovation. The American engineer Walter Hunt from New York invented a great many articles that became a necessity of fashion. Among more pedestrian items such as the fountain pen and the velocipede, the bicycle with the very big wheel up front, Hunt invented the safety pin and the lock-stitch sewing machine. He received a patent for the safety pin in 1849 but sold it later to pay off a debt. He invented the sewing machine in 1834, but it was never patented.

Sewing machines had been mechanized since the beginning of the nineteenth century, but they could only manipulate one thread through the fabric in a chain stitch. While highly decorative, the chain stitch was no good at holding clothes together. If one end came loose, the entire seam would ravel. Hunt's machine created a lock stitch, using two threads. The needle had an eye at the same end as the point that carried the top thread and shuttle that carried the bottom thread. When the needle passed through the fabric, it left a loop through which the small bottom shuttle could pass. When the next stitch was made, it pulled the preceding one tight around the shuttle thread. This interaction between threads locked the fabric between them and created a sturdy stitch. But this loop and shuttle system was not efficient and the machine had to be reset frequently.

Elias Howe, an inventor and engineer from Massachusetts, took the idea of the lock stitch sewing machine and refined it into a more efficient and workable apparatus. He patented the lock stitch sewing machine in 1846. He was forced to defend his patent on more than one occasion, as there were several engineers working on creating a lock stitch sewing machine. One of these was Isaac Merritt Singer who created his own version of the lock stitch sewing machine in 1850. Singer was also an American born in New York, like Hunt. While history has given Howe the credit for inventing the lock stitch machine, it was Singer who made it better and marketed it into a trade name synonymous with sewing.

Singer first came across an older version of a lock stitch sewing machine made by Orson C. Phelps and sold through the Lerow and Blodgett company out of Boston. After a careful study of the machine, Singer made careful notes about some of the issues with the machine and how he would address them. Instead of the shuttle going around in a circle, he would have it move in a straight line. In place of the needle bar pushing a curved needle horizontally, he would use a straight needle that moved up and down.[14] He spent forty dollars and eleven days on the project and came away with the prototype version of every sewing machine made in the world today. It featured a straight needle with the eye at the point and a transverse shuttle system. The needle apparatus was attached to an overhanging arm that positioned the needle above the shuttle. The movement of the two was coordinated by gears that ran through the needle arm and through the shuttle bed. The machine also had a presser foot to keep the fabric in place and a feed wheel that would drive the fabric evenly between the needle and shuttle. He built the machine into a table not only for stability, but to have a surface to rest the cloth that one was sewing. Older sewing machines used a hand-crank, which made it nearly impossible to simultaneously monitor the feed of the fabric under the needle and turn the machine to make it work. Singer connected his machine to a spinning wheel's foot treadle, thereby leaving both hands free to ensure a straight and even stitching of the fabric.

Not even one full year later, in 1851, Singer had been awarded a patent on his version of the lock stitch sewing machine and had formed his own company to manufacture and sell it. His partner and capital investor was Edward C. Clark, a lawyer from New York. Clark's venture paid off, and by 1853 the I. M. Singer & Company was the leading manufacturer of sewing machines in the United States. Singer then moved his corporate offices to New York City and started manufacturing the machines there, under the name of Singer Manufacturing Company, trying to capitalize on the growing ready-to-wear market there. The original Singer machines sold for $100 in 1853. By 1855, Singer Manufacturing had become the world's largest sewing company and opened its first branch office overseas in Paris. Singer and Clark were quite canny when it came to their marketing and knew when and where to take their machine to maximize interest and sales. Over the next thirty years, Singer branch offices would open in Scotland, Brazil, Germany, and England. And by the 1870s, Singer would also have several manufacturing plants in the United States and in Europe to keep up with the enormous demand.

Although the sewing machine was an early success, making Singer a very rich man, he did not stop improving on his original design. He patented a device to maintain tension between the needle thread and the shuttle thread, a device that would allow the operator to easily make ruffles, tucks, and bindings, and several shuttle improvements including the oscillating shuttle which is what is found in modern sewing machines.

Singer wanted more than to produce a quality machine; he wanted to make it available to as many people as possible. In 1856, Clark devised an installment plan that would allow people of the working class to be able to purchase their own sewing machine and set up a home-based tailoring or alterations business, or give someone the freedom to make his or her own clothes for much less expense than buying them.

By century's end, the Singer Manufacturing Company had patented the first electric sewing machines for commercial use. Electric home sewing machines would soon follow. The Singer Manufacturing Company also operated some of the world's largest factories and sold over 200,000 units annually.

Isaac Merritt Singer died in England in 1875, but his legacy lives on through the twenty-first century with the company he founded. Singer made sewing accessible to the world. Ebenezer Butterick made fashion accessible to the world. Butterick was another Massachusetts inventor and entrepreneur. He and his wife, Ellen, created graded tissue paper patterns to be sold to the home sewer. Paper patterns were not a new innovation, but prior to 1863, they only came in one size. A long process of grading and fitting would be required for a home seamstress to make a garment in a size other than the basic stock size the pattern came in. Butterick and his wife devised a grading system that would include a range of sizes for each pattern. They settled on tissue paper because it was lightweight and easy to pack and ship across the country and the world. The patterns were wildly popular and by 1864, the Buttericks had a factory in New York City with a team of workers printing various styles of the graded patterns. E. Butterick & Co. at first focused on children's clothing and menswear but expanded to include women's fashion in 1866.

In addition to producing patterns, the Butterick company published informational fashion magazines about clothing and textiles. After Ellen died in 1871, Butterick stayed active in the business. *The Delineator* began publication in 1873 and was the most popular magazine in America through the turn of the century. It reported not only on fashion, but on fabrics and textiles and gave advice on what materials to use for what kinds of clothes. By 1876 the company had over 100 branch offices in the United States, Canada, and Europe. In 1881, E. Butterick & Co. became the Butterick Publishing Company. Ebenezer Butterick would remain active in the company until his death in 1903. Butterick graded tissue paper patterns are still sold today.

In the 1850s, the discovery of synthetic dyestuff revolutionized fashion. Scientists had been hard at work trying to create a synthetic dye that would yield the bright, colorfast hues that the consuming public craved. Through the 1820s many European chemists were able to isolate the blue pigment from indigo and reproduce it with very limited success. Aniline was isolated from coal tar for the first time in the 1830s. Coal tar is a viscose biproduct of coal when it is used to make coke, a type of coal used for fuel that is highly concentrated and refined and does not smoke when burned. In 1856, the young English chemist William Henry Perkin was experimenting with using aniline to try and synthesize quinine, an anti-inflammatory, antipyretic (fever reducing), analgesic compound used to treat malaria. Instead of finding artificial quinine, his sample turned vividly purple and stained his labcoat. When he found that the stains were not only colorfast, but a very pleasing color, he realized that this could be a discovery greater than synthetic quinine. Perkin was an artist by hobby and recognized the impact such a dyestuff could have on the world. He went to work on the aniline project in secret, perfecting the means to scale up production to commercial levels and market it. He knew his dye would be a huge success as purple was a much-sought-after color and one of the most difficult to produce. This was why it was reserved for royalty only. Perkin named his color mauvine.[15]

It was quite serendipitious that Perkin made his discovery when and where he did. England had the industrial capacity to manufacture the dye and was an immense resourse for the raw materail, coal tar, which was a byproduct and considered waste. The tastes in fashion at the time were leaning toward more, and brighter, colors and a rebounding world economy gave many people a disposible income with which to buy fine clothes. The dye was a resounding commercial success and its discovery lead to the synthesizing of more colors, including black. Perkins became an exceedingly wealthy man but did not leave his beloved chemistry. He went on to synthesize not only other colors, but also synthetic bases for perfumes. He retired from the chemistry business in 1874.

Silk was the dominating textile of the second half of the nineteenth century. Although cotton imported from India and elsewhere remained a fashion staple, the desire for silk rose steadily through the century. Silk produced in Japan became a highly desired commodity after the Japanese ports were opened to the West in the 1850s. Stores across Europe and the United States opened specifically to capitalize on this trend. During the International Exhibition of 1862 held in London, delegates from Japan showcased their native arts and crafts, including silk production. In 1875, Arthur Lazenby Liberty opened a shop on Regent Street in London that he called East India House. It specialized in curiosities from all over Asia and the East and especially Japan. These included lacquerware, porcelain, and many different kinds of textiles. He arrayed his silks according to color and pattern, displaying them to catch the eye of passersby. His East India House shop was the next step for him after he had run the Oriental Bazaar department at the Farmer and Roger's Great Shawl and Cloak Emporium; the department had been the most profitable one in the entire store. Although he carried many items of interest from the East, silk textiles consistently sold the best. By 1884, Liberty had opened a dressmaker's shop and focused on "aesthetic gowns"[16] made from unique and unusual fabrics. He specialized in the importation of silk form Japan. In Japan, mechanization allowed silk producers to create a stronger and more uniform filament that made for a better quality textile. This advance paired with the silkworm blight of 1860 caused the demand for Japanese silks to spike. Liberty capitalized on this, bringing more and more of these silks into his shop and catering to an elite clientele. He created lavish catalogs and encouraged a mail-order trade.

The desire for silk was greatest during the opulent Second Empire in France. Empress Eugenie kept a very fashionable court and insisted that her court ladies be dressed in the finest garments that Paris had to offer. Both the domestic silk mills and the influx of Japanese trade gave women of fashion and station a treasure trove of silks from which to choose. Especially in the late nineteenth century, the wearing of a Charles Worth couture gown made in the finest of Liberty silks imported from Japan was the ultimate status symbol.

The textile industry changed dramatically between the start of the century and its end. Advances in weaving and coloring the textiles made modern styles possible. Innovations in sewing and pattern-making brought the world of high fashion within reach of the masses. Technology of the nineteenth century was seen as the great equalizer. Without even one of the many inventions and improvements, costume and society of the nineteenth century would have been entirely different.

THE EMPIRE PERIOD, 1800–1820

Art

At the opening of the century, the premiere painter of Europe was Jacques-Louis David (1748–1825). He was fond of the Neoclassical Greek style that was influencing the fashion and decorative arts of France. David tended toward simple lines that were inspired by the vase paintings of ancient Greece and fifteenth-century Italian art. In 1804, David was asked to paint Napoleon's coronation scene, "The Coronation of the Emperor Napoleon I and the Crowning of the Empress Joséphine," which was completed in 1807. David had also painted the iconic portrait of Napoleon signaling to his troops as they crossed the Alps in 1800. David's student, Antoine-Jean Gros (1771–1835) painted "Napoleon in the Plague House at Jaffa," a propaganda piece showing Napoleon's benevolence as well as an early interest in the dress and architecture of the East. As the central patron and inspiration, Napoleon was at the center of much of the art of Continental Europe.

Jean Auguste Dominique Ingres (1780–1867) was one of Europe's most renowned painters towards the end of the Empire period and well into the 1860s. He was a devotee of David's and adhered to the Neoclassical styles. He, too, painted Napoleon, but one of his most famous works from this period was "La Grande Odalisque," painted in 1814. He is best known for his portraits that were executed in stunning detail done both in paint and in pencil. He was famous for accurately capturing not only the fashion of the period with remarkable accuracy, but also of conveying the facial expressions of the models sitting for the paintings.

When the French occupation of Vienna, Austria, forced the Akademie der Bildenden Künste to close, two of the displaced artists, Franz Pforr (1788–1812) and

Friedrich Overbeck (1789–1869), formed the Brotherhood of Saint Luke (Lukasbrüder) in 1809. Their focus was on the emotional purity of art and keeping it as true to nature as possible. They studied late medieval and Italian Renaissance artists and works and drew their inspiration from the works of Dürer and Raphael. The Akademie was reopened in 1810, but many of the students were not readmitted and most them turned instead to the Brotherhood. In 1811, the Brotherhood relocated to the abandoned monastery of Sant'Isidoro in Rome and took up a monastic lifestyle, treating their art as a religion. They became known, rather derisively, as the Nazarenes. But a style emerged from the Brotherhood that was an amalgam of Germanic and Italian styles, portrayed most notably in Overbeck's work, "Italia and Germania," where two female figures clasp hands and lean their foreheads together. One is dressed in Italian styles and the other in Germanic. They are an allegorical representation of this stylistic exchange.

Neoclassicism also reached Rome. Roman sculptors of the time created large marble statues indicative of the country's ancient roots. Antonio Canova (1757–1822) created the statue "Perseus with the Head of Medusa" for Pope Pius VII to replace the original state taken as tribute by Napoleon, "Apollo Belvedere." When Napoleon heard about the artist's talent, he summoned Canova to Paris and installed him there as an Imperial sculptor. Bertel Thorvaldsen (1768/70–1844) was a Danish sculptor living and working in Rome. With the creation of his Neoclassical work, "Jason with the Golden Fleece," the too was catapulted into favor. Thorvaldsen went on to a long and prosperous career as a Neoclassical sculptor in Rome, one of the highlights of his career was the tomb of Pope Pius VII in Saint Peter's.

In England, Joseph Mallord William Turner (1775–1851), a recent electee to the Royal Academy, experimented with using watercolors in his landscapes. After studying the Old Masters such as Titian, Salomon van Ruysdael, and Claude Lorrain, he seeks to perfect the art of the landscape painting. In 1804, William Blake (1757–1827), an English poet and printmaker, begins on the ninth and last volume in his *Books of Prophesy* series. This poem took more than one hundred plates to illustrate and was an example of Blake's own style of "illuminated printing," which blended the traditional aesthetics of the illuminated manuscript with contemporary lithographic printing techniques.

Some of the world's most enduring works of literature were published during this time including classic novels by Jane Austen and Charles Dickens and the first edition of *Kinder und Hausmärchen* (*Children's and Household Tales*) by Jacob (1785–1863) and Wilhelm (1786–1859) Grimm, more commonly known as the Brothers Grimm.

Men's Clothing

In the preceding centuries, both in Europe and in the United States, men's clothing had become highly decorative, lush velvets and intricate embroideries were used on men's coats and breeches. By the dawn of the nineteenth century, fashion had changed dramatically. In the aftermath of the French Revolution, men in France turned away from the ostentatious costumes of the eighteenth century and embraced simpler attire that reflected the values of the republic, not the pop of the aristocracy. Knee-breeches had remained popular with the upper classes right through the Revolution, but in the aftermath, men adopted the long trousers of the working class. Many Revolutionary groups even used this fashion as part of their rebellion, calling themselves *sans culottes*, or "without breeches."[17] This fashion was often paired with the *bonnet rouge*, the red cap of liberty, one of the most important symbols of the Revolution.

But this Revolutionary fervor did not last long. Once Napoleon crowned himself Emperor in 1804, there was once again an aristocracy in France. Gone were the lavish costumes of the pre-Revolution era, but they were replaced with a more refined elegance. Colors of this period are often referred to as "somber." Breeches became fashionable as court dress once more, and few men wore trousers. Men did, however, wear pantaloons, which were worn long to the ankle like trousers, but were much tighter fitting, often including a strap worn under the foot to keep them from riding up. Pants were made with a fall front closure, a wide flap that buttoned on the sides. After 1807, trousers began to return to accepted fashion and had replaced breeches for general wear by 1810. By the middle years of the Empire period men had three choices when it came to pants: breeches, pantaloons, and trousers. Breeches were still considered the most formal and worn for evening and court occasions until about 1815. Wide-legged, Russian-inspired trousers were worn for casual attire.

Coats and waistcoats changed relatively little, even through the Revolution. They were made primarily from wool, but silks and velvets were seen on high-ranking men during formal or court occasions. Coats generally ended at, or just above, the waist at the front, with long tails reaching to the knee in the back in 1815 and lengthening to below the knee in 1820. The cutaway could either be a smooth curve from the center front to the tails in back, or the tails could, beginning at the side seam, make a right-angle corner from the waistline in front to the fall of the tails. Coat collars usually had a deep notch where the collar joined the lapel. This allowed for a man to turn his collar up in the fashionable manner. Often the collar and lapels had velvet facings. Pockets were placed in the pleats of the tails or at the waist. Coats of this period could be single- or double-breasted and were always worn with a waistcoat.

Nineteenth-century waistcoats were built like modern vests. They were sleeveless garments made to be worn beneath the coat. The front of the waistcoat was cut from a fashionable fabric, in this era, usually a contrasting color. The unseen back of the waistcoat was plain and inexpensive linen, cotton, or some other lining fabric. Waistcoats were made with stiffened collars and lapels that would show above the collar and lapel of the coat. When the coat was worn closed, a few inches of the waistcoat would be seen below the front hem of the coat. Often in cold weather, men would layer their waistcoats for warmth. Waistcoats could also be worn layered to show contrasting colors or weaves.

Overcoats were cut very full, made to cover the coat and waistcoat with ease. They were worn long, at least to the knee if not to the ankle. Overcoats also had wide lapels and collars that could be made to be worn tall. Some overcoats had short capes attached to the shoulder, either one or two to three layered. In England, this coat was known as a *carrick*. Full cloaks were worn only occasionally and usually only for travel. Overcoats were made of wool and in dark colors: black, dark brown, navy blue, or charcoal grey.

Underclothes for men remained unchanged since the start of the eighteenth century. Linen or cotton drawers were worn beneath the pants. Shirts were also made of linen or cotton and full cut. Drawers and shirts could be made from flannel for extra warmth in cold weather. The center front of the shirt often had pleats or ruffles and the collar was made to stand high, reaching to the cheek. These tall collars were perfect for wrapping cravats. Cravats were introduced in the seventeenth century and still popular at the beginning of the nineteenth century. They wrapped their cravats several times around the collar. Stocks were also becoming popular. Stocks were stiffened bands that were wrapped around the neck and fastened at the back. In 1815, Robert Pringle opened a factory in Harwick, Scotland, that specialized in stockings, hosiery, and underwear to meet the demand of a rapidly growing retail market. Within a few years, Pringle had expanded his business to include other knot and wool goods as well.

At the start of the century, shoes with decorative buckles were popular, but like many fashions of the previous era, they were an accessory that disappeared after the Revolution. Nineteenth-century shoes closed with a tie at the front instead of a buckle and had low, rounded heels and a rounded toe. Spats were worn over shoes to cover the stockings. Boots remained popular and the prevailing style after 1815. Fashion boots were made in a military style, but actually military boots covered the knee and were cut away behind to allow for walking, riding, and sitting. Some fashionable boots could be turned down at the tops to show fashionable linings and others were shorter and made to be worn with pantaloons. In 1800, shoes made to fit the left and right foot separately were being produced in small quantities, but it would be several decades before these types of shoes would be widely available.

Banyans and dressing gowns had also been introduced in the seventeenth century and remained popular through the nineteenth century as well. These robes were ankle length and made with a wide flare through the hem. Banyans were made from highly decorative fabrics that would not usually be used in menswear. Wool, silk, and cotton damasks and brocades were the most popular. The heaviness of the banyan would depend on the weather. In the winter, banyans were often thickly quilted. Occasionally, banyans had accompanying waistcoats and soft nightcaps. Although banyans had begun as a garment worn strictly in the home, by the nineteenth century they became acceptable as daytime casual wear.

Men wore their hair short. Faces were clean shaven except for side whiskers which were allowed to grow long. Hats were the primary accessory for men, especially top hats. Top hats had crowns that were very tall or shorter with a medium-sized brim that was rolled up at the sides and dipped down in the front and back. Tops hats were glossy and made out of silk or felt made from wool or beaver that was treated with mercury to give it sheen. Another popular hat was a bicorne. This hat had two points that could be worn with the points front to back or side to side. Bicornes were primarily made from wool felt. Some evening fashions called for the hat to be flattened and carried under the arm instead of worn on the head. This fashion was known in French as *chapeau bras,* "hat for the arm."[18] Napoleon was fond of the bicorne hat. Gloves were also an important accessory for men. They were made of cotton or leather. White gloves were worn for formal occasions. Hand-carried accessories such as walking sticks and parasols were also fashionable for men. Magnifying glasses mounted onto a long handle were also carried. Rings and watch chains were the most common jewelry for men. Occasionally brooches were worn on the coat, waistcoat, shirt, cravat, or stock. Only men who were fastidious about trends and fashions used makeup. Some used rouge on their cheeks, carried scented handkerchiefs, and bleached their hands very white. These styles were primarily associated with the Dandies.

The Dandy was an English phenomenon, although French men were known for chasing fads of fashion. The English Dandy was a man who not only followed the height of fashion, but was known to circulate in the highest echelons of society, and he was a charming and witty companion. Magazines, pamphlets, and books were published to advise Dandies how to dress to the height of each particular and ever-changing fashion. The wearing and tying of neckcloths were one of the hallmarks of Dandy style. There was even a book focused specifically on neckwear fashion printed in 1818 called *The Neckclothiana*; it was originally published as a satire, but it contained such detailed and valuable information that it became an important resource. During the early nineteenth century in England, the Regency period, the prince regent kept company with a very fashionable set. His closest companion was George "Beau" Brummell and he was the English fashion leader of the early part of the century. He was known for his impeccably tailored coats and the finest linen shirts. He also popularized buckskin breeches, very tight trousers, and a shorter-crowned beaver hat. Brummell's tailors labored to perfect every part of his ensemble, leading to the detail-oriented approach still used in modern men's tailoring. Cork Street in London was the Dandies' style center with famous tailors like Schweitzer and Davidson, Mayer's, and Stulze, who was the exclusive tailor to the Duke of Wellington, a renowned Dandy. Men across England sought to emulate this fashion with varying degrees of success. Even Napoleon admired Wellington's style so much that during the Battle of Waterloo in 1815 when he changed his customary black stock for a white cravat like those favored by the Dandies. Dandy styles appeared in France and the United States, but they were never as popular in either country as they were in England.

Fashion in England, aside from the Dandies, was much the same as it was in France except without the symbolism associated with the Revolution or the Empire. In the United States, style news traveled slowly. The climate differences between the United States and Europe also added to differences in the way Americans dressed, not to mention that Americans were quite reluctant to follow English fashion in the wake of the Revolutionary War and the War of 1812.

London quickly grew into a highly fashionable center for men's clothing. By 1803, Savile Row, Pall Mall, King Street, and Covent Garden were popular shopping areas. In 1819 the Burlington Arcade opened. It was a covered shopping district that boasted seventy-two small shops that sold everything from jewelry to shoes and handkerchiefs; all manner of fashionable accessories and ready-to-wear items such as drawers, shirts, and stockings. The Burlington Arcade was protected by liveried guards in traditional uniforms who enforced a strict code of conduct that prohibited running, whistling, singing, busking, carrying of very large parcels and packages, and opening umbrellas inside the building. But not far from this shopping finery was Rosemary Lane, a street that housed many shops that sold "slopwork," ready-made garments intended for laborers and others of the working class. It was near an area called the "rag fair," where there was a bustling secondhand clothing trade.

Women's Clothing

Women's costume of this period remains one of the most easily recognizable modes of fashion, the Empire dress. The Western world followed this new

French fashion with vigor. The Empire dress was characterized by a simple gown of unadorned cotton muslin with a very high waistline that sat immediately under the bust with very short sleeves. Necklines were often quite low and usually square. The cut of the gown was slim and narrow. The idea was to evoke the dress of antiquity in Greece and Rome and was originally modeled after what was depicted in sculpture. The dresses were primarily made white or cream colored in imitation of the white marble statues. The very wide *panier* hoops of the eighteenth century had vanished after the Revolution, leaving this simple silhouette that required no underpinnings whatsoever. Visible flesh was in vogue and women routinely bared their arms, especially during the evening. Dresses also came with detachable sleeves to go from day to evening wear with ease. Some women wore flesh-colored stockings to give the illusion of nude legs. The dresses were column-like and often worn with a train, even during the day. The bulk of the yardage was focused towards the back of the dress to enhance the train and to give the front a flat and smooth appearance. Although Napoleon banned the import of cotton muslin from India, which was under English control at that time, he could not staunch this fashion. Cotton was brought in from Egypt instead and the trend vigorously continued, although contraband cotton from India and England was highly coveted.

At the start of the period, a very simple dress was preferred, although these gowns were often worn with a colorful, woven shawl. These paisley shawls were carefully draped and arranged and there were entire manuals published to direct ladies how to wear them correctly for every occasion. But within a few years surface ornamentation on gowns began to become fashionable. Whitework embroidery of tiny repeating motifs covered the entire gown. Sometimes for daywear, metallic or colored threads were used sparingly. Another popular decoration was of a single band of color at the hem of the skirt, at the waistline, at the edge of the sleeves, or at all three places. In the early years of the century, this was usually in some Classical motif such as the Greek Key design. Between 1804 and 1807, Napoleon's excursions brought Eastern influences of Egyptian, Etruscan, and Oriental ornamentation. Printed cottons from Egypt and India became popular. For court functions, dresses made from colored silks that required hoops were still worn. Elaborate jewelry and accessories were paired with these formal gowns. After 1808, there was a heavily Spanish influence on dress, giving more attention to jewelry, beadwork, embroidery, and other accessories. A shawl much like a Spanish mantilla supplanted the paisley shawl for many women. By 1810, women began to add a vertical band down the center front of the dress to meet the horizontal dress at the hem, and they added ruffles and flounces along the hemline. Occasionally, a light robe decorated with embroidery or beadwork was worn over the top of the Empire dress. A Gothic influence in 1811 removed the last remaining classical lines and replaced them with a fuller, flared skirt with tiers of small ruffles at the hem.

The extremely high waist remained fashionable throughout the entire Empire period. But during the second half of the era, from 1810 and onward, changes could be seen. Dresses were no longer made exclusively of simple cotton muslin, but colorful silks and velvets were being used. The short dress sleeves became puffed and gathered down to a band to which an additional long sleeve could be attached. Necklines also became much higher and the bodices more structured and fitted. The extremely high waist gradually lowered to a point just above the natural waistline. After 1814, necklines were either very high and trimmed with lace for day wear, or cut wide and straight across in a boatneck style for evening. The slender, column-like shape of the gown was also disappearing, moving toward a silhouette that favored a flared skirt. Gores were added into the skirt to widen it and required wearing petticoats to maintain the fashionable shape. For day wear, skirts were worn shorter, just above the feet so the shoes could be seen. Decorative elements, which were already important at the hemline, were further focused at this area to draw attention to the feet. Late Empire gowns featured ruffles, pleats, and puffs trimming the bottom of the dresses.

The years prior to 1815 are considered to be Neoclassical in France. After 1815, when Napoleon was permanently exiled to the island of St. Helena, there was a gradual shift away from Empire fashion in favor of the newly emergent Romantic style. When the Bourbon monarchy was restored to France in 1814, there was a greater emphasis on fashions borrowed from England. There was also a resurgence of trends popular before the Revolution such as widespread use of the fleur-de-lis as a decorative motif. But throughout the first twenty years of the century, women's dress in France, as well as in the rest of the Western world, would be dominated by the Empire silhouette.

In addition to the ubiquitous wool paisley shawls, the Empire silhouette required special outerwear to accommodate it. Typical Empire ladies wore a short jacket known as a *spencer* or a long coat called a *pelisse*. The spencer was an English fashion that became a sensation across Europe and the United States. It began as a hunting jacket cropped short to the fashionable waistline and worn over the French Empire gown and the English round gown. Spencers could have long or short sleeves and could be worn indoors or out of doors. They were made in a rich color of wool or silk and worn either to contrast the white gowns or match the later, colored dresses. The Englishman Lord Charles Spencer is credited for creating this fashion which was originally intended to be worn as menswear. Popular legends tell of Lord Spencer taking a bet that he could start a new fashion in two weeks. The tales differ about how the coat tales were removed and why, but each story ends the same way: with Lord Spencer wearing his cropped jacket and causing a fashion sensation.[19] The pelisse was a French coat designed to be worn over the narrow, high-waisted silhouette. Full-length cloaks and shorter shoulder capes were also worn, but women craved an outerwear fashion that accentuated the Empire line. The pelisse was a full-length coat with long sleeves usually made in silk or cotton during warmer months and wool with a plush lining for colder weather. They were made with the same high waistline and narrow fit as the gowns that they were intended to cover.

Beneath these body-conscious gowns, women wore soft stays, not unlike modern "body slimmers." Instead of a stiff busk to keep the torso rigidly upright and rows of reeds or bone to constrict the figure, Empire stays were made of only a few layers of fabric with cording stitched between the layers to support the bust and help smooth the belly into a figure befitting such clinging garments. In 1808, Auguste Caron's *The Lady's Toilette* advised that the bosom should not appear too large, with breasts supported and separated. Caron also advised that the bosom should be kept as pale as possible and the height of fashion demanded that the blue veins should be visible on the surface of the skin. The chemise was still worn next to the body and beneath the stays.

Empire chemises were also of cotton or very fine linen and cut in the simple, narrow style of the dress. Under the chemise, some women wore pantalets: a long, straight-legged garment made of cotton or linen and edged with rows of frills, lace, or pin-tucking. Pantalets that could be seen at the hem of the dress did not remain in fashion for adult women, but they were often used for little girls' styles.

High-heeled shoes that had been popular for women since the seventeenth century fell out of fashion after the French Revolution. Flat-soled shoes were the most popular style for women throughout the Empire period. Shoes for evening wear were usually made of delicate silk and decorated with small silk rosettes and tied with ribbons. These fragile shoes could not be worn outdoors or very often and women of wealth had several pairs of each style. Grecian-style sandals were also popular for daytime and some evening wear and often laced up the calf to the knee with long leather ties. In 1810, a flat-soled low boot became fashionable for daywear. These boots were made of soft leather or fabric that matched the pelisse coat.

Hair was styled in a manner based off of Greek ideals. The hair was swept back from the face and gathered in ringlets or coils at the back of the head or nape of the neck. Wisps of hair were curled to frame the face. During the years just after the Revolution, a short cropped hairstyle modeled after the hair of those going to the guillotine was popular and it was known as *à la victime*. A style of short, sculpted curls was also fashionable for women known as *à la Titus* and it was based off the hairstyles seen of the statues of the Roman emperors. These short styles did not last well into the period; long hair that could be elaborately styled in the manner of Classical statues became far more desirable.

Hats were also indispensable for the fashionable woman. Bonnets with high crowns and wide brims made of straw, stiffened fabric, or a combination of the two, became popular. They were tied under the chin by wide, satin ribbons. Matrons favored small muslin caps trimmed with ruffles or lace that were reminiscent of older styles. These were worn primarily indoors and referred to as day caps. After Napoleon's campaign in Egypt, turbans became very fashionable. Hats were an important accessory for not only daywear, but for evening events such as the theatre, opera, and balls. Formal hats were often trimmed with ruffles, ribbons, and feathers. One such hat was the *casque à la Minerve*, a small cap that resembled the one featured on the statues of Minerva, the Roman goddess of wisdom.

In the turbulent years following the French Revolution, real gemstones were hidden or had been destroyed. Inexpensive semiprecious jewels were cut into faceted gems and set into metals that simulated gold. Pinchbeck was the most popular of these imitations; it was formulated from an alloy of copper and zinc and was golden in color. The market for this low-cost jewelry was large, such that the craftspeople who worked in these materials had their own designation as *bijoutiers* to differentiate them from craftspeople who worked with precious metals and actual jewels, *joailliers*. After Napoleon's coronation and the return of court life to France, real jewels began to be seen on nobility once more. Matched sets of necklace, comb, tiara or diadem, bandeau, pair of bracelets, pins, rings, earrings, and possibly belt or shoe buckles known as parures also came back into fashion. Some women also continued to wear *sautoirs*, long gold chains joined by a medallion, especially for daytime or less formal dressing. A new trend in jewelry created during this period was the cameo. A cameo is a carving done in positive relief where the figure is of one color and the background is another. Traditionally, cameos were carved from conch shell and the raised image was white or off-white and the background pink. But cameos can be carved from any type of shell, stone, bone, porcelain, wood, or any hard material. Cameos of this period were primarily conch shell, porcelain, and semiprecious jewels that could achieve the desired two-tone look. Napoleon had a crown that was decorated with cameos and it did not take long for a desire for cameos to take hold across Europe and the United States.

Other Empire accessories of note were the reticule, the muff, and gloves. The reticule was a small purse carried by fashionable ladies. It was just large enough to hold a woman's essentials that she might need for an evening out. These tiny purses were highly decorated with embroidery, beadwork, and other techniques and no well-dressed lady would be seen without one. Muffs had been in fashion for over two hundred years by this period. They were made of fur or plush, a very deep pile velvet. A woman would insert her hands on either side of the cylindrical muff in order to keep them warm. Gloves were essential for women for many reasons. Although showing the flesh of the upper arms was fashionable, hands and forearms were still covered by gloves. Gloves also kept the skin of the hands soft and fashionably pale. No woman wanted to have hands the looked as if they were tanned from working out in the sun. For evening wear, gloves reached to the elbow or just above it and arm bands were often worn between the top of the glove and the edge of the sleeve. For daytime, wrist-length gloves were worn. Evening gloves were usually white satin while gloves for day could be more varied in color and decoration and made of silk, cotton, or leather. In the winter, women often wore wool mittens alone or over the top of their gloves.

The main cosmetic used by the French was perfume. In 1806, Jean-Marie Farina arrived in Paris and opened the Roger & Gallet perfume shop on Rue Saint-Honoré. His Eau de Cologne formula was prized by both men and women, alike. Facial makeup was rarely used by women of fashion, except for the occasional powder, light rouge, or lip color. Makeup was still considered to be used primarily by whores and not socially acceptable for ladies of good breeding. If any facial cosmetics were used, care was taken to make the look as natural as possible.

Early on, the French recognized their position as a fashion leader and began to publish many magazines full of the latest styles and instructions on achieving the most current look. These magazines were popular in England and in the United States, as well as all over Europe.

Dress in England, while still echoing the fashionable French silhouette, was an entity all to itself in many ways. English dress at this time is commonly referred to as Regency, in honor of the prince regent who was the style leader of the country. At the start of the nineteenth century, everyday wear was strongly influenced by the Empire line. Dresses were simple, of plain cotton muslin and made with a dramatically high waist. But England's monarchy and court customs were still intact and dress for court occasions were quite different than in France. Formal court dress for women was still quite elaborate with wide dresses supported by hoops. The high-waisted fashion did not combine well with courtly attire, and like many of her predecessors, Queen Anne of Denmark during the seventeenth century especially, Queen Charlotte dictated what would be worn at her court, fashionable or not. But when the prince regent entertained, he allowed the Empire silhouette and gained a reputation of being a man of fashion. When he assumed the throne as George IV, he banished the antiquated hooped dresses from court in favor of the new silhouette. He did keep to the basic rules of courtly dress, however. Necklines were cut low and trains must be worn. Young, unmarried women were expected to dress in white and married ladies could wear whatever colors they chose. But the fashion for white, off-white, and cream-colored dresses from France meant that nearly everyone at court was wearing almost the same color.

England was known for superb cotton textile production, taking Indian fibers and weaving them into new and interesting fabrics. Sheer cottons such as organdy and leno were the most popular as were specialty weaves such as "windowpane," where alternating heavy warp and weft yarns into the wave created a checked design. Tambour embroidery was also prized. In this technique the fabric is stretched over a round hoop, much like a tambourine, and a hook is used to manipulate decorative threads over the surface of the fabric. Napoleon's ban on English and Indian cotton imports meant that these textile treasures were not sold to France, but they were very popular elsewhere in Europe and in the United States. Conversely, because of the animosity between England and France, England did not import French silks. When Napoleon was removed from power in 1815, trade between England and France returned to normal and the French enjoyed English and Indian cottons and the English once more reveled in French silks.

The mania for all things Greek was not restricted to France. In 1806, Lord Elgin brought pieces of the Parthenon from Athens to London; these consisted of statuary fragments from the large friezes that stood atop the front and rear entryways to the temple. The classically inspired white gowns were popular in both France and in England and English women also styled their hair in imitations of ancient Greek fashions. Hair was styled into knots and coils and held with fillets, headbands, and combs. Later in the era, a simpler style with the hair oiled and combed into two locks behind the ears became more popular.

English clothing styles for women reflected a similar construction, but they began to differ greatly in style. Necklines were not as deep and worn rounded rather than square, which gave the English dress of this period its name: the round gown. The overall column-like shape of the dress and the use of the train were quite similar to French styles, but while the waistlines were very high, they were not quite under the bust as French Empire dresses were worn. The elevated waistline was popular in England, but it was executed in a different way. English women used more yardage in their skirts, making them fuller and gathering them to the high waistband. A small pad was placed at the small of the back to help the fabric fall correctly from the waistline and drape into an attractive train. Although the bodice of the round gown was also unstructured, it featured gussets on either side of the bustline for shaping and support. English women also adored wool paisley shawls as well as more delicate tulle and sheer shawls often decorated with tambour embroidery. They also enjoyed the use of gloves, muffs, and reticules just as much as the French.

But one quintessentially English mode of dress was the riding habit. Although women throughout Europe rode, it was considered a particularly English pastime to ride and hunt. The woman's riding habit consisted of a tailored and fitted, almost masculine-looking jacket worn over a tailored white shirt. The skirt was wide and long, often made of a heavy fabric such as wool or a cotton coutil. These ensembles were normally dark in color and did not show dirt easily. In addition to riding and hunting, English women commonly wore riding habits while traveling because they afforded more modesty and were easier to care for than the delicate and sheer round gowns.

Round gowns remained pale and soft dresses for most of the period, but it was not long before women wanted change. Before colors and use of a wider variety of textiles was popular in France, the English were experimenting with silk taffeta and satin as well as differently textured cottons. Married women at court once more began to dress in color. Deep jewel tones like ruby red and deep blue became popular for autumn and winter by 1815. Women would also layer sheer colored fabrics over the white skirt, or reverse it using a dark-colored skirt beneath a layer of very sheer white cotton or silk. Printed cottons became very popular in England and small, repeated geometric and floral motifs appeared on the round gowns. As the Regency era progressed, dresses became more colorful and more structured. Like in France, the hemlines became more widely flared and required petticoats to maintain the fullness. Skirt and sleeve treatments grew more elaborate and necessitated a change to more substantial dress fabrics. Trimming and surface decoration began to take precedence in the design and construction of English gowns. English waistlines were highest in 1816 and began to lower by small degrees until it stopped just above the natural waistline by 1820.

Shoes in Regency England were just as delicate as French shoes, made from silk and other fabrics and made to be worn at formal, indoor events. They were tied with ribbons and decorated with similar trim as their French counterparts. Shoes at this time for women around the world were generally made with straight soles, with no differentiation between the left and right foot.

Hats in England were more focused on the fashion of bonnets than were hats in France. After 1815 bonnet brims widened considerably and were known as Leghorn bonnets because of the leghorn straw used in their construction. English bonnets were shaped into many different forms and decorated with ruffles, frills, ribbons, and feathers.

English fashion publications had been in circulation since 1693, but during the Regency period, they became very important. In 1770, the *Lady's Magazine* began to be produced monthly and was exported to the United States throughout the era. In 1806, two more influential magazines started production. They were *Ackerman's Repository*, which offered fashion news and hand-colored plates with fabric swatches attached, and *La Belle Assembly*, which was written by a seamstress in London and gave not only fashion information but the ability to have the author create the ensembles features in the articles. French publications such as *Le Journal des Dames et des Modes* and *Gallery of Fashion* were also circulated in England.

Overall English and French fashions moved in parallel lines, but they did not cross for much of the period. The design and construction of dresses while similar were unique to each country. In England, there was more of a sense of restrained elegance and modesty. Dresses were not as sheer or clinging and the décolletage was not as daring.

Dress in this period in the United States was also roughly parallel to the styles in Europe but executed in its own way. The distance between the United

States and Europe and the availability of materials were the two main causes for differences in fashions between them. It took a very long time for information and textiles to travel across the Atlantic. The population of the United States was also more diverse and subject to interaction with a variety of different cultures such as the Native Americans. In the Colonial period, which directly preceded this era, the influence was primarily English and Dutch. Up north in Canada, the influence was decidedly French, but there was little interaction between the two cultures outside of fur trapping and trading.

Fashionable American women had several ways of gathering fashion information, but all the methods were costly and time-consuming, constantly leaving them several months, if not years behind the prevailing European styles. Many women had a favorite dressmaker in London who kept a mannequin, of the woman's measurements and sewed dresses to fit the mannequin then sent them onto the United States. Small alterations that might have been necessary could be easily made by local seamstresses or by the woman herself. Women might also order dresses done in a cheap material to be sent over and replicated stateside in fashionable yardage that she had also purchased and imported. Other women used an early catalog method and shopped for English fashions out of books of fashion plates and early fashion magazines. The English publication of the *Lady's Magazine* was available in limited circulation on a monthly basis in the United States from 1770 through 1837. This magazine was the first one available in America to include engraved illustrations of contemporary popular fashion instead of simply describing it. By 1810, there were several fashion magazines available from England and France, such as *Ackerman's Repository* and *Le Journal des Dames et des Modes*.

After the French Revolution, many displaced aristocrats and those that had served them fled to the United States. This brought an influx of French fashion as many of the refugees were royal dressmakers, hairstylists, milliners, and designers. When the political situation normalized in France, many of these immigrants renewed their connections with professional peers still in Paris. A system of fashion dolls was introduced to the United States during this time. Small dolls were dressed in a miniature version of high-fashion garments and sent to the United States. Dressmakers could then make copies based on the doll's designs and sell them to their patrons in the correct sizes. These dolls would continue to be an important part of the dissemination of fashion for most of the nineteenth century.

American fashion centers were few and far between. Philadelphia was the nation's first capital and was a major trade hub dealing in luxury goods. Women of fashion could also find fine restaurants and elegant ballrooms for dancing there. Many displaced Parisians took up residence in Philadelphia and taught dance and etiquette. The influential style magazine *Port Folio* was published in Philadelphia from 1801 to 1827. It featured not only articles on literature, opera, and theatre, but also hand-colored fashion plates from London and Paris. These factors make Philadelphia one of the United States' most splendid cities and its first fashion centers.

New York City was not far behind. In 1814, the population there was over 100,000. As a port city rich with trade, New York attracted a sophisticated population. By 1802, the American Academy of the Fine Arts had been founded by Mayor Edward Livingston and his brother Robert R. Livingston who was the

American minister to France. They installed a collection of copies of French sculptures and paintings. In 1818, Henry Sands Brooks opened a men's clothing store in Lower Manhattan that would become the Brooks Brothers store, the oldest men's clothing store chain in the United States. Brooks offered a mix of inexpensive ready-to-wear items and upscale, hand-tailored suits made of the finest wools brought in from England and Scotland.

Other influential American cities included Boston, Charleston, Newport, and Baltimore. Women in these cities also followed fashion as best they could, often circulating European fashion plates and dolls among their group of friends. Although these cities were not as large as Philadelphia and New York City, they were also port cities with a good trade and access to European publications and textiles.

American women were not entirely cut off from Europe, but even if women could get information on the current styles, domestically produced luxury textiles were nonexistent. In 1818, a factory that produced machine-made lace opened in New England and there was numerous mills that created cotton and wool fabrics, but none that produced silks or any kind of complex weaves such as damasks and brocades. Even prosperous cities could not always guarantee supplies of luxury textiles due to the various political changes in France and in England creating trade blockages and embargoes, especially during the War of 1812. Decorator fabrics such as curtains and upholstery were turned into fashionable dresses on many occasions. Throughout the period, most American women wore homespun cloth produced locally and in small quantities. The average woman did not have the means to purchase costly imported materials, but she did have the ability to decorate them in ways that often rivaled the finest dresses in Europe. American women became renowned for their skills in embroidery, beadwork, lacemaking, knitting, and crochet.

Children's Clothing

Children were dressed as miniature adults. Boys were dressed in skirts and dresses until about age four or five. There was no "breeching" ceremony as there had been in previous eras; at about age five, trousers were then worn under the skirts. Skirts for boys were not as long, as full, or as decorated as skirts for girls. At about age six or seven, boys were dressed in a "skeleton suit," which consisted of a loose shirt with a wide collar that could be frilled. The trousers were wide in the leg and high-waisted, buttoning to the bottom of the shirt or a very short jacket. By the time a boy was eleven or twelve, he dressed like an adult in scaled-down versions of fashionable men's clothing. Young boys' hair was often worn curled, but as they grew older, they adopted hairstyles more like an adult's. Boys could also wear either leather shoes or soft boots.

Girls dressed like small adults from a much earlier age. Dresses were cut much like a grown woman's, but shorter and worn over pantalets. Girls wore the dress and pantalets combination until they were ten or eleven years old, then switched into more fashionable women's dress. Small girls wore their hair in a simple style, but adolescent girls adopted adult hairstyles as well as clothing fashions. Complicated Grecian-inspired styles were very popular. Bonnets were also worn by girls. Girls wore the same flat slippers made of leather or fabric as adult women. They also could wear soft, short boots.

Specialty Clothing

In the early nineteenth century, military engagement was commonplace across Europe and in the United States. With Napoleon's wide-reaching campaigns, the military was often the first contact with different cultures and styles, and there was often a great deal of exchange of ideas. The use of frogs as closures was adopted by the French military after seeing such closures on the garments of those in the East. Frogging originated in China and is comprised of a set of ornamental closures made of cording. One side has a loop and the other a knot that slips into the loop and holds the garment closed without an overlap. Frogs became popular in military dress and then moved into civilian dress. Both men and women used frog closures on their overcoats, spencers, and pelisses. In the United States, army regulations sought to pare down the uniforms to promote a less European look and the ornamental frogs were replaced with simpler cotton cord loops during the War of 1812.

The popular headwear for Western military was the shako. Based off a Hungarian helmet design, the shako was a tall, cylindrical hat often decorated with plumes or large pom-poms. While they were extremely popular from the outset of the nineteenth century, they had all but disappeared by the beginning of the twentieth. The shako, alternately spelled chako, czako, schako, and tschako, was as cumbersome as it was impressive. It was soon retired from actual use in battle and became part of the dress and parade uniform instead. It is still used in modern times for both military parade uniforms as well as in civilian parades and drum corps.

THE ROMANTIC PERIOD, 1820–1850

Art

Romanticism was the dominant genre of art and literature that gave this period its name. This movement is characterized by a sense of nostalgia, vivid emotional content, appreciation of nature in a raw and untamed state, and attention to aesthetics. It is thought that Romanticism was a reaction to the Age of Enlightenment, which focused on rationalization, science, and strict social and political mores that discounted emotion and intuition and the force of nature. Romantics also had a keen interest in the supernatural and the occult; they reveled in things that could not be easily and rationally explained. Authors and poets like Nathaniel Hawthorne, Lord Byron, Percy Bysshe Shelley, Mary Shelley, Henry Wadsworth Longfellow, and John Keats tapped into the feeling of this movement and were extremely popular. In the United States, the work of Washington Irving and Edgar Allan Poe also capitalized on the high emotions and interest in the occult.

The Romantic period also saw the beginning of the Pre-Raphaelite Brotherhood. This confederation of artists, craftspeople, and writers formed in England in 1848 and was led by Dante Gabriel Rossetti, William Morris, John Everett Millais, and William Holman Hunt. They espoused a return to an ideal of medieval simplicity where spirituality and creativity were closely linked and nature could be appreciated in all its many facets. Their paintings were often of religious figures portrayed in a very human, everyday manner and for this they were sharply criticized for being blasphemous. But the bulk of their inspiration came from myths, legends, and contemporary Romantic poetry such as Keats, Byron, and Tennyson. For many years the Brotherhood met in secret to keep the painters from being expelled from the Royal Academy. They published a newsletter called *The Germ*, which only ran for four months in 1850. In addition to painters, the Brotherhood also included crafters and was responsible for the renewed interest in handcrafts that were considered obsolete in the face of the Industrial Revolution. William Morris's company designed, created, and sold textiles and wall coverings printed by hand using hand-carved book blocks. The Arts and Crafts movement in decorative arts also stemmed from the Pre-Raphaelites and the Romantic movement. Although there would be many fissures in the group and it would cease to function as an organized society after 1850, the Pre-Raphaelites would continue to directly impact fine art, literature, architecture, and interior design throughout the nineteenth century.

In France, the writer François-René de Chateaubriand (1768–1848) is often referred to as the "Father of French Romanticism." He was a major influence on Victor Hugo, who emerged as a popular and influential writer later in the Romantic period. The painter Ferdinand Victor Eugène Delacroix (1798–1863) was the most famous of the Romantic period in France. Instead of the perfectionism embodied by the Neoclassical work of Ingres, Delacroix looked back to earlier centuries, just as the Pre-Raphaelite Brotherhood had, and drew his inspiration from Venetian artists of the Renaissance and Dutch masters of the seventeenth century. He was especially fond of Rubens. He did not subscribe to the overly sentimental aspects of Romanticism but enjoyed depicting the often-violent forces found in nature and focused on the purely optical aspects of painting, especially placement of brushstrokes and use of color. Delacroix, in turn, was a source of inspiration to the later artistic movement of the Impressionists. One of his most famous works was "Liberty Leading the People" painted in 1830. It was painted after the July Revolution against King Charles X who sought to return the French monarchy to an absolutist regime as it had been in the past. "Liberty Leading the People" depicted a scene reminiscent of the French Revolution where the allegorical representation of Liberty is seen bearing the tricolor flag of the Revolution and leading a citizen's army across a barricade strewn with corpses. The original was purchased by Louis-Philippe, the man who would become the next French king, in 1831.

Surprisingly enough, landscape art flourished during the Romantic period. Accurate portrayals of all of nature's majesty, both beautiful and terrible, played right into the Romantic ideals of emotional communication and appreciation of the natural world. The Barbizon School was founded in about 1830 and focused on landscape art. The practice of sketching outside was encouraged by the school to capture a truly realistic scene and not a stiff, stilted image of a perfect landscape like previous classically trained artists had produced. The invention of collapsible tubes of premixed paints in 1841 made this kind of outdoor painting as easy as painting in a studio.

But possibly the most world-changing invention of the Romantic period was the invention of the photographic image. The process produced the world's first surviving photograph in 1826 and was exhibited to the public in 1839. Louis-Jacques-Mandé Daguerre (1787–1851) used iodine vapors to fix an image onto a silver-coated copper plate, and he called the resulting photograph a daguerreotype. Although the Englishman William Henry Fox Talbot (1800–1877) invented a photographic technique five years before Daguerre, it was not as reliable a process. Talbot turned his attentions to refining Daguerre's technique and advancing the science of photography. Now truly accurate images of people, places, clothing, sculpture, etc. could be captured and preserved for future generations. In 1849, a French foreign minister went on an expedition to photograph and document the great monuments of Egypt and the Middle East. This had been a particular boon to scholars of costume history, because for the first time they were able to compare the actual garments with the idealized fashion plates.

The Romantic period also saw the first World's Fair in 1851. It was held in London and called the Great Exhibition of the Works of Industry of All Nations. Queen Victoria and her consort Prince Albert were its chief proponents and organizers.

And possibly the most romantic of all Romantic-era tales was the death of Lord Byron. He donated a considerable sum of his large fortune to outfitting a fleet to aid the Greeks in fighting the Turks of the Ottoman Empire. He personally went to the Greek stronghold city of Missolonghi to held plan the attack on the Turkish stronghold of Lepanto but fell ill there. When he died in April of 1824, he was mourned deeply by the Greeks. Although they sent his body home to be buried in England, they kept his heart and buried it with great ceremony in the city. But tragically, Missolonghi fell to the Turks in 1826. In a last act of desperation, the Greeks ignited their stores of gunpowder, killing the Turks but sacrificing themselves. Legend holds that they died honoring the memory of Lord Byron; who was perceived to have died for them. Delacroix immortalized the Greek sacrifice in his 1826 painting, "Greece on the Ruins of Missolonghi," showing an allegorical depiction of Greece mourning the dead among the ruins of the city.

Men's Clothing

The typical man's attire of tailcoat, waistcoat, cravat, hat, and trousers was well established by 1820. Nothing large-scale changed for men's dress, but several modifications were made throughout the twenty-year period. A tightly fitted silhouette was popular at the outset of the period, and extremely fashionable men took to wearing corsets in order to achieve the right look.

Breeches were rarely worn at all, not even for formal or court functions, only for certain ceremonial costumes and sportswear. Instead, men wore the very tight-fitted pantaloons for formalwear. Even trousers were worn fairly tight and often needed a stirrup strap below the foot to keep them from riding up and to ensure a smooth, unrumpled line from waist to ankle. By the end of the period, the terms "trousers" and "pantaloons" were used interchangeably as the style of the pants had become almost indistinguishable. Pants were close-fitting and snug to the leg ending in a foot strap or a very narrowly cut ankle that was slit to accommodate the foot and then laced up. By the end of the 1840s the term "trousers" was almost exclusively used for pants. Also by the 1850s, fly-front closures had almost entirely replaced fall-front closures.

Coats were also now tailored to fit tightly and accentuate a narrow waist and broad shoulders. Padding was used in the shoulders and chest to create the necessary silhouette, and men of high fashion even took to wearing corsets specially made for the male physique. Men also padded their hips and calves to appear appropriately curvaceous in their tight pants. This would be one of the last times that menswear was focused on a shapely, body-conscious style. Soon men's clothing would take on a looser, boxy appearance that would remain through the nineteenth and twentieth centuries.

Jackets and trousers for men were usually made in very somber colors: black, brown, gray, beige, tan. The waistcoat was the focus of color and decoration for men and was often made in silk damask or brocade, embroidered satin, or velvet. Waistcoats varied slightly in length but still ended at or just below the natural waist. They were made in both single- and double-breasted styles and had either small, standing collars or a small, rolled collar that folded over without a notch between the collar and the lapel in a style referred to as a shawl collar in modern fashion terms. For daywear, men had a wider variety of colors, textures, and decorative elements from which to choose, but for evening and formalwear, waistcoats were required to be black or white and of velvet, satin, or pique. English Dandies sometimes wore very colorful waistcoats with their evening wear. Waistcoats were commonly made single-breasted for daywear and double-breasted for formalwear. Through the 1830s, men could wear two contrasting waistcoats for extra style. In the 1840s, waistcoats lengthened and came to a point below the waist. This point was known as the Hussar front or the beak. Lapels became narrower and less curved at the start of the decade, but by the time the 1850s were nearing, lapels had grown quite wide again and could be worn folded over the coat's lapels and collar. Waistcoats for weddings, formal dress, and eveningwear were predominantly white or cream colored and made of satin, velvet, or cashmere.

Coats changed through this period. A Romantic version of the frock coat became fashionable for daytime and casual dressing. The frock coat had not been popular in the Empire period, but this less structured coat, with its full-skirted bottom reaching to the knee or just below became favored as daywear again in the 1820s. There was a trend toward military-inspired frock coats with martial details like piping and a standing collar with no lapels. Riding coats in the 1820s and 1830s had very wide lapels. After 1840, lapels on riding coats and tail coats remained very wide with a deep notch cut between the collar and the lapel. Frock coats remained to have slender lapels in the shawl collar style without notches. Tail coats were still primarily double breasted and worn for evening and formal occasions while frock coats were single breasted and preferred for casual wear. By the 1850s, the frock coat was considered almost as casual as the banyan robe. The frock coat was still worn with padding in the shoulders and full sleeves through the 1840s. The torso remained quite fitted, but the skirting was narrowed shortened to above the knee.

In the 1820s and 1830s, sleeves had been made very full and gathered into the armseye creating a puff at the shoulder. In 1832, this fullness disappeared in the tailcoat but remained in the frock coat, although the size of the puff diminished until it finally disappeared as well after 1840. Also at this time the tailcoat was changing shape as well. Instead of the square open front, the tails now scooped smoothly back from the center front. It was called the newmarket coat and it was a single-breasted riding tailcoat that featured side pleats and no back vent. The collars and lapels were small and notched and the pockets were low and could be made with or without flaps. The front closing was mostly straight but curved back above the waist to allow the tails to flare away over the hips.

Banyans and colorful robes were still worn at home and for very casual daytime wear. These were made of bright prints and weaves of silk and cotton that were either imported or domestically made.

The majority of innovations in menswear came with outerwear. Men had ceased to wear the spencer entirely before 1820 and several different kinds of coats were designed and marketed all over the world. The greatcoat was a catch-all term for a full overcoat that reached to the ankle. These coats were made with or without lapels and featured a deep collar. Greatcoats could be either single- or double-breasted. A box coat or curricle coat was a less structured greatcoat that was made with one or more short capes at the shoulder. These styles of coats had been around since the start of the nineteenth century and had changed very little, but in the 1830s several new types of overcoats were developed. The first was the paletot. The paletot was first advertised in the early 1830s and it applied to a variety of styles. By and large, the paletot was a short greatcoat that could be single or double breasted with a small collar and narrow lapels. It could be made with a waist seam or without. The chesterfield coat was named after the Sixth Earl of Chesterfield, who was quite a socialite in the 1830s and 1840s. The chesterfield coat appeared in the 1840s and was most commonly made as a double-breasted long coat with no waistline seam. It featured a velvet collar and no side pleats, only a small vent in the back. The chesterfield is still a popular modern coat style and made for both men and women. The last of the coat innovations of the Romantic period was the mackintosh. This coat caused a great sensation as it was the world's first truly waterproof overcoat. Charles Mackintosh patented his waterproof textile in 1823, calling it "India rubber cloth." Mackintosh coats were ankle-length and cut full to fit loosely. Although they were wonderful to guard against the omnipresent English rain, they were said to have smelled terribly, and mackintosh wearers often were not "admitted to an omnibus on account of the offensive stench which they emit."[20]

Shirts during this time were made with very deep collars that could be worn folded over a cravat or neckcloth. Sleeves were cuffed and closed with buttons or cufflink studs. The fronts of the shirts had insets at the front that could be changed out for day or evening attire. The insets for evening or formal wear were frilled. Men still wore stocks, wide neckpieces that fastened at the back, at the neck. Cravats were still popular and were worn tied into a knot or a bow at the front of the neck. Drawers were unchanged through this period.

Stockings for men were usually knitted from worsted wool, cotton, or silk for formal dress. Shoes were low heeled and toes were square. Many shoes laced up the front with three or four eyelets and formal footwear was open across the instep and tied closed with a ribbon. Boots were still very popular for riding. In 1832, rubber soles for shoes were invented and by the 1840s all manner of rubber overshoes such as galoshes were available. Spatterdashers or spats also remained popular. These heavy cloth gaiters were worn over the shoes to protect the stockings. Spats for riding and sporting were worn to the knee. Spats were elasticized in the 1840s. Bedroom slippers were an important fashion for men and many of the fashionable ladies' magazines included needlepoint patterns for making these slippers.

Hair for men was kept short to moderate and worn in curls or waves. Beards became popular again around 1825. Top hats were the headwear of choice and by this period they were quite varied. Some were very tall and others much shorter. Some crowns were simple cylinders and others grew narrower at the top and still others grew slightly wider at the top with a slight outward curve. Top-hat brims were still universally small, with most having curled up edges and a small dip in the front and back. The first collapsible top hat was also invented during this time. Called the gibus hat, it had a hidden spring inside that allowed the hat to be folded flat and carried under the arm. For casual wear, the rounded crown hat known as a Derby in the United States and a Bowler in England became popular at the end of the 1840s.

Gloves were still an important accessory for men. Doeskin, kid leather, wool, or cotton gloves were worn during the day and evening dress still required white silk or kid leather. Snuff, a finely powdered inhaled tobacco, use saw a return to popularity, and men who were habitual users usually carried handkerchiefs because snuff caused sneezing and the occasional nosebleed. Canes and umbrellas were also common accessories. Cravat pins, watch chains, and brooches were also frequently worn by men. Men also favored matching gold stud button and cufflink sets.

During the Romantic period, after silhouettes relaxed from the padded and constricted forms of the 1820s, menswear went through relatively few changes. Colors for men were muted and somber and menswear took on a uniform appearance.

Women's Clothing

Roles for women became rather complicated in this period. Open displays of "womanly emotion" such as sighing, weeping, and fainting were encouraged. Thinness went right along with the maidenly ideal and women dieted en masse for the first time in history, seeking to achieve the thin, delicate beauty that was so prized. Women were expected to live up to many often-conflicting standards including the waifish maiden who pines away for love and the capable, industrious wife and mother. Affluent women were primarily hostesses for their husband's social events and supervisors of the household servants. Well-to-do ladies were expected to be accomplished in sewing, embroidery, sketching, painting of china, and other decorative homecrafts. The constricting styles of sleeves in this period made it impossible to do anything much more than small crafts held in the lap. This was also a time of westward expansion, and pioneer women struggled to remain at least somewhat fashionable but yet be able to do the often-hard labor that homesteading required. The bulky petticoats required to attain the very full skirts popular at the end of the period were a cause of major health concerns for women and became the target of Dress Reform in the 1840s and 1850s.

The period of 1820–1825 was one of transitions between the last vestiges of the Empire style into a silhouette that was entirely Romantic. Dresses of this transitory period still had an elevated waistline and relatively narrow silhouette that was starting to bell outward at the bottom and the top in the form of larger puffed sleeves and a fuller skirt trimmed with rows of ruffles. Through 1835 skirts grew extremely full with several gores and sleeves became an enormous puff from shoulder to elbow.

Dresses of the early Romantic period were frequently and creatively named after the time of day when the dress would be worn or called by the activity meant to be done in the dress. Some examples out of fashion plates included the "morning dress," the "afternoon dress," the "day dress," as well as the "promenade dress," the "carriage dress," and the "dinner dress." Morning dresses were the most informal and often made of white or light-colored cotton of linen. These dresses were also the softest and most unstructured and often referred to as the lingerie dress. Day, promenade, and carriage dresses were still not considered formal but were far more structured than morning dresses. They were made of silk, wool, muslin, challis, printed cotton, and batiste in a variety of colors that followed the seasons. Colors such as rich yellow, blue, green, and red were popular. Dyestuffs were still derived from natural sources at this time: plants and insects. Red dye came from the madder plant and shades of blue and violet could be obtained from indigo and woad. Blue was an especially popular color. Colors were often combined in stripes, especially for daytime dressing. Dresses intended for day wear had lower waistlines, wide sleeves, and full skirts. Necklines could be deep, V-necked styles or high collars that ended at the throat and were finished with ruffles or lace. A popular neckline treatment was a surplice, or crossover. Deeper necklines might include a sheer white cotton or linen tucker or filler to maintain modesty. The pelisse robe was another sort of daytime dress that was adapted from the pelisse coats of the Empire period. It retained the look of a coat with its center front opening that closed with buttons, ribbon ties, or hooks and eyes.

The sleeves were the most remarkable fashion detail in early Romantic dresses. Although they were various in style, they were all very large and full. The earliest form of the hallmark puff sleeve was a leftover from the late Empire era when long sleeves could be attached to the short, puffed sleeves of the dress. This early convertible sleeve was worn through 1825 and often had decorative epaulettes on the shoulder. The Marie sleeve was full from shoulder to wrist but had the fullness controlled by bands tied at intervals creating puffs between them. This sleeve was very reminiscent of the German slash-and-puff sleeves of the Northern Renaissance and the virago sleeves of the middle seventeenth century. The *gigot* and *demi-gigot* were the two most popular sleeves and both were extremely full and puffed at the shoulder. The gigot sleeve, also known as the leg-o'-mutton sleeve, gradually tapered to a fitted cuff. The demi-gigot was very full from the shoulder to the elbow and became fitted at the elbow and down to the wrist. The idiot or imbecile sleeve was very full from shoulder to wrist where it was gathered into a fitted cuff. The imbecile sleeve was called that because it was supposedly based off of the kind of jackets used to restrain the mad.

Waistlines sat just above the natural waist, were straight, and often accentuated with a belt or sash. After 1833, waistlines began to be constructed with a V-shaped dip in front. Skirt lengths changed quite a bit over these early years of the period. In 1820, hems skimmed the tops of the shoes but had risen to ankle length by the end of the decade. These shorter skirts were fashionable until 1836 when hems once again lowered to the top of the foot. During the transition years of 1820–1825, skirts were still narrow through the hips with a flare at the hem. After 1828, the skirt was extremely full from hip to hem and pulled into deep gathers or pleats at the waist. At the height of this fashion, the silhouette resembled the letter X.

Accessory garments used to change the look of the dresses for added flexibility in styling were very popular. Sheer tuckers called fillers or chemisettes were placed in the neckline of dresses to raise them for modesty or for a change of pace. Wide collars that draped over the large sleeves and closed across the bosom were called pelerines. Pelerines could be made as a matching item to a dress or could be of contrasting fabric. They could be plain or trimmed with lace and ribbons. Some were single layers of fabric and some were tiered. The pelerine was the most popular accessory garment for early Romantic women. A variation was the fichu pelerine; it had two panels or lappets that hung from the center front and were worn passed beneath the belt or sash at the waist. Some women also wore a santon, which was a silk lady's cravat, and a canezou which was like a waistcoat for ladies made in the form of a sleeveless spencer worn over the bodice.

Dresses for evening wear were similar in construction to dresses for daytime but varied in silhouette. Necklines were daringly low, cut wide across the bust-line, and nearly off-the-shoulder. Sleeves were very wide in eveningwear but tended to be shorter, ending at the elbow. White gloves that came to the elbow or just over it were worn for evening. Formal dress fabric was predominantly lightweight silk, satin, or organdy and skirt hems were short to the instep or to the ankle.

After 1836, the extremes of width began to deflate, giving the dresses a drooping quality. The sleeve fullness gradually lessened but did not disappear entirely. The bulk of fabric moved down the arm until about 1840 when the sleeves became more closely fitted from shoulder to wrist. Skirts lengthened to just above the floor and lost the fluffy, bouffant quality they'd had in earlier decades. The fullness gathered to the waist and was held out by several starched petticoats. In 1840, some skirts were edged in decorative braid that not only added visual interest, but helped to protect the fabric from wear and tear. Pockets were also sewn into skirts for the first time in history during this period. Previously, a pocket was a separate article tied at the waist and accessed by a slit in the skirt and petticoats. The slim styles of the Empire prohibited this practice and gave rise to the trend for reticule purses, but the voluminous Romantic skirts allowed ample space for pockets. Waistlines now sat at the natural waist and generally came to a point at the front. Bodices closed with lacings, buttons, or hooks and eyes either at the center front or center back and were usually made attached to the skirt to create a one-piece gown. Ruching, flounces, scallops, and cording were popular trims. Two-piece skirt and jacket styles were also somewhat popular. The jacket-style bodice was called a basque and one of the most popular was the *gilet corsage* that imitated a man's coat and waistcost. A French name for fashion pieces was the accepted manner of naming, no matter the garment's country of origin. In this case, *gilet* was French for waistcoat and *corsage* for bodice. In the 1840s, some skirts were made with several tiered flounces. It does bear mentioning that in the 1840s there seems to have been a marked difference in fashions depicted in magazines and fashion plates and what is seen on extant garments. One example is the placement of trims. Many fashion plates show the skirt decorations arranged horizontally down the center front of the skirt, and other show a wide vertical band of trimming on the skirt. Neither type of decoration has been commonly found on any garments from this period in any costume collection.[21]

Sleeves in the second half of the period were often set so low as to be off-the-shoulder. The bishop sleeve was popular until about 1840 and was made by pleating the fullness into the shoulder and letting the volume expand down the arm before being gathered into a fitted cuff. The *sleeve en bouffant*, also called *en sabot*, resembled the Maria sleeve with the fullness puffed out between areas where the sleeve was tight to the arm. The Victorian version of this sleeve had its largest puff at the elbow. A popular new sleeve treatment that appeared after 1840 featured a wide sleeve that ended at the elbow in a bell or funnel shape. Undersleeves decorated with embroidery or trimmed with lace were then sewn or buttoned unto the underside of the wide oversleeves. This not only created an attractive layered look, but made the cotton or linen undersleeves easily removed for laundering or to change or update styles.

Evening and formal gowns of the second part of the Romantic period were similar to those of the earlier years. Dresses were very full in the skirt and featured a wide, off-the-shoulder neckline that was either cut straight across or made, *en coeur*, "of the heart," with a dip at the center front. The bertha collar, a wide deep collar that followed the open neckline, was popular for both evening and more formal daywear. Some evening gowns had overskirts that were open at the front or puffed over the top of an underskirt. Formal gowns were made of satin, organdy, velvet, and silk moiré; they were lavishly trimmed with lace, ruffles, ribbon, and silk flowers.

Clothing for equitation remained popular. Riding habits were finely tailored and echoed the lines of men's clothing, with a jacket fitted to the torso and flaring out over the hips in tails. A top hat and cravat were also worn with the riding habit along with a full skirt of heavy cotton or wool. Most women of station rode sidesaddle, but some chose to ride astride. Women that rode astride donned pantaloons of sturdy cotton drill or coutil.

The underclothes for these dresses included the chemise, drawers, stays, and several layers of starched petticoats. Down or fiber-filled pads called bustles were often used in conjunction with the petticoats to help support the very wide skirts of the earlier years of the era. Ladies of England had used pads like these during the Renaissance and the Regency periods to ensure the proper drape of their skirts. There were no substantial changes in drawers; they were still made of fine linen or cotton or flannel for cold weather and closed with a drawstring waist. Drawers of this period were a split-crotch style with no center seam between the two legs. Women from all over Europe and the United States in just about every social class wore drawers. Chemises of the time were wide and came to the knee or just below it, and sleeves were generally short.

The greatest advancement of underpinnings of this time period was the early rudiments of a true corset. Prior to this period, stays were used to smooth the silhouette and provide the proper posture and support for the gown; they did not change the actual shape of the body. Beginning in the 1820s, corsetry was actually constructed to change the figure of the wearer and pull the natural waist into the desired small circumference. In 1827, an American physician denounced corsets as a "slow and fashionable poison."[22] The first corsets with a split-busk front closures were invented in 1829 by the French corsetiere Jean-Julien Josselin. This allowed women to be able to put on and take off their corsets themselves without requiring assistance. These types of corsets did not become common until 1850, however. But resourceful women came up with a variety of devices to assist in the process of tying and untying one's own corset, so that even poorer women who could not afford to hire maids to dress them could dress themselves. Corsets were all but required wearing for women of all social strata in this time period and although many fashion magazines gave directions on how to make one's own corset, even women with little money would save up to buy one rather than trying to sew a homemade corset that looked fashionable and fit well. "Elastic" corsets were advertised in the 1820s and appear to have been made with metal springs and wires to allow them some degree of stretch and flexibility. But after vulcanized rubber was regularly available in 1830, corsets with rubberized elements were introduced. Metal eyelets were invented in 1828 and replaced eyelets stitched around the edges with thread. These metal eyelets made corsets stronger, less expensive, and facilitated tighter lacing. The French corset industry was well known for luxurious, custom-made corsets, while English and American markets focused more on commercially made, ready-to-wear varieties. Mass-produced corsets of this era came in standard waist sizes from 18 to 30 inches, although larger sizes could be ordered by special request. The first fashion plate to actually feature a woman dressed only in a corset and petticoats was not printed until 1830 and it was considered scandalous and indecent. No matter how structured and opaque corsets were, they were still considered underwear, and in some places it was against the law to publish pictures of women wearing them and nothing else. Until 1870, many advertisers featured images of disembodied corsets. During the 1830s, many humorous and erotic prints about corsets circulated through Europe. Many artists got around the bans on showing naked women by showing them dressed in a corset. Valerie Steele says in *The Corset: A Cultural History,* "The corset assumed the role of surrogate for the body; it also functioned as a sign of undressing and making love. The act of lacing and unlacing the corset was treated as a symbol of sexual intercourse."[23] The corset is probably the single most enduring item of nineteenth century dress.

Stockings were knitted from silk or cotton, and of worsted wool for cold weather. During the 1830s and 1840s, black silk stockings were popular for evening wear. Shoes continued to be flat and slipper-like with square toes made of delicate fabrics. After 1840, a small heel began to be added to the shoes. Also at this time, white satin evening boots and ribbon sandals became more fashionable than slippers for evening attire. Leather shoes and ankle boots were worn in cold or wet weather. Gaiters were made for women as well as men to protect their stockings. These gaiters often coordinated with the dress. Galoshes and other rubber overshoes for wet weather were introduced for women as well in the late 1840s.

The pelisse coat cut to accommodate this wide silhouette was favored for women's outerwear until the mid-1830s, when a variety of shawls, capes, and mantles became fashionable. Full-length mantles were worn until about 1836; after that year they were worn much shorter. Depending on the season, mantles could be lightweight wool or cotton for daywear, thick wool or quilted cotton for cold weather. For evening dress mantles were typically of velvet, satin, or very fine, soft wool and lined with silk satin. Common styles of mantles were illustrated and described in the popular magazines of the time. One the most popular styles was the mantlet, a short shawl-like mantle that draped over the shoulders and hung down into two points at the front. The pelerine-mantlet was long to the elbows with broad front lappets like the fichu pelerine, but the pelerine-mantlet was not meant to be tucked into the belt. The burnous was a longer, more voluminous mantle with a hood that was named for a Middle

Eastern garment. It was usually made of soft wool or cashmere. The paletot was knee-length and more like a cloak with slits for the arms. Up to three capelets fell from the shoulders. A pardessus was a full outdoor garment with a definite waistline and wide sleeves that could extend half-length to the elbow or three-quarter length to the forearm.

Hairdressing for women of the Romantic period started with a basic part down the center. In the 1820s, after the hair was parted, the length was pulled back into a knot or a bun for daywear and into ringlets for evening. The hair framing the face was curled. After 1824, a more elaborate style emerged of braided loops and falls of curls around the face that often required a woman to supplement her locks with false hairpieces. These styles eventually merged in 1829 into an arrangement of waves and curls around the face and the length of the hair drawn up into an elevated knot near the top of the head. The style was very loosely based on traditional Chinese women's hairdressing and was therefore called *à la Chinoise*. Variations of these styles continued throughout the period. In the 1840s, hair was parted in the middle and combed down around the temples where it was arranged in fat ringlets or simply looped over the ears before being pulled back into a bun or chignon at the back of the head.

Hair was arranged with jeweled hair pins and tortoise-shell combs. For evening-wear, women often wore their hair dressed with fancy ornaments in lieu of a hat.

White linen or cotton daycaps with lace or ribbon trimming were worn by adult women indoors. Hats for outdoor wear were large and ornate with tall, rounded crowns and trimmed with plume feathers and ribbons. Bonnets with wide brims were worn tied beneath the chin so the crown of the bonnet could frame the face. These hats were also trimmed with frills, feathers, silk flowers, and ribbon. They were popular for being not only charming and attractive but valuable sunshades for women who valued a pale complexion, as well as for pioneer women and those who worked outdoors to guard against sunburn. Spoon bonnets with an oval shape were popular at the start of the Romantic period, but they soon gave way to rounder shapes that more closely framed the face. A bonnet veil was sometimes paired with these later, rounder bonnets of the 1840s and it draped down the nape of the neck. Some lined the opening of the bonnet as well, creating a multilayered effect that was both charming and modest. A popular hat of this period combined a bonnet brim with a soft fabric crown was called a capote.

Women favored simple jewelry at this time. Gold chains with a cross, locket, or a scent bottle were popular because they were considered so very romantic. Chatelaines hung from the waist. Originally used as a medieval key-chain, the chatelaine cycled through periods of popularity for hundreds of years. In the Romantic period women hung small sewing necessities such as scissors, a needle case, a thimble, buttonhooks, and the like. Brooches were popular, especially pinned to the wide bertha collars, and were often sold as sets with matching drop earrings. In the 1830s, ribbon chokers bearing a locket, heart, or cross pendant was very popular, as were choker-length strands of pearls. Jewelry grew less and less popular as the period advanced and by the end of the 1840s the main item of jewelry was a watch worn on a chain around the neck or suspended from the waist.

Other accessories included gloves for both day- and eveningwear. Day gloves were short, reaching the wrist and usually made of cotton, wool, silk, or kid leather. Evening gloves were long to the elbow or longer through the 1830s after which they reached to the middle of the forearm. Evening gloves were made of silk or kid leather. A popular trend for gloves was to cover the hand but not the fingers. Fingerless gloves were worn for evening and called mittens or mitts. Reticules and other purses, parasols, fans, and muffs were still popular accessories throughout the period. In the 1830s and 1840s hats were so wide that parasols were unnecessary, but they were carried unopened anyway. By the 1840s a parasol was invented with a folding handle to better fit into carriages.

A pale complexion was highly prized. Women tried to look wan, even sickly, with shadowy circles beneath their eyes and faces powdered with white rice powder. Rouge and lip color were not used at all, not only did they not fit the ideal of the maiden pining away for her true love, face paint was still considered improper and only used by prostitutes. Homemade or commercially available creams and lotions were used to keep the skin soft and smooth.

Although this silhouette was very feminine and romantic, a well-dressed woman could wear up to forty pounds of fabric in the form of dozens of starched petticoats and the volume of sleeves, skirts, and mantle. This made getting from place to place a cumbersome task and was thought to be the cause of dozens of health concerns. Several movements seeking to liberate women from the cruel and confining fashions began to crop up in the 1830s. None were successful at changing the course of fashion, and few women turned to these reformed styles.

Children's Clothing

Dress for children of the Romantic period was similar to that of adults. Fashion plates show even the smallest children in full, cumbersome sleeves and with abnormally small waists. Both young boys and girls wore dresses, often with pantalets beneath. Corsets were used on boys and girls alike, thinking that it was necessary to promote a strong, straight spine. But both men and women were known to wear corsets, and the health concerns could be simply a justification of forcing such adult aesthetics onto small children. By the 1830s, corsetry for very young children was abandoned.

Boys were put into trousers by age six. During the Romantic period, boys had a wider array of styles from which to choose than ever before. The skeleton suit, which had originally become popular in 1790, continued to be worn until about 1830. The tunic suit comprised a jacket that was fitted through the waist and attached to a full skirt that was either gathered or pleated to the waistband. This skirt fell to the knee and was worn over trousers. The tunic buttoned down the front and could be worn with a belt. Sleeves could be fitted to the arm or be made in the fashionable gigot style of women's clothing. For very young boys, full drawers with frilled bottoms were worn with the tunic instead of trousers. The Eton suit was another popular mode of dress for boys. It worn by school-aged boys and modeled after the uniforms at the Eton School, a prestigious all-boys school in England. It consisted of a short, single-breasted jacket that ended at the waist. The front was square and the lapels were wide. A white shirt was worn with the outfit as well as slim trousers, a waistcoat, and a necktie. This suit would become the usual attire for school-aged boys for the rest of the century. Boys could also wear smaller versions of fashionable jackets and trousers like those of adult men. Frock coats or dress coats were not made in children's sizes, but Romantic interpretations of historical and ethnic costumes were. Boys were also sometimes dressed in nineteenth-century versions of doublets, hussar tunics, Scottish kilts, and Turkish national dress. Miniature sporrans, swords, and other authentic accessories were paired with these costumes. Boys wore caps and hats inspired by sailor uniforms and ethnic styles.

Little girls' dress was made just like that of adult women, but with shorter skirts and sleeves. Pantalets were worn beneath the dresses, but lace- or ruffle-trimmed drawers were also popular. The dresses of even the youngest girls often featured very full puffed sleeves and some even had the overly large gigot-style sleeves. Smocks were also popular for little girls to wear. The smocking on the bodice that gathered the volume of fabric into a wearable size provided an opportunity to display fine needlework and add color and surface interest to the garment. Smocks were often worn as play clothes and could be worn by boys as well. Girls' hair was styled in slightly simpler adaptations of what their mothers wore, and they never went outdoors without a hat. Bonnets of all kinds were popular for girls, as was a starched linen or cotton lingerie cap.

Boys and girls commonly wore white cotton stockings and ankle boots in black or brown leather. For more formal dressing, girls would wear slippers styled after women's shoes. Romantic styles were very charming to look at on children, but they were not as comfortable or as practical as Empire and Regency clothing had been.

Specialty Clothing

In the Romantic period, shopping for clothing began to grow into the large retail industry seen today. Industrialization had a variety of effects on the populations of Europe and the United States. Farmers and laborers migrated to cities to find work that paid actual money, instead of barter or trade. The lower classes began to amass a small disposable income that could be spent on clothing and other niceties. These items of fashion were much easier to come by, made affordable by the factory system, which produced large quantities of goods in a short time. The owners, managers, and distributors of the factories comprised a rapidly growing middle class that was able to afford luxuries previously reserved only for the wealthy. The combination of potential customers, desired goods, and spending money created a boom in the retail industry, especially for ready-made garments. The high-end couture market was not suffering in the slightest as ready-to-wear was aimed primarily at the lower classes. Technological advances in spinning, weaving, dying, and sewing made the ready-to-wear industry possible. Items like the measuring tape, which was invented in 1820, was a great help to the garment industry as a whole.

During the 1820s and 1830s, as dresses became more elaborate and detailed for women, dressmakers and seamstresses were able to find a great deal of work to keep them gainfully employed. In France, female dressmakers began to rise to prominence and take on some very influential clients such as Queen Marie-Louise, wife of King Louis-Philippe. Mesdames Vignon and Palmyre were notable dressmakers of Paris who catered to the French aristocracy. Tailors also had a great deal of influence, even though the age of the Dandy was all but past, and the newly restored French nobility were eager to keep up with the subtle changes in men's fashion.

As more and more people moved to the cities, the ability to produce homemade fabric and clothing diminished and the market for ready-made work clothes grew rapidly. In 1824, Pierre Parissot opened a shop in Paris that sold inexpensive work clothes tagged with fixed prices. This was a new innovation in shopping that proved to be a great success and led to changes in the way readymade clothes were made and sold. Clothing sold for fixed prices required that production had to be standardized within the company, something that no one had ever worried about. Other companies had to keep prices competitive and it required them to adopt the same production standards. During the Romantic period, the ready-made clothing industry was one of the fastest growing in Paris, and thousands of garment workers came to the city. The ready-made market at this time could not yet diminish the demand for higher-end tailoring and dress making, but it did compete with the old, established secondhand clothing trade on which many of the lower classes had relied for centuries.

Shops began to specialize in particular areas of dress. Fancy goods stores were the fastest growing market share of the ready-made industry. These shops focused on millinery, trimming, notions, and the like. Often they worked closely with a dressmaker to provide the nontextile elements of an ensemble such as buttons, hooks and eyes, ribbon, and thread. A milliner today is solely a hat maker, but in the nineteenth century a milliner was the person who made and sewed all manner of trims and decorations for dresses, shoes, outerwear, and, of course, hats. Fancy good stores served a number of needs and are thought to be the precursors to the modern department store.

In 1824, La Belle Jardinière opened on the Quai aux Fleurs near the Temple District in Paris on the block where the secondhand clothing merchants had once been. La Belle Jardinière was not considered a true department store, but it did cater to the lower-middle-class and sold ready-made clothing clearly ticketed with reasonable prices. By 1830, two more large ready-to-wear stores opened. Bonhomme Richard opened at 9 Place des Victoires and also sold to lower-middle-class people. The House of Coutard was a new breed of ready-to-wear clothing store. With large, brightly lit windows with mannequins dressed in the latest fashions displayed in them, the House of Coutard focused on upscale designs and better quality clothing that could command higher prices. Their customers included lawyers, doctors, politicians, and other members of the bourgeoisie. Several other fancy goods stores followed suit, and in 1837, Thierry Hermés opened a luxury leather goods store. Hermés, originally a saddlery, is still in business in the twenty-first century and is still renowned for their fine leather and couture fashion line.

But it would not be until 1838 that the first true department store would open in Paris. Called Le Bon Marché, the good market, it was a single store that offered a variety of goods separated into different departments. The store was owned and operated by Aristide Boucicaut and his wife. Le Bon Marché's prices were fixed and absolutely no haggling was allowed. Boucicaut did guarantee the satisfaction of each purchase and offered exchanges or refunds on merchandise.

England had a storied tradition of fine tailoring dating back to the seventeenth century. Savile Row in London is synonymous with English tailoring. In the 1820s, the tailor James Poole moved his shop from Regent Street to Old

Burlington Street, which was adjacent to Savile Row. In 1846, his son Henry took over the business and enlarged the premises. He built an impressive showroom with a new entrance that opened into Savile Row itself. He focused on a clientele of middle-class men. Soon, other tailors also moved to Savile Row and the area became a prime shopping location for elegant men's clothing. Department stores that catered to the middle class opened up in Newcastle in England and in Edinburgh, Scotland.

The United States also saw the benefit of a ready-to-wear industry. After the Erie Canal was opened in 1825, the transportation of people, goods, and information could flow much faster between the eastern seaboard and the American West. By 1835, the ready-to-wear industry was booming in New York City, Philadelphia, and Boston. New York City became a major commercial center, especially for fashion, and by 1837 it was producing an average of $2.5 million worth of ready-made clothing annually.

Henry Sands Brooks had already opened Brooks Brothers as a custom tailor in 1818, but by the 1830s he had added a ready-to-wear section. The Lord and Taylor's Department Store opened in 1826. Samuel Lord and George Washington Taylor put their store on Fifth Avenue in Manhattan, making it the first of the great department stores to open there. Charles Lewis Tiffany and John Young opened a stationery and dry goods store at 259 Broadway in 1837. They modeled their store after the retail clothing stores and offered each item for sale marked with a nonnegotiable sale price. Eventually, the Tiffany family would leave the dry goods business and found one of the world's most renowned jewelry stores. Alexander Turney Stewart opened the Marble Palace just down the street from Tiffany's; it primarily sold Irish linen and domestic textiles. But Stewart designed the store to look like an Italian Renaissance palazzo, completely decorated in white marble and black wrought iron. Stewart's was one of the first stores to employ grandiose architecture to entice customers into his establishment over his competitors.

Although the United States was achieving financial, commercial, and manufacturing independence from Europe, it still looked to London and Paris for fashion. It would be years before an essential American style would emerge. One of the most important American fashion magazines started in 1830. *Godey's Lady's Book* was the first purely fashion magazine published in the United States. Other culture magazines like *Port Folio* featured articles on fashion and even the occasional colored plate. The only magazines devoted entirely to style were imported from London and Paris. Although *Godey's* got its fashion information from Paris, it was still an American publication and geared toward women who may not live near a major city. Each issue included not only a hand-tinted fashion plate, but a pattern, fabric requirements, and instructions for a fashionable dress that could be made at home. Sarah Hale was *Godey's* editor from 1837 until 1877, and she was dedicated to keeping a specifically American flavor in the magazine and included articles by authors such as Edgar Allan Poe and Harriet Beecher Stowe. *Godey's* did have some popularity overseas and enjoyed a limited circulation in Europe. But most importantly, Hale kept an extensive archive and left behind a legacy of the progression of women's dress from the Romantic period onward covering both the prevalent fashions of Europe as well as Americanized adaptations of them.

American fashion varied greatly depending on class and geographic area. People near to cities and large towns could easily purchase fabric, if not ready-made garments. Those who lived in rural areas often had access to wool and either linen or cotton depending on the area of the country. Dyestuffs could be found among the plants and insects of the prairie, and small towns and villages often pooled their resources of raw materials and skills to create textiles that could be shared among the whole population.

Americans in the Rural West did not have much access to fashion information, nor did they have the right materials to create stylist garments. Most homesteaders and pioneers wore simple, practical clothes that hearkened to colonial times. Men wore a simple tunic shirt with full sleeves and deep cuffs and collar. The tail was cut long to tuck into the trousers and between the legs to shield the skin from the often scratchy wool of the trousers. Drawers for men were worn in cold weather, but in the warmer months, they often went without. The trousers were made with a fall front and straight, slim legs. Men did wear a waistcoat and cravat, which were likely to be the most fashionable items in their wardrobe.

Women dressed in simple gowns of cotton, wool, or linen that opened to the waist at the center front. Bodices were lined and had reinforced seams. Buttons, ties, or hooks and eyes were used for closures. Sleeves were generally long and practical, neither too tight nor too full. Necklines were not fashionably low but often women used a tucker anyway as extra protection from the sun. Bonnets were also worn more for sun shading than high fashion. Day dresses often had removable and interchangeable cuffs, collars, and occasionally capelets. This allowed ease of laundering as well as flexibility in dress. Aprons were an important accessory, adding not only a decorative element to the dress, but also protecting it from dirt and damage. Women even in the most rural of areas usually wore at least three petticoats. This was partially for warmth but also partially to echo the fashionable full-skirted silhouette of the Romantic period.

THE CRINOLINE PERIOD, 1850–1870

Art

A major artistic movement was developed in England by Frederic Leighton (1830–1896) and James Abbott McNeill Whistler (1834–1903) in the early 1860s that popularized the concept of "art for art's sake," focusing more on the aesthetic value of art, composition, color, and details, than the subject matter. Many disillusioned members of the Pre-Raphaelite Brotherhood supported this movement. This grew out of the Pre-Raphaelite style of painting of the 1840s and 1850s and into the Aesthetic Movement of the 1880s that could give rise to Art Nouveau in the 1890s.

William Morris (1834–1896), a periphery member of the Pre-Raphaelite Brotherhood, founded the design firm of Morris, Marshall, Faulkner & Co. in 1861. He employed several other members of the Brotherhood and created handcrafted decorative arts with an attention to detail and medieval and legendary inspiration and subject matter.

The Salon des Refusés exhibits paintings rejected by the annual Salon in Paris in 1863. Among the exhibitors are Cézanne, Pissarro, Whistler, and Édouard Manet (1832–1883). Manet's painting that year was "Luncheon on the Grass" ("Le Déjeuner sur l'herbe") and it was inspired by a grouping of figures in the Marcantonio Raimondi engraving after Raphael of "The Judgment of Paris" c 1510–1520. It featured a nude woman reclining among two clothed men and having a picnic lunch. Although Manet's offering in 1865 would be accepted to the Salon, it would be even more shocking than the "Luncheon on the Grass." "Olympia," painted in 1863, was modeled after the famous "Venus of Urbino" by Titian. In Titian's "Venus," the nude demurely avoids eye contact with the viewer. However Manet chose to have his courtesan gazing frankly out of the painting and directly at the viewer. While Titian's piece was seen as fine art, Manet's interpretation was decried as vulgar and indecent.

Jules Chéret (1836–1932) popularized the technique of color lithography in 1866 and immediately the line between advertising and art became blurred as the medium became used for commercial purposes.

In the performing arts, German composer Richard Wagner (1813–1883) published the essay *Oper und Drama* in 1851. In the essay, he describes his idea of the *Gesamtkunstwerk*, or total work of art, which is to unite music, writing, drama, and stagecraft into a complete opera that integrates each of these pieces into a work of art greater than the sum of its parts. He would premiere his own *Gesamtkunstwerk, Der Ring des Nibelungen* (*The Ring Cycle*), in 1876.

The Paris Opéra, designed by Charles Garnier (1825–1898), was begun in 1861 under the patronage of Napoleon III. It was designed to integrate Renaissance and Baroque architecture and decorative arts, both of which were en vogue during this period. The Opéra was completed in 1875, and it endures yet as a symbol of the opulence of the Second Empire.

The Crinoline period saw a great deal of revivals. Gothic, Renaissance, and Baroque/Rococo revivals were all very popular throughout the period, often overlapping one another. Dense decorations and layers of ornamentation were as common for home furnishings and architecture as they were for the lavish and highly ornamented gowns of the fashionable ladies of the Crinoline period.

Men's Clothing

The overall look of men's clothing did not change much from the end of the Romantic period through the end of the Crinoline period.

Suits still consisted of a coat, waistcoat, and trousers. Coats were not usually buttoned closed but left open to show the vest, which was a term beginning to be used interchangeably with "waistcoat." Tailcoats were still worn for evening and formal occasions and cut with a more squared opening in front and narrower tails behind. Tails reached to just above the knee in back. Tailcoats had been popular for both daytime formal and evening formal events, but by the 1860s they were worn only for evening attire. Tailcoats of this period were black and had narrow lapels often faced with velvet. The frock coat remained a popular garment for daytime wear and was constructed in the same basic shape as it had been in the 1850s. It had a very fitted torso and marginally full skirt, although the waistline was lowered and had become less defined. The skirting of these coats had grown fairly long and would remain so through the period. The riding or Newmarket coat was still popular. In this period it came to be called the morning coat. The curve of the coat at the waist became less defined and now fell straighter through the center front.

A new garment introduced during this period was the sack jacket. It had originated as a lounging jacket in England and featured a loose, boxy construction with no waistline. It had long sleeves without cuffs, a straight single-breasted center front closing, and small, short lapels. The sack jacket was the precursor to modern jackets and sportscoats. The reefer or pea jacket was also popular for casual wear. These loosely fitted double-breasted jackets had come from hunting styles and were also worn as overcoats. They had small collars and vents at the sides instead of the center back like the sack jacket.

Waistcoats also did not encounter any major stylistic changes during this period. They were still the focus of color and ornamentation of the ensemble and made in both single- and double-breasted styles. Double-breasted waistcoats featured wider lapels while the single-breasted variety had much narrower ones. Waistcoats for daywear ended above the natural waist, but for evening they were worn longer. Waistcoats for evening also tended to be single breasted.

Men's trousers differed slightly from the previous period in that the straps at the bottoms disappeared. Although trousers were fitted close to the leg, there were not so snug as to ride up like they had in the past. The fashion was for a pegged look where the trousers were full through the hips and seat and gradually narrowed to the ankle. After 1860, the legs widened giving the trousers a straighter, only slightly tapered look. Men fancied striped, plaid, and checked fabrics for daytime wear and many styles included a band of fabric running down the outseam from waist to ankle. Belts were not fashionable accessories; instead men wore suspenders, known as braces in Europe. Suspenders were not usually seen and were often highly decorated. Hand-embroidered suspenders were a common gift for a lady to give a gentleman. As in previous years, magazines often published suggestions and patterns for various types of needlework to decorate suspenders. Some trousers were made with a tab and buckle at the center back to better customize the fit of the waistband. These trousers did not need to be worn with suspenders.

After 1850, a new type of trousers emerged for men and boys. Called knickerbockers, these pants were cut very full and loose in the legs and gathered to a band worn beneath the knee. Knickerbockers replaced the knee breeches that had been previously worn for hunting, riding, and other outdoor activities. The term *knickerbockers* was shortened to *knickers* sometime later. "Knickerbocker" was the name of the pretended author of Washington Irving's *History of New York City* and was used to describe the descendants of the original Dutch settlers of New York City. The pants may have derived from the illustrations of these Dutch settlers pictured in the book.[24] New Yorkers are sometimes still refereed to as "knickerbockers" by some people, and that is the reason the major league basketball team that plays there is called the Knicks.

Colorful dressing gowns were still worn in the home, but the term *banyan* was all but abandoned by this time. A new type of housewear was the smoking jacket. It was constructed like a sack jacket but made of velvet, cashmere, brocade, quilted satin, or other decorative fabrics. It often had velvet or satin lapels in an unnotched shawl-collar style. Smoking jackets were worn with nightcaps or tasseled caps. Underclothes and shirts for men did not change much in construction from the last period; they were still made of cotton or linen.

Shirts for daywear were plain-fronted while shirts for evening still had the ruffles, tucks, and embroidery that they'd had throughout the century. Shirts were predominantly white with a collar that reached the jawline and worn with a cravat or a tie. Shirts for casual or sportswear could come in other colors.

Boots were very popular for men and they came in various heights, from very short boots often made with elastic sides to tall boots that reached midcalf. Most boots buttoned or laced closed. Leather shoes were also worn and these closed with laces. Spats were still a very popular accessory to wear, made from sturdy cotton and buttoning over the ankle to protect the stockings. They are also called gaiters or spatterdashers.

Overcoats for men varied greatly in design. Some were very fitted as they had been in the previous period, while others trended toward being looser. Overall, overcoats seemed to be becoming more comfortable garments. Many of the earlier styles of coat still persisted, like the chesterfield and the paletot. Mackintosh rubber coats were still being worn, as well. A longer, fuller version of the frock coat was developed for outerwear during this period. Two new types of overcoats were the Inverness and the raglan. The Inverness was reminiscent of the curricle coats of the 1840s with its attached capelet. The Inverness was a much looser-fitting coat than the curricle and had wider sleeves; it featured only cape that hung from the neckline and ended at the wrist. The raglan was called a "raglan cape" even though it was a coat with sleeves. It fit very loosely through the shoulder due to the new and innovative sleeve style of it. The sleeves were cut with a deep, diagonal seam that ran from the neckline under the arm instead of setting the sleeve into a round armseye. This sleeve treatment is very popular in modern garments such as baseball jerseys. It created a smooth, sloping shoulder with a much less defined fit. Cloaks and shawls for men were also popular for eveningwear.

Men of this period kept their hair short and styled in waves, curls, or simply slicked back. Side whiskers became very popular and were usually worn very long and full. These side whiskers came to be known as sideburns, possibly after General Ambrose Burnside, a Union general in the Civil War, who was known for his thick side whiskers that connected to his moustache. After the 1850s, moustaches became popular, and by the 1860s very few men were clean shaven.

Top hats were still the most often-worn style of hat for eveningwear. Derbies and other hats with a low crown were very popular as well. In 1865, John B. Stetson was traveling through the western United States and made a wide-brimmed hat from beaver felt and rabbit skins to shade himself from the sun. The hat was high crowned, had a wide brim, and was water repellant. It was also crushable and easy to maintain. It soon became a staple for the cowboys of the area and remains a symbol of the American West to this day.

Men were still expected to wear gloves. They also carried canes and umbrellas; both were often made with decorative handles. Watches and watch chains were the most popular type of jewelry for men. Stud button and cufflink sets were also popular and available in many styles and colors. Tie pins, wedding and other rings were also common, as well as the occasional devotional pendant, such as a cross or saint's medallion. Men's clothing remained as simple and somber as it had been throughout the Romantic period.

Women's Clothing

The Crinoline period is named for the use of the cage crinoline in fashionable dress. By definition, any kind of stiffened petticoat is a crinoline. The cage crinoline, also known as the hoop skirt, was introduced circa 1857. Soon the "cage" was dropped from the name and the garment came to be known as just the "crinoline" in the common vernacular. The term "crinoline" was, and still is today, used interchangeably with the term "hoop skirt," although "crinoline" covers a wider variety of stiffened petticoats made to hold out the dress, and "hoop skirt" refers specifically to the type of underskirt stiffened by a series of hoops.

The silhouette of this period was entirely dependant on the cage crinoline, although the shape of the crinoline would change throughout the period. The crinoline was entirely rounded in the early years, from its inception in about 1857 through the middle 1860s. It grew flatter in the front and fuller in the rear during the 1860s. The crinoline could be constructed in one of two ways. The first was like the farthingale hoops popular during the Northern Renaissance, where the hoops of wood, whalebone, or steel were encased in a channel sewn into a petticoat. The second would be to suspend each hoop from a series of tapes. Both types seem to be used throughout the period. The second version would produce a lighter-weight crinoline, but the first type would be much warmer. A single petticoat trimmed with lace and ribbon would be worn over the crinoline. In the summer months this petticoat would be cotton or linen and it would be wool in the winter. Additional underpetticoats might also be worn in cold weather.

Many dresses for daytime were made in two pieces, the bodice and skirt separate. This allowed women to mix and match tops and skirts as they desired. Bodices could be made to match the skirt or be a separate garment. Bodice separates generally ended at or near the waist and could close either at the center front or center back with buttons or hooks and eyes. They were shaped by use of curved seams and darts to the fashionable hourglass silhouette. Armholes were often placed very low, creating a smoothly sloped shoulder line. Early in the period, the "bottle neck shoulder" look was highly prized, that is to have the smoothly sloped look of the top of a bottle. This style, as with the Romantic period styles, seriously inhibited a woman's range of arm motion. The jacket style known as a basque, first popular in the 1840s, remained in fashion. The basque usually had a front placket that extended below the waist and was made in imitation of a man's waistcoat. Some basques were long through the hips and flared out in a uniform length, others were long at the front and the back but shorter along the sides, and some were short at the front and lengthened to the rear. Bodices that were made of silk or wool were lined with linen or cotton. Linen or cotton bodices could be with or without lining. Boning was also added to many bodices in the form of whalebone sewn into the seams. One-piece gowns with the bodice and skirt sewn as the waistband were still worn as well as a new type of gown that had no waist seam. The princess dress was made with gored panels cut to shape to the body.

Necklines for daywear were high and without an attached collar. Neckline edges were usually finished in bias piping. Collars and cuffs for day dresses were often removable for ease of laundering and for flexibility. Sleeve styles featuring wide oversleeves with removable undersleeves had begun to become popular in the 1840s and only grew in popularity through the 1850s and 1860s. The undersleeves were usually highly decorated with lace, embroidery, and other trimmings and called *engageantes* in the popular fashion magazines. Oversleeve shapes had many variations on a theme. Bell sleeves were narrow at the shoulder and gradually widened to an even, round shape and ended below the elbow. Pagoda sleeves were narrow that the shoulder but expanded rapidly into a wide opening below the elbow that could be even all the way around or could be longer at the back of the arm. The undersleeves were tied or buttoned or pinned into the wide oversleeve opening. Sleeves could also be made that did not require an undersleeve and were gathered to the wrist. Many of these sleeves were pleated into the armseye and gathered to a band at the wrist leaving the fullness of the fabric at the center of the sleeve. Other sleeves were very tight fitted from shoulder to wrist and featured cuffs at the wrist and epaulets at the shoulder. The Maria style, popular in the 1820s, consisting of puffs from shoulder to wrist, also remained popular. Sleeves on basques were constructed like a man's jacket without gathers or pleats into the armseye and a smooth fit from shoulder to wrist.

Blouse separates were now becoming fashionable as well. They featured high collars and closed sleeves. In the 1860s, the red Garibaldi blouse, made in imitation of the red shirts of the Italian unification forces of Giuseppe Garibaldi, was especially popular. Blouses could be cotton, linen, or silk and were considered very casual and for daytime, especially morning, dressing only.

Skirts had continued to widen through the 1850s and 1860s, growing to a maximum circumference of fifteen feet. Early in the period a dome shape dominated, but later it would change to focus the fullness at the back. The skirt fabric was joined into wide rectangles and gathered to the waistline through the 1850s, but by the 1860s the skirt constriction began to use gored fabric. Gores are cut on the straight grain to be very narrow at one end and wide at the other. Use of gores allows a full hemline but much less bulk at the waist. Skirts at the end of the 1860s had a more sloped and less domed appearance due to the gores creating a smooth line from the waist to hem. Crinolines were shaped to accommodate this change in aesthetics and were mostly of the second type discussed in this chapter, the kind made up of rows of hoops suspended by tapes. The waistline placement remained above the actual waist.

Skirts were usually lined. If not completely lined, they at least had a band of lining around the hem to help protect it from dirt and wear. Braid was still used to edge the hems and keep them from fraying and tearing. Skirts for adult women reached completely to the ground throughout the Crinoline period. Skirts could be very simple or very elaborate. Some skirts were made of deep flounces such as was popular in the 1840s and others were made to wear one over another and achieve a layered look. A popular double-skirt style was to have the underskirt trimmed with rows and rows of pleats, tucks, or ruffles and the overskirt lighter and more bouffant, often looped up or puffed.

Women employed many tricks to add flexibility to their wardrobes and to protect their garments as much as possible. One popular accessory of this time was an apron. Aprons had been popular as an accessory and means of protecting one's clothes for centuries. But many ladies of fashion who had no need for a protective apron still wanted to wear one because they were popular and frequently made them out of fine silks with elaborate embroidery. The removable cuffs and collars were both to elaborate a wardrobe, but also offer protection to easily soiled areas. Aprons, cuffs, collars, and even some undersleeves were made in white linen or cotton to facilitate washing and bleaching if needed. Some women still wore a fichu, a sheer white tucker for the front of the bodice. In this period they appear crisscrossed over the bust and tied in back. Fichus and other modesty accessories are referred to throughout the period as canezou, but that term is not used beyond the end of the 1860s.

Dresses for evening were primarily two-piece matching skirt and bodice. They were made with a much wider and lower neckline and of fine fabrics such as silk and velvet. Specialty silks were extremely popular, especially those with an iridescent quality and those which included supplemental wefts or warps usually of a contrasting color or a metallic called "shot silk." Evening dresses often had an off-the-shoulder neckline and could be straight across or have a central dip known as *en couer*, "of the heart." Many evening or formal dresses had a bertha collar, a wide band of fabric around the neckline. Sleeves were primarily short and often hidden by the bertha collar. In the late 1860s some dresses even were made sleeveless with shoulder straps or ribbons tied over the shoulders. Gloves were worn for all formal or evening occasions, usually to the elbow. Double skirts were very popular for evening dress, and waistlines often came to a point below the natural waist. Evening gowns were trimmed lavishly using lace, ribbons, ruffles, frills, rosettes, pleats, tucks, and silk flowers.

Underpinnings were more important in this period than they had been so far in the century. Women continued to wear a chemise made of cotton or linen. Chemises were short sleeved and full cut, falling usually to the knees. Drawers were worn beneath the chemise and were also of cotton or linen. Drawers were knee length and trimmed with tucking or lace. The crotch seam remained open throughout the era. Flannel drawers were worn during cold weather. The corset was then worn over the drawers and chemise. Corsets were being shaped differently in this period, using gores and other construction techniques to make them stronger and longer lasting. Innovations from the last period, such as metal eyelets, helped in the evolution of the corset. Steel also began to replace whalebone as a boning material. Corsets also became shorter, focusing on the bust and midriff rather than the hips. As the width of the crinoline began to decrease, corsets became tighter and sought to exert greater changes on the natural shape of the body. The term "stays" disappeared entirely and was replaced by "corset" worldwide. On top of the corset was the camisole or corset cover, a linen or cotton garment that reached the waist and was darted and seamed to fit snugly over the corseted figure. Corset covers typically buttoned or closed with hooks and eyes down the center front and were decorated with lace and embroidery.

Stockings were made of cotton or silk, or wool for winter. White was the most common color of stockings, but there were other colors available, as well as stockings knit into patterns like plaid. Shoes for daywear were square toed and had low heels. Boots remained a popular choice for ladies' footwear and made in black or brown leather. Boots were cut to above the ankle or could be taller to the low calf and closed with laces or buttons, some low boots used elastic. Evening shoes were primarily white satin or kid leather and often tinted to match the gown.

Outerwear for women was numerous and often different fashion magazines would give different names to the same garment. By and large, women's outerwear consisted of a variety of coats, both fitted and unfitted, and mantles. Articles from the previous period were still worn such as the pardessus and paletot, both fitted, sleeved outdoor garments, and the burnouse, a hooded cape worn draped around the body in imitation of Middle Eastern dress. A fashionable addition to outerwear of this period was the zouave jacket. The zouave was a lightweight collarless jacket that fastened at the neck. The center front was left open and it curved away toward the back. It was trimmed with braid, had straight sleeves of medium width, and was often paired with the Garibaldi blouse, although it could be worn with any other kind of blouse as well. The zouave jacket was inspired by the Algerian regiments in the French army.

Women in this period also enjoyed several styles of mantle that could be worn for day or evening. The mantle was not a shawl or cloak-like article as it had been in eras past, but a three-quarter-length coat that was fitted to the waist in the front and full at the back. Most mantles featured very wide shawl-like sleeves that were cut-in-one with the bodice portion of the mantle. It could be made for daywear or eveningwear, depending on the colors and fabrics used. The pelisse-mantle was a double-breasted unfitted coat with a wide collar and turned-back cuffs. The long, loose line of it was based on the pelisse coats in earlier periods. It was considered a daytime coat. The shawl-mantle was a cloak type of garment worn full and loose and reaching almost to the skirt hem. It could be made for either day or evening wear. The talma-mantle was also a cloak and it featured either a full, tasseled hood or a flat collar. The shorter version was called the rotonde. Talma-mantles were considered more formal than the rotonde.

Hairstyles were very simple for most women during the day for most of the period. They parted their hair in the center and drew it across over the ears and back into a bun, into braids, or into ringlet curls at the back of the head or the nape of the neck. Hair was also gathered back into a net snood that was often made of chenille or colored silk. Pads were often placed under the hair to give more volume to the style, additions of artificial hair were also used, but usually only for evening. The most popular style for evening was to arrange ringlets along the back of the head. Hair falls became extremely common through the 1860s as evening styles became more intricate and elaborate.

A wide variety of hats was available for women of the Crinoline period. Soft cotton or linen daycaps were still popular for indoor use and were trimmed with lace and ribbon, often with lappets that hung down the back of the neck and were drawn over the shoulder. Older and married women favored these daycaps. Bonnets continued to be worn by some, but their heyday had passed. Small hats and hats with low crowns and wide brims were the most popular. In the evening, women dressed their hair with ribbons, lace kerchiefs, beaded snoods, and flowered ornaments and jewels.

Jewelry for women included the usual pieces: rings, bracelets, necklaces, earrings, and brooches. Gold, or gold-colored metal, was the most popular. Coral, cameos, and cabochon stones were considered the most fashionable. Mourning jewelry was also becoming popular in this time as Queen Victoria in England mourned the death of her husband Prince Albert in 1861. Mourning items were primarily made of black jet. Articles like rings and brooches that incorporated the loved one's hair were also prized.

Accessories did not much change from the preceding period, women were expected to wear gloves whenever out of the house. Daytime gloves were shorter and fitted and made of leather or cotton, while evening gloves were still generally white and worn shorter in the 1850s and long to the elbow in the 1860s. Fingerless gloves or mitts were also popular for both day and evening. Evening mitts were made of lace. Women carried parasols, folding fans, embroidered handkerchiefs, and muffs. Parasols were silk with metal or whalebone ribs. Parasols with folding handles were still used for carriage riding.

Cosmetics for women still favored a pale complexion, but not the wan and delicate look of the Romantic era. Visible make-up such as rouge and lipstick were still considered in bad taste and only for use by prostitutes and low-class women. But ladies of fashion were encouraged to use a number of beauty treatments either concocted at home or bought from a reputable apothecary. There were treatments for blemishes, freckles, and facial redness, as well as mixtures to thicken and add luster to the hair.

By this time in the nineteenth century, communication between major fashion centers was generally good and clothing became fairly uniform throughout the Western world. The small exception to this is the American South during the Civil War. Many accounts drawn from diaries and magazine articles of the time describe the differences in antebellum dress. The "Southern Belles" mode of dress focused on the rounded shape of the crinoline and gathered skirts. During the time of the transition into the sleeker, gored skirt shape, the South was cut off from contact with the rest of the fashionable world by the Civil War, which lasted from 1861–1865. Elzey Hay wrote an article for *Godey's Lady's Book* in 1866 describing her life and dress during the war. She describes tearing apart old dresses and parasols for patching and trimming their worn-out dresses. They took pieces of one black silk flounced skirt for two years before turning to the parasol. She says that "no umbrella ever served so many purposes or was so thoroughly used up before. The whalebones served to stiffen corsets and the waist of a homespun dress and the handle was given to a wounded solider for a walking stick."[25] She also mentioned walking three miles to see some copies of the *Godey's Lady's Book* that were only six months old, otherwise they had no incoming fashion information whatsoever. Before the war, Southern women had often gone more of their own way as part of a social statement, but the war trapped their styles into a silhouette like that of the late 1850s. When Reconstruction came, they were shocked to find out how much had changed and hurried to catch up.

Children's Clothing

During the Crinoline period, more than ever, children were dressed like miniature adults. As styles changed for women from the full, rounded skirt to a narrower, gored skirt, the same change was also seen in the clothing of young girls.

Infants were dressed in long gowns until they could walk. Little caps trimmed with lace and ribbon were an important accessory for babies, because they were beautiful to look at and because they helped keep the babies' heads warm. Caps were made of very fine and soft cotton or linen, or they could be knitted or crocheted.

Both girl and boy toddlers were dressed in short skirts that reached about to the knee or just below. Pantalets or fuller, gathered drawers were worn beneath and seen below the hem of the skirt. Boys and girls also wore petticoats under the skirt to increase the fullness.

Boys began to wear trousers by age five or six. These were usually made in the same style as the clothing of adult men. A popular style of pants for boys was knickerbockers. They were full through the knee and gathered to a band then buttoned or buckled closed just below the knee. Knickerbocker suits were comprised of the knickerbockers, a short, collarless jacket, and a vest. Boys also continued to wear the Eton suit and the tunic suit, but the skeleton suit was no longer worn. Another popular outfit for boys was a sailor suit. Trousers or knickerbockers were paired with a blouse with V-shaped opening at the neck and a wide, flat, square collar that hung over the shoulders at the back. This blouse was called the "middy," which was short for "midshipman."[26] Outdoor garments for boys were directly based off of fashionable men's overcoats such as the Inverness, paletot, and chesterfield, as well as a variety of cloaks. Bathing suits were made of knitted wool jersey.

Clothing for girls was very much like what their mothers wore. As a toddler, a girl wore short dresses that ended at the knee with long pantalets or shorts drawers showing beneath. Although the wearing of pantalets would persist throughout the period, they would not be worn much after 1870. Little girls' dresses were worn with petticoats. Even the dresses for the very young were trimmed with braid, velvet, ribbon, and soutache, just as an adult's dress would be. As girls grew, their skirts lengthened and were worn in the manner of the prevailing fashion of the time: gathered and full early in the period, gored and slimmer later in the period. Older girls wore skirts that came to the ankle with a fashionably shaped hoop skirt underneath. Young girls were also corset trained from a very young age. Corsets for young girls were lightly boned, or not boned at all and not worn very tight. By their teenage years, girls were expected to wear a fashionably shaped corset.

Ankle-length boots were the primary footwear for both genders throughout the period. Occasionally for more formal dress, slippers were worn. Stockings for children were of wool or cotton and were striped or solid generally of black, white, or brown.

Boys' hair was kept short and neat. They wore caps, sailor hats, and scaled-down versions of men's hats like the derby or the top hat. Girls had their hair dressed in ringlets or pulled back from the face. They wore hats that were miniature versions of fashionable women's hats such as bonnets and pillboxes.

The overall look for children was that of small adult. Style was prevalent over comfort and children were expected to comport themselves as befitting such mature clothing.

Specialty Clothing

The specialty dress of the Crinoline period had a wide focus, from the very highest class to the lowest. This period saw the birth of couture, of the "Bloomer," and of blue jeans.

Charles Frederick Worth came to Paris in 1845 with 117 francs to his name and unable to speak a word of French. He became a salesman and an apprentice draper at Maison Gagelin, a store that specialized in shawls and coats. He was married to Marie Vernet, a French model at Maison Gagelin. Marie enjoyed modeling her husband's designs and helped his establishment of a dress department at the Maison. When Maison Gagelin showed Worth's dresses at the 1851

Exhibition in London, they caused quite a stir and earned the Maison a gold medal. He also exhibited at the Exposition Universelle in Paris in 1855 with much success. In 1858, he left Maison Gagelin and opened his own firm, the House of Worth. His timing could not have been better as France was entering the lavish era known as the Second Empire under the very successful rule of Napoleon III. The demand for luxury goods in Paris was the highest it had been since before the time of the French Revolution and Worth was set to capitalize on it. Worth was already winning much public acclaim in 1860 when he secured the patronage of Empress Eugenie. Her attentions secured his place as the "father of couture." *Couture* is French for "dressmaking" and *haute* means "high." The two combined are meant to reference the high art of fine dressmaking.

Through the 1870s, Worth was a major designer and attracted clientele from all over the world. His name was mentioned in nearly all the popular fashion periodicals of the time and he became one of fashion's first celebrities. He was best known for his innovative styles and use of lavish fabrics and trimming. While he was best known for his one-of-a-kind couture creations, he also created a system of prepared designs shown on live models that could be ordered and tailored to fit the customer. Worth's clients ranged from aristocracy like Empress Eugenie and Queen Victoria, to actresses like Sarah Bernhardt and Lillie Langtry, to Cora Pearl, the period's most illustrious courtesan.

Worth garments still survive in many costume collections around the world, a testament not only to his proliferation, but also to the quality of his work as many of these designs remain in a wearable condition. The House of Worth finally closed for good in 1956.

The idea of forming a Utopian Society was a major social and religious force in the United States. Many of these colonies established their own forms of dress; one of the most recognizable was the "Bloomer costume" which was espoused by Dress Reformers as well as Utopian societies. The heaviness of layers upon layers of petticoats worn by women in the 1840s was quite detrimental to their health. Feminists and suffragettes chose to adopt a more modern and healthful mode of dress, adding Dress Reform to their crusade. Lucy Stone, Elizabeth Cady Stanton, Susan B. Anthony, and Amelia Bloomer all adopted this style of dress. Amelia Bloomer did not originate this costume, historians believe it was an acquaintance and fellow feminist, Elizabeth Smith Miller who was the first to wear this ensemble in public. While in Europe, Miller had seen women in health sanitariums wearing a long, full tunic over very full trousers that were gathered to the ankle in the Turkish style. Bloomer did wear the ensemble when she lectured and endorsed the look in an 1851 article. After her article was published, the costume became synonymous with her and was forever after referred to as the "Bloomer costume" or simply as "bloomers." Very few women outside of the budding feminist movement indulged in wearing the "Bloomer costume" and it was ridiculed by the contemporary media.

Today, the term "bloomers" is very well known and now refers to a type of undergarment that is very full in the leg and gathers tightly to a band worn just above or below the knee.

The discovery of gold at Sutter's Mill in California in January 1848 caused a boom in immigration to the West Coast of the United States. Over 40,000 prospectors had moved to California by 1850. Along with those searching for gold in the ground were those who came to seek their fortune from the fortune seekers. Entrepreneurs of all kinds set up shop in San Francisco. Levi Strauss was one of those people. He came to San Francisco in order to open a dry goods store catering to miners, carrying with his sturdy canvas to sell for tents. The miners often complained that their pants wore out too quickly and Strauss saw an opportunity. He took the tent canvas and had them made into pants instead. They sold extremely well and he imported bolts of fabric and other useful items from his family's larger dry goods store in New York. He turned this fabric into more of the sturdy pants and sold accessories such as handkerchiefs, suspenders, and belts. The pants were extremely popular, but the main complaint was that the pockets were always ripping out.

Jacob Davis, a tailor from Reno Nevada wrote to Strauss with a solution to this problem. He found that using metal rivets at the stress points reinforced the pockets and greatly extended their lives. Strauss had Davis come out to San Francisco and put him to work for the company making his "waist overalls," as the pants were called, with rivets at the stress points of the pockets. The rivets were the only part of the pants that were ever patented. The modern blue jean was created in May of 1873 and Strauss had opened a large factory and warehouse space on Market Street in San Francisco in the early 1880s. The basic waist overall was known simply as the "XX" until 1890 when it was given the official lot number of 501.[27]

"Jean" is the generic term for a heavy cotton twill fabric. Strauss chose a warp-faced twill that was made with indigo dyed warp and white weft because of its strength, comfort, and colorfastness. "Serge de Nimes" was an indigo-dyed fabric made in Nimes, France. It was originally made of a wool/silk blend and dyed dark blue. Although both jean and serge de Nimes existed at the same time as two different textiles, there seems to have been some sort of cross-pollination during the nineteenth century when the twill became indigo blue and the name became "denim."[28] From its humble beginnings as miners' pants in the 1850s, denim has become a universal fashion staple.

THE BUSTLE PERIOD, 1870–1900

Art

At the outset of the Bustle period, the prevailing artistic movement was Impressionism. This avant-garde style of art took the world by surprise and caused a great stir in the artistic community. Although they began meeting and painting in the 1860s, the Impressionists had their first showing at the *Salon des Independents* in Paris, France, in 1874. The idea of Impressionism was to catch the fleeting quality of light and air with small, quick brushstrokes and use of vivid color to give the viewer a glimpse of life at the very moment it was painted. Original use of light, color, and angle as well as the sense of motion were essential to the style. Auguste Renoir, Claude Monet, Alfred Sisley, and Frederic Bazille were the first four artists of this new movement. They soon recruited Edgar Degas, Édouard Manet, and Camille Pissarro into their ranks and exhibited their first showing under the name of the Anonymous Society of Painters, Sculptors, Printmakers, etc. Early critics were harsh in their assessment of the paintings, criticizing what they felt was a rushed and unfinished sketch-like quality. More progressive critics were appreciative of the accurate portrayal of modern life and the masterful interplay of light and color. It was Monet's "Impression, Sunrise" shown as part of the 1874 exhibition, that gave the movement its name.

Innovations in synthetic colors gave the Impressionists a radically wide palette and they indulged in it. Manet's painting, "Boating," painted in 1874, was the first to use some of the new colors including Cerulean blue and synthetic ultramarine. His composition was also shocking to some conservative viewers as he used a very Japanese-inspired style of zooming in on the subject and cropping out everything else. Japanese influence had been growing in fine art, decorative arts, and fashion. Impressionists were also inspired by the popularity of vacationing in the country-side and often painted the beaches and picnic gardens of the areas surrounding Paris. The city itself was also undergoing many changes. Some were planned, like the ambitious and sweeping renovations of Napoleon III, and others were due to damage during the Franco-Prussian war. Some chose to paint cityscapes, others chose to paint people. Although the subject matter was as diverse as the painters themselves, their method of execution is what bound them all together.

The Impressionists maintained a very relaxed and unstructured membership that numbered anywhere from nine to thirty artists at any given time. The artists involved in the movement were Alfred Sisley (1839–1899), Berthe Morisot (1841–1895), Camille Pissarro (1855–1903), Claude Monet (1840–1926), Edgar Degas (1834–1917), Édouard Manet (1856–1833), Frederic Bazille (1841–1870), Mary Cassatt (1844–1926), Paul Cezanne (1839–1906), and Auguste Renoir (1841–-1919). Later members included Georges Seurat (1859–1891), Paul Gauguin (1848–1903), and Paul Signac (1863–1935). Vincent van Gogh (1853–1890) and Toulouse Lautrec (1864–1901) were never official members during the active period of the Impressionists but are considered to be Post-Impressionists. The group organized eight showings between 1874 and 1886 and Pissarro was the only one of them who participated in all eight exhibitions. After Bazille was killed in the Franco-Prussian war, the driving force of the Impressionists was lost and cracks began to form among the group members. The painters were beginning to develop new styles and move in different directions. By the time of their last exhibition in 1886, few of the Impressionists were working in the style any longer.

The defining factors in Impressionist style were the use of short, rapid, and often visible brushstrokes producing an almost pixilated effect. The painting was usually done *impasto*, meaning they used thick paint applied to the canvas quickly and leaving behind obvious and visible brushstrokes and palette knife marks. Paint was used undiluted with glazes for opacity. Bright colors were used and applied directly to the canvas with little mixing. Colors were also placed side by side to create contrast instead of being blended one into another. Paintings were also almost always painted outside, *en plein air*, rather than inside of a studio. Although the Impressionist movement itself did not last to the end of the century, the innovations and aesthetics born during the movement continue to inspire and affect all forms of art to this day.

The second major artistic movement of the Bustle period was the Aesthetic Movement that was dominant from the 1880s through the 1890s. The Aesthetic Movement was closely linked to the Arts and Crafts Movement, Dress Reform, and Art Nouveau, and had been inspired by the Pre-Raphaelites. It was considered a part of a larger European movement, Symbolism or Decadence in France and Decadentismo in Italy, and known scholarly under the general notion of Design Reform. The main idea behind the movement was "art for art's sake," to provide pure sensory pleasure without the need for a message of any kind. John Ruskin and Matthew Arnold had been pushing the idea that for a work to be considered art, it needed to have a moral and a purpose. Aesthetics rejected this definition and focused on not only the ideals of beauty and sensuality in fine art, but in dress and decorative arts as well. The Aesthetic Movement championed a relationship between art, dress, decorative arts, literature, and music. The adherents of the Movement focused on living a life in imitation of art instead of allowing art to imitate life.

Oscar Wilde was a devotee of the Aesthetic movement, exploring its tenets both in his writing and his attire. During his lecture tours of the United States in the 1870s and 1880s, he wore what he thought of as an Aesthetic costume consisting of a velvet suit with a loosely fitted jacket, knee breeches, a very wide collar, and a tie. He was basing his look off of a romantic version of the Cavalier styles of the seventeenth century. (Aesthetic dress will be discussed in greater depth in the Specialty Dress section of this chapter.) Wilde was lampooned in the Gilbert and Sullivan operetta, *Patience,* which made fun of the Aesthetes and parodied Wilde with the main character.

Aesthetics merged into the Arts and Crafts movement with the belief that beautiful objects are somehow inherently better than their ugly, mass-produced counterparts. William Morris reorganized his decorative arts company in 1875, ridding himself of partners that did not share his vision and renaming it Morris and Co. He and several of his Pre-Raphaelite Brotherhood friends focused on the time honored traditions of handiwork. He revived block printing using natural dyes and old world discharge-dye techniques. His firm also created woven textiles as well as printed, seeking to revive the art of the wall hanging and tapestry. Although his financial success was limited, his designs did become classics and Morris and Co. remained open until 1940. Christopher Dresser was another follower of the Aesthetic Movement who worked in decorative arts. He was trained as a botanist but believed wholeheartedly in the power of beauty. He was quoted as saying, "To ornament is to beautify. To decorate is to ornament."[29] He took a different approach than Morris. While Morris sought to undermine the industrialization process and bring about a revolution in handicrafts, Dresser recognized the inevitability of industrial progress and went to work as a designer of mass-produced items. He saw no reason why industry could not be made to create beauty. He turned to his botanical knowledge for his inspiration, creating elegant geometric designs for household goods and textiles. He sought to find the underlying essence of design and often came up with very abstract versions of common plants. He felt that by abstracting and stylizing the design, there would be no influence from the source, only the essence of pure beauty. Dresser was first introduced to Japanese art in 1862 and traveled to Japan in 1877. The minimalist and stylized art of Japan would become a major part of his designing. He opened his design firm, Art Furnishers' Alliance, in 1880, just down the street from Morris and Co. and Liberty's, a well-known importer of Asian textiles.

The idea of art as a multisensory experience meant to fill the world with beauty was one of the enduring ideas of the Aesthetic movement. Although

Morris and Dennis did not ever truly achieve their goals, they did set into motion a wave of new and innovative thought about design: Mechanization cannot replace the ineffable glow of something lovely created by hand. Utilitarian items did not have to be only functional and have no decorative value. These lofty ideals still reverberate through the decorative arts world today as the beauty and emotion associated with the appearance of even the most banal of appliances, like washing machines and refrigerators, is an important factor in their design and advertising.

Both botanical elements and influence from Japanese styles would continue to influence art of all kinds. The Aesthetic movement flowed into the Art Nouveau movement, which was the last major artistic movement of the nineteenth century. Art Nouveau became popular in about 1890 and would remain a popular mode until the beginning of the twentieth century. Although Art Nouveau claimed that it was an entirely new art—hence its name—that was not based in any earlier artistic styles, it clearly was a product, if not of the Aesthetic Movement itself, of the greater Design Reform movement as a whole. Proponents of Art Nouveau sought to clear the clutter of eclectic and often chaotic Victorian design. They utilized smooth curves and sinuous lines and took their inspiration directly from nature. Art Nouveau was rarely symmetrical, even if it was only the difference of one leaf or one flower petal, one side never exactly matched the other. Art Nouveau styles became extremely popular in textiles and ornamentation and there was a proliferance of jewelry and decorative items made in the style.

The term *Art Nouveau* was first applied to this style in the Belgian journal *L'Art Moderne* in the 1880s. The first group of Nouveau artists called themselves Les Vingt, "the twenty," because there were twenty members at the time. They took to heart the teachings of William Morris when it came to putting one's heart and soul into art and creating an item that is spiritually uplifting because of its great beauty. They sought to unite fine and decorative arts; they wished for fine arts to be accessible to the masses and for decorative arts to be revered the same as fine arts. Their focus initially was on architecture and furnishings. Hector Guimard designed the beautiful and sweeping subway station entrances all over Paris. They were made of black wrought iron and glass and created to be sculptural instead of institutional. There were few corners or straight lines in any of his glorious Metro awnings. This sinuous style was culminated in 1889 when Gustave Eiffel created the Eiffel Tower in Paris. Seen alternately as fine art and an eyesore, the towering metal structure was unlike anything else in the world and remains an enduring symbol of Paris and of the Art Nouveau movement.

Art Nouveau was also well known for its lithographic art. Artists such as Henri de Toulouse-Lautrec, Gustav Klimt, and Alphonse Mucha are three of the movements best known. Toulouse-Lautrec created colorful renderings of Parisian nightlife and is best known for his images of the Moulin Rouge. His artistic style borders the Post-Impressionists and early Art Nouveau. Klimt was fond of the rich color and sheen of gold leaf, sinuous lines, and nontraditional layout and model poses. Mucha, however, went on to be the very embodiment of the art. His posters were all bordered in stylized flowers and bands, curving, swirling lines dominated his style. His models were mainly women and always shown in flowing, classical, or medieval types of gowns and robes that were decorated like the Art Nouveau–styled garments of the time. His images conveyed a sense of motion. It was Mucha's idea that art should present the viewer with a profound, but personal, moment of spirituality. He longed to focus on more serious subject matter but the bulk of his work was commercial: advertisements for theatrical productions, soaps, candy, cigarette rolling papers, etc. Although his work was thought to be antiquated and terribly out of style when he died, it has experienced several revivals—there was a major revived interest in Mucha during the 1960s—and he remains one of the most recognizable artists in history.

Although jewelry design was rather low in the Nouveau hierarchy of design, it was, and still remains to be, a popular part of the movement. The art of jewelry design leant itself to Art Nouveau. Soft metals like gold and silver were easily manipulated into the signature curving styles. Colored metals, enamels, and stones could be formed into whimsical elements like leaves and flowers. Rings, bracelets, necklaces, earrings, brooches, hat pins, and hair ornaments were all crafted in the Art Nouveau style. Paris and Brussels were at the heart of Art Nouveau jewelry design. The greatest designer of this movement was René Lalique. He used a variety of precious metals with traditional elements such as gemstones and enamel, but he also mixed in nontraditional materials such as glass, bone, and horn. For Lalique, the beauty of the end product was the most important thing, not the intrinsic value of the materials used. He was inspired by nature and glorified it in his work. From his experience with Japanese art and culture, he favored dragonflies, bamboo, and ginkgo leaves in his designs.

Although Art Nouveau was relatively short-lived, it had a great impact on modern art. Although it failed to truly distance itself from artistic influences of the past, it did plant the seeds for future generations of artists to do just that in early-twentieth-century movements such as abstract art. Art Nouveau remains a popular style through the twenty-first century.

Most of the artistic movements of the late nineteenth century were heavily influenced by the opening of the Japanese borders in the 1850s. By the 1870s, the start of the Bustle period, Japanese imports were pouring into the West. Textiles, art, decorative objects, and furnishings were available for purchase across Europe and the United States. Japonisme became an undercurrent artistic style, never truly surfacing on its own, but guiding the designs of contemporary movements like the Impressionist, Aesthetic, and Art Nouveau. One of Europe's introductions to Japanese art was during the World's Fair of 1867 in Paris. Early on, the cultural encounter created a mania for all things Japonesque, regardless if they were truly Japanese in origin or not. Mary Cassat was inspired by the subtlety of composition in Japanese artwork. William Morris was inspired by Japanese woodcut printing. Toulouse-Lautrec was inspired by the colorful and grotesque Kabuki theatre prints. Japanese style was not only a breath of fresh air, but an inundation of truly exotic ideas from an island nation that had remained isolated for hundreds of years. Japan's influence in Bustle period design was as subtle and refined as was its art.

Men's Dress

Although men's dress did not change dramatically throughout the century, in the final decades of the nineteenth century, several elements still present in twenty-first-century men's attire developed. The fullness of the frock coat remained popular for daytime until the late 1890s, when it went out of style. It was replaced by the closer fit of the morning coat, with the center front curving back away from the waist to reveal the waistcoat. This contrasted with the very loose and unfitted sack jacket, which was worn as sportswear or only for the most casual of occasions. The sack jacket was made with no waistline seam and could be straight through the center front or curved away slightly. They were made in both single- and double-breasted varieties. Another popular item of sportswear was still the reefer. Its cut was similar to the sack jacket except that it was always square through the center front and double breasted. Through the 1870s and 1880s, reefers were worn as suit jackets and as overcoats, as they had been during the Crinoline period as well. But by 1890, they were preferred for overcoats and no longer worn as jackets. The reefer was supplanted by the Norfolk jacket, which was a sport jacket worn with a belt.

Paul Wayland Bartlett, 1890, American sculptor, by Charles Sprague Pearce. Bartlett wears the typical three-piece suit buttoned high on the torso, with the waistcoat showing. © National Portrait Gallery, Smithsonian Institution / Art Resource, NY.

Coats of this period tended to button high on the torso and the waistcoat did not show. By the mid-1880s, coats were worn open and attention was placed once again on the waistcoat. At that point in the period, they were made of colorful figured fabrics, stripes, plaids, and checks. Previously, they had been much blander, made in the same fabric as the jacket or the pants.

Trousers were straight cut and narrow, although trousers for daywear were cut wider. Men wore knickerbockers for popular outdoor activities such as golf, tennis, hiking, and bicycling. Knickerbockers were worn with knee-length stockings; argyle, plaid, and striped stockings were popular. Tall boots or specialty made shoes for activity were also worn.

Men's eveningwear still consisted of a tail coat. The tails were about knee length in back and were tapered toward the bottom. By the 1880s, the tail coat collars were shawl collars, one continuous collar and lapel with a smooth, unnotched edge. The collars were usually faced with velvet or satin or another high-sheen silk. Waistcoats for eveningwear usually matched the rest of the suit and continued to be double breasted. Trousers also matched the coat and were cut fairly straight and narrow through the leg. The outer side seam was covered by a braid or band that matched the trousers color. Dress shirts were white and simple with two stud buttons at the front. After 1889, the fronts of some dress shirts were made with vertical pleats. But the most far-reaching innovations in men's formal wear came when a formal version of the casual sack jacket was created. It was introduced in Tuxedo, New York, and still goes by that name today: the tuxedo.

Shirts of the Bustle period were very stiff. Formal daytime shirts had been pleated at the front but were worn plain again after 1870, becoming pleated once more in 1889. The amount of shirt that showed above the jacket or coat varied year to year. Shirts had been predominantly white, but in the 1890s they came in more color options. A popular style was a striped shirt with a white collar and cuffs. Collars were worn tall and they grew to their tallest and widest in the 1890s. In the 1880s, men's collars were removable and interchangeable. Like similar techniques used in women's dressing, the removable collars and cuffs made laundering them simpler and allowed for a man to change his look with a variety of collars in differing shapes and sizes. Some collars were tall and others folded over, and many came in matched sets with cuffs.

Cravats finally fell out of fashion and were replaced by the necktie, another modern staple of menswear that had its heyday in this period. Ties were worn long and simply knotted with the ends held in place with a tie pin. Bow ties also became popular and were frequently worn for eveningwear and formal occasions.

Drawers for men were now regularly made of a wool knit, but cotton knits were also available for warmer months. Drawers were fairly long, most reaching to the ankle. Some ended at the knees for wear with knickerbockers. Drawers construction included a button closure at the front and a drawstring at the back to adjust the fit. The legs also had a drawstring to adjust the snugness there and keep them from riding up. Drawers of this period featured a smoother, more snug fit than those of previous eras. Undervests also became an important garment. These undershirts could have sleeves or not and were also made of knitted wool, although cotton and even silk versions were also available. They were fairly close fitting and long to the hips with a front button closure. Combinations were also popular, they combined the drawers and undervest into one garment. These were also known as the union suit. The union suit buttoned up the front from hips to neck and featured a button flap in the rear.

Stockings remained the same as they had been, knit from wool, cotton, or silk, and available in black, white, or designs like striped, plaid, checks, or argyle. Knee-length stockings were worn with knickerbockers and were often decorative. Shoes were made in a wide variety of styles including the Oxford shoe, a low leather shoe that laces up, which is still worn today. The Balmoral was a lace-up boot inspired by Scottish shoes and was available in casual, dress, and athletic versions. The Congress boot was an ankle boot with a patent leather upper and elasticized sides. Athletic shoes were made in sturdy leather and rubber soles, and they were made for specific activities such as tennis, bicycling, or gymnastics.

Outerwear for men actually experienced several changes through the period, requiring men to pay close attention and update their garments in order to keep up with trends. Coat lengths began relatively short in the 1870s but grew steadily longer through the 1880s and 1890s. The frock coat remained popular as an overcoat style, though the full skirting was much narrowed and lengthened until it resembled the silhouette of many of the other coats of the period, except that it was fitted through the torso. The wide, unfitted chesterfield coat was also worn frequently. The Inverness coat was regularly worn by men of this period.

The shape of the shoulder cape lengthened quite a bit, and some were made to appear entirely cloak-like from the front but look like a regular overcoat with very full sleeves from the back. The Ulster coat was the longest coat of all, reaching almost to the ankle, even in the 1870s. It featured a hood, a cape, or both that could be detached, and it had a belted waist.

Men wore their hair very short during this period and parted it at the side or the center. Side parts were more popular than center parts, however. Trim beards with moustaches and full sideburns were popular at the outset of the period, but as the century wound to a close, the prevailing style would become a clean-shaven face and a moustache.

Hat styles remained consistent. Silk top hats were worn for formal and evening dress. Folding or collapsible top hats were popular for the opera and the theatre. Evening top hats were black while top hats for daytime formalwear could be light grey, fawn, buff, or white. Derbies and caps were still worn for casual attire, but new hats were being introduced. One of the most popular was the fedora. It was a felt hat with a low crown creased from front to back, symmetrical indentations at the front, and a medium brim that dipped in the front and back. The homburg was much like the fedora but without the indentations at the front of the crown. It also had a smooth brim that did not dip down in the front and back. The deerstalker was a fabric cap that had a bill at the front and rear and was straight through the sides. It was usually made of plaid, check, or hound's-tooth wool and was popularized by the illustrations of Sherlock Holmes in the Sir Arthur Conan Doyle books. In the 1880s and 1890s, straw boaters became fashionable for casual daytime wear. They were very low-crowned hats with a flat, medium-sized brim made of shellacked straw. Boaters would stay in fashion through the turn of the century. The baseball cap was a cap that fit snugly to the head and featured a bill to shade the eyes from the sun. They were made of wool with a leather bill and worn exclusively by early baseball players. But soon the baseball style began to mingle into the designs for other types of caps and by the 1900s started to be seen off of the playing field. The fedora and the baseball cap remained important elements in men's headwear through the twentieth century and the baseball cap is still a fashion staple for men of the twenty-first century.

Men went relatively unadorned in the Bustle period. Their jewelry choices were limited to wedding rings, tie pins, pocket watches, watch chains, and decorative shirt stud buttons and cufflinks. Any other form of jewelry was not considered masculine. Gold had been the prevailing metal of choice, but now silver was becoming popular.

Gloves and walking sticks were still the most popular accessory choices. Men's accessories were not as important in the Bustle period as they had been earlier in the nineteenth century. The foundations of modern men's dress were laid in the Bustle period and the rudiments would remain unchanged into the twenty-first century.

Women's Dress 1870–1890

The Bustle period was one of eclectic tastes and many revivals. There was a romantic sense of history and many articles of clothing were named for historic figures. There were "Medici collars" and "Louis heels" alongside "Marie

Antoinette fichus" and the "Anne Boleyn paletot."[30] Women had a great deal of choice when it came to selecting garments and accessories. Shops were full of delightful dresses and shawls and the latest in corsets and underpinnings. Throughout the period, the bustle was the main silhouette of women's fashion, defining the look of this period and giving it its name.

In the late 1860s, although the rounded cage crinoline was still being worn, the fullness was starting to focus towards the back. Skirts were being cut with gored panels instead of straight, square pieces that were gathered to the waist. This gored construction technique allowed for more control over where the fullness of the skirt could be placed. As fullness moved towards the rear, a new silhouette developed. The bustle went through three major stylistic changes from 1870–1890.

The full bustle, cascade, or waterfall bustle was popular from 1870-1878. It began simply as fullness from the skirt swagged back and was pinned or sewn in place and decorated with ribbons and frills. As this early period advanced, the crinolines were made with a layer of stiffened ruffles at the back to support the drapery at the rear. Skirts were made with drapery attached to further enhance the appearance.

From 1878–1883, the bodices grew extremely long and narrow and the bustle fullness dropped down to the floor in a train off of a slim-fitting skirt. A small, semicircular frame supported what fullness was left at the back of the dress. The bodices were called cuirass bodices and this middle period goes by that name.

The last bustle form was rigid and shelf-like. It dominated from 1884–1890. Skirts were cut to fall smoothly from the rounded hump at the rear created by sturdy metal bustle frames.

Throughout the period, two-piece gown construction was the most common. This allowed for a better fit between the tightly corseted torso and the bustled skirt. Dresses for daytime during the full Bustle period were very much like those of the Crinoline. Basque bodices, a jacket-type bodice with an extension below the waist, were very popular. Some were made with long extensions in the back that would add to the layering and draping of the bustle and act like a short overskirt. Necklines for daywear were high and V-shaped. Some necklines were fully closed and others were slightly lower and square. Lower, open necklines were filled in with a chemisette or lace. No matter how high or low the front neckline, the neckline at the back was very high and the curve from the center front to the center back was often decorated to frame the face and neck. Sleeves were close fitting and were three-quarter length. Sleeves were set higher into the bodice, allowing for a more natural shoulder line and greater range of motion. Skirts and bodices matched one another, but occasionally a blouse was worn as a separate. Skirts were full and long to the ground, sometimes having a drape across the front that looked almost apron-like. Skirts and basques were made with enormous fullness that could be pulled back over the rear and create the full, waterfall effect. By the middle 1870s, some basques were long to the knee or longer. The fullness was created by the drapery. At this time, the bustle only served to support the drapery, not to give it shape or much added fullness.

Although the changes in style seem very abrupt, in reality these changes were happening gradually over time. Through the 1870s the fullness of the bustle became less draped and organic and more structured. The fullness sank down the skirt until 1878 when it had vanished almost entirely. The introduction of the cuirass bodice in 1875 pushed this trend along. The cuirass was a long jacket that fit smoothly and snugly over the hips, ending at a point in the front. It required a smaller, lower bustle to fit properly. Women liked the elongating and slenderizing effect this bodice had on the torso and it became very popular. As the cuirass grew longer and tighter, the bustle grew smaller and lower until 1878 when it had nearly disappeared. Necklines and sleeves did not change with the cut of the bodice. The skirts however became very narrow as well, with a drape of fabric at the back, pooling into the floor is a short train. Decoration was low to the ground, focused on the hem of the dress. The narrow skirts and mechanisms required to keep the small, low, barely-there bustle draped properly were difficult to wear and impeded walking. While this silhouette was very modern looking from the outside, it was just as cumbersome as the petticoats and hoopskirts of earlier eras had been.

A slow return to the larger bustle began in the early years of the 1880s and it fully returned in 1883. This third bustle phase was very rigid and shelf-like. The bodices were tightly fitted and nearly all daytime dresses had high, boned collars. Bodice styles were of the basque and polonaise varieties, although some blouses were worn for day dressing. The polonaise was a bodice that had a long, full skirt attached to it. The skirt fabric was looped up, drawn up, or draped back over the hips. The front swag made an apron-like effect while the back draped over the bustle, exposing the underskirt beneath. Sleeves were generally fit snug to just above the wrist. Some sleeves in about 1883 had a small, puffed sleeve cap. By 1889 this puff was quite evident on many dresses and called a kick-up. Eventually it would lead to a return to very large leg-o-mutton sleeves in the 1890s. Skirts were much less full and fell in a relatively straight line around the bustle to end on a wide ruffle several inches above the floor.

Eveningwear in the first, full Bustle period was very similar to that of daywear. Many women would wear the same skirt but have a daytime bodice with a higher neck and an evening bodice with a low décolletage. Many evening bodices of this time were off-the-shoulder and could have a variety of sleeves ranging from small cap sleeves to elbow-length sleeves ending in ruffles. Evening bodices were much more decorative than daytime bodices, but they were sufficiently elegant on their own to dress up a skirt that could be worn during the day.

During the second, cuirass period, the only difference between day- and eveningwear was the fabrics and trimming used. Evening gowns were made from shot silk, silk taffeta, silk satin, and velvet with lots of trimming. Necklines and sleeve lengths were the same for evening as for day and generally followed the cut of daytime bodices of the full bustle period.

In the last incarnation of the bustle, the shelf bustle, again dresses for evening were not cut differently than dresses for daywear. Skirts were slightly longer and often had a train. Sleeves were all very short, frequently they were nothing more than a wide band over the shoulder that would get narrower through the end of the 1880s. Older and more conservative women wore their evening dresses with elbow-length sleeves. The fit of the bodice and the basic cut and shape of the skirt did not change for evening, only the fabric and trimming was markedly different. While silk was popular for daytime dressing, lustrous satins and taffetas were used for evening dress with a profusion of lace, frills, pleats, tucks, ribbons, and fringes.

Drawers and chemises did not change very much in the way of construction. Drawers were still made without a center seam and were trimmed with ribbon and lace. Drawers were made of cotton or linen for warm months and wool for cold weather. Chemises were knee length with a round neck and short sleeves. Through the period, chemises became highly decorated with lace, ribbons, and ornamental tucks. A combination chemise and drawers was introduced for women as it had been for men. Some combinations were made of woven fabric and others knitted. They were primarily made of cotton although wool was used in the winter. These combinations also had an open crotch seam. Knit combinations became very popular after 1870 as corsets grew tighter and women wanted a smoother fitting, less bulky undergarment.

Corsetry became very important in perfecting the look of the bustle. The corset was a longer affair now, covering the hips to add stability to the often-heavy bustle perched on the backside. The idea was to smooth and elongate the torso and create a properly proportioned bustline, a very small waist, and a round hip. These types of corsets were very important during the cuirass period. Corsets were made of whalebone, cane, or increasingly of steel. Spring steel was lightweight and resilient and made a very sturdy, snug corset. Corsets were routinely advertised and came in shapes and sizes to accommodate infants, toddlers, young girls, and teenagers.

Stockings often were made to match the color of the dress or shoes. Striped stockings and those that were decorated with clocks, small embroideries, were the most popular. In the 1870s, white stockings with colorful clocks were the favorite for evening. In the 1880s black was more popular. Shoes for daytime were now almost as delicate as shoes for evening. Silk or kid skin slippers and heeled shoes were worn in matching colors to the dress. Silk flowers or ribbons trimmed the tops of the shoes near the toe. There was no difference between shoes for day and shoes for evening throughout all three bustle periods. Boots were not considered fashionable and usually only worn by children. Rubber-soled shoes made of canvas or sturdy leather were worn for popular sports such as tennis. Rubber-soled boots were worn for hiking and boots were made with blades for ice skating.

In the Crinoline period, cloaks and capes had been popular and easily accommodated the allover round shape of the skirts. In the Bustle period, the shape of the skirt was not conducive to traditionally shaped outerwear garments. Most coats and jackets were made close fitted and short in the back and worn loose well past the waist in front. The fashionable coats each year were shaped according to the fashionable bustle of the time. Sleeves were of a basic style, not too tight nor too full, and usually made with a turned back cuff. Many familiar names from coats of years past were recycled into new styles. The paletot and pelisse were both three-quarter length to floor length depending on the date and the early differences in their structure were now forgotten as they both were cut and constructed to conform to the prevailing bustle. An Ulster coat was made for women with the same features as the men's version, only shaped to allow the bustle. Some capes and cloaks were used, again, shaped to fit the dominant style. A new innovation was the dolman coat. It was a semifitted garment in which the full sleeves were cut-in-one with the bodice of the coat and had no armseye, only an underarm seam than ran from cuff to hem.

Hair was typically parted down the center and put into waves around the face before being pulled back into a bun or knot at the back of the head.

Bangs, or fringe, as cut, curled across the forehead. In the 1870s, hair was arranged in braids, a cascade of curls, or in a chignon. The hair draped and fell like the bustle did. False hair was used to augment the very full and cascading desired look. As the cuirass period came and dress became more refined, so did hairstyling. A simple bun or series of curls was worn low on the back of the head, again mimicking the bustle. During the third bustle period of 1884, high, boned collars were fashionable and hair could no longer be dressed around the nape of the neck. Instead, it was gathered to the top of the head in a bun or a pile of curls.

In the 1880s, only older matrons still wore the white linen day caps indoors. Fashionable hats were large and decorative with feathers and ribbon and lace and all manner of trimming placed upon them. When hair placement was at the back of the head, hats were worn forward or with the back tilted up. As hairstyles became simpler, hats became more lavish. They were made with taller crowns and stocked with even more trimming. Some nearly brimless styles became popular. A straw sailor hat with a low crown and wide brim that was nearly devoid of decoration was popular for sportswear.

Jewelry was more often worn with evening dress than during the day. Brooches were common for daytime wear, but in the evening women put on their necklaces and earrings and bracelets and wore hair ornaments. Gloves were expected to be worn for both day and evening and the glove length would vary by sleeve length. Gloves worn long to the elbow or higher were part of evening dress. Muffs were not used as often in this period, although large fur muffs were still available, most women preferred smaller ones.

Folding fans were a very important part of a woman's wardrobe. More than just a method of keeping cool, an entire language had developed around the opening, closing, and motions of the fan. Women could communicate easily to one another without uttering a word. Popular evening fans were hand painted, but feather fans were also popular. Tortoise shell and ivory were used as sticks and handles. Parasols were also still popular and they were very large and decorative at this time. Lace and fringe trimmed the edges and the handles were usually long enough to use as a walking stick.

Rouge and other colored cosmetics were still not used by upper-class women. Powders and face creams were acceptable, as was the wearing of perfume.

Since the 1840s, there had been a push towards athleticism for women. And in the 1850s and 1860s some women did indulge in outdoor activities such as bicycling and tennis. By the 1870s, women were far more interested in active pursuits. Lillie Langtry, a famous English actress, sparked a fashion for clingy wool knits for active wear. The story goes that she was known as the "Jersey Lily," having been born on the British island of Jersey and that the fabric she wore also came to be known by that name: jersey.[31]

Wool knits became very popular for outdoor activities, especially bathing. A typical bathing costume of the 1870s and early 1880s consisted of bloomers, an overskirt, and a bodice, all made of dark wool jersey. The trousers became shorts after a time and stockings were then worn to the knee. Bathing shoes or slippers were worn on the feet and a bathing cap was worn on the head. In the 1880s, sleeves were decreasing in size and length and by 1885, many bathing costumes were sleeveless. Women were not actually swimming in these outfits but only wading in the shallows and splashing around.

1890–1900

As the century drew to a close, women's dress changed radically from the bustles of the preceding decades. Although fullness was maintained with deep pleats at the back of the skirt, no supporting structures were used beneath the skirt. The silhouette of the 1890s was very hourglass shaped and reminiscent of the Romantic silhouette of the 1820s. Sleeves were very full and large and skirts had a bell-shaped flare. In between, the waist was squeezed as small as corsets were able.

Dresses were constructed in two pieces. Bodices were lined and ended at about the natural waist, although some had a pointed waistline. Some bodices had small basques. But the main focus of bodice construction was the sleeves. The shoulder area was usually cut with a yoke and a full sleeve gathered into the armseye created a puffed top. Although pulls at the shoulders were seen with the kick-ups of the 1880s, by 1893 the sleeves had grown substantially. By 1895, only two years later, the sleeves were positively gigantic and often lampooned by the media. The typical leg-o-mutton style was made with a very full puff from shoulder to elbow with tight-fitted sleeves at the forearm. Some sleeves gradually lessened in size to the wrist, but these do not seem to have been as popular. The puff and fitted sections were often made in contrasting fabrics for visual interest. But this fashion could not continue and the sleeves were already decreasing in size just two years after they hit their peak. Epaulets and smaller puffs would remain fashionable through the end of the century.

Skirts were gored during this period to fit smoothly over the hips and flare out into a bell shape. As mentioned, pleats were commonly seen at the center back of the skirt. The hem of the skirt was stiffened slightly with a lining of horsehair braid or buckram on the inside. Skirts were fully lined inside, as were bodices. Although fashion plates show women wearing skirts floor length, contemporary photographs show that most women wore their skirts two to four inches off the ground.

This simple, elegant style inspired a new type of women's ensemble; the tailor-made jacket and skirt combination made in matched fabric. They were made by tailors instead of dressmakers and were often very masculine in appearance, save for the full, puffed sleeves. Women also wore blouses regularly and paired them with skirts or a tailor-made set. The blouse of the 1890s was known as a shirtwaist, or simply a waist. It, too, was made like a man's, short except for the full sleeves and the dramatic taper to the small waistline. They could be worn plain and simple or be quite elaborate with frills, pleats, tucks, lace, and embroidery. Shirtwaists were one of the first things that were available as ready-to-wear for women, and it was a mainstay of the growing ready-made garment market in the United States.

Evening dresses were shaped like the two-piece daytime dress. They had a deep neckline and off-the-shoulder styles, these would grow more common after 1893. They were made with the same large, puffed sleeves when they were popular and small shoulder puffs when they were not. Evening dresses looked much like daywear but were cut from a more formal fabric and often included a train.

Women could choose between wearing combinations or a chemise and drawers separately. Trimming and ornamentation was at an all-time high on underwear. The construction did not change from earlier decades in this period. Corsets, however, did change. The corset of the 1890s was an underbust corset, fitting from the hips to just under the breasts. This allowed the waist to be cinched tighter without having to account for the breast size and it fit with the fashion of a less structured bustline that would become prevalent in the early 1900s. But now a means of supporting the bust had to be found. Breast supporters had been patented in the 1860s and were meant to be used as an alternative to corseting. Although women were looking for comfort, the breast supporters could not achieve the fashionable silhouette so women continued to wear corsets instead. By the 1890s, magazines were filled with advertisements for all manner of breast supporters to be worn with the new underbust corset. These support garments were known by a variety of names, mostly describing the item as a bust girdle or bust bodice, but some advertisements called the article a strophium, the bandeau breast supporters worn in ancient Rome.

Bust improvers were sold at many stores that sold breast supporters. They were designed to help fill out the front of the dress and add shape and volume to the bust, something the corset had previously done. They were made in a number of ways, usually pads or pillows of cotton. The corset cover was now exclusively known by the term *camisole* and it was an even more important garment now that there were fewer layers covering the breasts.

Although there were no more heavy supporting devices and the skirts were stiffened at the hems, women still wore one to two full petticoats to maintain the fashionable hourglass silhouette. Stockings were usually of cotton for daytime wear and black or colorful silk for evening.

Shoes had rounded toes and medium heels. These were of leather or of silk. Boots were coming back into fashion and were worn laced or buttoned very tightly and reached either the ankle or the midcalf.

Due to the massive fullness at the shoulders, capes usually were worn instead of coats with sleeves. During the height of large puffed sleeves, capes were cut with the sleeve puff shape in them for a more accommodating fit. Collars on the caps and cloaks were high, often boned, and finished with a standing frill or ruffle. Some kinds of Ulster and chesterfield coats were produced with wide enough sleeves to be worn, but they were not as popular as capes.

A curled fringe across the forehead was still popular for women. The length of the hair was coiled onto the top of the head in a wide bun. At the turn of the century, when the "Gibson Girl" was popular, women brushed their hair into soft waves around the face and built up the front of the hair in a tall, bouffant style then coiled the rest into a wide bun. The puffed-up style required pads and false hair in order to achieve such height and volume.

Hats were worn only when going out of doors. Hats of this decade were small to medium sized with a low crown and a small brim or no brim at all. Trims were sculptural in quality and often rose in tall spires from the hat. Ribbons, lace, and feathers, sometimes the whole wing of the bird, were the most popular trim styles. Sheer veils were popular for some hat styles. Women also favored straw boaters and a small, feminine version of the fedora for casual and sportswear. For evening hairdressing women wore combs, feathers, clips, and other decorative ornaments.

Gloves continued to be worn, short for day and long for evening. Folding fans and boas were popular evening accessories.

Art Nouveau jewelry designs dominated the market after 1890 and women began to wear more jewelry with daywear than they had in previous decades. A watch pinned to the bodice with a watch chain was a popular item.

Rouge and facial coloring agents were still not acceptable for ladies to wear, but some face creams were slightly tinted. Powder still remained an appropriate and popular cosmetic.

Women's interest in outdoor activities only increased through the 1890s. Full knickers were worn by many women for bicycling and tennis. They differed from bloomers because they were shorter, more tailored though the waist, and constructed of studier fabric. Some knickers were more like divided skirts than pants. The knickers were paired with a matching jacket and a blouse that fit the ensemble, much like the tailor-mades. For bathing costumes, women's dress did not change. Wool jersey was still worn for beach attire. The bathing costumes were cut to match the fashionable silhouette which included large, puffed sleeves and full, bell-shaped skirts. Bloomers and stockings were worn beneath the skirts and like the bathing costumes of the previous decades, these were very cumbersome and uncomfortable to wear for anything more than wading and splashing. One might also imagine that once wet with salt water, the bathing costumes were not pleasing to smell, either.

The styles for women in the last few years of the century changed faster and more often than ever before. Greater communication through magazine and telegraph allowed women to be more active in fashion and find out about trends sooner. Industrialization and the burgeoning ready-to-wear market also created an atmosphere of affordable fashion. Women were able to go out to the stores and buy inexpensive garments that would suit them for the season while that fashion prevailed, and then be able to go out and buy more things for the next season and so on. More women were able to actively participate in trends as they were happening. The end of the nineteenth century also saw the inevitable march towards modernity, and the eventual end of idle beautiful women. Women of the twentieth century would seek to balance motherhood, fashion, and equality in the new century.

In the late nineteenth century, the beginnings of the fashion industry as it is known today were born.

Children's Dress

The manner of dress for children did not change very much throughout the entire century. A prevailing artistic movement did have more of an impact on Bustle period children's clothes than it had on clothes of other periods. The Aesthetic movement was echoed in dress for both women and men and eventually found its way into children's attire. Kate Greenaway was an illustrator of children's literature and an adherent of the Aesthetic movement. She depicted children in simple, sweet clothing. Little girls' attire was reminiscent of the Empire period, with high waistlines and a loose fit. Dress for boys was also inspired by the Aesthetic movement and literature. Illustrations depicting aesthetically romanticized cavalier dress, used in Frances Hodgson Burnett's *Little Lord Fauntleroy*, created a trend in boys clothing. Breeches and a full jacket were worn with a wide white collar, a bow, and large, white, turned-back cuffs. Knee boots or low boots and white or black stockings were worn on the feet. Hair was worn long and cut in a pageboy style, or left full and curling. Although this style was lampooned widely, evidence shows that very few boys ever actually dressed this way. Overall, the Aesthetic movement influenced fashionable children's clothing more than it did fashionable clothing for women.

Babies were dressed in long gowns until they were old enough to walk. Boys and girls in their toddler years were both dressed in shirt skirts, as they had been in previous eras. But also as in previous eras, the dresses and skirts reflected the dominant style of dress for women in the particular period. During the Bustle period, toddlers dresses had the bulk of the yardage focused at the rear of the dress and sometimes even had a drapery effect swept back over the hips like that of a woman's early bustle gown.

By 1890, young boys were breeched as early as three years old and as late as age five or six. As the period went on, boys ceased to wear skirts at earlier ages. By 1900, all boys were wearing knickers or short trousers by age three, and by 1910 skirts for boys had disappeared altogether in favor of rompers. Knickers for young boys at this time became very fitted after 1870, looking much like eighteenth-century knee-breeches. In the 1880s short trousers were introduced for boys as an alternative to knickers and knickers all but disappeared.

Older boys still wore the Eton suit and tunic suit as well as the sailor suit. These were cut of whatever colors and fabrics were popular at the time. The fit of these suits, especially the tunic suit, was narrower and more fitted and had a lower waistline. Reefer jackets were also popular, as were blazers, especially those made of striped or solid colored flannel with patch pockets. Blazers were often paired with knickers and had a very sporty appearance. Shirts were made with high, stiff collars, just like those of adult men. Boys also wore scaled-down versions of adult men's outerwear and hats as well.

As in the Crinoline period, young girls wore dresses in the same silhouette of adult women, but shorter. And just as was seen in crinoline, this included underpinnings. Early in the Bustle period, the bustles for young girls were full, imitating an adult's. During the cuirass style of the 1880s, girls' dresses were cut straight from shoulder to hip with a belt or a sash placed at a dropped waistline that hit at the hips. When bustles returned, miniature bustle constructions were seen in girls' dresses as well. In the 1890s when the leg-o-mutton sleeves returned, they were replicated in children's wear. Sailor dresses adapted from the popular boy's suit were also very popular and would remain so though the majority of the twentieth century. Smocked dresses obviously influenced by Kate Greenaway's art became a large commercial success as did ethnic-inspired styles such as the Russian blouse and Scottish tartan dresses.

Hair for boys was allowed to grow somewhat long until school-aged when it was cut short and styled in the manner of adult men. Young girls' hair was worn long in soft, natural curls instead of ringlets. Large bows were a popular ornament as well as the sailor hat and smaller versions of women's hats. Young boys predominantly wore caps but moved into more adult styles as they got older.

The Aesthetic movement gave children the most freedom and comfort in their clothing that they'd had since the Empire period at the opening of the century. This would start a trend in children's clothing that would encourage comfort, freedom, and safety and eventually lead to an entire segment of the fashion industry devoted just to children's clothing toward the end of the twentieth century.

Specialty Clothing

The Aesthetic movement was more than just an artistic one; it spilled over into fashion as well. The Aesthetic Dress movement was somewhat of a continuation of the Rational Dress movement which sought to liberate women from yards upon yards of encumbering petticoats and constricting corsets. Aesthetic Dress had more philosophical origins but was basically interested in the same ends: a softly styled look that was functional, comfortable, and flattering.

As discussed in the Art section of this chapter, the Aesthetic movement sought to beautify their world and produce art that inspired personal joy on a sensual level. The Aesthetic movement had been inspired by the Pre-Raphaelite Brotherhood, a group of artists and designers that rejected modernity in favor of a simpler medieval style. They painted scenes derived from medieval, Biblical, mythological, and legendary tales and dressed their models in the appropriate garb. Many of these dresses were so lovely and comfortable that the models kept them and wore them at home. Many of the models were the wives and girlfriends of the members of the Brotherhood. The women of the Brotherhood soon began making these simple, flowing dresses for themselves. The costumes were an amalgam of medieval lines combined with Victorian sensibilities and came together in a unique and anachronistic style that was neither one nor the other. When Japan was opened for trade in the 1850s, a distinctly Eastern influence could be felt in the lines, colors, and ornamentation of the clothes.

In addition to the style and fit of the clothes, the Aesthetics were against the usage of synthetic, aniline dyes and preferred to color their textiles with natural, plant-derived pigments. This gave the clothes a less vibrant, old-fashioned look, especially when compared to the rich, brilliant colors being produced at the time. The Gilbert and Sullivan operetta *Patience*, from 1881, took a satirical look at the movement and dubbed the soft, muted colors favored by wearers of Aesthetic Dress "greenery-yallery."[32]

The Aesthetic Dress movement gave women an opportunity to reject the prevalent fashions and instead dress in a manner that suited them. Corsets were not boned for Aesthetic Dress and dresses were not tight fitting. Women who chose to put on this fashion knew that they were going to be the target of ridicule as "loose clothing was often equated with loose morals."[33] The women braving these fashions were few and primarily artists, activists, and intellectuals.

The fashion of the loose and languid drapery of the Aesthetic Dress did eventually make it into high fashion. In the 1870s, loose-fitted, unboned tea gowns were introduced and became very popular for women of station. They were meant to be worn to High Tea with only other women in attendance. At first they consisted of a simple silk tunic with an overdress that could be embellished in some charming way. By the 1890s, they had become quite lavish and elaborately decorated, but still maintained their soft quality and loose fit. The ladies of the period were found to be much appreciative of the break in the often-exhausting ordeal of wearing such tight, cumbersome, and uncomfortable clothes. Most of these ultrafashionable women would never recognize the irony in their choice of attire.

The costumes and customs of mourning were quite notable in this period. Although the custom of putting on specific clothes to signify bereavement was not new nor singly confined to Europe, it held a special place in the cultural history of the Victorians. When Queen Victoria's beloved husband, Prince Albert, died in 1861, she went into mourning and remained that way for the rest of her life. Her very public mourning helped make bereavement a part of popular culture in England. Prior to Prince Albert's death, mourning was already established as a rigid set of codes that determined the length of time each period of mourning should last and what to wear during each, depending on the relationship of the mourner to the deceased.

Popular fashion magazines such as *Godey's Lady's Book* and *Harper's Bazaar* reported on mourning and gave tips on mourning etiquette. A detailed article on mourning was published in April 1886 in *Harper's Bazaar*. Aimed at women, it explained the exact allowances for dress and appropriate time periods for each stage of the wearing of mourning clothes in the United States. While a person was in mourning, no society interaction was allowed until the requisite time had passed. At that point the mourner would take calling cards to friends and acquaintances so that they would know she was through with the private time of mourning. The private aspect of mourning was not required for the relative of a husband that the wife had never met, but she was prohibited from venturing out in public in her mourning clothes and engaging in social events such as parties, balls, or the theater. Mourners were encouraged to keep their spirits up by visiting with close friends and family. The author of the article called the mourning clothes "a shield to the real mourner, and they are often a curtain of respectability to the person who should be a mourner but is not";[34] meaning that even someone who was happy that the deceased had passed away must still go through with the proper mourning rituals.

The period of mourning for a widow in the United States was eighteen months, although in England it was twelve months or the traditional time period of a year and a day. Mourning for a parent, grandparent, or sibling lasted twelve months and the mourning for a child lasted no more than nine months. No matter the length, there were three stages of mourning. This first stage of mourning was considered deep mourning and required the entire dress to be made of, or covered with, crape.

Crape is a crinkled silk fabric and is referred to as "crepe" or "crêpe" in modern spelling. Victorian mourning fabric, however, is spelled "crape."[35] Women were expected to wear gowns of crape, bombazine, or Henrietta cloth during first mourning. The crape of the Bustle period was made of silk that had not been degummed to remove the seracin and therefore had a matte, lusterless finish. It was uncomfortable and quite flammable and tended to shrivel in the rain. *Harper's* recognized the discomfort and even danger of crape veiling around the face as well as its health risks, including nose and eye irritations that could lead to disease and blindness. The author bravely states, "It is a thousand pities that fashion dictates the crape veil, but so it is. It is the very banner of woe, and no one has the courage to go without it."[36] The author then advises to wear a swatch of tulle over the face to shield it from direct contact with the crape.

Bombazine was a silk and wool mix and usually worn by the middle class or lower. Henrietta cloth was another silk and wool mixture. *Harper's* allowed for a dress of Henrietta cloth so long as it was covered in crape. A woman's head had to be covered in a long crape veil known as the weeping veil and at her wrists were long, full cuffs made of white lawn or muslin known as weepers. Presumably these articles were for the purpose of wiping away the tears. Black mourning bonnets were also worn, but a woman had a choice between a bonnet and a widow's cap of white crape, much like the Stewart cap worn by Queen Victoria. Kid leather gloves in black were also worn. The only jewelry allowed except for wedding rings and articles made from the deceased's hair was simple jet jewelry. The main idea of first mourning was that the dress be as dull and unadorned as possible. The full mourning ensemble was colloquially called "widow's weeds."

When in mourning for a child, many of the harshest elements of first mourning could be omitted as it was not considered as deep a loss as was the loss of a husband. *Harper's* explains:

> No [mother] is ever ready to take off mourning; therefore these rules have this advantage—they enable the friends around a grief stricken mother to tell her when is the time to make her dress more cheerful, which she is bound to do for the sake of the survivors.... It is well for mothers to remember this when sorrow for a lost child makes all the earth seem barren to them.[37]

When mourning a parent, grandparent, or sibling, the crape veil was not placed over the head but hung from the back of the bonnet. When mourning for an in-law, a woman could go directly into second morning for one month, and then directly into half-mourning after that. The period of mourning for an uncle, aunt, or cousin was three months.

After six months of mourning, the heavy crape veil could be removed and replaced with a lighter weight one. After twelve months the widow's cap or bonnet could be removed and the woman would go into second mourning. At this point the widow could wear some ornamentation but only black jet jewelry was still allowed, except for diamonds in wedding rings. Dress was still dull black. This period typically lasted for nine months.

The third stage was called half-mourning and was usually three to six months in length. At this time all manner of black cloth could be worn, it did not need to be lusterless. Veils were also not required and a woman's everyday jewelry could also be worn. During half mourning, a woman slowly eased back into the wearing of colors and fashionable dress. In full mourning, women were expected to keep the proscription against color and luster down to their underclothes. Stockings, drawers, chemises, corset covers, and petticoats were all made in black. As mourning lessened, the colors that a woman was allowed to wear included grey, mauve, purple, lavender, lilac, white, and toward the end of the century, dark red.

Jewelry was an important accessory for all women of this era, even during mourning. Jet was the popular stone of choice. It is a fossilized form of coal and highly prized by the English. Jet jewelry was allowed throughout the mourning process and popularized by Queen Victoria. Items made from the deceased's hair were also popular. What started as a simple keepsake token was developed into an elaborate trend of weaving or braiding the hair into rings, bracelets, and brooches. The hair was also often clasped into a locket. Hair jewelry was acceptable throughout mourning and some grieving women wore their beloved's hair with them for years after, if not their whole lives. At second through half-mourning, gold and gold-colored metal was allowed to be worn.

Children were not kept in mourning longer than one month and girls under the age of seventeen did not wear crape or go into full mourning. A widower was expected to mourn his wife for two years, but he did not have to wait the full twenty-four months to remarry. Men could go about their daily lives and wear what they liked just as long as they wore a black armband of mourning. A woman was allowed to marry after her first year of full mourning only if she would be destitute without a husband, and especially if she had children. Her remarriage, however, did not exempt her from fulfilling the required mourning period for her first husband.

When Queen Victoria died in 1901, it was the last time this sort of elaborate mourning was seen. The massive causalities during World War I in Europe put an end to involved mourning etiquette. The same had happened in the United States during the Civil War. Victoria's wake was the mourning of Mourning and an end to a very peculiar chapter in costume history.

NOTES

1. "Porphyria is not a single disease but a group of at least eight disorders that differ considerably from each other. The symptoms arise mostly from effects on the nervous system or the skin. Effects on the nervous system occur in the acute porphyrias. Proper diagnosis is often delayed because the symptoms are nonspecific. Skin manifestations can include burning, blistering, and scarring of sun-exposed areas." http://www.porphyria foundation.com/about_por/index.html (accessed August 30, 2007).

2. The failure of the entire Irish potato crop in 1845 was caused by a fungal blight. This blight lasted from 1845–1849.

3. Marjie Bloy, "The Irish Famine: 1845–49," http://www.victorianweb.org/history/famine.html (accessed August 30, 2007).

4. Phyllis G. Tortora and Keith Eubank. *Survey of Historic Costume, Fourth Edition.* New York: Fairchild Publications, 2005: 264.

5. J. M. Thompson, *Napoleon Self-Revealed.* Oxford, UK: Blackwell, 1934: 294ff.

6. http://www.presidentsusa.net/1840slogan.html (accessed September 5, 2007).

7. David Herbert Donald, *Lincoln.* New York: Simon & Schuster, 1995: 576, 580.

8. George Alfred Townsend, *The Life, Crime and Capture of John Wilkes Booth.* Whitefish, MT: Kessinger Publishing, 2004: 3.

9. http://net.lib.byu.edu/~rdh7/wwi/comment/huachuca/HI2-03.htm (accessed September 5, 2007).

10. Jennifer Harris, ed. *Textiles: 5,000 Years.* New York: Harry N. Abrams, 1993: 106.

11. Harris, *Textiles:* 107.

12. Tortora and Eubank. *Survey of Historic Costume: Fourth Edition.* New York: Fairchild Publications, Inc., 2005: 256.

13. Ibid., 256.

14. http://www.singerco.com/company/history.html.

15. "Mauvine." *Webster's Revised Unabridged Dictionary.* MICRA, Inc. 13 Sep. 2007. Dictionary.com http://dictionary.reference.com/browse/mauvine.

16. Aesthetic dress was derived from the Pre-Raphaelite Brotherhood and their quest to simplify life. This mode of dress was usually worn without stays and was characterized by the soft, draping style. There is a more detailed description of the mode later in this chapter. Phyllis Tortora and Keith Eubank. *Survey of Historic Costume: Fourth Edition.* New York: Fairchild Publications, Inc., 2005: 331.

17. Ibid., 262.

18. Ibid., 274.

19. Ibid., 268–269.

20. C. W. Cunnington, and P. Cunnington. *Handbook of English Costume in the 19th Century*. London: Faber and Faber, 1970: 142.

21. Tortora and Eubank, *Survey of Historic Costume*, 287.

22. Valerie Steele, *The Corset: A Cultural History*. New Haven, CT: Yale University Press, 2001: 77.

23. Page 45.

24. Tortora and Eubank, *Survey of Historic Costume*, 205.

25. Elzey Hays, "Dress Under Difficulties: Or Passages from the Blockade Experience of Rebel Women," *Godey's Lady's Book* July 1866: 32.

26. Sara J. Oshinsky. "Christopher Dresser (1834–1904)". In *Timeline of Art History*. New York: The Metropolitan Museum of Art, 2000–. 12 September 2007 http://www.metmuseum.org/toah/hd/cdrs/hd_cdrs.htm.

27. Phyllis Tortora and Keith Eubank. *Survey of Historic Costume: Fourth Edition*. New York: Fairchild Publications, Inc., 2005: 330.

28. Phyllis Tortora and Keith Eubank. *Survey of Historic Costume: Fourth Edition*. New York: Fairchild Publications, Inc., 2005: 335.

29. Jane Ashelford. *The Art of Dress: Clothes and Society 1500-1914*. New York: Harry N. Abrams, 1996: 242.

30. Ashelford, 229.

31. Ashelford, 229.

32. Phyllis Tortora and Keith Eubank. *Survey of Historic Costume: Fourth Edition*. New York: Fairchild Publications, Inc., 2005: 353.

33. "Mourning and Funeral Usages", April 17, 1886 [electronic edition]. Harper's Bazaar, Nineteenth Century Fashion Magazine, http://harpersbazaar.victorian-ebooks.com (2005). 12 September 2007.

34. "Mourning and Funeral Usages", April 17, 1886 [electronic edition]. Harper's Bazaar, Nineteenth Century Fashion Magazine, http://harpersbazaar.victorian-ebooks.com (2005). 12 September 2007.

35. Tortora and Eubank, *Survey of Historic Costume*, 322.

36. Lynn Downey, "Levi Strauss: A Short Biography," *Levi Strauss & Co.* 2005, http://www.levistrauss.com/Downloads/History_Levi_Strauss_Biography.pdf (accessed September 11, 2007).

37. "The History of Denim: Lifestyle Monitor Denim Issue" *Lifestyle Monitor Trend Magazine*. 2007. Cotton, Incorporated. http://www.cottoninc.com/LifestyleMonitor/LSMDenimIssue/?Pg=4 (accessed September 11, 2007).

FURTHER READING

Ashelford, Jane. *The Art of Dress: Clothes and Society 1500-1914*. New York: Harry N. Abrams, Inc., 1996.

Boucher, François. *20,000 Years of Fashion: The History of Costume and Personal Adornment*. New York: Harry N. Abrams, 1967.

Coleman, Elizabeth A. *The Opulent Era: Fashions of Worth, Doucet and Pingat*. Brooklyn, NY: The Brooklyn Museum in association with Thames and Hudson, 1989.

Cunnington, C. Willett, and Phillis Cunnington. *Handbook of English Costume in the Nineteenth Century*. London: Faber & Faber, 1970.

Ginsburg, Madeleine. *Victorian Dress in Photographs*. London: Batsford, 1988.

Gontar, Cybele. "Art Nouveau." In *Timeline of Art History*. New York: The Metropolitan Museum of Art, 2000–. http://www.metmuseum.org/toah/hd/artn/hd_artn.htm (accessed October 2006).

Harris, Jennifer, ed. *Textiles: 5,000 Years*. New York: Harry N. Abrams, Inc., 1993.

Humphries, Mary. *Fabric Glossary*. Upper Saddle River, NJ: Prentice Hall, 2003.

Humphries, Mary. *Fabric Reference, Third Edition*. Upper Saddle River, NJ: Prentice Hall, 1996.

Ives, Colta. "Japonisme." In *Timeline of Art History*. New York: The Metropolitan Museum of Art, 2000–. http://www.metmuseum.org/toah/hd/jpon/hd_jpon.htm (accessed October 2004).

Kadolf, Sara J. and Anna L. Langford. *Textiles: Tenth Edition*. Upper Saddle River, NJ: Prentice Hall, 2006.

Krick, Jessica. "Charles Frederick Worth (1826–1895) and The House of Worth." The Costume Institute, Metropolitan Museum of Art. http://www.metmuseum.org/toah/hd/wrth/hd_wrth.htm

Le Bourhis, Katell, ed. *The Age of Napoleon: Costume from Revolution to Empire: 1789–1815*. New York: Metropolitan Museum and H. N. Abrams, 1989.

Mandell, Richard D. *Paris 1900: The Great World's Fair*. Toronto, Canada: University of Toronto Press, 1967.

Meller, Susan and Joost Elffers. *Textile Designs: Two Hundred Years of European and American Patterns Organized by Motif, Style, Color, Layout, and Period*. New York: Harry N. Abrams, 2002.

Montgomery, Florence M. *Textiles in America 1650–1870*. New York: W. W. Norton, 2007.

Milbank, Caroline Rennolds. *New York Fashion: The Evolution of American Style*. New York: Harry N. Abrams, 1989.

"Mourning and Funeral Usages," April 17, 1886 [electronic edition]. *Harper's Bazaar*, Nineteenth Century Fashion Magazine, http://harpersbazaar.victorian-ebooks.com (accessed 2005).

Perrot, Philippe. *Fashioning the Bourgeoisie: A History of Clothing in the Nineteenth Century*. Princeton, NJ: Princeton University Press, 1994.

Ribeiro, Aileen. *Ingres in Fashion*. New Haven, CT: Yale University Press, 1999.

Riegel, Robert E. "Women's Clothes and Women's Rights." *American Quarterly* 15, no. 3 (Autumn 1963): 390–401.

Samu, Margaret. "Impressionism: Art and Modernity." In *Timeline of Art History*. New York: The Metropolitan Museum of Art, 2004. http://www.metmuseum.org/toah/hd/imml/hd_imml.htm (accessed September 2007).

Steele, Valerie. *The Corset: A Cultural History*. New Haven, CT: Yale University Press, 2001.

Thieme, Otto Charles. "The Art of Dress in the Victorian and Edwardian Eras." *Journal of Decorative and Propaganda Arts* 10 (August 1988).

Tortora, Phyllis, and Keith Eubank. *Survey of Historic Costume: Fourth Edition*. New York: Fairchild Publications, Inc., 2005.

Troy, Nancy J. *Couture Culture: A Study in Modern Art and Fashion*. Cambridge, MA: MIT Press, 2003.

Worth, Jean Philippe. *A Century of Fashion*. Trans by Ruth Scott Miller. Boston: Little, Brown, 1928.

MOVIES

The Age of Innocence (1993)
Bram Stoker's Dracula (1992)
Forsythe Saga, BBC (2002)
The Heiress (1949)
House of Mirth (2000)

Howard's End (1992)
The Importance of being Ernest (2002)
Impromptu (1991)
Micahel Collins (1996)
A Midsummer Night's Dream (1999)
Nicholas and Alexander (1971)
Pickwick Papers (1952)
The Prestige (2006)
Room with a View (1986)
Tess (1979)
Titanic (1997)
Washington Square (1997)

1900–1918

Ellen Hymowitz

TIMELINE

1912	*Titanic* sinks; Balkans War
1913	New York Armory Show bring ideas on modern art to the United States
1914	World War I begins when Archduke Ferdinand is assassinated; Panama Canal opens
1916–1922	Dadaism art movement founded in Zurich spreads to New York, Paris, and Berlin
1917	United States enters the war; Russian Revolution
1918	War ends
1919	Treaty of Versailles; Bauhaus School of Design opens

THE EDWARDIAN PERIOD AND BELLE ÉPOQUE, 1900–1914

The gorgeously evocative period known in France as the Belle Époque retained the opulence and hierarchies of an earlier time. In 1914, as World War I approached, the era disappeared like so many pale satin frocks down a passageway, leaving the ghost of idle pleasures in its wake. Spanning the turn of the century and capitalizing on fortunes accumulated before the democratizing notion of income tax existed, the Belle Époque held out a lavish style of life to the relative few who could afford it. Many of the Parisian couture houses established in the nineteenth century continued to supply their high-gloss designs to clients of near-limitless means. These patrons ranged from aristocrats to renowned actresses. Wives and daughters of American "merchant princes"—a newfangled aristocracy based solely on wealth—pursued objects of luxury to affirm their high rank in the world. With the onset of World War I, everything changed, including fashion for both men and women.

In turn-of-the-century Rio de Janeiro, the fashions of Paris were seized upon as emblems of modernity. Wanting to distance themselves from the vast lower classes, elite and upper-middle-class Cariocas viewed Paris as a heaven of high style, "civilization," and superiority. Not just French fashions but also French literature, furnishings, and language were adopted for use in Rio. In 1908, this extreme Francophilia was satirized by a writer in Brazil. While acquisition of Paris originals or, more commonly, local re-creations of them was desirable, it was but one step on the way to a dreamed-of destination. It was not enough to have a shadow of it, but rather one must have the thing itself. To dress in Parisian clothes was to shed one's sluggish provincial fate.

In 1900, a writer for the *Atlanta Constitution* described a subterfuge used by *modistes*, corset makers, and milliners to attract American clients. After checking newspaper lists of visitors—those reckoned worthy of having their arrivals announced—members of the fashion trade scanned hotel registers, then sent saleswomen directly to the rooms of the hoped-for clients. The shop representative, an invariably appealing "little solicitor of patronage," would then make an unabashed and often-successful pitch for business. By using lovely-looking salespeople, dressed in the same types of goods for sale, makers not so subtly implied that human loveliness lingered as the essence of a purchased item.

With French fashion dictating what women wore around the world, the passionate American shopper in early twentieth-century Paris was poised for flattery and enthusiastic spending. She sought a quantity of dresses that pertained to different occasions and different parts of the day, merging conformity with a peculiarly American brand of ostentation and hoarding fashionable dresses and accessories. American fashion journalists admonished their readers to take a lesson from the average Frenchwoman, who was seen to shop more sensibly and not lose herself in fads. One recommendation to Americans was to follow the French wife's habit of having her husband pass judgment on the purchase of her clothes, not to monitor cost so much as to inject his purported sense of fashion. It is not clear how many French husbands were recruited for such missions, but it is certainly true that female consumers felt new trust in the capabilities of men as fashion arbiters. They felt, too, a new ease in dealing with the intimate proximity of couturiers in the process of shopping, a shift from the female realm of the personal dressmaker.

While Edwardian London remained the capital of men's tailoring, the lure of Paris as a near-holy destination for fashion pilgrims suggests the international sway of couture and the worldwide conformity, for women, to an established French ideal. American expressions of style were fueled by a French paradigm ready to be investigated. Situated at the heart of the fashionable world, the 1900 Exposition Universelle in Paris asserted the global dominance of Parisian dress, while demonstrating and promoting an international exchange of trends in decorative arts. The sprawling World's Fair captured in its profusion of ideas and wares the threshold sensation of one century giving way to the next. An inventory of its contents would describe how the nations represented at the exposition assayed the material future of the world. Not just the objects showcased but even the choice of which countries and enterprises would participate suggests many of the remarkable aesthetic and technological achievements, as well as the cultural biases, that would suffuse the century to come.

Despite pressures for women to wear conventional and constricting dress, in the period before World War I, the dress reform movement of the previous century lost momentum. The reality of women's freedom overtook the symbolic nature of restrictive clothing. Increasingly, women enrolled in universities, entered the workforce, and earned their own money. Women's magazines advised female office workers to wear dark colors that resisted staining and avoided attracting male attention. Participation in sports, including tennis, swimming, and cycling, demanded suitably fluent—if, by today's standards, cumbersome—clothes. In 1913, *Vogue* devoted a special issue to fashions, such as long coats and large veiled hats, for "motoring." The need for these styles reflected the availability, in the United States, of mass-manufactured cars.

Several aspects of the 1900 Exposition relate in particular to fashion history. One of the fair's many pavilions, the Palais du Costume, offered a waxwork overview of dress from ancient times until the present, providing a historical context for the contemporary examples that concluded the exhibition. Mannequins for each style of dress—from Byzantine to Napoleonic—were set in tableaux intended to recreate the settings in which the clothes originally were worn. Another exhibition, this one organized by designer Jeanne Paquin, showcased Parisian *haute couture*. Many of the most prominent couturiers took part, including Callot Soeurs and Jacques Doucet. The seminal Parisian couture salon, the House of Worth, displayed its lavish gowns in an arrestingly modern style, on wax mannequins arranged under artificial lighting.

Jean-Philippe Worth, along with his brother, continued the business started by their father, Charles Worth. Jean-Philippe suggested that he had the forethought to reproduce the indoor nighttime atmosphere in which the evening gowns would actually be worn, although in truth, such adjusted lighting was a feature of various dressmaking salons and the use of waxwork mannequins was certainly not restricted to Worth's particular display. The designer's exaggerated claims, however, fit the image-making thrust of his salon. Self-promotion, then as now, played a key role in the success of an enterprise. According to Worth's account of the event, admiring crowds at the firm's exhibit were huge enough to require a policeman to manage them. For the House of Worth, as for most other prominent fashion concerns, connections to "high society" reflected and created the value of the company. The designer's boasting of these ties suggests, too, the social distance in place between the businessman and his clients.

Many signs linked status and fashion, as they had for centuries. The House of Worth continued to flourish after Charles's death in 1895 and offered gowns heavily constructed from silks, voided velvets, heirloom lace, and other costly materials. The firm applied lavish trimming, including quantities of lace, to already lush fabrications. At times, a machine-made version was substituted for heirloom lace, in the belief that the difference between the two would not be easily discernible. The decorated fabrics were set upon a lining that was closely fitted to the body. Oversized hats, often garnished with feathers, added substance to an already substantial figure. The silhouette of a Worth couture gown depended largely on its wearer's reconfiguring undergarments.

Legendary fashion designer Gabrielle (Coco) Chanel, who was born in 1883, recalled that the women of her youth lacked a human form and that Worth dresses "contradicted nature." Corsets of the 1900s pushed the bosom forward and the rear in the opposite direction, suggesting a reverse *S*-curved silhouette. Though originally intended to free the waist and diaphragm from earlier corsets, the newly devised foundation garment was, as a critic noted, equally cumbersome and uncomfortable.

This S-curve has been linked to the sinuous lines of the Art Nouveau movement in fine and decorative arts that pervaded the 1900 Exposition. However, if there was any connection between the disjointed thrust of a Worth gown and the organic curves of Art Nouveau motifs, the two strains of turn-of-the-century fashion were mostly separate and distinct from each other. Worth's gowns were part of a continuum of structured fashions.

Though Art Nouveau arose in the nineteenth century, its roots lay in the renegade Art and Crafts movement advanced by John Ruskin and William Morris. An idealization of the handmade (vs. machine-made) and the natural—in fabrics, silhouettes, motifs—Art and Crafts conflated a variety of social and political preoccupations. In colonial India, the growing nationalist movement found paradoxical inspiration in the theorizing of British proponents of Arts and Crafts. The shift to locally made, as opposed to imported, textiles would lessen Indian dependence on Britain and help the colony break free of British control. Later, Mahatma Gandhi promoted the hand weaving of textiles, using the spinning wheel as a symbol of Indian independence. Concerns about the depersonalizing aspects of mass production merged in the West with an interest in dress reform.

Already, women were choosing loose-fitting, more comfortable tea gowns to wear at home. Expressed differently in London, Paris, Glasgow, Vienna, and other European cities, the same desire arose to unify all the aspects of one's surroundings, including the clothing that surrounded one's body. Architecture, fashion, interiors—all contrived from the same sensibly organized (if deceptively costly) point of view. The Japanese manner of integrating applied arts, and endowing even utilitarian items with beauty, offered consumers in the West a novel way to regard their own domestic surroundings.

Apart from their assumptions of ethnic Otherness, based on doubtful ethnographic showcases, visitors to the Paris Exposition were tricked into believing that exotically costumed individuals floating through the crowds were also, in fact, from distant, fabled lands. These, however, were actors, Europeans paid to impersonate cultural strangers.

While the Paris Exposition as a whole could be regarded as spectacle, theater and theatricality played a variety of roles in the world of fashion. Couturiers costumed actresses for their onstage roles and provided wardrobes for their offstage lives; theatrical costumes influenced the design of ordinary clothes; actresses were dressed by the best modistes on frequent trips to Paris. While lingerie gowns were commonplace for at-home dress, actresses pioneered their acceptance as streetwear.

Shop windows offered up another sort of theater, those of Paris considered to be more dramatically focused than their American counterparts, with fewer types of items mixed in each window. In 1910, a competition was held in Berlin for the most artistic shop window design. German Expressionist artist August Macke made shop window displays a recurring subject of his paintings.

From the turn of the twentieth century until the war, a masculinizing influence held sway in both boys' and women's dress, culminating in the military uniformity of true army clothes. Young girls adopted boyish knickerbocker suits for play. For men, a premium was placed on the inconspicuous sameness of business suits. One critic noted approvingly of this sea of drab men: "They are so well-dressed, in fact, that they are scarcely noticable."

Japanese Inspiration

Following the opening of Japan to Western trade in the mid-nineteenth century, Siegfried Bing, a German-born art dealer based in Paris, began to collect and sell

Japanese prints, textiles, and decorative objects, initiating a Western fascination that erupted in *Japonism* or Japanese-inspired styles of art and design. The movement reflected a more generalized interest in the exotic, as interpreted within the confines of European culture. The appeal of Japonism extended to the styling of women's hair into the "pompadour à la Japanese," a roll at the base of the head around the back and sides. Orientalism, Western imaginings of Eastern dress and culture, overlapped with Japonism and was sometimes conflated with "primitivism," although the latter term is more frequently associated with projections of Western assumptions onto African or South Pacific tribal cultures. Bing's Art Nouveau Pavilion was an offshoot of his gallery in Paris. The design movement of Art Nouveau, which borrowed its name from Bing's shop, had stylistic roots in organic, asymmetrical forms, echoing the Rococo style of the eighteenth century. Japanesque motifs of scrolling waves, tendrils, and flowers such as peonies were used in the earlier movement of Arts and Crafts.

One source of Japanese-inspired clothing and textiles was Liberty of London. In 1905, the department store published a catalogue of fashions in the domestic context of furnishings also for sale. The catalogue's illustrations suggested a natural habitat for fashionable creatures inclined to comfortable but still beautifully fabricated gowns. Liberty gowns mixed historicist (making reference to long-ago styles) and pan-Asian motifs, including, for at least one gown, the figure of a dragon.

As visitors to the 1900 Exposition flocked to intimate, if inanimate, exhibits of sophisticated dress, interior decorations, textiles, and mechanical inventions, they were mesmerized as well by "savages" who were displayed in what were imagined to be their own natural habitats, ones far removed from the idylls of a Liberty catalogue. The fair's human dioramas—actual living people transported from distant countries and exhibited as curiosities—reflected a European fascination with the "primitive"; in fact, such traveling displays of "natives" were not unique to the Paris Exposition. From a Eurocentric viewpoint, these "envoys," exposed in states of provocative undress, satisfied expectations of Otherness and exoticism.

One French writer offered his bemused impressions of natives in the Congo. It was this reporter's perception that the members of a tribe—called the Pahouins—would shed, at the drop of a hat, their skimpy monkey-skin coverings in order to dress in Western clothes. Not just any Western clothes: these were a hodgepodge of aged masquerade costumes, gifts of explorers and missionaries. The hapless natives appeared as firemen, *zouaves* (Algerian soldiers in bright-hued uniforms), clowns, or, in one case, Tyrolean dress. Meanwhile, Parisian couturiere Paquin used monkey skins to add a note of exoticism to outerwear such as capes and coats.

Colonial Africa, India, and the Far East

Conversely, beyond the temporal and geographic confines of the Paris exhibition, individuals in far-flung parts of Africa and Asia expressed their own fascination with ungimmicky Western dress, adopting it to conform to colonial expectations or to express qualities of sophistication and modernity. Missionaries, colonial administrators, and trading companies brought with them exposure to European dress.

As a late-twentieth-century writer describes the Congo: "In 1901, a priest visiting the sick in Brazzaville found 'Christians from Senegal and from all the West Coast.' Most of them imitated whites in everything detestable; and on the roads, we meet the crudest sort of dandies." Describing these lapsed Christians disapprovingly, the priest noted that they were wearing "real trousers, jackets, soft brimmed hats, carried canes and had a cigarette hanging form their lips." The most resourceful people were wearing worn-out shoes long forgotten by some explorer. In the years immediately before World War I, starched white and khaki suits modeled after the wear of white colonial officers were high fashion among the Congolese riverboat workers who came ashore on Sundays. Diversity of styles and the development of local styles is also hinted at in European accounts. Young men wore their shirts outside their trousers and wore their finest clothes such as trousers and frock coats, which they had bought secondhand.[1]

For a short time in Britain and the United States, khaki was styled into women's gowns, but the color was so unflattering that it was a short-lived trend. The drab material was identical to that used for men's military uniforms. Eerily, but perhaps conveniently, the same gowns could double as mourning dresses.

Korean Clothing

In Korea, political events at the turn of the century shifted women's dress away from the tradition *hanbok* and into accordance with Western styles, though many still clung to the indigenous style. Men were compelled, all at once, by an 1899 government decree, to adopt Western dress, following the example of diplomats.

A more measured and organic pace applied to changes in women's clothing, more along the model of Western fashion evolution. No sudden politically motivated change was imposed; rather, the Western style adopted by wealthy or royal women who had lived abroad or who had worldly connections heralded, with their own clothing, a preference for foreign dress. In 1899, one such citizen returned to Korea in

> an entirely new look that marked the beginning of Western-style fashion in Korea—an S-line art-nouveau style dress that was in vogue in Europe at the time, silk socks and low-heeled pumps, a hat decorated with ribbons and feathers, and carrying a parasol.[2]

Later, the American style of separate blouses and jackets for women roused interest, and in 1905, a version of dress reform led to a revision of the traditional dress. Women paid new attention to their hair, with younger women adopting the pompadour style, though not the "Japanese" version in vogue in the West.

Chinese Clothing

In the first decade of the twentieth century, upper- and middle-class Chinese citizens wore some components of Western dress—fancy socks for men or other similar novelty items. The founding of the Chinese Republic in 1911 brought with it a reconsideration of national dress. For some, Western clothing was a vital indicator of progress, a way for China to access and connect itself to the modern world. For others, adoption of Western dress was yet another way China would be ruled by outside forces. In addition, the importation of Western clothing threatened the stability of a long-established silk industry. Questions were raised, too, about the healthfulness of Western corsets, not to mention the productive time potentially wasted on chasing after fashion trends.

A spokesperson for the endangered silk industry mocked the republicans' sudden embrace of Western dress:

> Let's first mention the things that a lady can't do without: a pair of sharp-toed, high-heeled, premium leather shoes; a pair of "violet mink" gloves; two or three plain or jewel-encrusted gold pins; a white lace … handkerchief; a pair of gold-rimmed, new style eyeglasses; a curved ivory comb; and a silk kerchief. Now let's address the things a man can't do without: a Western suit, greatcoat, Western hat, and handkerchief, with the addition of a boutonniere, a pince-nez, and a few words of pidgin English.[3]

Futurism

The Italian art movement known as Futurism proposed, beginning in 1909, to inject the dynamism of modern cities into shapes of modern fine and decorative arts, including fashion. Futurists placed clothing within the context of architectural space, suggesting that bright, geometrically patterned textiles would reflect the dazzling geometry of cities. Futurist clothes, devised of intricate colorful shapes, would resurface decades later in the work of Italian designer Emilio Pucci. In 1900, Giacomo Balla, a founder of the Futurist movement, traveled from Rome to view the Paris Exposition. He expressed his vision of an artificially lighted, electrified city—the Palais de l'Électricité—first in painting and then in the future and clothes.

Women's Clothing

Belle Époque styles for all women persisted with luxurious and extravagant fabrics, styles, and beautiful finishes. Soft colors in discreet tones were popular, and anything bold was a jolt to the fashion senses of women in Europe. Women's tailor-made suits consisted of matching skirts and jackets that were tailored and stiff, reflecting the style worn by men—jackets with lapels and single- or double-breasted styles, but with enlarged, bishop, more feminine sleeves. Cuffs were either very wide or buttoned tight on the wrist with lace decoration or ruffles. Lace added a feminine twist to the white shirts. Daytime dress was generally a one-piece garment with both the skirt and bodice top attached, unlike the separates of the tailor-made suit.

With clothing reform, simpler designs and livelier colors with Art Nouveau–inspired designs were the rage. The princess cut for women's dresses returned by 1909. Hobble skirts were introduced about 1910, but were unpopular because they drastically restricted movement and made it very difficult to walk. These outfits had a raised waistband that landed just below the bust and had very long sleeves that were narrower than the previous century's leg-o-mutton sleeves but could be exaggerated as well.

Until a more relaxed silhouette took hold, the ideal of ample, blossoming flesh demanded, paradoxically, a means to configure restraint. Corsets, despite the dress reformers, were still needed in order to push the bust up as part of the reverse S-curve. As reform dress gained popularity, the gowns flowed more freely from the shoulders or breasts and were less tightly constraining.

By 1910, the voluptuous S-curve had given way to the narrow, if not sandwich-board, sheath dress. As World War I approached, women's hemlines rose to accommodate physical movement, including that of dance; the craze for animated ragtime music extended from its African-American roots to the dance halls of Paris, Vienna, and other cities of Western Europe.

For women's gowns, exquisite and labor-intensive trimmings and ornamentation of beads or sequins gave physical embodiment to prosperity, before the "symbolic" wealth of financial investments eclipsed this, as the literal gold standard of fancy dress. Applied ornamentation, including heirloom laces, moved the implied value of women to the surface of their clothes.

Affluent women and men dressed for dinner. How much flesh a neckline would reveal depended on the time of day, with daywear always more modest than that for evening occasions. Women could choose between *décolleté*—lowered neckline—and long-sleeved, neck-concealing styles.

Below the rarified ranks of aristocrats and debutantes, middle-class women in England, Europe, and America sewed their own clothing or used local dressmakers to produce approximations of the latest trends. These dressmakers varied in skill: many were true artisans, expertly interpreting the dictates of Paris. Others struggled to keep up; by the time they mastered the complicated drape of a new skirt style, its ideal construction would have changed. The dressmaker served the whims of clients, and her accommodation to these whims preserved an established imbalance of social power. Within the moral restrictions of Victorian society, the hands-on intimacy of fitting a dress to the exposed body naturally excluded men from the role of seamstress. Through their acknowledged superiority of taste, couturiers reversed the entrenched positions of manufacturer and client.

Increasingly, department stores offered reliable ready-made clothes for women, men, and even children. These stores and smaller shops published advertisements for clothing of a wide range of quality and cost. The availability of mass-produced items, in department stores and by mail order, helped to democratize the consumption of fashion. Affordable replicas or approximations of stylish, often Parisian, clothing narrowed the gap between the highest tiers of society and a new middle class.

In newspaper columns, journalists tracked fashion trends in Paris, suggesting how these might be adapted by American women, including by those of "slender purse." By 1905, a fashion reporter for the *New York Times* produced such high-octane recommendations that, to a modern reader, her advice blurs into a confounding stream of color, collar, skirt width, and millinery urgings.

Blouses, known as shirtwaists or "waists," were worn with "tailor-mades." These masculine-influenced day or walking suits composed of long skirt and jackets were fitted and produced, as their name suggests, by tailors for women. In 1900, *Harper's Bazar* recommended day suits with short dark jackets and a lighter-colored skirt. Four years later, *Harper's* suggested women economize by applying surface decorations to ready-made gowns.

Women's magazines included sewing patterns in their articles, with the presumption that readers were competent seamstresses or had easy access to local dressmakers. In 1911, after a strike for higher wages staged by 10,000 American dressmakers and tailors was settled by arbitration, women were able to obtain their designer gowns from patterns by Worth and Paquin without being rejected by their local tailors or seamstresses.

Parisian-American influence was reciprocal. By 1905, the firm of couturier Jeanne Paquin was designing "hundreds of dresses," to be sifted through by American department store buyers. As is still done today, the buyers chose the styles of interest to them, then requested changes in their design to accommodate the taste of American women.

Footwear

Women's shoe and boot styles were long and heeled, with slightly rounded toes and two-inch (5 cm) heels. These shoes were mostly made of leather in brown, black, or other colors. As skirts were long to the ground, only the toes peeked out from underneath. The foot was fully supported with straps up to just below the anklebone and button fastenings.

Hairstyles and Headwear

Hair was worn tightly waved and close to the head, tied at the back of the nape of the neck. With this style, women wore smaller hats, but as hair piled up on top of the head and protruded out the sides, the hat styles followed with the "picture hat," which was large and richly decorated with exotic looking feathers, ribbons, flowers, and bows. Hats were worn outdoors only, and face veils became popular and were pulled down over the face.

Accessories

Women continued to wear and carry many of the accessories of the past century. Gloves and handbags were essential for outdoor activity in both winter and summer, and some sort of sunshade (in the form of a parasol, for example) was also required, as was a muff in the colder climate. Women sported feather boas for eveningwear and carried fans with orientalist themes to match their similarly themed gowns. Women wore cotton stockings for daywear and, for evening, wore silk colored stockings to match the gown.

Fashion for Older Ladies

Bluntly worded newspaper advertisements and articles recommended suitable outfits for the "old" and "elderly," making practical suggestions about flattering colors (purple was good) and forgiving, shapeless waists. Shapeless, however, was not to be confused with the loose garments of the Arts and Crafts variety. "Old" women were exhorted not to dress like their daughters and granddaughters, but the very presence of such warnings hinted at an undercurrent of change.

Paul Poiret

Paul Poiret, a renowned designer of the time, described the influx of American buyers to the firm of Jacques Doucet (where the avant-garde designer worked early in his career). At the time, Poiret stayed within the bounds of conventional dress, catering to the buyers who would arrive in Paris frequently and pore over the designs. In 1900, Poiret was granted an early discharge from the army because he was a former pupil of the Institute of Living Oriental Languages. Early on, the designer who would gain fame for his orientalist fashions had shown an affinity for the East. Poiret took a position at the House of Worth, where his mandate was to design everyday fashions.

Poiret eventually set out on his own, opening a salon in 1904. His designs broke with the silhouette and ornament of contemporary dresses, and instead he offered straight sheaths, open at the neck. By 1905, he had dispensed with corsets entirely. His fame was intently calculated; he dressed renowned actresses, as well as famous dancer Isadora Duncan. His parties were lavish, original, and theatrical, effectively promoting his orientalist designs. Poiret drew upon the talents of artists, including Georges Lepape, to illustrate promotional brochures for the firm and employed additional artists, including Raoul Dufy, to create textile designs.

When Sergei Diaghilev's Ballets Russes appeared in Paris, Poiret found inspiration in the dance costumes of Leon Bakst, using the language of the Orient—some amalgam of Japan, Arabia, and Russia—to create vividly colored dresses and harem pants to be worn with feather-cocked turbans. Poiret's wife served as an effective, even exotic, model for her husband's designs. Later the couturier launched a perfume, setting a precedent for future designer branding of fragrances. As would be seen in later decades, items such as designer perfumes, makeup, or underwear physically touch the consumer's body, offering her entree into an otherwise impenetrable and dazzlingly fashionable world. That perfumes and other relatively cheap offshoots of couture are mass manufactured does not diminish their power to infuse ordinary lives with glamour, and this glamour remains firmly embedded in every material homage to it.

In 1911, Poiret put forth the hobble skirt, a tease of silhouette, promising its wearer freedom at the waist, then tripping her up with a fettered hem. Years later, a musical composition called "The Lame Duck" had the alternate title of the "Hobble Skirt Step." After splitting the hobble skirt to allow its wearers to dance and, more pertinently, walk, Poiret created the *lampshade*. A strange combination of kimono and hoop skirt, the style featured a stiffly wired tunic that stood away from the body. For the couturier's most famous and extravagant party, "The Thousand and Second Night," his hundreds of guests were asked to wear harem pants and other orientalist fashions of his design. The host appeared dressed as a sultan, his head wrapped in a turban.

Poiret was not alone in capitalizing on the craze for the Ballets Russes. Jeanne Paquin created gowns in equally vivid colors, and, like Poiret, used distinguished artists to illustrate her products. The firm Callot Soeurs applied glittering *Japonesque* surface decorations to their conventionally shaped gowns. Jean-Philippe Worth sniped that Bakst's costume designs were "rather difficult to dance in" and provided his own orientalist theater costumes in 1912. In addition, the designer Lucile's friendship with Bakst may have accounted for her use of intense and original color schemes with her tea gowns. In 1909, New York dressmakers Farquharson and Wheelock fashioned a raspberry-colored silk gown from an Indian sari fabric possibly supplied by a well-traveled client. Designer Mario Fortuny devised a way to lock pleating into textiles and in 1907 created the Delphos gown, a columnar sheath based on the draped garments of Greek statues and cut in a flat, *Japoniste* style.

The "King of Fashion," as Poiret called himself, was the first couturier to travel to the United States to promote his work. Once there, he encountered clothing that he had not designed, but that bore faked versions of his label. Under the law of the time, he had no recourse to prevent such piracy. Charles Worth, too, saw his own distinctive labels counterfeited, a practice familiar to modern consumers of fake designer bags.

Poiret expanded his business to encompass interior decoration. This urge to design not just clothing but also furnishings paralleled the pan-European interest in a totality of design, an approach known as *Gesamtkunstwerk* (German for "total artwork") was seen in the productions of the Wiener Werkstaette in Vienna. In fact, Poiret's designs influenced fashions in that city, where women began to wear Haremhosen, or harem pants. In 1913 the Viennese firm of Fa. Koellner & Weigener staged a show of orientalist fashions, despite widespread Austrian antipathy toward France and its emblematic French couture.

Rites-of-Passage Dress

Theatricality itself was a kind of primitivism, a provocation valued for the release it offered to conventional audiences. It could be argued that the conventions of ceremonial dress, worn for weddings, graduations, communions, and even mourning, thrust the wearer into a temporary state of stage performance. However, rather than gaining the latitude of inventiveness permitted to actors on the stage, "lay" individuals found rites-of-passage dress at least as proscriptive as everyday wear.

Women's magazines detailed appropriate gowns for graduations and, of course, weddings. Famed couturiere Coco Chanel recalled in a memoir of her childhood that her choice of outfit for her first communion set her apart from the other girls, who wore simple bonnets on their heads. Subjecting herself to ridicule, she wore a distinctly fashionable dress, with a purse, and a *couronne* (a crown-like circle) of roses in her hair. In Eastern countries where Western clothing was the norm, the use of traditional indigenous costume persisted for ceremonial occasions.

Mourning Clothes

In 1904, the average life span in the United States was less than fifty years, with children and relatively young adults often finding the need for mourning dress. For men, women, and children, mourning was subject to the concerns of fashion, having to be not just respectful but flattering to its wearer. Mourning dress was worn not only by immediate members of a grieving family but also by aunts, cousins, and other relatives. In a 1900 edition of the *Chicago Tribune*, a fashion writer gushed about the unlikely topic of fashionable mourning outfits. These traditionally somber garments were made of black satin with different sorts of trimmings made of velvet. Black velvet decorations on the hats (cherries, grapes, flowers, and leaves) were beautiful.

Mourning clothes for women encompassed not just gowns but every accessory, including gloves, moving through a somber scale of color changes, from black to gray and sometimes to lavender, and worn for months or even years. In 1909, *Harper's Bazar* spoke of the "luxury of grief," a poetical-sounding term that referred, in fact, to the luxurious dressmaking fabrics available to those few mourners wealthy enough to indulge: "Ottoman and other ribbed silks, all in jet dye, and usually veiled with crepe-bound filet or tulle.... Included in that list, too, are the jet-dyed grenadines, which take crepe folds beautifully." In the same vein: "Marie Antoinette bonnets bordered with dull jet beads. They are worn with a long veil (which is almost a burnous cloak in dimensions) of heavy crepe."

For men wondering how to dress appropriately for mourning, the *New York Times* offered advice. They were to wear a black suit, with a white shirt and pearl buttons, and a bow tie. Black ties were worn only with dinner jackets, and a black ascot with a pearl stickpin was appropriate. Particular hat and glove styles were also recommended, including gloves made of dark gray suede and black seams.

Men's Clothing

Men wore a suit in a fitted style buttoned fairly high at the waist showing the bottom of the vest and tops of high-waisted long trousers with pressed creases and turned-up cuffs. Over time the suit became more fitted and the lapels longer. For formal occasions, a gentleman wore a dinner jacket (also known as a smoking jacket or tuxedo) without tails for evening and with tails for formal daytime occasions.

Men's clothing was grist for near-constant review. Differences between handtailored and ready-made frock coats were analyzed, as were the benefits and drawbacks of detachable shirt collars. It was suggested that shirts with attached collars could be worn just once and then discarded, though it is unclear what the destination for these items might be.

Outerwear Garments

Men could choose from a variety of coats, depending on the style of suit worn underneath. The chesterfield was elegant, while the Ulster was more casual and a raglan-sleeved coat the most comfortable. These were for the most part long to the knees. Shorter coats were introduced as the sportswear fashions became necessary and the ease of movement was welcome.

Hats and Accessories

Men wore the stiff round bowler hat, a top hat, or a boater with a shallow, flat, wide crown and medium brim. The occasion dictated which hat was appropriate, but it was unusual for a man to be seen without headwear at this time.

A man wore a handkerchief in the breast pocket of his jacket. On his hands, he wore gloves, and he continued to carry a cane or sometimes a riding crop.

To decorate the neckties that were now commonly worn, a jeweled tie pin was worn. Ascots were worn with stickpins. Other types of decoration included shirt buttons and cufflinks to close the shirt cuffs below the jacket. These were often made of gold and could contain an engraving of the man's initials.

Domestic Servants

Affluent women were advised to loosen up on the uniform requirements of their domestic employees so as not to risk losing them over such a trivial matter as an imposed white bonnet. Maids who resented the stigmatizing bonnets as symbols of menial labor were likely to flee to the plentiful jobs in shops or factories. Despite this edging toward democracy, a contrary set of boundaries remained stubbornly in place, not just of wealth and social class but also of age, gender, and size. Newspapers advised different styles for "short, stout" man as well as for the "angular chap."

Children's Clothing

The constriction imposed by women's corsets extended, until the beginning of the twentieth century, to the swaddling of infants. The custom persisted until, in a climate of growing social independence and freedom of movement for women, a similar lack of inhibition was allowed to babies.

Infants and very young children of both sexes were dressed in nearly identical ways, with boys in dresses and kilts. The use of blue and pink to distinguish between genders didn't come into play until the 1920s. It was less important to differentiate boys and girls at an early age. It became very important, however, to distinguish between children and adults. For very young boys, skirts and blouses offered the benefits of freedom and warmth "for the most vital parts of the body." By 1910, this genderless latitude had narrowed, as short pants or trouser suits replaced loose clothes for little boys.

As they grew older, girls "stayed young," never abandoning the skirts of their infanthood, while growing boys progressed to knickers and then long pants. The exact age for promoting a boy into his gender varied, often depending on a mother's choice. The extravagance of children's dress was a subject of debate; early in the century, an American elementary school teacher published "A Plea for the Inconspicuous Child," faulting mothers for expressing their own vanity by way of their children's clothing.

Mothers purchased their children's clothing ready made or sewed them at home; women's magazines published sewing patterns. Military themes—sailor suits, even, for special occasions, an admiral's costume—were safe and traditional looks for boys, particularly in the transitional years between toddlerhood and adolescence. Girls wore their own sailor-inspired frocks. Older girls might wear designs very much like those of their mothers with ribbons, lace, and patriotic medallions on their dresses' hems.

Older boys followed the proper, if monotonous, example of their fathers, abandoning distinctive outfits—knickerbockers, golf suits, Russian blouses—for the "dignity" of "sameness," a sober world of darkly colored suits.

In the rarified setting of couture, Jeanne Lanvin got her start designing "mother/daughter" dresses. Coco Chanel reversed the direction of grown-woman-to-girl influence. Her modest shifts for women were, essentially, young girls' styles. From 1908, when she started selling small hats and simple jersey dresses, the designer crossed accepted notions of mature women's clothes.

1914–1918

In August 1914, American shoppers in Paris found themselves stranded in paradise by the unexpected outbreak of war. Having planned on leisurely return trips to the States, instead some made panicked arrangements to sail home by way of London. Others clamored to board the limited number of civilian ships still leaving from France. Sailing away from Paris, too, was its solo status as fashion arbiter of the world. Parisian sketches and mockups of fall designs, transported like stowaways in the luggage of a few American buyers, briefly sustained a dominant French influence on American clothing design. Among the last arrivals from France were high-waisted Directoire or Empire "picture gowns," modern interpretations of styles worn in the nineteenth century by Napoleon Bonaparte's wife, Empress Josephine. With a nod to the sweeping militarism of the Napoleonic era, new fashions heralded the start of a new kind of war.

At first, it was widely assumed by both soldiers and civilians that Germany's attacks on Russia and France would end within a few months. Each side—the Allied Forces and the Central Powers—predicted its own quick victory. Life, including the pleasures of self-adornment, would emerge unscathed. However, the initial attacks and counterattacks—violent but almost ceremonial in their brevity—turned into years of stalemate and loss. Trench warfare, poison gas, and the use of air power all made their grim debuts. No one could predict the conflict's ultimate duration, the demands it would make on industry, or its repercussions for global trade.

The lack of preparedness for what would become the most technologically advanced war so far in history—the first to use air power and chemical weapons—showed itself most absurdly in the initial outfits of French soldiers. Men entered the fray dressed in the equivalent of charming targets—blue jackets and red pants. In an attempt at remedy, entire uniforms of a conspicuous blue were substituted, before the logic of camouflage took hold.[4] An artist in the British Admiralty worked out a disruptive pattern called "dazzle painting." This form of camouflage—a carefully engineered chaos of colors—was used on ships to confound enemy targeting years before it was applied to textiles.

At the request of the British government, Burberry transformed one of its casual coats into a walking arsenal, the newly dubbed "trench coat," with metal rings from which to dangle map cases and special flaps to conceal grenades.[5]

At the front, the living and dead shared the same cramped underground quarters; infectious disease carried the purgatory of trench life out into the world. Spread in part by troops on leave or returning home, influenza ravaged American cities as well as remote areas otherwise untouched by warfare. Between 1918 and 1919, more people perished in the "Spanish flu" pandemic than had died in the whole of the war.[6]

In this context of grief and fear, the idea of fashion for the sake of fashion lost much of its allure. At the same time, changing roles of women, along with severe shortages of basic materials, effected profound changes in the silhouette and purpose of clothing. In the course of World War I, dress forged modernity from privation.

Restrictions in dyes—most American dyes had been imported from Germany—subdued the available palette. As the stockpiles of chemicals dwindled, American textile designers minimized the use of colorants. Stripes, widely spaced prints, black, pale colors, and white (the color of undyed leather or fabric) replaced more color-saturated fabrics. Oxford cloth, which combined pure white with colored thread, gained popularity. Textiles were printed on one side only, rather than woven of predyed thread. Leather gloves tended to come only in white. The stuff of uniforms—excess khaki cloth and navy yarn—gave an unavoidably militaristic look to women's day suits and sweaters.

By October 1914, many of the leading couturiers of Paris had closed their fashion houses and gone to war. These new recruits included Poiret, Doucet, and both Worth brothers. As a military tailor, Poiret—the great fantasist of pre-war costume—devised a streamlined and sober overcoat. Poiret's two daughters, lacking their father's talent for invention, maintained a diminished workshop until the business reopened in 1918. Callot Sisters and other couture houses already owned and run by women had the advantage of gender when men were called away for service.

The very few books on clothing published during the war favored thrift over fashion. Magazines, on the other hand, continued to flourish. Often these included patterns for dresses and nurses' uniforms. In 1916, when it grew difficult to ship issues of American *Vogue* to England, Condé Nast established a British edition.

In the United States and Britain, war drew together upper and lower economic classes in a common goal, without quite erasing all social distinctions. In the face of enemy fire, social stratifications fell away as rich and poor suffered the same fate. A small contingent of French and American women had the means to obtain couture designs even after the outbreak of war. Some couturiers, most famously Chanel, opened shops outside of Paris that were satellites of their Parisian salons to accommodate these women of means. Paris-based go-betweens, called *commisionnaires*, managed to purchase fashions for some American customers, while a very few society figures had their Red Cross uniforms made by Lanvin and other couture salons.

Whatever the glamorous source of their uniforms, socially prominent women contributed to the war effort, sometimes with absurd results. Mrs. William K. Vanderbilt, wife of one of the wealthiest men in America, took charge of the American Ambulance Hospital in Neuilly, France, taking care of wounded soldiers. A reporter noted both her democratic compassion and ties to her social class: Mrs. Vanderbilt dressed in the white Red Cross uniform and comfortable, distinctly unglamorous white shoes. Her pearls and silk stockings perked up the drab uniform. The famous American-born writer Gertrude Stein, author of *The Autobiography of Alice B. Toklas*, abandoned her home in Paris for the safety of the French countryside. Accustomed to presiding over a dazzling salon of artists and writers, she lurched into the fray as a game but inexpert ambulance driver.

With uncertainty about their future, men in uniform were the subjects of widespread admiration, gratitude, and female attention. The word *khaki* owes its origin to the Hindi term for "dust"; for soldiers, the trip from uniform to dust was not complicated. Fearing a loosening of morals, women were warned against the irresistible appeal of uniforms. Khaki and girls, they were told, were a dangerous mixture.

Of course, women, too, wore uniforms, some more naturally romantic than others. Nurses tending soldiers on the front endured the same mortal threats as men yet retained feminine outlines in their dress. For women in dangerous occupations, protective gear transcended and even disguised their gender. Similarly, war blurred, but did not eradicate, divisions between social classes. Even women doing high-level government work were discouraged initially from wearing standard uniforms. Since they were not engaged in active combat, it was felt that their display of khaki would trivialize the fabric for "real soldiers."

It was not just khaki that could lose its profound meaning; men's work itself could be demystified and cheapened if done by wives and daughters. At the outset of the war, many women were rebuffed in their desire to take over jobs vacated by men going off to war. The same labor unions that that eased their wartime restrictions against women would later play a role in restoring the status quo, urging female workers to hand back their hard-won jobs to returning soldiers.

For women, everyday dress bore the imprint of war, displaying military-inspired details—insignias, gold braid, brass buttons. In the United States and Britain, sharply cut, tailored suits in blue serge or other utilitarian fabrics and colors reflected the increasing shift of women into the masculine working world. Emphasis on practicality over decoration made for a kind of civilian uniform. But American women drew the line at National Standard Dress. This social movement proposed a depressingly homogenized "utility" garment, equally appropriate for day, evening, and sleep wear; women could dine out in their nightgowns, or go to bed in the equivalent of a business suit. Women were not all satisfied, patriotic as they were, to dress in standard prescribed clothing.

If not standardized, clothing for women grew more practical and allowed for a new ease of movement; skirts rose from ankle length to midcalf. Bus conductors and business commuters could not, it was clear, hobble their way to work. Even pants worn with a blouse and jacket could be appropriate daytime wear.

The wristwatch, first introduced to troops as a practical alternative to the pocket watch, appealed as well to men not in uniform. This shift to wristwatches had implications for the design of men's suits. Without a pocket watch, the vest had little purpose in life. Just as women were abandoning constricting undergarments, the relaxed two-piece "sack suit" gained popularity for men. The "sack" style, influenced by leisure clothing, challenged the precision and anonymity of military dress. For men, daywear grew increasingly acceptable for all but the most formal evening occasions.

For women on lower rungs of the social ladder, war work in offices and factories held the promise of attractive wages and free uniforms. Women worked in shifts as telephone operators and translators, in close proximity to men on the frontlines, picking up and moving from one location to the next as troops advanced. More than 100,000 British and American women served in the Red Cross or auxiliary units of the army, navy, or air force. Women took on a wide range of jobs, from chauffeurs and cooks to intelligence officers. Convicted by the French government as a double agent in the war, the infamous "Mata Hari"—Gertrud Zelle, a symbol of French degeneracy, the woman behind the veils—was more a projection of orientalist fantasy women in intelligence, an exotic dancer who veiled her intentions and identity as well as her body.

The diversion of ordinary chemicals to the war effort diminished the availability of textile dyes, since explosives and dyes depended on the same raw materials. British department stores guaranteed that garment fabrics would be just as advertised—red would be red and blue would be blue—subject to the requisition of dyes for explosives. Conflicting alliances mapped new and distinct patterns of trade, closing off the usual avenues for the exchange of materials and finished goods. In the United States, shipments of dyes and textiles from Germany were embargoed. Some countries, including the United States, saw the closing off of imports and outside influences as a boon to domestic production and proud nationalism. Ads urged American women to "buy American." American industry, in particular, benefited from the double luxuries of time and distance. The United States delayed its entry into the war until 1917, and no fighting took place on American soil.

Nationalism—sometimes to the point of racial eugenics—was promoted in Germany, Austria, China, Japan, India, and Ireland. At war with France, German shoppers could no longer look to Paris as a fashion muse. Instead, the government promoted German-made clothing as a matter of nationalistic pride as well as economic necessity. French social weaknesses, it was felt, could be discerned in the details of Parisian dress. Merchants sought to define a strong, independent, and wholesome German woman in relation to her cosseted, even perverse, French counterpart. Moral lapses were asserted in relation to dress: French women dressed not for their own needs but only to please men; their clothing revealed too much flesh and was too complicated even to be put on without assistance; tight clothing worn by pregnant Frenchwomen increased the likelihood of their giving birth to damaged infants, so that the wearer's vanity overtook her maternal concerns. According to this German propaganda, unstructured clothing for women accounted for the robust nature of German babies, and babies were needed to repopulate the country. Whether she dressed for maternity or work, the ideal German woman expressed her nationalism through practicality and comfort. Paradoxically, this unconstricted style led directly to the decadent chemises of flappers in the 1920s.

Britain's call for military recruits throughout its empire met with a mixture of enthusiasm and resistance. The dominions of Canada, Australia, New Zealand, and South Africa readily sent reinforcements. Following the Easter Uprising of 1916, Irish Loyalists, subject to the political rule of the British Empire, felt little desire to join in the cause of their own oppressor. Irish clothes were a "subversive mix of Irish material and British designs." Interest in traditional Irish dress, previously on the wane, gained new currency as an emblem of nationalism.

> The "Irish costume" never became a strict uniform; each group, and individuals within each group, wished their expression to reflect or conceal their particular social, economic, and political history. It would seem that the various expressions of condescension, aspiration and contempt that are part of these costumes are so complicated and so open to interpretation and misinterpretation that they are, in fact, quite representative of Anglo-Irish relations.[7]

JAPAN

Although it sent troops in support of the Allies, Japan remained isolated from the struggles abroad, and as a major exporter of silk, the country's wartime economy soared. Japan supplied more than 90 percent of silk imported by the United States, and flush with prosperity, its consumers showed a passion for Western-style manners and dress. Wool, a material long foreign to the Japanese market, had been used before the war to make traditional Japanese garments, a standard application of a new material. Then, no longer just the stuff of warm kimonos, wool was applied to the manufacture of desirable Western-style suits. Still, status was no match for comfort, and once back in the intimacy of their homes, even proud owners of Western-style garments shed them in favor of traditional clothes. As always, this shift included the first step of exchanging one's shoes for slippers. Every front door opened onto a special entrance hall equipped with a cupboard or rack devoted to storing shoes. Working women wore Japanese underwear under Western dress, while the highly fashionable yet traditional obi, which in 1915 sold for as much as five thousand yen. Geisha women, not regular Japanese women, bought these beautiful garments. Such lavish display gave geisha the kind of cachet now attached to Hollywood stars in designer gowns.

CHINA

That modernity took the shape of the Western invention was, in the Far East, a source of political ambivalence. In China, books promoted the idea of the "perfect" young woman—healthy, educated, and, in isolation from the rest of the world, ready to perpetuate and improve the Chinese race. These women were seen as the nexus of modernity and its attendant anxieties. Encouraged to wear traditional dress, young women were drawn, too, to more worldly Western styles. The term *jianquan* was intrinsically related to the eugenic mission of strengthening the Chinese race and appeared frequently in texts on hygiene and education. The word could also be translated as "perfect" or something much less politically charged, such as "robust," "sound," or "in good health." Citizens resisted the influence of outside cultures even as the Eastern country admired the material trappings of the West.

In China, the seasons dictated what people wore. In winter, thick fur and cotton-padded garments were needed, while in summer, light gauze, silk, and even grass cloth was used. Clothing in China was not dictated by fashion and the dressmakers in the capital (Peking) but was more practical.

Westernization of men's dress throughout the world imposes monotony and a certain sameness in terms of fashion. In the Peking parliament, the official form of dress was the frock coat for day and swan coat for evening. Diplomats abroad were told to adopt local dress for busines during the day but go back to traditional Chinese clothing when at home. Men more than woman were anxious to emulate Western dress.

While some saw the westernization of Chinese dress as progress, others did not. At a time when foreign fashion was being flogged at newly established tailors, dressmakers, and shoe shops, the traditional typical Chinese tunic was being discarded. Parliament kept a close hold on and dictated as much as it could, what Chinese people wore.

After protests from national silk industry fearful of losing business, parliament authorized two clothing styles, a mix of Western and Chinese shape and decoration. These costumes were to be manufactured in Chinese fabrics.

INDIA

India sent supplies and nearly a million troops in a spectacular demonstration of allegiance to its own oppressors hoping to be rewarded for its sacrifices with release from British rule. Sikhs, just 2 percent of the Indian population, made up 20 percent of the British Indian Armed Forces. Distinguishable by their religiously imposed turbans, or *dastaar*, Sikh troops fought in trenches alongside English soldiers. At war's end, despite the sacrifices of its volunteers, India's reward was only partial independence. A total break from British domination would not be achieved until 1947. *Khadi*, a domestically produced fabric, came to symbolize the goal of Indian independence, cutting the country's reliance on goods imported from Britain. The *Khadi* movement, begun in 1908, persisted through the war.

THE UNITED STATES

With no subtext of resistance, the United States, unlike India, had only itself to represent when it joined the Allies. Despite the burden it would place on domestic manufacturers already taxed beyond their limits, American forces rejected offers by European allies of available but generic uniforms. The troops preferred to stand out as Americans, retaining a distinctly national identity even as it was submerged in a common cause. In fact, the production of military uniforms was, in the First World War—as throughout the history of warfare—the ultimate expression of dress-related nationalism.

With more than 120,000 servicemen off to France by December 1917, the American clothing industry scrambled to keep up with an unstoppable need for raw materials and finished fabrics. Cotton and linen, diverted from domestic consumption, were incorporated into the very structure of airplanes and ammunition; linen lined the wings of airplanes. In 1917 and 1918, the military requisitioned the entire American production of wool. The rush to sew and distribute uniforms confounded systems accustomed to a slower pace. Ground, air, and naval troops, nurses, women's auxiliary forces, even canteen and other quasi-military workers all required outfits that could identify members of a group while distinguishing rank.

In 1917, the U.S. Navy accepted women into the official ranks of the Naval Reserve. Army and Navy women's auxiliaries contributed directly to the war effort. War succeeded where years of social and political protest for suffrage and dress reform had failed. In both Britain and the United States, patriotic efforts subsumed both the suffragette and reform dress campaigns.

By 1918, more than 500,000 Americans were serving in the U.S. Navy. Each sailor was issued four pairs of trousers and three middies of white cotton, two pairs of trousers and two middies of blue flannel or serge, one overcoat, three white cotton hats, and one blue flannel cap (the last paid for out of the sailor's own wages). All garments needed to be replaced as they wore out. Complicating the logistics of production and distribution, at first Navy uniforms could be manufactured only in Brooklyn, New York, and Charleston, South Carolina. The initial efforts at enlarging existing factories were an uncertain venture. Before the war, machine sewing at home had complemented factory production. While condemned as an inferior system, home-based work at the outset of the war had, at least, the advantage of a stable infrastructure. A report from the Committee on Women in Industry of the Advisory Commission of the Council of National Defense analyzed the home work system, where women took home the pieces and sewed them in their homes, delivering the finished product back to the manufacturer. The committee concluded that in Brooklyn, home and piece workers produced excellent uniforms. Large garment manufacturers in the area did not have proper sewing machines to produce key details on the uniforms such as eyelets and decorated collars. Uniforms needed double rows of stitching for durability, and buttons and buttonholes required special methods to meet strict uniform standards.

In sewing factories, gender determined how the work would be divided. Men did the most important tasks, the cutting and bundling of cloth and inspecting of finished garments. Despite the hectic need for goods, women workers confronted extrarigorous entry requirements into the network of factory production. Charleston produced only cotton garments, the dungarees used by mechanics, and its factories were overwhelmed.

In 1918, 21,000 women in just one area of Indiana engaged in home sewing of Army shirts. According to a critical government report, "home," as opposed to factory, work was a wasteful method, with only a small number of Army shirts produced by each seamstress. The decentralization of houses complicated the transport of fabric and finished shirts. Home work, however, was an established means of family support, with assignments doled out to as many women as possible in order to distribute income. Though accomplished at home, machine sewing setups differed little from sweat-shop conditions. Piece workers labored ten-hour days, six days a week, and were paid just under 15 cents an hour—a rate far lower than the standard for factory work. Contractors worried that contagious diseases could be transmitted—by way of clothing—from unsanitary homes directly to soldiers. Because they lived in the greatest poverty, African-American producers of home-sewn shirts came under suspicion as possible sources for disease, with a consequent falling off of work.

CHILDREN'S CLOTHING

Military influences on fashion, widely seen in women's civilian dress, showed up in outfits for children, as well. Sailor clothes remained a staple of children's wardrobes. For the few families who could afford them, military tailors in France ran up uniform-inspired play suits for boys, while dresses for French girls mimicked the uniforms of English marines. Mothers in France could dress up their children as "télégraphistes," complete with "telecommunications" insignia on the collar; a child could pretend his finger tapping on a school desk was sending out secret messages.

Children celebrated religious rites of passage, such as confirmations, not in church but in school, with their economical school uniforms doing double duty as fancier dress. Incredibly, Girl Guides—the British equivalent of American Girl Scouts—served as official messengers for classified documents. Girls in uniform waited outside ministry offices for the chance to run errands in the cause of war.

Books for school-age boys—even those written by men fresh from the horrors of war—narrated a sanitized, even jaunty, view of the conflict. Fiction offered a cool distance from trouble; from these books, boys gleaned only the nobility of service. As portrayed in stories, uniforms marked adulthood and the purely theoretical pleasures of sacrifice.

In 1918, the American magazine *Ladies' Home Journal* supplied the makings of a rainy-day pastime for children. A cherub-faced paper doll could be cut out and dressed up in an array of playful costumes. No distinction was made between improbably silly and staunchly patriotic examples of dress. A clown suit and an eighteenth-century fancy-dress outfit, complete with powdered wig, shared the page with a choice of three different war uniforms. The paper doll could be dressed up as a farmer holding a lamb, or an officer set for likely death in the trenches.

Far from dreams of pure adventure, children's clothing in wartime bore the imprint of deprivation. In Italy, as elsewhere, even middle-class children wore conspicuously outgrown clothes. Rather than buying new outfits for their families, women patched together fabric from worn-out garments to make wearable "new" clothes. To make these additions as inconspicuous as possible, they were presented as "decorations," a band of contrasting fabric sewn around a hem or inserted into the bodice of a dress.

Infants, one expert advised, were not to be handled by visitors for the first few months after birth and were to be toilet trained at two months of age. For these reasons, no clothing for "show" would be needed. Once house broken, the baby could be dressed up to receive guests. Newborns were wrapped tightly around their torsos to ensure proper growth. Care was to taken to put comfortable outfits—buttoned in front and not pulled over the head—on top of this binding.

LIFE DURING THE WAR

Like jazz, the tango threatened to introduce wildly exotic life into the subdued orderliness of wartime fashions and behavior. The Catholic Church categorized the tango as a sin worthy of confession. The pope, who had, unsurprisingly, never seen the dance, nevertheless condemned it. All the furor had to do not just with "indecent" tango dresses and vulgar dress-seam to pant-seam contact but also with a perceived connection between the dance and savagery. One historical theory traces the origin of tango to Africa. Argentina, however, the country most associated with the dance and where it probably originated, was directly responsible for this invasion of indecency. By all accounts, tango first gained popularity in Argentinean brothels. Air travel and the dispatch of troops to distant places spread cultural ideas and misconceptions. Not having gotten their land legs yet, sailors fresh from foreign ports might have waddled into dance clubs, presumably to throw themselves at scantily dressed Parisians. More decorously, working women in demure dresses flocked to afternoon tea dances. They served their country by mingling in a civilized fashion with enlisted men. They provided welcome entertainment and distraction from the war and dressed to please the men they met.

In 1914, everyday coats could be trimmed with monkey fur or other "peltry," while metallic fringes rippled from the hems of tango dresses. The craze for the tango was only one of the frivolities amok in prewar Paris, London, and the United States. Stores promoted flattering "starvation gowns," cut to give the illusion of successful dieting. Even tailored suits could be constructed to accommodate dancing. Advertisements extolled the "dismountable" (collapsing) hat for men, perfect for motoring, rail travel, and trips to the theater. (Professional baseball players—young, healthy, and mysteriously unenlisted—played on, acknowledging the war with flags on the sleeves of their lively uniforms.) An American society figure—"the Apostle of Diamond Heels"—promoted "pantalets." When bird plumage was banned as decoration for hats, live bugs took the place of jewels. Iridescent beetle casings had been used in India since the nineteenth century as decoration for export gowns, but casings were just that, the equivalent of empty houses.

A vogue emerged for arrestingly colored hair, and wigs took hold first in Paris and London and then in the United States. Decades before the advent of Punk, women turned their hair blue, green, pink, "tango red," or "rainbow" with powders or wigs. Fashionable women with neon hair strolled the avenues and danced at fancy-dress balls. American shoppers heard predictions of "eccentricity and ugliness" and also of a fantastic array of disparate styles. "Ugliness" had a comic swing to it. There was something for everyone. Some men and women tangoed in identical outfits, oblivious to gender. One couple copied the fractured colors of stained glass and came as saints, complete with halos. Bizarre colors for clothes and hair mirrored developments in modern art, particularly Futurism. The Futurist movement, originating in Italy and Russia, embraced all facets of art, including poetry, music, and clothing design. The fracturing of bright solid colors in art and design might represent the power of shrapnel to shatter a body into pieces.

In 1917, the British War Office published a pamphlet detailing "protective clothing for women and girl workers." No single type of garment could meet the needs of women engaged in a startling new range of tasks and situations. These occupations included brick, gas, and glass works, metal processes (including acetylene welding and crane driving), farming, food production, sand-blasting, and exposure to hazardous chemicals. The War Office identified the risks as dust, wet processes, heavy machinery, excessive heat, and extremes of weather. Overalls, knicker suits, leather bibs, knee-high weatherproof boots, heavy gloves, goggles, and materials that included "jean" protective clothing transcended style and held no pretense of seduction.

Working or traveling, women required practical, unconstricting clothing. Corsets belonged to another, distant age. In Britain and the United States, women in offices wore menswear-inspired business suits. Skirts grew wider and shorter, stopping at midcalf. Nurses in the field pared down their uniforms, removing unnecessary fabric trailing from the back hems of their skirts. What use was style if it got in the way of saving lives?

While nurses and female yeomen filled military roles, civilian women's organizations of all kinds worked on the home front. In fact, such groups composed three-fourths of the wartime organizations just in the state of Virginia. The state's Equal Suffrage League temporarily suspended agitation for women's voting rights and joined with dozens of other organizations, including the Virginia Association Opposed to Woman Suffrage, to support the war effort. In Richmond, suffragists transformed the Equal Suffrage League headquarters and worked tirelessly for the suffrage auxiliary of the Red Cross. The auxiliary had sewing machines and purchased a knitting machine and pledged to provide mittens for the 100 nurses assigned to U.S. Base Hospital No. 45. By November 1917, the women already had produced 1,244 garments, including bed shirts, bathrobes, pajamas, pillowcases, sheets, and towels and had knitted sweaters, mufflers, mittens, and socks. Elsewhere, men too old to serve, children, and women of all political views also turned to knitting. New Zealanders knitted thousands of socks, scarves, and sweaters for the British troops.

Inevitably, bereavement took on a communal and not just personal dimension, with widespread attention paid to mourning dress. Dye shortages allowed for a slightly more relaxed version of mourning dress, adding touches of white to otherwise black fabric. A small minority of women boycotted the custom of mourning dress, arguing that the constant acknowledgment of death denied the existence of an afterlife. Lack of fashionable dress was seen as "defeatism." Mourning dress continued to be conservative and, as earlier, lightened as the mourning period progressed.

CONCLUSION

During the war, luxuries of the past were cast aside and the serious world of conflict replaced the frivolous café society and snobbish setting of the Edwardian period. This lasted for the four years of the war. Finally the war ended, with U.S. president Woodrow Wilson offering to moderate a settlement as the two sides agreed to lay down their arms.

The Germans were given no effective voice in the treaty negotiations, and the Allied forces laid down the severe conditions under which Germany was to live for the next twenty years. The Versailles Treaty not only made Germany responsible for all the death and suffering of the war but also deprived it of Alsace and Lorraine (which went to France) and some of its overseas colonies as well. New frontiers were drawn, and seven new states got their independence: Poland, Latvia, Czechoslovakia, Finland, Estonia, Lithuania, and Yugoslavia. Hungary and Austria were divided into small independent states. Of course, despite the new boundaries put in place with the treaty, ethnic groups were unhappy with the new borders, some being left on the what they considered to be the "wrong side." Often these unhappy minorities were ignored by the governing ethnic majority.

This unrest continued until World War II, which will be discussed later. From 1918 until 1939, however, those who had profited from the war, and there were many who had, took their newfound wealth and sense of renewed life and made the 1920s a decade of fun, frivolity, and love of life. The black mood of the war was replaced with bright attitudes, a fierce loathing of ugliness, and fashion that was bright, light and joyful. The restrictive corsets of the past were never reclaimed, and the newly emancipated women dictated their own fashions.

NOTES

1. Phyllis M. Martin, "Contesting Clothes in Colonial Brazzaville," *Journal of African History* 34, no. 3 (1994): 401–26.
2. Seong-hee Joo, "An Overview of Modern Fashion in Korea," *Koreana* 15, no. 1 (Spring 2001): 4–9.
3. Quoted in Peter, Caroll, "Refashioning Suzhou: Dress, Commodification and Modernity," *Positions* 11, no. 2 (Fall 2003): 444.
4. Diana Condell, curator of medals and uniforms at the Imperial War Museum.
5. The company has continued to market disarmed versions into the twenty-first century.
6. The disease did not originate in Spain, but since the earliest descriptions of it emerged in that country, the misnomer stuck.
7. Hilary O'Kelly, "Reconstructing Irishness: Dress in the Celtic Revival, 1880," in *Chic Thrills: A Fashion Reader*, ed. Juliet Ash and Elizabeth Wilson (Berkeley: University of California Press, 1993).

FURTHER READING

Byrde, Penelope. *The Male Image: Men's Fashion in Britain, 1300–1970*. London: B. T. Batsford, 1979.
Quoted in Caroll Peter. "Refashioning Suzhou: Dress, Commodification and Modernity." *Positions* 11, no. 2 (Fall 2003): 444.
Field, Jacqueline. "Dyes, Chemistry and Clothing: The Influence of World War I on Fabrics, Fashions and Silk." *Dress* 28 (2001): 77–91.
Hoare, Philip. "I Love a Man in a Uniform: The Dandy Esprit de Corps." *Fashion Theory* 9, no. 3: 263–81.
Joo, Seong-hee. "An Overview of Modern Fashion in Korea." *Koreana* 15, no. 1 (Spring 2001): 4–9.
Martin, M. Phyllis. "Contesting Clothes in Colonial Brazzaville." *Journal of African History* 34, no. 3 (1994): 401–26.
McDaid, Jennifer Davis. "'Our Share in the War Is No Small One': Virginia Women and World War I." *Virginia Cavalcade* 50, no. 3 (2001): 114.
Mulvagh, Jane. *Vogue History of 20th Century Fashion*. London: Viking, 1988.

MOVIES

Dr. Zhivago (1965)
Lawrence of Arabia (1962)
Nicholas and Alexander (1971)

The Twenties

Ellen Hymowitz

TIMELINE

1920	Prohibition goes into effect; U.S. women get the right to vote
1922	Mussolini leads the Fascists in Italy; Russia builds the Socialist state based on Communism led by Lenin
1923	Hitler attempts a coup against Bavarian government
1924	Lenin dies in Russia, and Trotsky and Stalin battle it out for control; Surrealist movement born
1924	Rayon fabric becomes available to replace silk
1924–1929	Period described as the Roaring Twenties
1925	*The Great Gatsby*, by F. Scott Fitzgerald, published
1928	First complete "talkie" film
1929	Stock market crash

In the 1920s, opponents of women's suffrage poked fun at the "flapper vote." Yet their term, belittling as it was, neatly encapsulated the mix of fluff and sobriety that marked the postwar years. In the "Jazz Age," nations around the world faced the loss of huge swaths of their population. Damage to physical terrain, industry, ego, international trade—all these injuries needed to be erased, confronted, and overcome. The reconfiguration of national boundaries applied to morals as well as empires. In Britain, the behavior and fashions of women directly reflected the postwar shortage of men. According to one observer, the "social butterfly"—a scantily clad, jazzed-up "flapper type"—proliferated in the middle and upper classes and set her sights on nabbing one of the disproportionately small number of marriageable men who had survived the war. At least one observer blamed the "caprice" of these in-demand men for influencing what women should wear.

To accommodate men whose tastes veered between artlessness and blatant eroticism, women dressed themselves in everything from modest suits to exotic wraps with lush fur collars. Dress, however, was determined by more than the whims of the opposite sex. Independence—even rebelliousness—was, for women, a self-propelled by-product of the war. Much of this freedom was confined to the middle and upper classes. In the United States, a 1921 newspaper headline captured—for working-class women—the prim bossy voice of convention: "Dowdy Girl Loses Job; Gets It Back after a Shampoo."

THE FLAPPER

An international phenomenon, the "flapper"—a slender, short-haired, short-skirted young woman, her bosom subdued to an androgynous flat silhouette—conveyed in her dress and behavior what in the 1920s was radically new and openly allowed. The term *flapper*—meaning a flighty young girl of questionable morals—originated in a British word for a kind of perch that thrashed about when thrown into a hot pan, suggesting these girls, like fish in hot oil, moved by reflex and not intention.

In fact, whole countries and not just young girls were forced after the war to be enlivened—socially and economically—by defeat. The influence of American clothing designers remained strong, while Paris, with its revived couture industry—including the houses of Worth and Poiret—put a French spin on American fashion. American film stars shopped for luxurious clothing in Paris; New York girls made a splash abroad, their bold independence overshadowing the more conformist *jeunes filles* in France; from an American point of view, French women came into their own only after they were married. The New York girl replaced royalty and were at the center of the international stage.

In a changed political and social landscape, optimism suffused American industry and its international trade. For much of America, upbeat fashions reflected a desire to shut the door on a horrifying past. The color black, once a symbol of mourning, turned into a sign of chic. A skin-baring black dress could be cut very low in the back or held up simply by narrow shoulder straps. In 1926, expensive black gowns concocted of faille or chiffon and rhinestones were described—with an editorial wink—as perfect for the Lenten season.

As in the mod 1960s, to be young in the 1920s was to traffic in the

Rep. T. S. McMillan of Charleston, S.C., with flappers who are doing the Charleston on railing, with the U.S. Capitol in the background. Courtesy of the Library of Congress.

marvelous and shocking. Older women, advised against wearing short skirts, were offered the dubious honorific of "dignified." Hiked-up girlish clothes conveyed ambiguous meaning, with innocence as likely deceptive as real. Flappers were criticized for their short skirts that barely covered their knees, forcing them to walk in a peculiar mincing manner. Girls as young as eleven or twelve might be referred to as flappers, or flappers *manquées.*

With bobbed hair and angular bodies, true flappers threatened social order not just because they could resemble prepubescent girls but, more perversely, because they might be mistaken for young men. The signature bob of actor Louise Brooks had a fresh and winsome look. In France, some women took the look further, wearing their hair so short they appeared like "female men"—*les garçonnes.* In Vienna, the bob haircut was known as the *Bubikopf*—"boy's head." Greta Garbo and, later, Marlene Dietrich, cross-dressed on- and off-screen, mixing female beauty with men's clothes.

Greta Garbo, 1922, wearing a swimsuit. Courtesy of the Library of Congress.

Androgyny signaled frank homosexuality or female empowerment, or both at once. Not only had women assumed the male role in wartime industries and in the structure of families, but, in the "Roaring Twenties," they entered without blinking into the speeded-up world of cars and planes. Aviation pioneer Amelia Earhart, who famously posed for photographs in masculine leather helmet, goggles, and pilot overalls, was also photographed in a ruffled blouse and pearls.

In 1925, Paris couturier Lucien Lelong rejected a straight up-and-down silhouette to promote what he called "kinetic dress." He constructed clothes with the means to spring into motion—to flare and swing with the movement of their wearer. For Lelong, costume design took a rightful place among the other arts of the age, sharing the *Zeitgeist*—the prevailing spirit of the era. In the 1920s, this spirit was motion, the speed of cars and airplanes, the fracturing gestures

Amelia Earhart Putnam, 1932. Courtesy of the Library of Congress.

of Futurism, even—according to one fashion writer—the explosion of poetic form into free verse.

MEN'S CLOTHING

The "new" woman, uninhibitedly independent, emerged in the Far East, Austria, Germany, South America—essentially, around the globe—a sociopolitical souvenir of the World War. Men's dress, on the other hand, didn't keep up with the revolutions in women's fashions, with men's posture straightened by years of military stiffness and suits concerned more with rectitude than comfort.

In Germany, Dada artist Raul Hausmann associated constricting menswear—the disregard for ease in movement and lack of body consciousness—with "Germanness." While the *Neue Frau* shared a universal postwar identity with the New Woman, German men's suits and shirts betrayed a persistent nationalism. Berlin tailors, were said to make suits stiff as sheet metal, while American and British suits were soft and comfortable. In 1926, Haussman demonstrated—by putting on loose pants to dance in a Berlin art gallery—the stylish comfort of the "Oxford Bag." He praised the wide-legged, British-inspired pants as un-German and unregimented in their construction. They were modern because they freed the body to move.

Perhaps it was postwar humiliation, shell shock, and nihilism in Germany, and men expressed themselves through lack of expressiveness in clothing. In America and Britain, more optimistic men embraced sporty outfits, knickers, and loosely fitted suits. In some cases, the "Germanness" of modern fashions was condemned because the clothes were dispensed from the mostly Jewish-owned department stores and smaller shops.

Spared the political turmoil of postwar Germany, American men had the luxury to fret about changing styles in menswear and the etiquette of dress. Tight suits, descendents of wartime uniforms, loosened up.

In 1922, the *Chicago Tribune* began publishing—first three times a week, then every day—a column devoted to the minutiae of men's fashions. The comprehensiveness of the coverage and know-it-all pointers revealed a

TWYEFFORT, Inc.
580 5th AVENUE
NEW YORK

A man modeling a walking suit, 1925. Courtesy of the Library of Congress.

feminized way of considering clothes. Men, it seems, were as uneasy as women about what they should shop for and when and where to wear it. Readers learned that the jazz suit was a fad, appropriate only for the lower classes. They were fed descriptions of ties, sack suits, handkerchief cravats, felt hats, shoes, dinner jackets, wedding clothes, walking sticks, raglan sleeves, Navajo bathrobes, and snap-on ties. "Stout" men should dress to conceal their bulk and "thin men need curves." On men with the wrong-shaped feet, spats could look ridiculous—like bandages. Gray was a good color for pale complexions; one type of hat was best for men with full faces. "Every man can use three straw hats." Advice was offered on proper dress for golfing, motor-ing, and bathing (swimming). Running out of ideas, the column probed which suits and ties would be most flattering for a circus giant and the "world's smallest man."

One *Hartford Courant* writer in 1927 theorized—half-jokingly—that rule-driven dress drove men to join fraternal organizations. The black-tasseled red fez that identifying members of the Shriners was introduced by a stage actor who helped found the organization, transferring customs of theatrical disguise—like the Turkish fez—to men having nothing to do with the Bosporus.

For men as well as women, once fashion styles migrated from upper to lower classes, they lost their original cachet. By 1926, the full-cut Oxford bag—once worn exclusively by men at that elite college—lost its charm when men in the "East End," a working-class section of London, adopted the style.

BUENOS AIRES

The tight-fitting suit, once all the rage in Britain, was deported by trendsetters "back to Argentina." In truth, affluent men in Buenos Aires preferred to iden-tify themselves as decorously European, backing away from what they regarded as an indolent and lower-class "tropical" population. One way to maintain this class distinction was to avoid acknowledging the tropical weather. It was only with reluctance that, in 1921, Argentinean men abandoned formality and adopted American-style lightweight suits for the heat of summer.

Known as the "Paris of South America," Buenos Aires in the 1920s was Paris on the sunniest of days. Paris fashions—chic hats, shoes, coats, dresses—arrived in the city a remarkable two or three seasons ahead of the U.S. market. Latitude determined at least part of this advantage—when winter was descending on the Northern Hemisphere, women in Buenos Aires were scouting summer clothes. Strong trade agreements meant that goods arrived from not just Europe but also the United States and the Far East. Well-heeled Buenos Aires women devoted their mornings to window shopping and, finely attuned to shifts in Paris fashions, they embraced the trend toward radically short skirts months before it took comfortable hold in New York.

JAPANESE CLOTHING

The woman in short skirts—the New Woman—was everywhere. She cut a swath through 1920s Japan, whose great postwar prosperity set it apart from other nations. For most of the conflict, Japan's balance of trade had tilted pre-cipitously in its favor. The country manufactured and exported huge quantities of goods unavailable from other sources. With a monopolistic hold on key international trade, businessmen grew wealthy practically overnight. Reportedly, some entrepreneurs even made fortunes from selling coffins for victims of the flu pandemic. While this wealth did not extend beyond a small percentage of the population, the *narikins*, or *nouveaux riches*, were exuberant consumers with a penchant for Western dress. Literally, a *narikin* was a chess piece that morphed—symbolically and magically—from pawn into gold as it advanced across the game board.

Abandoning habits of thrift and simplicity imposed by Buddhism and Shintoism, narikins built ostentatious Japanese- or Western-style homes, collected expensive art, and only occasionally dispensed funds for philanthropic projects. Hypersuccessful men wore Western-style suits; their wives alternated between Paris fashions and traditional dress—*kimono* and *obi*.

Accessories reflected the mix. In 1923, the most popular item of jewelry—worn by both men and women, and with both Western and traditional dress—was the wristwatch. This was followed by the exclusively feminine *obi-dome*, a silk ribbon fastened with a catch of silver, platinum, or gold, sometimes encrusted with precious stones. Other distinctly traditional and gender-specific items included hair combs and pins topped with jade, quartz, lapis lazuli, or filigreed silver or gold. Some less conservative women wore diamond rings, even with traditional clothing. Men in Western dress sported stickpins and cufflinks. With the exception of American-made wristwatches, nearly all items of jewelry were domestically produced.

For the nouveaux riches, even the glacially changing kimono and obi were not immune from the impositions of consumerism. Materials and decoration changed rapidly enough to subject traditional costumes to the whims of fashion and the newly wealthy *narikin* bought more kimonos, which changed in detail from season to season in much the same way they would purchase Paris fashions. Details and accessories made fashion statements and showed how up-to-date the wearer was. Worried that less affluent citizens would spend beyond their means in their efforts to stay in fashion, it was rumored that the government ordered a popular department store to restrict offering new fashions more than twice a year.

In the 1920s, two new styles of obi (sash) appeared, called the *Fukuro* and *Nagoya*. Though the role obi played in traditional dress did not change, both new styles were less formal and more comfortable to wear than the unforgiving, stiff version that preceded them. Even women who dressed in traditional costume dressed their children in Western-style clothes, which were considered more comfortable than traditional outfits. Businessmen in the largest cities of Japan wore western clothing while women largely still wore the traditional garments such as long kimonos with padded hems.

Far from the world of the geisha, the *Modan Gâru* (Modern Girl) emerged in Japan; a living banner of modernity, she was greeted with both admiration and fear. Dressed in Western clothes she purchased for herself, she did not conform to a rigid demarcation between genders. The Modern Girl was seen as the wave of the future, for better or for worse. Her self-fulfilling way of life, for some, was a forecast of the downfall of Japanese culture. Her emotional and material independence could be interpreted as rampant consumerism and self-indulgence. Looked at this way, the Modern Girl's self-reliance placed her, correctly or not, into the world of the *narikin*.

CHINESE CLOTHING

U.S. manufacturers of cheap wristwatches anticipated a huge market for them in China. In Taiwan, the anti-foot-binding movement liberated even lower-class women to wear leather shoes. Most men and children, and the upper classes of women, had by the 1920s already switched from traditional to Western dress. As in Japan, the phenomenon of the Modern Girl in China threatened traditional values with her perceived self-absorption and materialism. At the same time, the potentially corrupt Modern Girl held the appeal of a modern nation, economically and socially competitive with the Western world.

INDIAN CLOTHING

Following the war, asceticism, for the vast majority of people in India, stemmed from abject poverty and not a considered rejection of materialist values. The most impoverished men wore loincloths simply because they could not afford more sheltering clothes. Political leader Mahatma Gandhi made a direct connection between India's reliance on British imports and its inability to break from British colonial rule. Traveling all around the country, he proposed a return to hand spinning and weaving of *khadi*, a rough-hewn material of nondescript or white color. He advocated the sacrifice of finer, colorful fabrics of British manufacture in exchange for self-sufficiency. India imposed a tax on British exports of cotton, which sent the English manufacturing center of Lancashire scrambling to produce its goods more cheaply so it could compete with the domestic Indian sources.

Gandhi progressively nationalized his own appearance, moving as far away as possible from the image of an "English gentleman." Ultimately, he wore only the loincloth, a form of dress—or undress—invested with layers of meaning. His choice was meant to be temporary—to draw attention to the poverty of the nation, to establish different conceptions of moral decency between the cultures of Britain and India, to imbue himself with a saint-like aura. At other periods in the struggle for self-rule,

Gandhi at his spinning wheel aboard a ship enroute to London, 1931. Courtesy of the Library of Congress.

Gandhi wore a longer *dhoti*, also made of khadi. After much consideration of regional origins, fabrics, and forms, he chose to wear a special white woven cap for men. The cap was accepted widely and worn as a sign of protest—not just against the British but also the customary divisions of class and caste that historically had undermined cohesive nationalism in India. (Once a year, during the Indian celebration of Holi, such divisions are briefly suspended, and the transformation of clothing expresses the translocations of status. For a day, castes are temporarily reversed. Normally servile men and women are permitted to hurl brightly colored dyes at individuals of any class. By the end of the day, color-saturated clothing, skin, and hair obscure social distinctions.)

The Gandhi white cap turned into a flashpoint of controversy. Members of the Indian Congress were compelled to wear it; it was banned from British government offices. The British hounded wearers of Gandhi caps; nonwearers were hounded by Indians who wore them. Clothing was a central tool used by Gandhi to communicate his beliefs in a country of largely illiterate people who spoke a dizzying range of languages. The national flag of India has a spinning wheel at its center in tribute to Gandhi's campaign; the flag—like that of any country—is another way for cloth to convey meaning without text. Eventually, class distinctions emerged even for this emblem of inclusion. The fineness of weave could be adjusted to accommodate the demands of wealthy men.

There were other, internal objections to khadi. White khadi was too plain for women who missed the independence of aesthetic choice in color and pattern. In addition, in a society where white symbolized widowhood, the lowest status for women, it seemed an unlikely choice. Some would-be adopters of the dhoti were hesitant to wear it, questioning if they met Gandhi's definition of sanctity. Others chafed at Gandhi's insistence on the wearing of khadi for members of the Non-Cooperation Movement. As it had been the case for the British Arts and Crafts movement that inspired him, painstaking hand production of objects ended up making them more expensive—and less accessible—than the mass-produced goods available from Britain.

British politicians complained that the tariffs on imports from Britain had been imposed by "millionaire merchants," whose goal was motivated less by politics than by greed. In either case, the cooling effect on British industry was the same. Displaying no urge toward asceticism, the maharajah of Kapurthala brought along two valets, a secretary, a cook, and twenty-seven trunks full of clothing for a 1925 visit to Atlantic City, a seaside resort in New Jersey. In a tweed suit and straw hat and carrying a Punjabi walking stick, its ivory handle ornamented with jewels, the maharajah mixed Eastern opulence and Western rectitude. (He also—according to an American observer—admired the rolling chairs on the boardwalk.)

ART AND CULTURE INFLUENCING CLOTHING

In the 1920s, women occupied a variety of roles related to art, as objects and object makers. Zelda Sayre Fitzgerald, an icon of the Jazz Age, described the flapper's life as art: "I believe in the flapper as an artist in her particular field, the art of being—being young, being lovely, being an object." In fiction that only thinly disguised their lives together, Zelda's husband, F. Scott Fitzgerald, offered variations of his wife and himself in novels that included *The Great Gatsby*, *This Side of Paradise*, and *The Beautiful and the Damned* and in the short stories "Bernice Bobs Her Hair" and "Diamond as Big as the Ritz." Fitzgerald frequently lifted, without crediting them, his wife's words for use in his own works.

In paintings by men, the New Woman might be depicted as a symbol of debauchery, her flapper dress cut to reveal a gaunt body. In contrast, women artists took active roles in designing textiles and clothing and graphically recording the visual world from their own perspective. German Dadaist Hannah Hoch incorporated images of women's dress and real textiles into her collages, manipulating the feminine uses of clothes.

In New York, artist Florine Stettheimer, with her two sisters, presided over a salon. The ongoing gathering of illustrious figures included famed Dadaist-surrealist Marcel Duchamp. Dressed in haute couture and immersed in "haute conversation," the Stettheimer salon had a decidedly feminine atmosphere, filled with "dandies and social butterflies." Florine captured on canvas her sisters and their guests, many of them homosexual or bisexual men. In her paintings, she bestows upon all her male subjects, whatever their sexual orientation the same thin waist and svelte physique. In a 1923 double portrait of the artist and Duchamp, the female figure, in a slender rose-colored gown, and the male one, lounging on a fringed pink chair in black suit and socks, share the same wasp waists, high-rounded shoulders, and masculine short hair.

Man Ray, whose avant-garde fashion images appeared in *Vogue, Harper's Bazar, Vanity Fair,* and many other stylish magazines, photographed Duchamp dressed as the artist's trademark alter ego, a female double he called "Rrose Sélavy" (a pun on "Eros, that's life"). Duchamp, in cloche hat and full makeup, looks every bit a lovely woman.

German artist Christian Schad captured the slithery coldness of Weimar cabarets. His 1927 painting, "Count St. Genois d'Anneaucourt," portrays an

Undated photograph of F. Scott and Zelda Fitzgerald on their honeymoon. Courtesy of the Library of Congress.

elegant man in black tie, bracketed by women in see-through diaphanous gowns, their eyes kohl smudged and hair scissored into flapperish bobs. On closer inspection, it becomes clear the two deadpan women are not women at all.

Russian-born painter Sonia Delaunay trained in Germany and lived in Paris, then Spain and Portugal, before returning to Paris at the war's end. When she opened her own textile-printing factory in 1924, Delaunay mixed motifs of ethnographic African art, Ukrainian peasant embroidery, and orientalist Egypt in her designs. Influenced, too, by the Russian Suprematist art movement, Delaunay substituted textiles for the flat canvas of fine art. Her block geometric–patterned textiles in bright colors suited the flatness—what fashion historian Richard Martin called the two-dimensional planarity—of 1920s dresses. She exhibited her geometrical designs at the 1925 Exposition de l'Art Décorative—where the common themes of geometry, motion, and African motifs came together in what would later be known as the Art Deco style.

POSTREVOLUTIONARY RUSSIA

Fashion in Russia succumbed to the Revolution. While affluent Parisians were quick to adapt peasant motifs in their gowns, women in postrevolutionary Russia struggled to clothe themselves in facsimiles of Parisian dress. After 1917, it was impossible to find new sewing patterns or fashion magazines. Women coveted European and American magazines of any type if they showed women in up-to-date clothing.

In 1921, an attempt at reviving couture in Moscow ended in pathos. Far from the gilt chairs and mirrored walls of Paris salons, the few daring women who showed up for the Moscow collection gathered in a dismal room, its discolored plaster walls lit by a single bare light bulb. A total of three outfits made up the whole collection—one each from Lanvin, Paquin, and Chanel—and rough wire frames stood in for sleek mannequins. Acquiring Paris fashion was, from a Socialist perspective, an act of sedition; of the handful of women nervously in attendance, a lone woman made a discouraging purchase—a copy, not the original—of a Paquin dress shown in blue silk. Informed that the only fabric available in blue was a heavy, military type, the shopper accepted a brown satin with stains that, saleswoman suggested, could be covered with embroidery. The silk stockings and chic heels needed to complete the outfit were nowhere to be found. Only heavy shoes and wool stockings were available in Moscow; a fragment of elegance was the best a woman could hope for.

By 1923—six years after the Revolution—mass-produced clothing was largely of poor quality and dreary design. The First State Cotton-Printing Factory recruited two Constructivist artists—Liubov Popova and Varvara Stepanova—to design textiles and dresses. Incorporating elements of French Cubism and German Bauhaus design, the Russian Constructivist movement embraced fine and applied arts. Its mandate was to create fashionable—even chic—items while meeting the stringent production and distribution demands of a Socialist economy. Popova arrived at the factory with some experience in costume and window display, but none in the complicated chemical and technical aspects of printing. These she taught herself so she could specify the dyes and processes needed to accurately reproduce her geometric op-art designs.

Exiled in Paris, Russian aristocrats arrived stripped of everything but their empty titles. The triumph of the Revolution lay in their reversal of fortune: the dazzlingly privileged were reduced to driving taxis and sewing clothes. In 1923, Gabrielle (Coco) Chanel hired Countess Orloff-Davidoff—once one of the richest women in Russia—to sell dresses at Chanel's shop in Biarritz. To supplement her income, the countess hand-knit jerseys, soon selling enough of these to establish her own business. She, in turn, hired friends as knitters. Chanel sold these jerseys of fantastical provenance in her shop. In Paris, some American department store buyers were quick to purchase Ukrainian-style embroideries from the workshops of princesses. An American critic, however, suggested that Russian-inspired gowns—vividly colored, "peasant cut"—should be reserved for costume parties.

> ### SURREALISM IN FASHION
>
> In Paris, designer Elsa Schiaparelli found Armenian women whose traditional knitting technique matched her needs for trompe-l'oeil ("fool the eye") patterned sweaters. Armenian knitting permitted two colors of wool to be combined so that one color could come to the foreground while the other remained subtly detectable, creating the illusion of depth. Schiaparelli put the traditional folk technique to avant-garde use, making her fortune with a sweater that seamlessly—and humorously—incorporated the image of a "real" bow knot. Schiaparelli's witty use of Surrealism in fashion—the bow that was not a bow—preceded the appearance of Surrealist René Magritte's iconic painting "The Treachery of Images" ("This Is Not a Pipe," 1928–1929).

BLACK AMERICAN INSPIRATION IN CLOTHING

As fashion historian Palmer White relates:

> In the twenties, everything black came into vogue, thanks to the French Colonial Art Exhibition of 1922 which introduced the eroticism of African sculpture to a wider French if not international public. In 1925 the Art Deco exhibition reflected the influence of black African art on weaving, carpets, drapes.... [Designer Elsa Schiaparelli] adapted the savage colours and forms to her hand-knitted sweaters.... She added masks and idols from various countries in French Equatorial Africa, and magical symbols from the French Congo.... She then used these sweaters as backgrounds for barbaric accessories [including] strand necklaces and bracelets made of horsehair.[1]

Designers used the exotic-sounding (and dehumanizing) "Tête-de-nègre" to refer to a dark brown fabric.

In the wake of antiblack racism that had extended even to the status of soldiers, the "New Negro" of the 1920s signaled a departure from culturally imposed stereotype and a radical movement toward black self-definition. As the term *black* is today, *Negro* in the 1920s was an imprecise way of identifying individuals, lumping together Southern-born blacks and immigrants from Africa and the Caribbean—disparate groups related only by skin color. Harlem was the "Negro Mecca" and birthplace of the Harlem Renaissance, an eruption of genius—

Josephine Baker

Phot. v. Gudenberg

Undated photo of Josephine Baker. Courtesy of the Library of Congress.

writers, artists, dancers, and musicians who profoundly influenced the cultures of America and Europe. Black performers introduced jazz to Europe and to white America, and jazz—with its off-kiltering steps and improvisations—came to define the age.

Paris-based American performer Josephine Baker emblemized all that was exotic and animalistic in the Jazz Age. Baker toured European capitals, with all dancers performing in scanty costumes improbably designed by the Wiener Werkstaette für Dekorativ Kunst in Vienna. Jazz was a new form of popular music with disregard for the stiff formality of music from previous centuries. It was a great leveler and considered democratic. The idea of breaking down social barriers by way of "frankness" was far from a universal goal for all black people in the 1920s. The jazz spirit did not animate every social event; many formal dinners and weddings still reflected the aspirations of white society.

COUTURIERS AND REPRODUCTIONS

Dressmaker-designed clothes are by definition original. Most designers dealt in reproductions, counting on the cachet of original designs to feed interest in copies. The subject of design reproduction was a tricky one. Couturières feared that replicating a creation would diminish its value. At the same time, outside manufacturers might illegally copy and market a dress, taking away income rightfully due the designer.

Madeleine Vionnet

Madeleine Vionnet was one of several couturières who only reluctantly permitted their fashions to be copied, manufactured in quantity, and distributed by department stores. Known as a technician of fashion, Vionnet cut her gowns on the bias, sometimes from a single piece of fabric, making them, in fact, nearly impossible to copy She wanted as much exposure of her couture designs as possible—through fashion shows, magazines, ads, movie costumes—but initially feared this would increase demand for inexpensive copies. Vionnet registered her designs, protested unauthorized production of copies, then decided to capitalize on the mass market, still worrying this would destroy the exclusivity and desirability of the original designs.

Coco Chanel

Coco Chanel did not hesitate to sell approved copies of her work, including clothing she designed for famous actresses, such as Broadway star Ina Claire.

However, hijacking of designs took income away from Chanel and other creators. In 1927, a New York man faced counterfeiting charges for selling imitation designer perfumes. Police searching his apartment found thousands of bottles, either empty or containing plain water—and many fake perfume labels.

Chanel put a twist on the meaning of counterfeiting with her frankly faux jewels—cheap fake pearls and pins, to be worn with expensive copies of her original creations. She sold accessories to accompany her black dresses such as rhinestone necklaces and bracelets and shoulder pins. This nonchalant high/low mixing of the real couture clothing and fake jewelry defined the look and helped make it modern. Chanel's clothing looked simple, but the devil was in the details—the cut, the hand (or feel) of the fabric, the designer's own compelling way of life. Chanel acutely understood that simplicity in design was the best guide to good taste.

Gabrielle "Coco" Chanel, 1910. Courtesy of the Library of Congress.

The designer's glamorous personal life was inextricably tied to the marketing of her products; in truth, she invented and packaged herself. She wore bangles and ropes of pearls and brooches, all defiantly not what they looked like. Her distinctive appearance—underwrought, gamine, steely—and her involvement, both rumored and real, with aristocrats and royals made her a celebrity of tabloid proportions. For years, the press linked her to the preternaturally wealthy Duke of Westminster, known as a huntsman and sportsman. In 1928, it was reported that the Duke had spent a million dollars to spruce up his yacht in

CHANEL NO. 5

Coco Chanel was apparently superstitious about the number five. She always played the number five when gambling in Monte Carlo, and her most famous perfume is known as No. 5. It sold, at the time, for 5,000 francs ($200) per liter. She usually chose February 5 and August 5 as her opening days for her collection for fall and spring lines.

preparation for marriage to a "dressmaker."

Even if she did not invent the little black dress—and there is good reason to think she did not (the honor may fall to Poiret)—Coco Chanel made it essential. She thought garish colors worn by women made them look ugly and thus started her fascination with black. It was speculated, as well, that she turned to black out of mourning for a dead lover. Her black dresses, though, appear to have nothing to do with sadness.

Chanel translated the ease of sport clothing into daywear—knit tops and uncomplicated frocks. In 1923 she showed a gray jersey knit "sports costume," an unbuttoned jacket casually tied at the neck, worn with a side-pleated skirt. She used wide stripes—horizontal and sailor-like—in her sweaters. The designer used the same sportive horizontal stripes for beaded evening gowns.

This photo shows the daring styles women were willing to wear in the Jazz Age. Courtesy of the Library of Congress.

SPORTSWEAR

In the United States, demand for sport-related dress increased dramatically after the war. Summer and winter resort vacations called for sport-specific clothing—items for skiing, swimming, tennis, tobogganing—and production of athletic dress more than doubled.

In Paris, both Jean Patou and Chanel translated aspects of Cubism into sportswear, from tennis sweaters to swimwear made from unshrinkable jersey. With clothes designed by couturier Patou, French tennis star Suzanne Lenglen blurred the line between sport and fashion. Patou replaced the long, petticoated tennis costume with a short white pleated skirt that barely covered the knees. He substituted a menswear-inspired, short-sleeved vest for the usual long-sleeved "feminine" blouse.

The "sporty" woman was modern and, increasingly, "masculine." In Germany's Weimar Republic, the sporty woman was suspect because she appeared sexually ambiguous—more boyish than maternal. At the same time, critics recognized that the athletic body was better suited for industry and childbirth. After 1928, fitness for German women was actively promoted and athleticism lost its wayward connotations.

THE HOLLYWOOD INFLUENCE ON CLOTHING

The Sporty Woman, Modern Girl, Flapper, or New Woman—whatever the jargon, the image sprang in large part from the movies. It would be hard to overestimate world interest in Hollywood films and their stars. The worlds of fashion and film intersected: clothing designers created costumes and dressed film stars for their off-camera hours; moviegoers got ideas about dress—and life—from the larger-the-life figures on the screen. In the Art Deco period, the two-dimensional outlines of women's dress fit the flat screen of film projection. Women derived fashion inspiration from the iconic bob of Louise Brooks and the demure charm of Mary Pickford. It was the sister of fashion designer Lucile who came up with the term "It Girl," and the actress Clara Bow was the most famously "It."

CONCLUSION

In the age of anything goes, of jazz clubs and speakeasies, of masculinized women and feminized men, even regulations on the dress of schoolgirls loosened up. In response to a demand for personal freedom, schools relaxed uniform requirements.

The stock market crash of 1929, which led to the Great Depression, was preceded by a time of great extravagance and prosperity that allowed fashion to evolve and modernize as society changed. The market crash was like an overlooked grenade—hidden from sight since the war, then accidentally kicked into action a by a distracted passerby. A decade after the Great War, the lost grenade remembered its destination and shot the Roaring Twenties back into a pitch-black sky.

NOTE

1. Palmer White, *Elsa Schiaparelli: Empress of Paris Fashion* (New York: Rizzoli, 1986), 52–62.

FURTHER READING

Gordon, Rae Beth. "Fashion and the White Savage in the Parisian Music Hall." *Fashion Theory* 8, no. 3 (September 2004): 267–99.

Makela, Maria. "The Rise and Fall of the Flapper Dress: Nationalism and Anti-Semitism in Early Twentieth-Century Discourses on German Fashion." *Journal of Popular Culture* 34, no. 3.

Martin, Richard, and Harold Koda. *Waist Not: The Migration of the Waist, 1800–1960.* New York: Metropolitan Museum of Art, 1994.

Sichel, Marion. *History of Children's Costume.* London: Batsford Academic and Education, 1973.

MOVIES

Cabaret (1972)
The Godfather: Part II (1974)
The Great Gatsby (1974)
Male and Female (1919)
Mantrap (1926)
Pandora's Box (1929)

The Thirties

Ellen Hymowitz

TIMELINE

1930s	Communism, Fascism, and Socialism all gain strength thanks to global depression and poor economies
1931	Glass fibers developed
1932	Shirley Temple makes her film debut
1933	Nazi takeover in Germany; Hitler comes to power; Prohibition repealed in the United States
1934–1935	Long March occurs in China
1936	King Edward VIII of England abdicates in order to marry the divorced Wallis Simpson
1936–1938	Spanish Civil War
1938	Germany annexes part of Czechoslovakia and Austria in preparation for war; DuPont introduces nylon fibers
1939	*Gone with the Wind* wins the Academy Award for Best Picture; Germany invades Poland and World War II breaks out in Europe

In England, it was called "the Slump"; in the United States, the "Great Depression." By either term, the vibrant, flowering economy and decadence of the twenties was, in the thirties, a grand rose that had lost its bloom. The previous decade skidded to a halt with the stock market crash of October 1929.

European countries still faced the costs of postwar reconstruction, and many Americans had bought their futures—houses, cars, stocks—recklessly on credit. Wealth in the United States was split between a handful of spectacularly wealthy individuals and the vast horde of ordinary citizens who, as often as not, lived hand-to-mouth or mostly on hope. When the middle class slid into debt and much of the working class depended on government subsidy, daily life turned into a slog, a hopelessly Sisyphean push upward and inevitable fall.

As far as clothing was concerned, fantasy was solace, and the devastatingly beautiful gowns worn by stars offered not just remote diversion but also inspiration. Shirley Temple, an impossible mix of innocence and precociousness, captured an adult longing for a preternatural childhood in the face of adult woes. With her signature curls and puffed-sleeved, doll-like dresses, the valiant child star dominated American movies of the 1930s. Mothers curled their little girls' hair and dressed

WINDSOR WEDDING

In England, King Edward VIII abdicated his throne to marry Wallis Simpson—a twice-divorced American. Her "Wallis blue" wedding dress, designed by Paris-based American couturier Mainbocher, was widely copied and available at "bargain basement" prices. Peculiarly, Simpson's wedding dress was buttoned at the back in a puckered zig-zag that suggested a stitched-up wound. Paradoxically, considering the Windsors' conspicuous consumption, fashion writer Holly Brubach notes that Mainbocher's designs were inspired by his belief in conserving during a time when so many were destitute.

them in "Shirley Temple style." Their own hairstyles imitated the movie stars as well. Women's hairstyles got longer and fuller due to the increased popularity and availability of the Marcel Wave, also known as the permanent or "perm." Women's hats grew less substantial and more feminine and impractical throughout the 1930s.

The beginnings of international air travel and the worldwide distribution of Hollywood movies put a Western spin on clothing styles as far away as China and Japan. Consumed by fashion, the British Duke and Duchess of Windsor were as frequently photographed as Hollywood stars and shared the stars' concerns about the ten pounds "added" by photography and film. Throughout the Depression, the Windsors' privileged circle lost neither their desire for ravishing clothes nor the means to obtain them. They had outfits made to their specifications for travel to resorts on the Riviera and at St. Moritz, for sporting activities and evenings out.

In contrast, "used clothes brigades"—charitable drives throughout the United States—solicited secondhand clothing for indigent families. Clothes for children were intentionally bought too big, in order to accommodate several years' growth. In 1939, with the declaration of World War II, clothing became a battleground of restrictions. Nationalism took the form of not just military uniforms but also the diversion of domestic materials for war use. Synthetic fibers and substitutions such as artificial silk were the order of the day; necessity was the mother of stylish invention.

WOMEN'S CLOTHING

Hemlines were already dropping by the end of the 1920s, and the female silhouette grew more conventionally feminine in the thirties. From the flapper wilderness of loose clothes and loosened morals, a determined waistline reappeared. Trousers—long but body-freeing—offered a transition point between the short dresses of the twenties and the midcalf ones that followed. Shorts remained the desirable, and distinctly feminine, costume for tennis. Long pants, however, were another phenomenon. Their implied androgyny made people nervous. Trousers suggested not just comfort but also an emphasis on sport and work outside the family. Lesbians had long borrowed the look of men's clothes, an association not lost on heterosexual men.

In Hollywood, Katharine Hepburn, Greta Garbo, Ginger Rogers, and Marlene Dietrich wore trousers on and off the set. They were style leaders and inspired copycats worldwide. Their assumption of men's style was at once alluringly feminine and vaguely threatening. Hepburn's passion for sport furthered her androgynous image. American movies were the overwhelming global influence on women's dress, eclipsing fashion magazines as a source of inspiration.

American sportswear designers in New York and Los Angeles grew increasingly prominent, though Parisian couturières, including Madeleine Vionnet, Elsa Schiaparelli, and Coco Chanel, still set trends. A shift in power was noted in the American press: Paris "offered" but did not "dictate" fashion. Both American and French designers, including Chanel, created costumes for movies, while costumers hired by film studios gained fame with styles linked to particular stars. Women of limited means sought to copy the sylph-like gowns, leisure ensembles, and sport clothes worn by their idols on and off the screen, and manufacturers adapted stratospherically expensive designs for a low-end mass market.

Home sewers continued to be supplied with commercially made patterns to help them stay in style, on a budget. Fashion historian James Laver observes that the Depression democratized fashion. A 90-percent duty was slapped onto the cost of the original models of fashions brought to the United States by 1930. Dress packages with the garment pieces already cut out in linen and full instructions on how to assemble them were called *toiles*. These were allowed into the United States duty free and allowed women to have the look of the original 100,000-franc dress for perhaps $50, depending on the fabrics she chose. *Vogue* pattern books offered knitting instructions for designer sweaters.

After a decade of experimentation, the DuPont chemical company introduced nylon in 1938. Initially it was used for women's stockings, but the military soon requisitioned the material for parachutes for the war that started in Europe a year later. Nylon was an exciting prospect for women who could not obtain or afford the coveted silk stockings, and nylons were a hugely popular garment when introduced.

Silhouette

Film stars Garbo, Dietrich, Rogers, and Jean Harlow epitomized the ideal 1930s silhouette. Departing from the straight up-and-down lines of the flapper, the thirties shape was more womanly than girlish. Triangulated, the new

> ### ON THE GO
>
> A year after the stock market crash of 1929, there was still a demand for chic travel clothes. Two-piece calf-length dresses in tricot were teamed with fur-lined coats that recalled the Roaring Twenties.

Greta Garbo, 1931, Hollywood movie star. Courtesy of the Library of Congress.

ANTI-JEWISH SENTIMENT AND THE FASHION WORLD

At the outbreak of war, responding to increasing anti-Semitism, some costume (and fashion) designers dropped their identifiably Jewish last names, Adrian Greenberg being the most prominent example.

look emphasized shoulders at the expense of the knees and skimmed the body in a narrow sheath. Height for women was newly valued; small hats and narrow skirts acted like vertical stripes, visually lengthening the body.

Vionnet's revolutionary bias-cut crêpe-de-Chine, originally used only as lining fabric, appeared over and over as the outside fabrics of sheath-like long gowns. Her gowns were made up of bias-cut triangles carefully put together to be form fitting without side or back openings. The pull and the fall of the fabric were stunning and seductive. Often cut to a low swooping curve in the back, elegant evening dresses mirrored revealing suits for swimming and sunbathing. The nakedness of backs suggested a sophisticated ambiguity: seduction could be accomplished by women through the act of walking away.

Once again, an interest in Classical Greece and Rome pervaded the bias-cut gowns of thirties couture. With their draped and pleated gowns, both Vionnet and couturière Madame Grès alluded to ancient Greek statues and lyre-playing figures on Greek vases in Renaissance art. A renewed interest in classicism heralded a change to balanced and pleasing form. At the same time, fashion photography of the decade frequently subverted Classical images for the purposes of Surrealism. In a 1937 fashion spread photographed by Man Ray for *Harper's Bazaar*,[1] Madame Grès—herself trained as a sculptor—juxtaposed her white "Grecian column gown" with ancient Greek statues. In films and art, surrealists Jean Cocteau and Salvador Dalí put stark images of Classical pillars and statuary to eerie use.

Both costume designer Adrian and couturière Vionnet feared wholesale reproduction of their designs and tried to make their creations too hopelessly difficult to reconstruct. Throughout the decade, the popularization and replication of original designs teetered between economic windfall and a cheapening lack of quality control. Reproduction of their designs did not necessarily benefit fashion innovators. Film stars' gowns—often riffs on Vionnet's distinct bias cut—had little impact on the income of Vionnet. A dress designed by Adrian for Joan Crawford for the 1932 movie *Letty Lynton* was copied and reproduced on a mind-boggling scale. Macy's cinema shop sold 500,000 of the dresses; its style retained currency

MASS-MARKETING MOVIE CLOTHING

To satiate the industry of desire for film clothing, Bernard Waldman's modern merchandising bureau was set up to serve as the fashion middleman for Hollywood studios. The studios provided him with sketches and photos of the costumes designed for the stars up to a year in advance, making it easier for copies to be made available when the movie was released. The bureau then contracted with manufacturers to produce and advertise the clothing in time for release of the film. Waldman started a chain of official Cinema Fashion Shops, selling expensive copies of gowns, which remained pricy in order to maintain their status, identified with particular stars.

throughout the decade. The dress, of starched white chiffon, featured gigantic puffed sleeves. Every little girl all over the country, within two weeks of the picture's release, felt she would die if she couldn't have a dress like that, and the country was soon flooded with little Joan Crawfords.

Millions of people went to the movies every week, seeking an escape from their daily grind in the glamour and beauty portrayed on film. Movies telegraphed ideals of athletic, slender bodies. In fashion magazine spreads, spectators and participants in sporting events were casually but elegantly dressed in distinctly American clothes. Fashion shows were sometimes inserted into 1930s movies, where some shifts to "real life" were more plausible than others. Audiences were perfectly willing to interrupt the plot of a film to admire what were essentially commercials.

In England, department stores had become a main source of fashion for men and women. They sold a mixture of haute couture–inspired dress and Hollywood-inspired dresses and mixed together all the fabrics and trimmings needed to make these at home. Those who could not afford the ready-made clothing had the option to make them at home.

Chanel continued to innovate on the part of women and made an institution of the clean, pressed, crisp, white-collared, button-down shirt and knitted sweaters, jackets with trimming, and well-made, well-thought-out skirts with pockets in logical spots for easy use. These pieces are all now known as classics in fashion, but they had their origins for women's fashion at this time. For eveningwear, Chanel created romantic flowing styles on the bias with fitted tops and wide flowing sleeves.

MEN'S CLOTHING

White-tie full dress with a tailcoat popped back into men's evening fashion in the thirties. It is as if the world felt that the Great Depression was a judgment on the fast times and youth culture of the 1920s and was prepared to grow up and do penance in the 1930s.

Men's fashion was inspired in the same way as women's by Hollywood stars and their wardrobes. Smoking jackets and suits worn by Cary Grant and Fred Astaire offered a sadly unobtainable ideal of suave evening dress. The Duke of Windsor set clothing trends, including the Windsor knot and the mixing of different patterns, such as tweeds and checks, for daywear. The Duke was the first to insist on zippers instead of buttons, for the trousers of his Savile

Cary Grant (as Dr. David Huxley) in Howard Hawks's 1938 film, *Bringing Up Baby*. Courtesy of Photofest.

WESTERN WEAR

Cowboys, secondhand clothes, zoot-suiters, and the Men's Dress Reform Party defined, in a polyglot fashion, the menswear of the 1930s. Cowboy shirts, once the exclusive domain of the Wild West, spread to the East Coast and then boomeranged back when fans of Westerns demanded mass-market copies of clothes that drawled. Levi's became the first company to put a brand identifier on its clothing. Years before clothes became walking billboards for designer logos, Levi-Strauss put its identifiable red tab on the back pocket of its jeans.

Row suits, and spurned dowdy braces (suspenders) and belts for a sleeker line. The masculine ideal was suave.

Men wore fitted jackets that lay at the hips and emphasized broader shoulders (the English drape suit). The jackets had shorter lapels but were largely the same design as before and could be either single or double breasted. The business suit, used by men out in white-collar jobs, were made of worsted wool, linen, and fine gabardine in the summer. The patterns were often muted pinstripes in dark colors, but a trend toward color and lightness was seen after the character Jay Gatsby wore his lovely light summer whites for his fantastic parties in the book *The Great Gatsby*. These were, however, more for the increased number of sports and leisure styles that appeared for men. Knitted shirts and sweaters became popular, remaining so to this day. Shirts differed only in patterns (not all shirts were white) and the style of collar. The Windsor collar was specially designed to accommodate the wider Windsor knot of the tie.

From 1929 until it fizzled out in 1937, the Men's Dress Reform Party in England fought to free men from their usual lot of stiff collars, choking ties, ugly braces, unwashable heavy suits, and drab colors. The Reformers said that trousers were ill favored and unsanitary and that there was no place and no excuse for the hideous and ridiculous *plus fours* (full knickers) introduced in the twenties. The campaign encouraged men to go "back to nature" (in moderation) and wear sandals instead of shoes, and shorts or kilts in place of trousers, insisting that skirts are not solely a female garment! Men were urged to pay attention in their dress—as women already did—to climate and season. Freed from the constrictions of stereotypically manly dress, men would reveal more of their bodies, because covering the body produced immorality by creating mystery. (Only for very young children would expanses of bare skin be viewed as unerotic, and what the Men's Dress Reform

THE ORIGINS OF THE ZOOT SUIT

Swing music, a kind of jazz, was hugely popular in the 1930s. African American–inspired swing dancing dictated looser suits for young men. The forties' *zoot suit* evolved from the roomy *Oxford bag* style of the 1930s. This style of trouser emerged in Harlem and other lower-class neighborhoods in cities across America. Then came the flamboyant, conspicuously expensive suit worn on the East Coast by African Americans and on the West Coast by Latinos as an assertion of self-worth and of identity, as an act of rebellion, and sometimes as a marker for criminality. It became more popular in the early 1940s.

Party promoted was very much a return to an idyllically androgynous ease and innocence.)

Though ridiculed in their time, the ideas of the movement took hold in later decades, when men's clothing was freed up and even in the 1960s and 1970s when styles were feminized. In the 1930s, though, the Duke of Windsor appeared frequently in kilts, owing to his position in Great Britain, which included Scotland. A 1934 photograph shows him (then the Prince of Wales) in a plaid kilt, checked jacket, tie, shirt, knee socks, and laced-up ghillies. The gender of his clothing derails at the waist, with the upper half masculine and the lower, feminine. The codpiece-like sporran (the hide pouch that is a traditional part of Scottish national dress) hanging from the front of the kilt further blurs gender lines.

The manufacture of menswear shifted from the provenance of men to women. Custom suits were still made by tailors who were highly skilled and invariably men. Mass-manufactured suits were another story. Factory sewing was considered "light" industrial work—unskilled, and therefore feminine. Virtually all the creators of factory-made men's suits were women, who manufactured with female hands a form of masculinity.

Hairstyles, Hats, and Accessories

Whatever his economic status, every man wore a hat in the 1930s. They wore soft or stiff trilbies or sportier peaked caps. Their hair was parted in the middle

Young men wearing zoot suits at a dance at the Washington Hotel in D.C., 1942.
Courtesy of the Library of Congress.

and not as thickly plastered with pomade as the previous decade. Older men often wore mustaches, which went out of fashion in the 1940s. A man's shoes were narrow and usually two-tone in color, and he finished his look with the regular accessories commonly seen for decades: a watch, tiepin, cufflinks, and perhaps a ring.

CHILDREN'S CLOTHING

In the 1930s, girls past early childhood dressed in versions of their mothers' clothes with the same longer skirts and natural waists. Children's clothes were ordered from Sears catalogs, purchased in department stores, or sewn at home. McCall's, for example, sold patterns for adult clothes in children's sizes. Styles worn by adult film stars influenced the clothes manufactured for girls as well. Actress Deanna Durban set a trend for bolero jackets. Far more pervasively, mothers smitten with Shirley Temple chose the actress's baby-doll-style dresses for their little girls.

Manufacturers of zippers launched an aggressive "self-help" campaign to promote the use of zippers in children's clothes. The industry pitch: Busy mothers could save time by freeing tots from the daunting task of buttoning their own clothes. Instead of fumbling with buttons, it was argued, zippers made it easy for very young children to dress themselves.

The hemlines on ready-made aprons (costing 39 cents) and dresses (65 cents) for girls two to eight years old stopped at just above the knees. Flowers, bunnies, and even a winged fairy were popular decorative motifs. Mothers were expected to finish off the garments with embroidery done at home; cotton floss was available for an extra 20 cents. Smocking was popular for the bodices of dresses for younger girls. Girls could play in one-piece (or two-piece made to look like one) trousers and sleeveless or short-sleeved tops.

Department stores offered one-piece sleepers, sometimes with feet attached.

Short rompers for boys of up to age eight had ready-to-be-embroidered motifs of sailors or puppies. For boy three to eight there were tailored suits with short pants. With or without a jacket, long ties were worn with short-sleeved shirts.

In 1931, a full, forty-one-piece infant layette could be purchased for $9.95. Items included knitted wool booties, sweaters and bonnets, and flannelette kimonos.

By 1934, it was clear that money was short. Stores advertised children's outfits as "Bargains, every one!" Good quality at low cost was assured. Mothers were encouraged to outfit their sons in "double duty denim overalls" and jacket, "built in every respect like Dad's—Cut over big, roomy patterns." Oversized, nonripping denim work clothes were "extra long-wearing bargains." For younger boys, stores offered tweed and corduroy knickers, cotton long-pant playsuits, and shorts useful for "sport or camping." Styles for older girls stayed resolutely grown-up. Dresses were midcalf length, and suits were accessorized with short gloves, court shoes, and beret.

In 1937, dresses were still fitted at the waist, but hemlines crept up to approach the knee. Military styles resurfaced in 1938, a year before World War II was declared. A patriotic suit for boys might be a white fabric with gold-colored braid, buckles, and buttons on a navy trim in a sailor mode. Detachable white collars and cuffs, in white pique or organdy, and a variety of belts could extend the life of a dress, making one garment seem like several.

YOUTH MARKET EMERGES

The rumblings of a youth-centered market were beginning to be felt. More than ever, parents took to heart the style preferences of their children. Department stores made the tentative step of organizing clothing displays not just by gender but also by age. The first bras meant for developing figures were introduced in the 1930s. The clothing and beauty industries began to perceive the purchasing power of the not-quite-adult.

From its start in 1935, *Mademoiselle* (or *Mlle*) magazine aimed its fashion and advice columns at "smart young women." In 1939, *Glamour of Hollywood*, a magazine offering tips from film stars, lost its *from Hollywood* tag and became simply *Glamour*; it competed with and copied *Mademoiselle*, while targeting a less-sophisticated readership. Both magazines were attuned to mass market fashions.

GERMANY

The ideal German body type of the 1930s was essentially androgynous. Vigorous exercise was expected of both men and women. Sports outfits for women included bathing ensembles—one-piece swimsuits cut to midthigh and often belted. The suits were coordinated with long robes, capes, and even a fishnet "coat" and worn with high-heeled sandals. By 1930, women in Berlin were seen wearing more revealing swimsuits, with tight braless tops and no sleeves. Biking wear consisted of pedal pushers with a matching below-the-knee wraparound skirt and a tucked-in, short-sleeved, lightweight blouse. For tennis, women wore a white pique sleeveless bloused top with a defined waist, and a loose skirt that stopped above the knee. Suitable hiking clothes included shirtwaist-style dresses worn over knickers, or loose pants, just covering the calf, worn with a full-sleeved, tucked-in shirt.

Germany's attempts to promote the country as a fashion center generally failed. Adolf Hitler's takeover of Germany in 1933 ended the economically unstable but prodigiously artistic Weimar era. As anti-Semitism grew increasingly harsh, the government outlawed all Jewish ownership of businesses. Shopkeepers and department store owners had their businesses taken from them without compensation. The banishment of Jews had a profound effect on the fashion industry in Germany. Designers, artists, and factory owners were exiled or murdered, their talents and skills disappearing with them.

The brown shirts worn by Hitler's private army—the Sturm Abteilung ("Storm Section")—were recycled World War I uniforms. Nazi soldiers wore the skull and crossbones, imagery later appropriated by Punks. As the decade progressed, work clothes for women gained importance.

ITALY

In Italy, where more than forty fashion magazines were available at the start of the decade, lavish spending on clothes was promoted as a boon for the economy. Later, when foreign imports were condemned, Mussolini promoted at a "made in Italy" campaign. This did not stop the dictator's daughter from wearing fashions from Paris, however.

Up until World War II, military women—even Fascist Party inspectors—did not wear military uniforms. Rather, they dressed in well-styled gabardine suits, elegant walking shoes, and perhaps an inconspicuous fur stole as outerwear.

AFRICAN INFLUENCE

Americans who looked to Paris for the latest fashions were thus also influenced by African themes. The most influential themes within French and American fashion were North Africa and orientalism, sub-Saharan Africa, images of Africans, and jazz. The strongest similarities between French and American fashion were in textiles and garments based on North African textile design and costumes. Jewelry was evidence that the harem associations of slavery had shifted, linking African Americans to the exotic people of slavery. Sub-Saharan influence was strong in the use of animal furs or prints. Images using Masai shields were important in the United States.

CHINA

In 1935, the Chinese government, alarmed at "exhibitionist flappers," outlawed immodest dress. Western dresses had to cover both elbows and knees. Traditional dress had to be worn with long pants, so the thigh-high slit in the skirt would not reveal bare skin. For men, pajamas and coatlessness were forbidden out of doors. Government workers and students were made to wear uniforms. The rigorous dress reform arose not just out of concerns for modesty but also because the government had built a new textile factory and needed to guarantee a market for it.

THE SOVIET UNION

Soviet women, in the face of communism and the radical changes they had experienced in the previous twenty years, had acquired a severe distaste for anything that showed signs of bourgeoisie idleness, such as high-heeled shoes and fashionable dress. The lack of aesthetics as an important part of the daily lives of women was to the point where some even broke their mirrors and paid no attention to personal adornment. Any emphasis on clothing was in terms of work clothes, and many women dressed like men, in caps and clothes held together with safety

---

WEST AND EAST INSPIRATION

The influence of and resistance to Western dress was felt everywhere from Turkey to Iran. Early in the decade, Japanese women were receptive to aspects of Western clothing. Some younger women embraced the entire look, abandoning traditional costume for the short sleeves, narrow waists, and calf-length skirts of American girls. Japanese girls at the same event might appear in a kimono or fitted dress. Older women resisted a complete switch. American designers in Japan adapted conventions of modesty and material to dresses with long sleeves and skirts.

pins. The predominant color throughout Soviet style was brown, which women knit into shawls they wore over their heads for warmth. Black and blue coats and shabby black skirts with loose cotton stocking did the minimum to protect women against the elements. Clothing was made in the same factories where military uniforms were made. They dressed to work, and that work took them alongside men in the fields, building sites and driving trams. They were often hard to distinguish from the men. Mass production meant that there was very little in the way of choice of goods. If women were interested in smelling nice or wearing cosmetics, it seemed there was only a limited choice of scents and all the lipstick colors looked the same.

In 1932, the government relaxed the rules and allowed the first public fashion show in Soviet Russia. It was attended by 40,000 women, including factory girls and farmworkers. At this show, they voted en masse to approve fifty new styles that would then be on offer for women who were complaining that there was too little choice in their clothing and that it was unattractive. The fashions were all designed by women, one of whom was sent by the Soviet government to apprentice with a French couturier in order to learn some of the trade to bring back to Russia.

In 1936 French couturier Elsa Schiaparelli spent time in Russia and observed the women and their dress habits. It seemed to her that women were dressing better than they had at the beginning of the decade, with the peasants dressed in one fashion (the old black coat and shawl over the head), while the intellectual workers dressed better in a trim figure wearing a proper hat. Red was a dominant color for communism but also in fashions from Russia long before, and she hoped it would catch on and allow for livelier fashions for women.

TURKEY

Inspired by Gandhi's khadi campaign, President Kemal of Turkey announced in 1930 that although he would continue to wear "Bond Street" (i.e., London-style) clothes, he would insist that they be made from Turkish fabrics. Kemal's goal was to increase Turkey's domestic economy while endorsing Western modernity, and to this end he increased tariffs on foreign incomes. Working-class men had no trouble buying Western-style suits. Previously veiled women followed trends from Paris, even refashioning their discarded veils into stylish turbans. Men in the peasant class wore the traditional baggy "sultanate" trousers and purchased their Western suits from purveyors of secondhand clothes. The import of even used clothing was restricted by the new import taxes. The government's plan was to acquire foreign

> ### IRAN
>
> In a bid for modernity, Persia (now Iran) banned traditional dress for women and aggressively enforced the change in favor of Western dress. Veiled women feared going outside, where they risked having their *hijab* (head covering) yanked off by officers. Forced to abandon their customary dress, unveiled women found an acceptably Western way to achieve modesty—choosing baggy, ankle-length overdresses and head scarves.

equipment to create a domestic clothing industry in Turkey. Kemal observed that Gandhi's insistence on hand-loomed cloth was impracticable and ultimately doomed by the import of cheap Japanese textiles made to look hand-woven.

NOTE

1. In 1929, *Harper's Bazaar* was rechristened with a new spelling after decades as *Harper's Bazar*.

FURTHER READING

Kirke, Betty. *Madeleine Vionnet.* San Francisco: Chronicle Books, 1998.
Laver, James. *Costume and Fashion: A Concise History (World of Art).* London: Thames & Hudson, 1995.
Schrum, Kelly. *Some Wore Bobby Sox: The Emergence of Teenage Girls' Culture, 1920–1945.* New York: Palgrave Macmillan, 2004.
Stern, Radu. *A Contre-Courant, Against Fashion: Clothing as Art, 1850–1930.* Cambridge, MA: MIT Press, 2004.

MOVIES

Bringing Up Baby (1938)
Curly Top (1935)
Jezebel (1938)
The Jungle Princess (1936)
Letty Lynton (1932)
Mata Hari (1931)
Morocco (1930)
Romance (1930)
Tea with Mussolini (1999)
Top Hat (1935)
The Women (1939)

The Forties

Ellen Hymowitz

TIMELINE

1939	World War II begins after Hitler invades Poland
1941	Japan bombs Pearl Harbor, bringing the United States into the war; wartime rationing of textile products declared to aid in the war effort
1945	Germany surrenders; atomic bombs detonated over Japan; war ends with surrender of Japan; United Nations formed
1946–1949	Chinese Civil War
1947	India and Pakistan gain independence from Britain
1947–1948	Palestine partitioned and Israel established
1949	North Atlantic Treaty Organization (NATO) formed; Germany divided into East and West

From its start in 1939 to its end in 1945, World War II was the prevailing influence on fashion and every aspect of life of the 1940s. For the first half of the decade, wartime rationing of textiles, clothing, and leather led to abrupt changes in styles for women, particularly in England, France, and the United States. New synthetics were substituted for the nylon, silk, and other desirable materials diverted from fashion for military use. American man-made fabrics included Celanese rayon and *celbrook*, which resembled sharkskin.

With the ever-present threat of bombing or gas attack in London came the need for outfits called "siren suits" that could be zipped into quickly for lightning-fast escapes to underground shelters.

After the occupation of Paris by the Nazis in 1940, women in the city relied on bicycling and the Metro to get around, and their clothing had to be weather resistant and easy to move around in. The occupation had a profound and paradoxical affect on the couture industry. Some couturiers closed up shop but remained in Paris. For example, Gabrielle Chanel shut her couture salon but continued to market her perfumes; for the war's duration, she lived at the Ritz Hotel with her Nazi companion (later she was quoted as saying, "When a woman my age has an offer from a man, she does not look at his passport"). Some foreign designers working in France, notably

Harry Hopkins, President Roosevelt's chief advisor (left), Diana Hopkins, his daughter (center), and Prime Minister Winston Churchill (right), wearing his "siren suit," pose with Falla, President Roosevelt's dog, in Washington, c. 1945. Courtesy of the Library of Congress.

Italian Elsa Schiaparelli and Mainbocher, left Paris for the United States.

At the start of the Occupation that he had masterminded, Adolf Hitler wanted to add luster to the Nazi image by transferring the Parisian couture industry to Berlin or Vienna. After much negotiation, he was convinced by Lucien Lelong, a designer and the president of an organization of couturiers, the Chambre Syndicale de la Couture Parisienne, that the intrinsic value of couture could not be separated from the traditions and skills in France. An arrangement was struck to limit distribution of couture creations to Nazis and their wives in Germany and Occupied Paris. French customers retained the right to shop couture. Ultimately sixty fashion houses were exempted from the fabric rationing system imposed in the rest of Paris. Even with enough money to pay for clothing, a lack of ration coupons made shopping impossible for the average Frenchwoman.

With its reprieve from rationing, the couture industry produced lavish clothing with a devil-may-care disregard to the privations of the average French citizen. Lelong's bargain put in place what were essentially sumptuary laws. Parisian couturies supplied the wealthy Vichy collaborators and German officers' wives with elaborate clothing. Though the newly installed Nazi government did take advantage of the luxuries of Paris, the great majority of couture clients during the war were still French. The couture industry did better financially during the German occupation than it had done previously during the troubled economic times of the 1930s.

At war's end, couturiers offered a variety of patriotic explanations for what appeared to have been self-serving collaboration. The strongest case for the continuation of the couture industry was the potential loss of employment for at least 12,000 workers in Paris. Less convincingly, some couturiers maintained that the peculiarly French high styles of fashion were a form of protest against the Occupation, a visual assertion of pure "French-ness." Others argued that the soldiers at the front were sustained by memories of the fashionable wives and girlfriends waiting for them at home.

The important American market, closed off from French imports during the war, had to be wooed back at war's end. In the interim, a characteristically breezy American style had blossomed. In the latter half of the decade, even

A young man, wearing a straw hat, reads aloud to two men, Harper's Ferry, West Virginia, c. 1942. Courtesy of the Library of Congress.

when Parisian designers regained their global influence, the impact of fashion persisted—as it does to this day. England, too, cut off from French fashion directives during the war, built on its own distinctly British style, characterized by tradition, stability, and references to the tweeds of sport and country life rather than taffeta.

The Blitz—Germany's constant and shattering 1940 air raids on London—destroyed much of its urban landscape. England's defense efforts relied not just on its military but also on the "home front," with the citizens who stayed put, working crucial jobs, running households, and maneuvering within the system of ration coupons. Even then Princess Elizabeth used ration tickets in 1947 to purchase fabric for her wedding gown.

The term *teenager* first came into use in 1941, labeling a generation situated behind childhood play and adult sophistication. Magazines such as *Seventeen* and *YM* catered to a new audience of consumers. For young men in their late teens and very early twenties, the jazzy zoot suit that had emerged in the 1930s reached its heyday, entering the common parlance of men's clothing styles.

Christian Dior's "New Look," a style introduced before the war but then stopped in its tracks, reappeared as the postwar anti-uniform for women. Intensely feminine, fabulously profligate in its use of fabric, Dior's nipped-waist invention was radically new, though arguably not modern. It built upon the extravagant couture styles that had continued to flourish—for a relatively small audience—throughout the war.

For many men, military uniforms alone were the extent of their dress parade. At a turning point in their lives, bridegrooms—half in and half out of ordinary life—posed in uniform for their wedding pictures. In 1941, when a wedding dress would use up nearly a third of a woman's annual allotment of coupons for clothing, most British brides wore uniforms, too. Marriage, at least as it started out, looked like war.

WOMEN'S CLOTHING

The commen women's wardrobes consisted of an overcoat, a suit with a blouse, a day dress made from utility cloth, and perhaps eveningwear. Wealthy women continued to dress well, only slightly limited by rationing for the war effort.

The German occupation condemned Paris to a state of solitary—if, for some, fashionable—confinement. Deprived of French exports and media coverage of Paris inventions, stylish women around the world were suddenly bereft. Who would tell them what to wear? Compounding the dilemma, clothing supplies from any source were in desperately short supply.

A lack of dictates from Paris helped to heighten the "democracy" of American sportswear. The clothes were created mostly by women for women. Women adjusted wrap dresses, for example, to suit their own comfort and sense of style. The addition of pockets—long a feature of men's clothing—freed women from the necessity of carrying handbags. Further evidence of democracy was that the same clothes were appropriate for different times of day and different occasions. These were mass manufactured in a range of prices, making them accessible to most women, and could be put on and taken off with ease. Designer Bonnie Cashion added patch pockets and luggage closings to coats and dresses that managed to look simple, sturdy, and dashing. This kind of innovation was common and helped to spark the fashions of America that so dominate later decades.

New York designer Claire McCardell, the most prominent of the American sportswear designers at the time, confronted head-on the restrictions of war. Responding to the shortage of leather, she commissioned Capezio to produce ballet flats in a variety of textiles to coordinate with her clothing designs. McCardell used cheap and unlikely materials, including denim, plaids, and men's shirting, to create appealing and wearable designs. In 1941, she produced a line of interchangeable separates that made nine variations from five separate pieces that could makeup an entire wardrobe; they were comfortable for travel and adaptable for any occasion. The pieces included a taffeta shirt, rayon jersey harlequin-print slacks, a long taffeta skirt, a jersey top with push-up sleeves, and a jersey jacket with taffeta lining. McCardell added detachable hoods to many of her tops. Her designs flattered women of different body types. A two-piece middy blouse outfit emphasized a small waist; a short, unfitted bolero jacket shifted attention from waist to shoulders. McCardell designed a separate collection of so-called junior fashions, including a popular *dirndl* skirt. Rejecting the stiff lines of a military silhouette and the mannish lines of ultra-padded shoulders, she designed more feminine and softer looks for women. For McCardell, who was herself an independent successful woman, feminism was enhanced by feminine dress.

During the war, General Limitation Order L-85-1942-46 in the United States forbade woolen wraps, evening dresses, and bias-cut dresses and skirts (which wasted fabric), or the full dolman sleeves. Jackets were restricted in length, cuffs were banned, and belts could be no more than two inches (5 cm) wide. Women wore narrow dresses that emphasized the shoulders and knee-length skirts and had a silhouette that stressed the waistline at its natural position. Styles were unembellished in the face of restrictions on fabrics and trims. Necklines were generally high and conservative, adding to the military feel of the era.

Women's shoes were sturdy and comfortable, with sensible heels, and were made without leather, which was needed for the war effort. Sisal and cork soles were the base for fabric uppers on shoes. Women wore scarves in contrasting colors, and jewelry was important to embellish the drab clothing. Brooches and pins adorned the lapels of their suits, and bracelets and necklaces decorated the wrists and necklines.

The housedress was popular among housewives for the washable and versatile nature of the fabric and the fact that the informal dress was suitable for everything from kitchen chores to moviegoing. The style could be made up in synthetics, calico, or gingham—any material not needed for the war effort.

Women who had been dependent on domestic servants to perform all their housework were suddenly without help because maids had moved out of the homes and into factory jobs or war work. Many of the women were new to housework, and they demanded housedresses (or coats) styled like sport clothes that were distinct from maids' clothing. Clothing for domestic chores had to be practical and protective, sparing not just the woman herself but also her better outfits. Working women who rushed home to cook dinner had with no time to change clothes. For them, the pretty apron—often a frock-like pinafore—was prescribed. Housedresses had to be washable, easy to iron, well made (so they didn't fall apart after repeated washing), and colorful to keep up a woman's morale. Claire McCardell's "popover" dress more than fit the bill. Manufactured in the thousands, the popover had three-quarter-length sleeves, deep armholes, and a surplice closing at the neck. Available in checks or plaids, the popover featured a large quilted pocket, big enough to fit the matching oven mitt that hung on fabric ties from the waist.

Los Angeles rivaled New York as a center of fashion. Californian clothing was more casual; New York, more business oriented. Movie costume designers set or reinforced fashion trends with styles for famous stars. Movie costumer Adrian gave Joan Crawford her signature mannish suits with padded shoulders and defined waist and dressed Katharine Hepburn in somewhat softer but still masculine daytime suits and trousers. He used a bias cut for evening dresses when restrictions on fabric forbid its use for ordinary clothes. Adrian also branched off from movie work to design a line of mass-marketed clothing.

In contrast to the extravagant gowns worn by Nazis and their wealthy collaborators, the average Frenchwoman scrambled to make the best of what she could find. Women were forced to make do with the fabrics that were easily available to them and had to adapt styles so that they didn't use up more than their share of rationed fabrics. This meant sleeveless dresses and shorter shirts. Pleats were not allowed on skirts or trousers, because they took too much fabric. Fabrics that pulled double duty as household textiles became eveningwear. Ticking used for mattresses was sometime used for clothing and other previously utility fabrics were used for clothing production. There was only a set amount of fabric allowed for any garment, and it depended on the type. Women's dress was inspired by the military look, boxy and mannish, but with a certain glamour attached.

When the Nazis seized ownership of cars, trucks, and buses for their own use, women in Paris started to wear large shoulder bags, practical for bicycling through the city and fitting the military outlines of women's clothes. When leather was hard to find, synthetic fabrics took their place, including a "curled rayon pile" that looked like black Persian lamb. Similarly, cork and wood platforms were used in place of leather for women's shoes.

When everyone in London had to carry a gas mask with them at all times, the "gas mask bag" became a designer item. Women decorated them to match their outfits, and the canister-style bags were copied by stylish women as far away as Argentina and Brazil, where the shape lost its sinister meaning and was associated simply with European chic. Perfume and lipsticks were marketed in containers shaped like tiny gas masks.

Unlike clothing, accessories were not rationed, but the materials to make them were often in short supply. A black market arose to accommodate, illegally, the desire for luxury goods.

Magazines

Fashion magazines gained in popularity during the war, though French *Vogue* was shut down when its editor refused to collaborate with the Nazi regime. In the short time before it was shut down, French *Vogue* offered features on such topics as what the well-dressed women were wearing in bomb shelters.

American *Vogue*'s subscriptions increased dramatically, and the magazine spelled out the new American style—confident, independent, sporty, and patriotic. American clothing was in every way democratic and was available at different price points and manufactured by unionized workers. *Vogue* showed American women engaged in sports and dressed stylishly by designers who took government restrictions as a challenge. Even socks instead of stockings could be seen as an advantage: "socks can contrive to look charming." Fashionable clothes were photographed in Blitzed London against backgrounds of destruction.

In 1943, American *Vogue* tendered advice to have a single article of clothes—coat or suit or even one hat—made to order or have ready-made clothes tailored to fit. Styles should be "square-shouldered, close fitting, below knee." Magazines offered sewing patterns for converting men's suits into women's.

The New Look Introduced

Before the war, Christian Dior's New Look was introduced, though it only became well established after the war. Christian Dior's New Look had an enormous swirling skirt, fitted top, and nipped waist creating a wasp silhouette. With the outbreak of war in 1939 and subsequent fabric rationing, this look was put on hold until 1947, when it was reintroduced. During the war, though, elements of the style were seen in the bigger shoulders and nipped waist. Skirts, of course, were necessarily skimpier than the New Look of 1947 but were still smart looking and feminine. This look had an essentially military feel, and reflected the all consuming mood of wartime.

Hardy Amies

British designer Hardy Amies, later to be the Royal Dressmaker, promoted a traditional, and distinctly not high-fashion, look to enthusiastic American audiences. His tailored suits and dresses were made from hard-wearing British fabrics and capitalized on the relative stability of the English upper-class or country look.

After the War

The end of the war ended the isolation of Paris but did not immediately restore couture's international status. Lucien Lelong—who, by collaborating with the Nazis, had kept the fashion industry in Paris going—organized a marketing effort to restore Paris couture to its prewar luster. Turning to a custom begun in the eighteenth century, Lelong sent dolls wearing miniature versions of fashions to customers far from buying centers. The 1946 "Theatre de la Mode" featured two hundred small, exquisitely made mannequins, their wigs coiffed by the leading hairdressers of Paris, their outfits miniature versions of the latest Paris fashions designed and made by the most eminent Paris couturiers, including Worth, Paquin, and Balenciaga. Each doll was placed in a setting created by a different artist—Christian Berard, Jean Cocteau, and notable others. The Theatre de la Mode traveled all over the world, transforming the state of Parisian couture back to full-size stardom. The show garnered rave reviews in New York and across the United States and set the stage for Dior's stunning New Look.

British women initially clung to the timelessness of their traditional, conservative styles, embodied by the wardrobe of Queen Elizabeth II. But the New Look seduced Britain (though not the queen).

In 1946, a purely American style burst onto the scene, its extreme skimpiness having nothing to do with rationing. The wallop caused by the revealing suit was compared to the explosive effects of American bomb testing on the pacific atoll of Bikini.

MEN'S CLOTHING

During the war and as men were demobilized and moved from their military uniforms to regular street clothes afterward, there was a certain continued sameness that prevailed. When not in uniform, many men continued to wear clothes they had bought before the war. In Britain, utility regulations extended to men's suits. Compared to prewar suits, utility ones were made of lower-quality fabric, often a mix of wool and cotton, used sparingly with purely decorative features omitted.

Male model wearing a single-breasted gray flannel suit and hat. Courtesy of the Library of Congress.

YOU ARE ENTITLED TO
1 SUIT   1 TIE
1 RAINCOAT 1 HAT
1 SHIRT   1 PAIR SHOES
2 COLLARS 2 PAIR SOCKS

YOU WILL SERVE
YOURSELF
CIVILIAN EXPERTS ARE
HERE TO ASSIST YOU

One of the first British RAF servicemen to be demobilized is measured for his civilian suit at a demobilization center in London, 1945. © AP Photo / Eddie Worth.

THE ZOOT SUIT

The zoot suit was colorful suit—in lime green or canary yellow, for example—and could have a bold printed fabric. The jacket was loose and had wide shoulders. The trousers were exaggerated and wide but had a narrowed cuffed ankle worn over two-tone, lace-up shoes. The shirt had a tight collar and a V-knot tie. The whole look was topped off with a flat hat and a strut of confidence that enhanced the look of the suit. The style filtered into mainstream men's fashion. The look was also picked up in Western Europe, Canada, and the Soviet Union. In Paris, where jazz was king, the suit was called the *zazou*.

Vests, trouser pleats and cuffs, shoulder-padding, double-breasted styles, and buttons on sleeves were all eliminated to save on materials. Only three colors—brown, navy, or gray—were available, making civilian dress not that different from uniforms. Like a prisoner let out of jail, each demobilized soldier entering civilian life at war's end was given a single suit by the government. These "Demob suits" (short for demobilization), cheap and mass produced, depressingly reflected the continuing utility restrictions.

By contrast, in an era of cheerful austerity, the voluminous *zoot suit* first seen before the war was an unpatriotic slap at the American nation. It consisted of an oversized drape jacket with exaggerated shoulders and high-waisted trousers full at the leg but tapering sharply. The suit and tie were all in bright flashy colors. The suit could not be separated from the swagger of its wearer. The "hip" zoot-suiter was defiant, often associated with criminality. Some zooters were involved in racketeering; others, just hanging out unsupervised on street corners, were accused of "juvenile delinquency"—a new addition to the American psyche and English vocabulary.

The zoot was possibly the only article of clothing to incite actual riots, when off-duty Anglo servicemen in Los Angeles violently attacked "unpatriotic" Hispanics, some of whom were promptly arrested. Zoot riots, defended as political protests but more accurately about race, spread from Los Angeles to Detroit to Harlem and even to Montreal, where the dominant English attacked minority Italians and French (the seeds of Quebec's French Separatist movement can be traced to such attacks).

Two men who in their youth fit the stereotype of criminal zoot-suiters are remembered today as defiant figures in American politics who had long since shed their zoot identities. Cesar Chavez, an outspoken and influential union activist in Los Angeles, spent some early time in jail for criminal acts unrelated to union organizing. Malcolm Little, a self-acknowledged pimp, rapist, and drug dealer known as "Detroit Red," learned about the Black Muslim movement while serving time for criminal activities. Little, who changed his name to Malcolm X, was influenced by zoot suit riots in Harlem, going on to lead the radically antiwhite Black Muslims in their struggle for black equality. The cut of the zoot suit moderated but nevertheless influenced men's suits in the 1950s and beyond.

CHILDREN'S CLOTHING

British and American children, like their parents, experienced strict wartime limits on new clothing and shoes. Restrictions of materials outlawed even the most ordinary details of children's clothing; pocket flaps, trouser cuffs, and pleated skirts were not allowed. Even the number of buttons was regulated.

Rationing posed particular hardships for children who outgrew their clothing before it was possible for families to purchase replacements. An American newspaper reported that the usual thirty-coupon allowance for British boys restricted them to one suit, one pair of shoes, one shirt, and one pair of socks per year, although extra-large or tall children received a few extra coupons. Not surprisingly, swapping outgrown clothing replaced sales of new items. By 1943, more than five hundred Children's Clothing Exchanges had been established in Britain, many of these in schools. The exchanges operated on a barter system, with donated used clothing awarded points to be applied to the "purchase" of replacements.

In addition, the "Make Do and Mend" scheme was applied with ingenuity to the problem of outfitting growing children. In 1942, a special "Make Do and Mend" fashion exhibition offered examples of imaginative recycling: corduroy riding breeches reappeared as a boy's lumber jacket; a woman's white tennis costume was cut down to make a suit for a toddler. Old silk stockings were worked into such useful items as slippers and hats, while old felt hats were resurrected as handbags. Seamstresses used flour bags and even architects' linen tracing squares to make handkerchiefs; girls wore overalls made from their mother's slacks or a dungaree suit fashioned from a discarded blazer.

At the sound of an air raid siren, residents of London had to dash to shelters. Some spent nights in chilly London Underground (subway) stations that acted as bomb shelters. Many children went to bed in hooded "siren suits." Much like snowsuits, these one-piece washable outfits kept them warm in the cold night air. Adaptations of the siren suit, some very stylish, were worn by adults. Similar one-piece outfits are still popular for babies.

From the mid-1940s on, British boys' and girls' clothing was either home-sewn or bought through catalogs. They both wore pants with suspenders or elastic waists. Young girls subscribed to *Calling All Girls* (later renamed *YM*), and boys to its brother publication, *Calling All Boys*. First published in 1944, *Seventeen* magazine captured a teenage audience eager for advice on fashions and teen life. In the same year, singer Frank Sinatra's appearance at the

Paramount Theater in New York attracted 25,000 fans, the girls in sweaters and bobby socks, boys in zoot suits. (Not all Sinatra fans were teens. Designer Adele Simpson brought out an $85 "swoon suit" for women, its cutaway jacket styled like Sinatra's.)

While rationing continued in England, American teens in 1946 dressed in bright colors for exercise or "loafing" and changed into well-pressed conservative clothes for going out. Too old to be cute, too young to be taken seriously by adults, teens preferred the company of their peers. Conformity was the order of the day. Mothers worried that their youngsters would risk scorn by dressing differently from their classmates; some waited to outfit their daughters until school had started, so the popular styles could be ascertained and followed. The concept of the "inferiority complex" entered the vocabulary of parenting and, postrationing, weight became a concern. The New Look's constricted waist also filtered down to the young girls.

WEST AND EAST

India

Before 1945, Indian women dressed in *saris*, the beautiful and colorful classic long dresses. These garments, however, were not a common sight on the streets of New York or Washington, so when Indian women, usually part of diplomatic contingents, began to appear in the garments after the war, they were a source of fascination to Americans. The sari's graceful and flattering lines were also comfortable, and appropriate for any occasion. In the West though, where style was a matter of trying to stay up-to-date, even a successful garment such as this was part of the fashion cycle and as attractive as it was, it would go out of style.

Japan

In Japan, as in France and the United States, war propaganda was the subject for textile designs, particularly striking in its use for women's and children's clothing. The design for one Japanese kimono made in the 1930s or 1940s and meant for a baby boy bore a design incorporating battleships, submarines, destroyers, and other objects of mass destruction. A woman's kimono was printed with a design of Nazi and Japanese flags.

At the government's direction, Japanese women remade worn-out kimonos into loose workpants called *monpe*. After the war, women wore the "American Style," a long skirt that widened from a small waist, pulled together with a wide belt. Fashion changes from Paris were channeled to Japan by way of the United States. A year after American women adopted Dior's New Look, the "American style" in Japan was essentially Parisian.

China

In postwar Taiwan, new fashion magazines made it easy for women to see and copy what the women of the West were wearing. Professional tailors and home sewers alike learned how to make the desirable new styles. Women wore a mix of Japanese, Western, and updated traditional clothing.

Japanese-style school uniforms and ordinary dress were popular for young men in China during the period of Japanese rule, from 1937 to 1945. After that, many Chinese women returned to traditional Chinese styles, including the *cheongsam*, the long fitted-to-the-body dress with side slit and mandarin collar.

Korea

Korea restricted wartime consumption clothing. The "simple dress" resembled the utility garment, and even hair was stripped of glamour when permanent waves were outlawed. Women wore the Japanese-style loose work pants called *monpe*. Prewar Western-style clothing gave way to stringent military-style cuts for civilian clothing. Even after Koreans gained their freedom from Japanese rule, Korean women lacked the resources to make or buy Western-style clothing. Unlike Britain, where rationing was imposed by the government until 1952, Korea retained no official restrictions, but the simple dress and military blouses persisted, eventually to be replaced by Western dress.

FURTHER READING

Alford, Holly. "The Zoot Suit: Its History and Influence." *Fashion Theory* 8, no. 2 (June 2004): 224–36.

Baker, Patricia. *Fashions of a Decade: The 1940s*. New York: Facts on File, 2006.

De la Haye, Amy, and Cathie Dingwall. *Surfers Soulies Skinheads and Skaters: Subcultural Style from the Forties to the Nineties*. Woodstock, NY: Overlook Press, 1996.

De Marly, Diana. *Christian Dior*. New York: Holmes & Meier, 1990.

Goodnow, Cecelia. "MOHAI Fashion Exhibit Offers Glimpse into the History of Postwar Paris." *Seattle Post-Intelligencer*, March 13, 2006.

Steele, Valerie. *Fifty Years of Fashion: New Look to Now*. New Haven, CT: Yale University Press, 1997.

Veillon, Dominique. *Fashion under the Occupation*. Trans. Miriam Kochan. Oxford, UK: Berg, 2002.

MOVIES

Aviator (2004)
The Big Sleep (1946)
Double Indemnity (1944)
Gilda (1946)
Guys and Dolls (1955)
Mildred Pierce (1945)
The Philadelphia Story (1940)

The Fifties

Ellen Hymowitz

TIMELINE

1950	Acrylic fibers introduced
1950–1953	Korean War
1952	Elizabeth II becomes queen of England
1953	Polyester fibers become widely available for clothing
1954	French withdraw from Indochina
1955	Frank Lloyd Wright designs the Guggenheim Museum in New York
1956	Suez Canal built
1957	European Common Market established; Russia launches the first satellite (*Sputnik*) into space
1958	National Aeronautics and Space Administration (NASA) established in the United States
1959	Cuban revolution

HISTORY

The postwar period was a feral cat waiting to pounce and the cat was the 1960s. Around the world, World War II had ended, but the threat posed by communism in Eastern Europe and China kept the West on the alert. As much as could be set in order—the reparation of the economic and physical ravages of war, reassertions of traditional gender divisions—the disorder of the 1960s was a murmur in the background; the first of the American troops to serve in Vietnam died in 1959.

"Mod" and hipster styles associated with the sixties had their start in the fifties. Designer Mary Quant, who would later be hailed as the inventor of the miniskirt, opened her first shop—Bazaar in London in 1955. There she sold inexpensive clothing in young, but still below-the-knee, styles. Around the same time, Quant teamed up with hairdresser Vidal Sassoon, who was beginning to refine his "wash and wear" cuts.

Even without the firm directives imposed by rationing, individuals in the 1950s tended to look outside themselves for instruction on how to dress. In the United States, even the apparently rebellious, leather-jacketed bikers inspired by the actor Marlon Brando had their own hierarchy of leadership, of alpha males and followers, who willingly kept themselves in their place. Revived after the war, the Paris couture industry reasserted its dominant influence on women's dress. Christian Dior's New Look, introduced in 1947, persisted into the decade. An American postwar plunge into conformity—the "gray flannel suit" of the businessman, the "preppy" look for young men and women—was subverted by a burgeoning underground of beats and beatniks, bikers and hipsters.

The 1957 movie *Funny Face* traced an arc of a French fashion world that made a god of a couturier, in this case, Givenchy, and a con man of a black-clad, philosophizing "beat." The only truly independent thinker in the film is a fashion editor, based on Diana Vreeland or Carmel Snow, the real-life editors of *Vogue* and *Harper's Bazaar*. In the movie, the magazine staff is commanded to "Think pink!" As obedient young women scramble to fill glossy pages with pink clothes, the editor declares of the color pink that she "wouldn't be caught dead in it."

The growing affordability of televisions meant that TV programming helped create and reinforce hierarchies of gender, ethnicity, income, and age. The name of one series summed up the ideal: *Father Knows Best*—affluent white family, spacious and well-furnished home, housewife mother, slightly (but only slightly) rebellious son, wholesome and cheerful teenage daughter, and adorable little sister.

The teenager was an ever more visible phenomenon in the 1950s, edging toward a rift from adult society that would upend the world in the 1960s. In Britain, the "Teddy Boys" picked up where the 1940s zoot-suiters had left off. Teddies wore dandified suits whose style extended to women's clothes.

And Elvis Presley was on nearly everybody's mind. From the moment of his first hit in 1954—"That's All Right"—to his 1958 draft into the Army, Elvis was the stuff of teenage ecstasy and parental fear. His honeyed voice and suggestive body moves spoke of an overt sexuality at a time when sweetness and repression were expected of young girls. With Elvis on their side, the young were a force to be reckoned with. By the end of the next decade, youth itself would be idolized like Elvis.

WOMEN'S CLOTHING

With great emphasis on conformity and newfound postwar affluence, women wanted to look "right" and had the means to do so. Fashion magazines once again dictated exactly what style of dress should be worn for dinners out—which was a different style from cocktail wear. Outfits for cocktail parties that started at different hours might demand subtly different clothes. Evenings at the theater required yet another change of clothes. Afternoon outfits were to be accessorized with matching handbags and shoes, and hats and gloves, and it would be embarrassing indeed to be seen wearing day shoes with evening dress.

Accessories could make or break an outfit; the worth of even an expensive dress could be sacrificed with the wrong choice of costume jewelry or hat. It was up to each woman to internalize a uniform; no army was outfitting her, so every fashion decision was fraught with anxiety. Fabrics considered right for evening clothes were unacceptable for day. The smallest details had to be minded. A married woman's trousseau could provide a foundation of a wardrobe. Not just heirloom table linens or fine silver, the trousseau included new clothes provided by the bride's parents, as had been the tradition for centuries. The burden of paying for future clothes would then be handed over with the bride when she married. To economize, the color range of fashions could be limited, with accessories changing the look of each outfit—a leftover from war rationing.

Women were expected to feel, if not tightly girdled, then "constrained" in their clothes, even when doing housework—and the amount of housework increased when women gave up war work to concentrate on perfecting domestic life. The 1950s saw the rise of the suburb, an impressive lowering of the average age for marriage, and a dramatic boost in the number of children considered desirable to make a normal (heterosexual) two-parent family.

Cars played an increasingly important role in daily life. The constant redesign of car profiles and colors has been likened to the market-driven changes in fashion, and car advertisements often featured stylish women dressed in outfits that coordinated with the latest in car designs. The three-quarter-length car coat emerged to foster comfort while driving, though the first of these coats was not short enough to accomplish ease. Suburban women were expected to look feminine and to dress with their husbands in mind, even with a houseful of young charges. Most women shopped in department stores or in local shops; a very small percentage traveled to Paris for couture clothes of flabbergasting expense. Outfits were as expensive as cars. The innumerable fittings that were—and remain—an essential step in the couture process meant a substantial investment of time, further moving such purchases out of the reach of the average woman.

There were, however, other mechanisms in place to make high-end Paris designs available to a wide range of shoppers. In her examination of the commerce of 1950s transatlantic fashion, historian Alexandra Palmer (2001) spells out the hierarchy of couture. At the highest level, copies of haute couture garments were available in selected American and Canadian stores. These "exact copies" were available in the same fabrics as the original, although at substantially lower prices. Next best, "line-for-line" or "reproduction" copies followed originals closely in design, but the fabric might not be of the same quality, and machinework would be used in place of time-consuming handwork that required skilled workers. In addition, couture originals could be purchased secondhand. Socialites who required a constant stream of new gowns for charity galas might sell and buy gowns through resale outlets. By the end of the fifties, couture designers had branched out into their own second- or third-tier markets, establishing "prêt-à-porter" lines—ready-to-wear versions of their high-end designs. In 1953, designer Elsa Schiaparelli signed on with eleven American manufacturers to control and profit from the mass-produced reproduction of her designs.

Back in Paris after World War II, Schiaparelli still had war in mind when she brought out her winter 1950–51 collection (less than a week after the start of a new conflict in Korea). She punningly named the collection "The Front Line"—referring both to battle and to the nearly two-dimensional construction of the clothes, their strikingly linear, anti-anatomical shape. For one suit, she added a large wooden stay to the front of the girdle to further flatten the wearer's stomach. The strict narrow line of the suit was accentuated by a stiff peplum that flared out from the bottom of the jacket. The diagonal closure of the jacket was echoed by high heels with wide diagonal straps forming a tight ellipse around the ankle.

In her winter 1951–52 collection, Schiaparelli used a silhouette she called SHAPE—for "Supreme Headquarters Allied Powers Europe." At the same time, she began her first ready-to-wear lingerie line. Branching out still further, she produced a line of eyeglass frames, including one pair based on the outline of a Vespa motor scooter. In the tradition of the late-1940s couture marketing scheme of the "Theatre à la Mode," Schiaparelli licensed dolls to be outfitted in her designs and sold in the United States. These spectacularly well-dressed dolls anticipated by eight years the introduction of the American doll Barbie, who arrived with her own wardrobe of collectible fashions.

Promotional shot of Audrey Hepburn, taken sometime in the fifties. Courtesy of Photofest.

Of course, there's cloth and then there's cloth: In fall 1953, Schiaparelli produced a formal unfitted coat made of "angel hair"—a shaggy, fur-like material made from rayon threads. The color of the angel-hair coat graduated from white to bright pink.

In 1954, just as Schiaparelli was bowing out from the business of fashion, her archrival, Gabrielle Chanel, reentered the world of Paris couture with her first collection in fifteen years. In that time sales of her signature perfume, Chanel No. 5, had flourished, although it had lately faltered enough to compel the designer to revive market interest in her name. Chanel's return collection was widely condemned by the press but was later even more widely embraced by critics and consumers. Chanel's classic suit look offered a welcome alternative to the extremes of the Dior New Look and its descendents. In its mix of casualness and formality, the suit fit the American desire for simple, if still costly, clothes. Chanel's "2.55" leather bag, famously quilted and hanging from a flattened chain interwoven with leather strips, was named for the date of its introduction. The designer weighted the hems of her suit jackets with metal chains and now brought what had been hidden and private into public view. The move could be considered the equivalent of placing a designer's label on the exterior of clothes.

The Ideal Beauty

Not surprisingly, there was more than one "ideal woman" in the 1950s and more than one ideal figure. Audrey Hepburn, ballet-dancer slender, with her swan neck and hybrid Euro-British accent, was one side of the coin; on the reverse was the iconic Marilyn Monroe. Voluptuous, artificially blond, artificially dumb, Monroe tantalized the ordinary man, a psychological transaction used to comic ends in the Billy Wilder film *The Seven Year Itch*: With wife and child ensconced in a second, summer home, the perfectly domesticated Tom Ewell encounters a new summer neighbor—the disingenuous Monroe—who just about knocks his socks off. Monroe as an actress was not a pinup, not a fashion plate.

Actress Grace Kelly, a former model who later married into royalty, had an icy, "upper-class" demeanor and looked

Marilyn Monroe stars in Billy Wilder's 1955 film, *The Seven Year Itch*. Courtesy of Photofest.

adult without crossing the line into the near self-parody of Monroe. In 1956, the top-flight leather company Hermès paid tribute to the actress—and princess—by naming what had been an anonymous 1930s handbag "the Kelly bag."

Silhouette

The 1950s silhouette relaxed into shapelessness, going from the exaggerated cinched waist and full skirt of Dior's New Look to Balenciaga's midfifties chemise. The look was still somewhat structured but was inspired by the drop-waist twenties silhoutte. The dress skimmed the body and avoided emphasis of the waistline, making it quite different from the dramatic silhouette of Dior. The Trapeze dress that followed foreshadowed the later 1960s A-line dress and swung straight out from the shoulders straight down and slightly flared.

The Marimekko line of clothing from Finland, first introduced in the United States in 1951, took off when it was worn by Jacqueline Kennedy in 1960. Marimekko clothes deemphasized the shape of the body, and their bright patterns of oversized flowers in cotton fabric made the clothes almost suitable for children (and in fact girls' versions were available, too). The late 1950s Empire cut—its waist elevated to just under the bustline—was another in the steps toward 1960s freedom.

U.S. President-elect John F. Kennedy and his wife, Jacqueline Kennedy, leave their Georgetown home for the inauguration day ceremonies in Washington, D.C., 1961. © AP Photo.

Footwear

There were many styles of shoes in this period, and the variety became more diverse as the decade closed. Shoes could be ultrafeminine. Replacing the clomping great shoes worn during the war, styles became less utilitarian and included stiletto heels and pointy toes. Audrey Hepburn looked the part of a stylish casual dresser when she appeared in ballerina flats and simple ankle-length black trousers. Saddle shoes (white tie-up shoes with black insteps) were also worn by the younger women with their full skirts and ankle socks.

Hairstyles, Hats, and Cosmetics

Women carefully matched their shoes and purses to the outfits they wore and wore gloves when they left the house. The hair was short and curly or straight, in a wash-and-wear look. Hats were either broad-brimmed and shaded the sun or were decorative. Wide-brimmed hats were wrapped with fabric that was also meant to match the outfit the woman wore. Smaller-brimmed hats were taller and straighter in the vertical. Women wore heavy eye makeup, especially mascara and black liner, and plucked their eyebrows. Lipstick was essential when leaving the house and meant a woman had a pulled-together, ultrafeminine look.

CANADIAN FASHION

While not rejecting all that Paris and America had to offer in the way of fashion, Canadian women were drawn to timeless British styles, like the wool suits made by Queen Elizabeth's dressmaker, Hardy Amies. Expensive but comfortable, unyielding to the whims of fashion, his clothes were appropriate in terms of style and also weather.

MEN'S CLOTHING

Mainstream American clothing for men in the 1950s was conservative and conformist, unofficial uniforms demanded by corporate jobs. Gregory Peck starred in *The Man in the Gray Flannel Suit*, a movie that came to define the faceless businessmen who made up the affluent postwar workforce. With the introduction of a wider range of synthetics, suits were lighter in weight but still virtually unchanged in design. One factor in the sameness of men's (and women's) fashions was economic. Manufacturers gained by increasing the mass production of a single style, able to purchase materials in larger quantities and not have to remake patterns. Late in the decade, the influence of Italy was seen in a narrowed and more overtly sexual suit. Off-hours, men had different choices for casual dress, and options for menswear increasingly merged with those of teenage boys as the decade progressed. Jeans, identified with certain underground or aggressive looks, became more commonplace. A revival of a Depression-era staple, jeans shed their association with heavy labor and extremely limited resources. Denim pants and jackets were part of the "Rockabilly" look.

Paving the way for future British menswear designers such as Paul Smith thirty years later, designer Pierre Cardin began supplying men's clothes in the 1950s. His name became synonymous with men's exclusive design. He supplied collarless jackets such as those worn by the Beatles in their early years, and other pop stars adopted the new, less conservative or boring styles that men had been tied to since before World War I. In 1953, Elsa Schiaparelli also licensed menswear designs and became part of the men's designer clothing segment.

While many young men dressed conservatively, others wore clothes that identified them as outside the mainstream. Popular music and musicians were strong influences. In the early fifties, the bebop "cool cats" wore clothes tied to a kind of music and looked like slightly deflated zootsuiters. Their jazzy, double-breasted suits were cut large, and accessories, including suspenders and a soft satin tie, played a major role in defining the image.

Men who wanted to show off or just look as if they had a privileged, collegiate (or prep school) background wore casual clothes that were as formulaic as business suits. "Preppies" kept their hair clean and short and wore blazers, pants with no extra fullness and narrow cuffs, and—most iconically—cotton shirts with button-down collars through which a necktie was threaded.

> **FASHIONS FROM OUTER SPACE**
>
> In 1957, *Sputnik* and space exploration reverberated in the futuristic styles of clothing designed by Pierre Cardin and Courrèges, who used cutting-edge synthetic fibers to further the space-age look of their designs.

Gregory Peck stars in Nunnally Johnson's 1956 film, *The Man in the Gray Flannel Suit*. Courtesy of Photofest.

SNEAKERS

While sneakers had been invented at the turn of the twentieth century, they were at first used only for athletic purposes. In the 1950s, they were adopted to wear as fashion footwear. For example, Andy Warhol wore them with his regular clothing. Teens also adopted the Converse All Stars high-top basketball shoe and wore it with rolled up jeans and T-shirts.

The "Beats" were hipsters of an intellectual bent. Their clothes combined leather jackets with cotton T-shirts and cotton work pants. Jack Kerouac, author of *On the Road*, and Allen Ginsberg, poet and author of the long poem *Howl*, were Beats associated with the scene in San Francisco. "Beatniks"—their name suggesting a miniaturized, more playful Beat— wore lots of black. Their female equivalents wore dance clothes such as leotards and ballet shoes.

CHILDREN'S CLOTHING

Young boys and girls in the fifties enjoyed dressing like horse wranglers in a western rodeo. In 1952, Simplicity offered a pattern for "frontier shirts" for children, illustrated with cowboy hats for both sexes. Complete western outfits for boys included a fringed jacket, cowboy boots, a holster, and a (toy) gun. Girls were similarly armed with holster and gun but wore a fringed vest and skirt. The 1955 movie *Davy Crockett* set off a craze among little boys for fake fur "Davy Crockett" coonskin hats, distinguished by the bushy fur tail hanging from the back. When not in rodeo dress, little girls wore dresses with fuller skirts (the New Look filtering down) that stopped at or above the knee. The princess-style coat had a fitted waist. In 1958, classic middie blouses were shown with very full skirts, and the next year, the "baby doll" shortie pajama appeared for girls. Cowgirl, doll, or princess—the choice of roles was vast.

The image of the "bobby sox"–clad teenage girl is indelibly linked to the decade of the 1950s, although not every girl, even among Americans, wanted to be a bobby-soxer. Fads like poodle skirts and saddle shoes were fun and identified girls as belonging to a group. For evenings out, teenage girls wanted to look adult and continued to dress like their mothers. Teen boys could sport a preppie look, with buttoned-down shirts. These were only two of the great mix of group identities available to teens. Some were clean cut and suggested chastity for girls and moderation for boys. Within other styles lurked the dark possibilities of promiscuity and lawlessness.

Whether or not the impression was accurate, certain clothing styles suggested juvenile delinquency. The dandified "teddy boy" look assumed to be worn by working-class British teens held the same dishonorable place in the public eye previously reserved for the zoot suit. They borrowed from the Edwardian look of the turn of the century, which included the longer coat trimmed with velvet collar, short lapels, and cuffed sleeves. Underneath the jacket, they wore waistcoats (vests) in the same fabrics as the jacket and trousers. The pants were short and narrow and showed off the broad brogue-style or eventually narrower pointy leather shoes and colored socks. Two of the trademark features of the whole ensemble were the narrow black ribbon tie and distinct duck-tailed hairstyle.

KOREA

With the outbreak of the Korean War in 1950, women's fashion went through another period of stagnation. However, even during the war, foreign clothing and textiles that made its way into the country by way of the black market were highly sought, with velvet, which had been introduced earlier, becoming very fashionable. Nylon debuted during this time and became especially popular in the postwar years. It was considered a symbol of sophistication and was used even for underwear and socks. Because nylon was not locally manufactured at the time, it was viewed as a luxury item. During the war, flared skirts and suits of nylon were also thought stylish.

In 1956, Korea's first fashion show was staged by designer Norano. Reactions to Norano's show were mostly "strange" and "curious." Nonetheless, with this show, the designer emerged as the forerunner of modern Korean fashion, while shows by Seo Su-jeong and Choi Gyeong-ja (currently chairperson of the International Fashion Institute) soon followed, generating much enthusiasm among the fashion industry. At that time, there was only one woman's magazine in Korea, *Yeoseonggye* (*Women's World*). And with its inclusion of a section called "Yeowon" ("Women's Garden"), the fashion spread was introduced to Korean magazines, giving a huge boost to the promotion of fashion for women.

The modified *hanbok* was still widely worn, but new trends were also introduced and gained popularity, including flare skirts influenced by Dior's New Look style, the H-line skirt, the A-line skirt, the sack dress, and the Empire-line dress. Tight-fitting one-piece dresses also debuted, but dresses with wide flare or ample gathering were favored for everyday wear. Skirts were generally long and mostly pleated, gathered, or flared, but after the mid-1950s, the tight skirt suit became commonly worn in various styles. In the late fifties, the slim style came into vogue, replacing previous styles with a slim or tight skirt. Later, with the introduction of the spindle line, French-sleeve blouses were worn in spring and fall with sweaters or vests.

Military-style suits with square padding remained popular until the mid-1950s, when, with the gradual emergence of the French-sleeve style, suits took on a feminine look, showing an accentuated waistline and a rather high hemline. One of the most popular items at this time was the coat. Overcoats were worn even with a hanbok, and to prevent wrinkles on the bow-silhouette hanbok sleeves, the sleeves of the coat were tailored in a similar style. Flare- and box-style coats were preferred, with collars being shawl, tailored, and wing. Mambo pants became chic with the popularity of the mambo dance, while such fashion items as sandals, stiletto heels, handbags, and gloves were also trendy.

FURTHER READING

Ewen, Stuart. "Form Follows Value." In *All Consuming Images: The Politics of Style in Contemporary Culture*, 177–89. New York: Basic Books, 1988.

Goldstein, Lauren. "What We Wore: The Best and Worst of 100 Years of Business." *Fortune* 140, no. 10 (November 22, 1999): 156–58.

Guinn, Muriel. "'Cats' in Fairfax Split over Blue-Jean Ban." *Washington Post*, August 26, 1957.

Joo Seong-hee. "An Overview of Modern Fashion in Korea." *Koreana* 15, no. 1 (Spring 2001): 4–9.

Palmer, Alexandra. *Couture and Commerce: The Transatlantic Fashion Trade in the 1950s.* Vancouver, BC: UBC Press in association with the Royal Ontario Museum, 2001.

Wilson, Elizabeth. "Deviant Dress." *Feminist Review*, no. 35 (Summer 1990): 67–74.

MOVIES

À bout de souffle (*Breathless*; 1959)
And God Created Woman (1957)
Funny Face (1957)
Grease (1978)
How to Marry a Millionaire (1953)
Man in the Gray Flannel Suit (1956)
My Favorite Year (1954)
North by Northwest (1959)
Pillow Talk (1959)
A Place in the Sun (1951)
Pleasantville (1998)
Rebel without a Cause (1955)
Sabrina (1954)
The Seven Year Itch (1955)
A Streetcar Named Desire (1951)
To Catch a Thief (1955)
West Side Story (1961)
The Wild One (1954)

The Sixties

Sara M. Harvey

TIMELINE

1960	The Pill is approved in the United States; John F. Kennedy elected president
1961	Bay of Pigs invasion in Cuba; Berlin Wall erected
1962	Cuban missile crisis
1963	Washington civil rights rally; Kennedy assassinated
1964–1975	Vietnam War
1966–1979	China's Cultural Revolution
1967	Six-Day War in the Middle East
1968	Martin Luther King Jr. assassinated
1969	Woodstock music festival

The 1960s was a decade of great change in all facets of life—from advancements in technology brought about by the "Space Race" to social ramifications from the assassinations of three of the decade's most prominent political figures to sweeping changes in music, film, and television. From the artistic influences of Andy Warhol to the trend-making music of the Beatles, these attention-grabbing personalities began to shape the world around them far beyond the scope of their media. The antiwar and civil rights movements became the focal points for the youth of this decade. For the first time, the counterculture movements in the United States and in Europe, England specifically, became an integral part of the overall flavor of the decade and began to have a large influence of change that still reverberates in the current sociopolitical climate.

Advances in textiles and dyestuffs opened fashion to varieties of colors and textures never before available. The civil rights and feminist movements also affected what people were wearing and how they wore it. Ethnic influences and women in pants threw fashion for a loop as diversity became the norm.

The world also experienced a new sense of internationalism as world events brought focus to countries such as England, France, the Soviet Union, and Vietnam. Profound changes in the very fabric of social structure came to the fore in this decade as well. The approval of the birth control pill changed women's lives when it came to family planning and began the sexual revolution. African Americans sought the equality that had been denied them for a century since the end of slavery. Starting in small ways with individuals, the civil rights movement was soon a major point of debate across the United States and throughout all levels of government, from local to federal.

Art and music experienced a renaissance. Experimental, esoteric, and aesthetic art and music became the voices of a generation that sought to challenge authority and shake up the status quo. This generation became the foundation of the youth movements that sought power and influence to make the world a different place than it was, to bring about change that they thought would make the world better. And for the first time, fashion began to experience change "from the streets," where these counterculture youth groups became the driving force behind trends all across the world.

Never before had both fashion and history experienced such a surge in globalization and fast-paced change. Events in the 1960s brought the attention of the world to places like Cuba and Vietnam, countries unknown to most of the population. And for the first time, people were able to see the surface of the moon. Fashion was inspired by London, San Francisco, Africa, and space. Like the branches of a tree, trends split off from a central silhouette into myriad variations. From the 1960s on, there would no longer be a single overarching silhouette that would define fashion. The age of the individual had arrived.

HISTORICAL CONTEXT

The 1960s opened with a series of far-reaching events. In 1960, the federal Food and Drug Administration (FDA) approved the birth control pill, which was most commonly referred to simply as "the Pill." This advancement in science would be a major component in the budding women's movement. This was also the year that John F. Kennedy was elected president of the United States.

Kennedy declared that the United States would put a man on the moon by 1970. Although the White House had announced plans to launch an orbiter in 1955, the Soviets had gotten there first. The Russians had launched the first satellite into orbit, *Sputnik I*, in October 1957 and touched off the Space Race between the United States and the Soviet Union. Americans were "shocked by the gap in technology between the United States and Russia that this feat represented."[1] Throughout the decade, the National Aeronautics and Space Administration (NASA) was a major focus of government funding and media attention. In 1961, both the Soviet Union and the United States were successful in implementing manned space travel; Russian Yuri Gagarin and American Alan Shepard made it into space in April 1961. John Glenn was the first American to orbit the Earth, doing so three times in 1962. The United States was victorious in the Space Race, however, landing *Apollo 11* on the moon in 1969.

These early years of the decade were not entirely rosy, however. Communism was a major concern to the West, especially the United States. In the rocky post–World War II landscape of Europe, Germany was literally torn by allegiances to democracy and communism. The London Protocol of 1944 had laid the groundwork for the division of Germany. East Germany fell under the control of the Soviet Union and West Germany remained under the protection of the other victorious Allies: Great Britain, France, and the United States. Between August 1961 and August 1962, despite the promises of the East German government, Walter Ulbricht, the head of state and the leader of the East German Communist Party, erected a fortified wall through the heart of the city of Berlin. This Berlin Wall became a larger-than-life and lasting symbol of the division between communism and the West. It was also a focal point of political maneuvering between the United States and the Soviet Union. The already-tenuous balance became even more strained in 1962 when an East Berliner, one of many who desperately risked the border crossing, was shot and died for lack of medical attention in the no-man's-land near the wall, making international headlines.

The Berlin Wall was only one facet of the escalating Cold War between the United States and the Soviet Union. The 1961 Bay of Pigs invasion of communist Cuba by Cuban exiles covertly sponsored by the United States was another thread in this tapestry. Originally conceived under President Dwight D. Eisenhower, the Central Intelligence Agency (CIA) trained the exiles and outfitted them with weapons for the invasion, which came early in Kennedy's presidency, in an effort to overthrow communist dictator Fidel Castro. This action prompted Castro to form closer ties with the Soviet Union.

The next year, Soviet premier Nikita Khrushchev and Castro agreed to place nuclear missiles in Cuba to protect the island from an anticipated U.S. invasion. The CIA learned of the Soviet plans and Kennedy warned Khrushchev not to send the missiles to Cuba and enacted a naval blockade of the island. Finally, after receiving private assurances that the United States would not attack Cuba, Russia backed off and removed the missiles. Known as the "Cuban Missile Crisis" in the United States, it was referred to as the "Caribbean Crisis" in Russia and the "October Crisis" in Cuba. The crisis lasted twelve days and was the closest the United States and the USSR came to the brink of a nuclear war.

A year later, Kennedy was shockingly assassinated in Dallas in November 1963. This was viewed as a major turning point in the history of the United States, as it proved to be very traumatic to the country as a whole, symbolizing a loss of hope and innocence, a theme that would reverberate throughout the decade.

The Vietnam War, another clash between communist and Western forces, also underscored the decade with conflict. Beginning in 1959, it was a constant issue throughout the 1960s and into the 1970s. Although Kennedy had promised aid to the government of South Vietnam to quell the spread the communist Viet Cong, the United States did not become highly involved in the war until 1965 under President Lyndon B. Johnson. The war was a brutal engagement and came at a high cost. By the official end of the war in 1975, more than 50,000 Americans had died or were listed as missing in action, and hundreds of thousands of the United States' allies had also been killed. Opposition to the war not only helped to change the political course of the engagement in Vietnam but also fostered worldwide fashion revolutions and spawned the counterculture that still lingers on through the new millennium.

Elsewhere in Asia, some economies were booming, especially in Japan. Political freedom and economic freedoms were intertwined in Japan as the postwar era brought industrial expansion. Because they were new, many of these Japanese plants were more modern and state-of-the-art than those in America and

Europe. Japan set the model for economic and industrial growth throughout Asia. Japan, South Korea, Hong Kong, Singapore, and Taiwan soon became known as technology centers creating items such as tape recorders, radios, binoculars, computers, televisions, and automobiles. Led by Japan, Asian superpowers took advantage of weak trade unions, low wages, high savings rates, and a culture that prized education and lifetime employment. With investments in emergent technologies and efficient production, Japan emerged as a major economic power in the 1960s.

Other places in the world struggled during this time of abundance in some countries. Europe was letting go of its colonies in Africa. The decolonization of Africa, reversing political controls that in some places had been in place since the seventeenth century, began in 1957. The Gold Coast was the first African colony granted independence from the British Empire and was renamed Ghana. By the middle of the 1960s, Belgium and France had joined England in releasing most of their colonies. Algeria was the last of the European-held African colonies to be freed. The French government, supported by French citizens living in Algeria, opposed the independence. But war forced the issue in 1962. Although granted freedom, famine, war, and coups have plagued Algeria and other former colonies through the decades and into the twenty-first century.

Europe was ready to rebound from any loss of economic stability without their African colonies. Begun in 1958, the European Common Market was a loose economic collective consisting of Belgium, France, Italy, Luxembourg, the Netherlands, and West Germany. By 1967, the member nations also included Great Britain and had changed their name to the European Economic Community (EEC) and forged a more solid union. They pooled their collective resources into a single market, abolished tariffs between themselves, and set up a standard set of tariffs on goods imported from other, nonmember countries.

Outside of the EEC, the Communist Party of the Soviet Union still held tight control over most of Eastern Europe. The Czechoslovak Communist Party tried to gain popularity by granting greater freedoms of the press and of speech. In 1968, the Soviet Union sent in troops to solidify control of Czechoslovakia back into their hands, putting a stop to all attempts at establishing a moderate government in communist-controlled Eastern Europe.

Human rights and social justice, or the lack thereof, were highly charged subjects in the 1960s. In the United States, discussions were focused on women's rights, "hippies" and antiwar protests, and the civil rights movement.

Starting with the availability of the Pill in 1960, women began to expect and demand a different role in American society. They shrugged off the "traditional values" that had been in place for generations and embraced a new age of not only sexual freedom but also more power in family planning as well. In the 1963 book *The Feminine Mystique*, Betty Friedan addressed the frustration of the modern woman, challenging college-educated women to rethink their place in society. "To Friedan, the middle-class home was a 'comfortable concentration camp' for women."[2] In 1966, the National Organization for Women (NOW) was founded to help establish equal rights for women, including equal opportunities, equal pay for equal work, and an end to discrimination based on gender.

It is difficult to think about the decade of the 1960s and not think of the hippies. This youth movement was an expression of opposition to the values of adult society known as the "Silent Generation." Students banded together to protest the Vietnam War and other social injustices. They burned their draft cards and staged demonstrations blocking the entries to military installations and draft centers. Colleges became the staging grounds for many of these youth activities.

The movement was attractive to Caucasian, middle-class, college-age students who were responding to, among others, Timothy Leary, a psychologist, writer, and proponent of psychedelic drug research. Leary coined the catchy phrase that defined the entire LSD movement: "Turn on to the scene; tune into what's happening; drop out of high school, college, grad school."[3] This saying was more commonly shortened to "Turn on, tune in, drop out." The hippie movement began about 1966, shortly after the United States entered into the Vietnam conflict. The Haight-Ashbury district of San Francisco was the birthplace of the movement, and it soon blossomed across the entire United States. Known as a drug-using counterculture, the hippies described themselves as embracing love and freedom from "the Establishment," the strictures of the older generation perceived to be too restraining. By 1967, the hippie movement had gained many followers from coast to coast. That spring, in both New York City and Philadelphia, thousands of young people assembled in public parks to celebrate love and to honor the notion that every person has a right to exist. This movement culminated in the greatest hippie event of the decade, the Woodstock Music and Art Fair in 1969.

By the middle of the decade, protests, demonstrations, and unrest on college campuses across the United States were drawing international media attention. It was generally known that students were rebelling against their parents' boring, middle-class, comfortable existence. Once again, California was the forefront of this movement, as the University of California at Berkeley became a hotbed of these types of student activities. But these youth movements were about more than just shaking up the status quo. The hippies and other student movements were very successful in bringing about social awareness to environmental issues, such as the dangerous use of the insecticide DDT, as well as social issues such as antiwar protests and civil rights.

The civil rights movement was the defining issue of the entire decade. With reverberations around the world, African Americans fought for equal rights. For nearly a century, "Jim Crow laws"[4] had enforced segregation across the country, especially in the South, where racial tensions had run high since long before the Civil War in the 1860s.

Beginning in 1961, African-American youths and their supporters from all over the United States engaged in "freedom rides."[5] These young people boldly rode segregated buses designated whites-only from Washington, D.C., to Montgomery, Alabama. These students encountered arrests and violence in their fight to gain attention for the Supreme Court rulings that declared segregation on such interstate travel illegal and unconstitutional. In 1962 and 1963, federal troops were enforcing the desegregation of the University of Alabama and the University of Mississippi by escorting African-American students to class.

The year 1963 was a formidable one for civil rights, as more than 250,000 people peacefully marched to Washington, D.C., where they heard Martin Luther King Jr. give his historic "I Have a Dream" speech. The assassination of President Kennedy did not stop the growing civil rights movements he had supported. During the Johnson administration, civil rights was a major focus of lawmaking, culminating in such landmark legislation as the Civil Rights Act of 1964 and the Voting Rights Act of 1965. These were some of the most far-reaching and comprehensive laws to ensure equal rights to all Americans, regardless of race, ethnicity, color, or national origin. Despite the passage of these laws, racially motivated riots were unfortunately common across the United States between 1965 and 1967.

It was obvious that many African Americans felt unsatisfied by the nonviolent tactics of King. Many were turning instead to the burgeoning "Black Pride" movement led by the Black Muslims and their charismatic leader, Malcolm Little, who renamed himself "Malcolm X"—the "X" was said to symbolize his lost African surname. Eventually, Malcolm X broke with the Nation of Islam to form his own organization to promote the alliance between African Americans and the rest of the nonwhite people of the world. Malcolm X was killed by assassins from within the Nation of Islam.

In 1968, the civil rights movement lost its great leader. Martin Luther King, a Nobel Peace Prize recipient, was shot in Memphis, Tennessee, in April of that year. His death was mourned by all races around the world and touched off violent riots in Chicago and Washington, D.C. The movement lost another great proponent when Robert F. Kennedy, President Kennedy's brother and a Democratic presidential nominee himself, was also shot and killed in 1968. When Richard Nixon was elected president in 1968, he was initially uncertain about supporting the still-controversial civil rights legislation, but more schools were desegregated under Nixon than had been under Kennedy and Johnson combined.

The vast changes, advancements, and social upheavals throughout the decade had a profound impact on fashion. Increased globalization brought in ethnic flavors, and new technologies allowed for innovative synthetic textiles, all combining to create unique designs. The sixties was a time of using dress for expression of ideology and group affiliation. Style was malleable, flexible, and in constant flux, a reflection of the historical background of the decade.

ART AND MEDIA

The 1960s saw an explosion of styles in art. "Optical Art," known commonly as Op art, specialized in bold, vivid graphics often containing bright colors and geometric patterns. These images were easily transformed into fashion. Op art was screened onto T-shirts, dresses, and pantyhose. The most famous example of Op art crossing over into fashion was the Mondrian dress designed by Yves Saint-Laurent in 1965. He took the popular blocky paintings of twentieth-century Dutch painter Piet Mondrian and basically wrapped them around the female form in a simple shift dress that was complementary to the geometric-colored squares and thick black lines.

Pop art, short for "Popular art," was also a major movement. With artistic powerhouses such as Andy Warhol, Pop art showcased the mundane as fine art. Paintings and silk-screened canvases depicted celebrity or comic book images, soup cans, and other everyday objects. Advances in dyes and printing techniques made these often oversized pieces of art possible. While both Op art and Pop art were larger than life and usually geometric, interest in Art Nouveau and Art Deco was renewed in the 1960s. Art Nouveau was extremely popular in its original form but was often reinterpreted in psychedelic colors and styles and transformed into posters for concerts. These reinvented old-fashioned styles were right in line with the "Mods" and hippies who recreated Victorian, Edwardian, and other folk styles in their clothing and lifestyles.

Mass media also had a profound impact on the world of fashion, both haute couture and styles from the streets. For the first time, through the use of color television, fashions could be seen within minutes across the country and around the world. The new prevalence of media in the lives of people created style icons that also helped to impact fashion. Musicians such as the Beatles, the Rolling Stones, Jimi Hendrix, and the Grateful Dead helped to disseminate and cement styles, especially with their fans and followers. Popular media had much more influence over what young people wore than the offerings of Paris or any individual designer did.

WOMEN'S CLOTHING

The sixties was a time of great advancements in fashion for women, not only in haute couture but also in the burgeoning prêt-à-porter market. Early in the decade, a recognizable silhouette was still foremost, but by the mid-1960s, fashion had branched off in so many different directions that there was no longer one defining look. Trends for women were fast moving, ever changing, and subject to fads. The sixties saw great changes in the fashion industry as some of the scions of the previous era's best designers broke away to form their own houses and one of the greatest houses ever known, the House of Chanel, returned to prominence. By the middle of the decade, the emergent prêt-à-porter, or ready-to-wear, market began to be taken seriously as a fashion force and was covered by the top industry media as well as by popular news sources. Television, glossy color magazines, and movies all helped to disseminate fashion information quickly around the world.

Additionally, the women's rights movement's social and sexual emancipation of women had a profound influence on what types of fashions were accepted by the female buyer and even what sort of fashions were designed and sold. Although women had been wearing pants in limited circumstances since the 1930s, by the 1960s, women demanded that pants be brought into the realm of feminine fashion. Designers around the world jumped at the chance to offer a new and innovative garment.

This freedom from previous social mores was also apparent in underwear and beachwear. A two-piece bathing outfit that exposed the entire midriff and was cut fairly high in the leg soon appeared on beaches around the world. These tiny tops and bottoms were said to "have the same effect on the world as the atom bomb tests on Bikini Island."[6] A summertime icon, the "bikini," was born. Many designers took to the flowering bathing suit market with outrageous designs of their own. Rudi Gernreich was famous for designing very startling and often-outrageous pieces. His "monokini," introduced in 1964, was a one-piece bathing suit with a modest bottom that ended well above the waist in two thin straps and left the breasts completely bare.[7]

The overall theme of the 1960s was one of receding formality. Early in the decade, in the United States and beyond, the grace and style of First Lady Jacqueline Kennedy was an elegant influence on fashion for women. Pillbox hats, gloves, Empire-waist gowns, and perfectly coiffed hair were popular throughout the abbreviated term of President Kennedy. After his assassination, although Jackie Kennedy still remained an influence in fashion, she was not quite the international style-maker that she had once been.

Beginning in the middle years of the decade, casual clothes began to be accepted in social situations, and the days of hats, gloves, and matching purses worn with a sensible dress became a memory. Hats and gloves were reserved almost entirely for weddings and solemn occasions by the middle of the decade. The designer Balenciaga was the initiator in what was referred to as the "relaxed spirit in fashion."[8] Yves Saint-Laurent also exploited this new, pared-down look. He said, "Elegance is no longer significant; clothes have to be fun."[9]

Fabrics and Color

The sixties was also a time of experimentation in color, form, style, and materials. In 1966, paper dresses debuted, originally as a commercial promotion. They soon became a small fad as designers and customers clamored for this new and avant-garde style. The paper dresses were a short-lived trend and were passé by 1968. But breakthroughs in design and construction of undergarments would last into the modern day, especially the fashion for colored and patterned tights and pantyhose.

Skirts

Beginning in the late 1950s, skirts were gradually shortening. The world of fashion was still transitioning from the New Look–influenced styles popular throughout the previous decade. A less fitted, A-line silhouette would dominate the better part of the 1960s. From womenswear to clothing for little girls, from formal dress to sportswear, a short, unfitted silhouette was in style for the entire decade.

Fashion influence was in flux, as inspirations were coming not only from Paris, the traditional heart of the industry, but also from Italy, England, and the United States. Mary Quant, a British designer, emphasized a youthful look with her short dresses that were based on children's clothes. Although *Vogue* started to take notice of these designs in 1963, it was not until 1965 when André Courrèges introduced his miniskirt line that the fashion really took off. Quant's focus was more on short shift dresses, and Courrèges designed super-short skirts to be worn with a coordinating top. Both of these designers were designing for the modern woman without reference to the past. The ideal was a sense of uncomplicated and active youthfulness. Simple lines and plain grosgrain piping in a single contrasting color were some signature details of Courrèges design.

In 1967, Pierre Cardin also joined in the short slip dress fashion, but in true Cardin style, he did it with a twist: he created his own type of wrinkle-proof synthetic textile called "Cardine."[10] His short A-line shifts were made in Cardine and embossed with large geometric shapes that gave his dresses a three-dimensional appeal.

Interest in new genres in fine art also found an outlet in high fashion. Saint-Laurent designed his own version of the short shift dress, but his were made with geometric blocks of white and primary colors bordered by thick black lines, a direct interpretation of the Mondrian's most famous Op art works.

New materials were very popular for high fashion. Vinyl, PVC, plastic, metal, and new inventions in synthetic fiber were all utilized in the clothes of the major designers. The most famous of all these designers was Paco Rabanne. He began to make his name in the fashion world in 1966. Rabanne was known for his elaborately detailed garments that were made of discs of plastic held together with gold links, or dresses sewn with elaborate embroideries that often incorporated pieces of metal. His creative use of materials in his designs also included chains, hammered metal plates, crystals, cellophane, pebbles, buttons, ostrich feathers, plastic, and celluloid. He used African masks in the bodices of his dresses and created molded raincoats. Although Rabanne's designs were often considered too extreme for the average consumer, he did influence other designers to experiment in materials and forms and added to the rich textural nature of the 1960s.

Paris designer Paco Rabanne presents a long-sleeved minidress of black and white plastic discs revealing the upper torso in his spring and summer collection in Paris, 1969. © AP Photo.

But there was conservative movement in the midst of the ultramodern, ever-changing trends. Coco Chanel, a pioneer of fashion for the liberated women in the prewar era, had closed her house and retired from fashion at the outset of World War II in 1939. When things returned to normal in the 1950s, she felt she could not adapt to the new, capricious nature of the industry. However, she eventually saw that the modern society maven and businesswomen needed a classic, stable wardrobe available to them to see them through the fickle trends of current fashions. So, in 1954, Chanel had returned to fashion. Her creations were reminiscent of her previous designs but tried to incorporate the love of texture that was an overarching theme for the decade. True to form, Chanel never designed skirts that were cut above the knee. She created matched skirt and jacket combinations of Scotch tweed and wools in staple colors such as navy, black, blush pink, cream, and white. For eveningwear, she used more sumptuous fabrics such as jersey and shantung. Jackets were fairly short, with cinched waists and decorated simply with pockets, piping, and tasteful gold buttons. But even Chanel was not immune to the effects of Rabanne: playful gold chains and other fanciful jewelry became an integral part of her designs. These suits were meant to remain a classic element of wardrobe for several seasons and indeed remained fashionable into the 1980s. A new worry for designers was the emergence of cheap copies of high-fashion pieces, yet Chanel was confident that her superior workmanship and materials were more important that just the look of her designs.

Pants

Pants for women became a major point of interest and conflict in fashion. Although bifurcated garments had been common throughout history for women in the East, Europeans and Americans were slow to accept pants on women. *Women's Wear Daily* reporters, for a story published October 17, 1966, donned fashionable pantsuits and went around New York City to see what the reaction would be—and they were almost universally barred entry to major establishments. The reporters were even denied entry at a fashionable restaurant where they were regular customers and had a reservation. Another restaurant allowed them entry initially, then when the maitre d' saw their attire, he announced suddenly that the kitchen was closed "and it is not the policy of the house to serve women in pants." Another high-profile restaurant let them in—after they explained that they were writing a story on the acceptance of pants for women—but made them sit in a corner out of the way and asked them to remain seated and not to dance or take pictures.[11]

MEN'S CLOTHING

Menswear as designer fodder came into being only in the late 1960s when younger designers saw a need and demand for stylish men's clothing. The clothing they produced was for a young man; it was colorful, had more variation in style and look, and was more affordable, to appeal to the younger man. Their designs were sold in small shops, which eventually became the boutiques that pepper our streets now.

All fashion went through many changes in the sixties—even fashion for men, which is traditionally very slow to evolve. At the outset of the decade, men's fashions had not come a long way since the 1950s. The newest trends in fashion were already brewing in London at the outset of the 1960s, although they would take another few years to reach the United States. Across gender lines, the major defining themes in the United States and England were the counterculture influences. Couture in Paris and the burgeoning prêt-à-porter market also had an effect on menswear. For the first time in modern couture history, menswear became the focus of many designers' work.

In the 1960s, women wore trousers as fashion dictated. What followed was a boom in design for women that borrowed heavily from menswear. These designs were very feminine but used a number of men's tailoring techniques. The opposite, however, was not true; men's design took nothing from womenswear. Designers made some attempts at revamping the look for men to try to bolster flagging sales, but the male public was not inclined to accept new innovations right away.

At the start of the decade, a trim and conservative silhouette was fashionable. Colors were muted and patterns were understated. A three-piece suit and hat were still considered to be necessary for the well-dressed gentleman. Since couturiers designed only for women at this time, well-to-do men patronized tailors for their clothing needs. By and large, if a man was going to be seen in public, he would be dressed in a suit. But some department stores were beginning to attract the male consumer by carrying good-quality garments that almost rivaled the offerings of tailors.

Pierre Cardin became the premier designer of men's fashions in the 1960s. He began to design for men in 1957, but his designs were not fully accepted by the male customer until after 1965. By then, Cardin's signature trim pant legs, long jackets with zippered closures, and patterned sweaters began to find a solid market appeal. Men's clothing early in the decade began to sacrifice comfort for easy-care, permanent-press, synthetic fabrics, but Cardin's line changed the expectation of fashionable attire for men. This was supported by the fashion press of the time, including such standards such as *Esquire.*

In less fashionable attire, changes appeared more slowly. Soon, the lapels had grown wider, shoulders more padded, and jackets more fitted through the torso, with a slight flare over the hips. Turtlenecks became accepted as an alternative to collared shirts, as they were colorful and versatile, although many restaurants and other high-end establishments refused admission to men without neckties.

Another fashionable piece of menswear that was popular with the consumer but not always acceptable to society was the Nehru jacket. It was originally designed by Michel Schreibner based on a traditional Indian coat that buttoned up the front from the neckline to the hem, had no lapels, and had a small, standing collar. The Nehru jacket—named after the prime minister of India, Jawaharlal Nehru—was constructed of soft fabrics and was light, unlined, and comfortable. It was often combined with the turtleneck. The Nehru jacket gained wider popularity after Cardin incorporated the look into his signature gray flannel suit jackets. Although these jackets were very popular and many notable figures in society wore them, Nehru jackets were never truly accepted as formal attire.[12] The Nehru jacket fad lasted about two years, while the turtleneck remained exceedingly popular for decades to come.

The sixties ushered in the "Peacock Revolution," which allowed men more variety of color in their dress. With much influence from overseas, especially England, American men found new avenues for self-expression in dress. Mods and hippies used many colors and textures and utilized clothing to articulate their beliefs through dress. The establishment of certain styles as part of a counterculture was a new idea that was very willingly embraced.

Even though most men were not a part of the counterculture, the influences of it moved up from the street level and affected the ideas of top designers. Wide, bell-bottom pants in various colors and weaves, as well as blue jeans, became common sportswear for casual occasions. Advancements in synthetic fibers and dye technologies made popular colors and textures easily accessible and affordable to both designers and the buying public.

The 1960s was a decade of great change for men. They were offered an unprecedented array of choice from colorful European Mod styles to more tailored and modern styles offered by top designers like Cardin and Ralph Lauren. Boutiques geared specifically to menswear began to open in the middle of the

Stuart Walker, left, and Andy Johnson model creations by Allare by the House of Worth at the menswear fashion show in London, 1968. © AP Photo.

decade in Paris, New York City, and London. Cardin was the first major designer to open up a boutique specifically for men. John Weitz, a popular American designer, opened one of the first men's boutiques in New York City in 1965. Designer styles became increasingly important in the 1960s as the fashion community moved toward catering to this new market segment. Throughout the decades to come, the modern menswear market would evolve into an industry that has nearly caught up with the dominating force of design for women.

Undergarments

The advancements in technology also brought changes to men's undergarments. Boxer shorts, knit briefs, ribbed sleeveless knit shirts, and T-shirts had been common for years, but the range of prints and colors available for men sharply increased. In the 1960s, briefs and undershirts began to be available in colors for the first time, although plain white would remain the classic and most popular color. Undergarments influenced active sportswear and vice versa.

Colors were paramount in the selection of clothing. This was a new avenue of choice for men, but they embraced it.

The small knit briefs worn for swimming in Europe gained some popularity in the United States and other countries. Called a "slip" in Europe, the small suits were colorful, dried quickly, were wrinkle free, and flattered a toned and youthful physique.

Hairstyles, Hats, and Accessories

Fashion of the 1960s centered on the young. Bright colors, fads, and long hair were three common characteristics of this decade. Gender lines became blurred as men grew their hair long and women took to wearing pants. Early on, long hair was seen as a mark of the young protester turning against middle-class values. Hair worn longer than shoulder length was primarily limited to young men in high school and college, although some older men sought to associate themselves with the protest movements by growing their hair out. Moustaches, sideburns, and full beards were also popular but, along with long hair, had limited acceptance in society.

With more focus on the hair, products for hair care targeted toward men gained popularity, and hats for men declined. Beginning with John F. Kennedy's bareheaded inauguration, hats for men became less and less popular throughout the decade. In Europe, hats for older men remained fairly common, but in the United States even the older generations gave them up.

Ties were fashionable with older men, but not with the younger set. In 1967, Ralph Lauren began to design men's apparel. He began his career specializing in ties, some as wide as three inches (8 cm). Wide ties came into vogue and would remain popular through the 1970s.

CHILDREN'S CLOTHING

The 1960s saw few changes in children's clothing, but major innovations in infant wear. Although designs for adults did have some impact on what their children were wearing, overall the look remained steady and "classic." What did change was the materials used in clothing for children. Among these advances was the invention of disposable diapers for babies. Introduced in 1960, these innovations made the life of the modern mother much easier, freeing her of a substantial portion of the laundry and the inconvenience of diaper services. Today, no mother can imagine being without such an important part of modern baby care.

In the 1960s, concerns for child development and safety were included in the design process. Utilizing new materials such as polyester and modacrylic could provide for waterproofing, stretch, and the application of fire retardants. Child development experts also encouraged loose-fitting garments to allow freedom of movement.

Clothes for infants and toddlers remained relatively unchanged throughout the decade. Garments were delicate and decorative for babies, appealing to the gift-giving market and primarily aimed at grandparents. For everyday wear, manufacturers took advantage of new fibers that allowed for more stretch and better stain resistance. The stretchy, all-in-one, footed terrycloth garment that is so ubiquitous in the current market was introduced in the early 1960s. These garments provided consistent warmth, protection for baby's delicate skin, and easy access for diaper changing. Combined with disposable diapers, baby care had never been easier.

Garments for toddlers and young children began to show elements of adult styles. Young boys were dressed as miniature versions of their fathers, with permanent-press polyester. The Nehru jacket and Mod-inspired styles even made their way into youth fashion.

Young girls had a wider selection from which to choose, just like their mothers. The popular A-line dresses were made in little girls' sizes. They were created in princess-line sundresses for summer and corduroy jumpers for winter. Skirts were generally short for even very young girls, often paired with colorful tights, again in a children's version of adult fashion. Preteen and adolescent girls wore the white, calf-length go-go boots that were all the rage, although boots designed for girls were usually made of vinyl or some other imitation leather and had thicker, lower heels than did their adult counterparts.

Another item of children's wear that is commonplace in today's world is the yellow rain slicker. This was another piece of children's clothing that was introduced in the 1960s. Advances in technology made it easy to create a truly waterproof outerwear garment. Imitation furs were another popular innovation used in clothing for both boys and girls. Imitation fur trimming on collars, hats, and hoods, as well as full coats, began to be seen in the children's department of major stores by the end of the decade.

Hairstyles for children did not change much through the decade. Curls, braids, and pigtails for girls were very popular. Older girls often wore their hair long and very straight like their mothers. Young boys also wore their hair styled in a classic manner. Children of the subculture social groups styled their hair like their parents. Hippies and Mods had long hair for both boys and girls. The Afro was popular for both African-American boys and girls.

STYLE TRIBES AND OTHER FASHIONS

The term *style tribe* was coined in 1994 by Ted Polhemus to describe the small, ardent factions of fashion adherents that developed through the sixties. Young people sought to set themselves apart from the mainstream and connect themselves to their chosen peer group. Polhemus explained his theory in his book *Street Style* and explained that they were interested in looking different from the mainstream of their parents' generation, but at the same time they all wanted to look alike and feel connected. They were part of a style tribe of young people who looked alike and thought alike and had the same goals and ideals.

In previous decades, these "street styles" were popular in both England and the United States as seen in the English Teddy Boys and the American zoot-suiters and beatniks. Early in the decade, the beatnik style from the 1950s merged into other more disparate British styles to create the Mod look. The Mods were based in the boutiques and clubs of Carnaby Street and Portobello Road in London. They featured a romantic, poetic look with long hair, round glasses, and elegant, handsome clothing for both men and women. A competing subgroup was the "Rockers," who strove for an edgier look with black leather and a motorcycle gang attitude. While the Mods won out in popularity in the 1960s, the Rockers would have their day in the next decade.

The Mod look was introduced to the rest of the world via the Beatles in 1963. In 1965, the American sportswear designer MacGregor brought Mod-inspired fashions to the United States. His designs were extremely popular and well received by the fashion press initially. There was a backlash against the look in 1967, but a resurgence in interest in 1969.

Just as the Mod influence was disappearing in 1967, the hippie movement was beginning. Begun by peace activists in San Francisco, the fashion of gypsy-like mix-and-match culled from thrift stores soon sent ripples throughout the country and then the world. The longer hair of the fashionable Mod became the shoulder-length or longer hair of the hippie. The hippie look went along with a lifestyle of drug use and mystic religions, culminating with the Woodstock Festival in 1969. Although elements of the hippie style would reverberate throughout the 1970s and beyond, the true nature of the movement would be lost to the commercial appeal of this style tribe.

Another iconic style that emerged during the 1960s went hand-in-hand with the civil rights movement. African Americans adopted traditional African styles to highlight their sense of "Black pride." The most popular garment was the *dashiki*, a simple tunic with wide sleeves that was made from colorful natural fibers such as cotton or linen. Fabrics such as kente cloth, a complex weave made on narrow strip-looms by Ashanti men in Bonwire, Ghana, were popular, expensive, and highly prized. Mud cloth was a simpler textile stamped in blocky, basic designs with a mineral-containing mud. Creative ethnic jewelry was also popular, made from traditional materials such as ivory, ebony, African beads, and cowry shells. The look was complete with the Afro, a full and fluffy arrangement that took advantage of the natural curl of the African-American hair. Pared-down versions of these styles were worn to work by many African Americans, but by the close of the decade this was less popular and traditional styles became reserved for primarily leisurewear.

There was one constant across all of the popular style tribes of the 1960s and that was the popularity of blue jeans. Blue jeans had been developed as a working-class garment, but by the 1950s had begun to be associated with the youth culture. During the 1960s, the various youth movements adopted blue jeans as almost a sort of uniform that visually separated them from the mainstream. Jeans were often personalized by their wearers with various embellishments that ranged from drawings and paintings to elaborate embroidery and appliqué. In isolated, communist Eastern Europe, jeans became a symbol of Western progressive ideals and a most coveted commodity.

By the end of the decade, these style tribes were an integral part of the fashion world as a whole, influencing and gaining influence from the top designers. For the first time, the true power over fashion was coming from the streets, as designers began to cater to the desires of the masses instead of dictating to them what they should wear.

CONCLUSION

The 1960s was a time of great advancements throughout the fashion industry. Prêt-à-porter manufacturers found that the emergent youth market with a large disposable income and a taste for ever-changing fashions could provide them with income and prestige. All around the world, folk costumes of native populations began to diminish as the availability of mass-produced and easy-to-acquire clothing took over. This was the first major expansion of the fashion industry since its inception in the thirteenth century.

NOTES

1. Phyllis Tortora and Keith Eubank, *Survey of Historic Costume: A History of Western Dress*, 4th ed (New York: Fairchild, 2005), 458.

2. Tortora and Eubank, *Survey of Historic Costume*, 461.

3. Tortora and Eubank, *Survey of Historic Costume*, 461.

4. "From the 1880s into the 1960s, a majority of American states enforced segregation through 'Jim Crow' laws (so called after a black character in minstrel shows). From Delaware to California, and from North Dakota to Texas, many states (and cities, too) could impose legal punishments on people for consorting with members of another race. The most common types of laws forbade intermarriage and ordered business owners and public institutions to keep their black and white clientele separated" (National Park Service, "'Jim Crow' Laws," http://www.nps.gov/archive/malu/documents/jim_crow_laws.htm).

5. Martin Luther King Jr. Research and Education Institute, "Freedom Rides," http://www.stanford.edu/group/King/about_king/encyclopedia/freedom_rides.htm.

6. François Boucher, *20,000 Years of Fashion: The History of Costume and Personal Adornment* (New York: H. N. Abrams, 1987), 425.

7. Tortora and Eubank, *Survey of Historic Costume*, 477, 479.

8. Boucher, *20,000 Years of Fashion*, 427.

9. Gerda Buxbaum, ed., *Icons of Fashion: The 20th Century* (Munich, Germany: Prestel, 1999), 83.

10. Boucher, *20,000 Years of Fashion*, 433.

11. Tortora and Eubank, *Survey of Historic Costume*, 468.

12. In a "Weird Al" Yankovic song titled "Everything You Know Is Wrong" off of the *Bad Hair Day* album released in 1996, the narrator laments at his death, "Now I'm up in heaven with St. Peter by the pearly gates and it's obvious he doesn't like the Nehru jacket that I'm wearing. He tells me that they've got a dress code." This indicates that even in the 1990s, the retro look of the Nehru jacket was still not accepted as formal attire.

FURTHER READING

Boucher, François. *20,000 Years of Fashion: The History of Costume and Personal Adornment*. New York: H. N. Abrams, 1987.

Buxbaum, Gerda, ed. *Icons of Fashion: The 20th Century*. Munich, Germany: Prestel, 1999.

Tate, Sharon Lee. *Inside Fashion Design*. 5th ed. Upper Saddle River, NJ: Pearson/Prentice Hall, 2004.

Tortora, Phyllis, and Keith Eubank. *Survey of Historic Costume: A History of Western Dress*. 4th ed. New York: Fairchild, 2005.

MOVIES

Belle de Jour (1967)
Blowup (1966)
Breakfast at Tiffany's (1961)
Bullitt (1968)
8 1/2 (1963)
A Hard Day's Night (1964)
Ocean's Eleven (1960)
That Touch of Mink (1962)

A portrait of Madame Charles-Maurice de Talleyrand-Périgord de Bénévent (later Madame George Francis Grand), c. 1808, shows the empire style of gown. © The Metropolitan Museum of Art / Art Resource, NY.

An English engraving of a millinery shop in Paris, 1822, shows good examples of both men's and women's clothing and accessories. © The Art Archive / Bibliothèque des Arts Décoratifs Paris / Gianni Dagli Orti.

"Mr. and Mrs. I. N. Phelps Stokes," John Singer Sargent, 1897. This portrait shows the structured style of women's clothing with large leg 'o' mutton sleeves and long skirt. The man's suit is a good example of the softer structure of men's clothing. © The Metropolitan Museum of Art / Art Resource, NY.

An elaborate silk ball gown by
Frederick Charles Worth. c. 1872. ©
The Metropolitan Museum of Art / Art
Resource, NY.

"Too Early," James Jacques Joseph Tissot, 1873, shows the formal dresses and accessories for women and black
suits for men. © HIP / Art Resource, NY.

Frederic Leighton's "The Countess Brownlow," 1879, is a good example of Artistic Dress reform. National Trust / Art Resource, NY.

The cover of *Life* magazine's February 18, 1926, edition, showing a well-dressed old man dancing with a flapper, by John Held, Jr. Courtesy of the Library of Congress.

Vogue magazine's 1941 cover pays homage to women fighting in the war. Courtesy of the Library of Congress.

Shown (from left) 1970s fashion icons: Jaclyn Smith (as Kelly Garrett), Kate Jackson (as Sabrina Duncan), Farrah Fawcett (as Jill Munroe) star in *Charlie's Angels* on ABC, 1976–1977. Courtesy of Photofest.

Michael Douglas (as Gordon Gekko) stars in Oliver Stone's 1987 film, *Wall Street*, wearing the typical shirt style and suspenders associated with high-powered Wall Street executives of the 1980s. Courtesy of Photofest.

Pearl Jam (left to right, Stone Gossard, Dave Abbruzzese, Jeff Ament, and Eddie Vedder) celebrate their MTV award for best group video at the MTV Video Music Awards in California, 1993 in their "grunge" style clothing. © AP Photo / Kvork Djansezian.

Supermodel Kate Moss struts the catwalk in a short blue and gold dress at the Gianni Versace Spring/Summer 1999 collection unveiled in Milan, 1998. © AP Photo / Luca Bruno.

Italian fashion designer Gianni Versace, left, poses with supermodels Claudia Schiffer, center, and Naomi Campbell during fashion week in Milan, Italy, 1996. © AP Photo / P. Castaldi.

Fashion designer Zac Posen poses for a portrait in his New York studio, 2004. Posen won a Council of Fashion Designers of America award for emerging talent. © AP Photo / Gino Domenico.

Jennifer Lopez poses with models wearing hip-hop style clothes from her line of clothes called "J.LO by Jennifer Lopez," 2001. © AP Photo / Jill Connelly.

British fashion designer Vivienne Westwood poses at her exhibition "Retrospective," which was showing at the NRW-Forum in Düsseldorf, Germany, 2006. © AP Photo / Martin Meissner.

The Seventies

Sara M. Harvey

The 1970s was a period of transition. The mercurial changes of the previous decade continued. The United States began diplomatic relations with communist China that not only forged a tenuous alliance but also ensured lucrative trade between the two countries. An armistice was declared between the United States and North Vietnam that finally ended the Vietnam War after much loss of life, finally bringing the peace that the youth of the sixties had been demanding. But where there were great strides in statesmanship in some countries, relations broke down in others. Regime changes in the Middle East shook up oil production and caused gas prices around the world to rise sharply.

The visionary youth movements turned away from their ideals, and some collapsed altogether, allowing new movements to emerge. What came about in the 1970s was indicative of their time, a mix of lost innocence with a kind of optimism that led to young people caring about environmental causes and social injustices more than ever. The women's movement continued into the new decade as women demanded equality and a place in the workforce. Expectations in relationships also changed. The divorce rate was at an all-time high, as was the number of couples cohabitating instead of getting married. With laws ensuring desegregation and other civil rights, African Americans as well now focused on finding true equality.

Fashion went through another shocking change. Fashion was still, for the most part, being controlled from the consumer level by subcultures and "style tribes." When consumers refused the offerings of the fashion mavens, the media declared that fashion was "dead." Ethnic looks, wearable art, and unique styles superseded what designers had to offer for the average consumer. But in the menswear sector, fashion was just beginning. Boutiques specializing in men's fashions appeared first in Europe, then in the United States. Major designers increasingly focused on men's clothing through this decade. Near the end of the 1970s, designers also discovered the merchandising magic of the label. For the first time, consumers began to shop exclusively for certain designers' names displayed prominently on the garment, especially on the back pockets of blue jeans. This trend would become a major factor in fashion in the coming decades.

The sense of individualism that was born in the 1960s continued to grow and evolve through the 1970s and beyond. People all over the world discovered that they could not only drive the direction of fashion but also affect the course of history.

HISTORY

The decade of the seventies was turbulent from start to finish. At the close of the sixties, the world had watched as Neil Armstrong walked on the moon, and people across the United States and overseas were captivated by the culmination of the hippie movement at Woodstock. But these "feel-good" days were soon to come to an end.

In May 1970, National Guard troops were sent to quell a large student demonstration against the Vietnam War held at Kent State University in Ohio. Although the students and other protesters were not armed, the guardsmen opened fire into the crowd, killing four students—two protesters and two bystanders. While such demonstrations had been met with violence in the past decade, never had it resulted in deaths. This incident galvanized the antiwar movement against the U.S. government and attracted more than 200,000 protesters to march on Washington, D.C., the following year.

This was only the start of Richard Nixon's problems as president. Nixon had been elected in 1968. He was successful in his dealings with China in early 1972, securing trade agreements and China's assistance in pressuring North Vietnam. The new trade between China and the United States furnishes his country with cheaper clothes, toys, and other goods. Nixon was confident that with China as an ally, he could turn the tide of the rapidly disintegrating situation in the Vietnam War. But he had overestimated the sway China had over the Viet Cong guerrillas. Finally, in 1973, Nixon signed an armistice and agreed to remove troops from Vietnam. Although it was a popular decision among the American people to finally bring the troops home, it went down in history as the first-ever military loss for the United States.

Nixon's presidency was steeped in scandal and disappointment. From 1970 onward, he was bogged down in rumors of secret dealings with the Central Intelligence Agency (CIA). In 1972, he was implicated in a burglary of the Democratic National Committee Headquarters at the Watergate Hotel and Office Complex in Washington. Five men, one of whom professed to be a former member of the CIA, were arrested at 2:30 in the morning on June 17, 1972.

The act itself perhaps would not have caused such scandal had it not been for the corruption and cover-up that followed. Among other things, Nixon tried to destroy incriminating audio tapes and paid one of the Watergate burglars $25,000 that went to a complex network of spying on the Democrats.

These events only slowly became known, however, and the American people, who had no idea what was afoot, reelected Nixon easily in 1972 in a landslide victory over Democratic candidate Senator George McGovern of South Dakota. But in 1974, when allegations of the spying and sabotage ring against the Democratic Party surfaced, Nixon was forced to resign in the face of impeachment. He resigned the presidency on August 9, 1974, the first and only American president to resign from office. Vice President Gerald Ford took Nixon's place as president of the United States. Ford, who had been appointed to his position following the earlier resignation of Spiro Agnew, became the first president who was never elected. The "Watergate Scandal" became a household term and has come to mean political scandal and abuse of power. When Ford came into office, he was faced with tremendous distrust by the public, which was only heightened by the steep rise in oil prices brought on by the 1973 Yom Kippur War.

The Yom Kippur War was fought between Israel and its Arab neighbors. Egypt and Syria attacked Israel on October 6, 1973—Yom Kippur, the holiest day of the Jewish calendar. The fighting was brief but intense. The Arabs underestimated the Israeli army and were soundly defeated. Egypt accepted a cease-fire in November 1973, with Syria following suit in May 1974. This caused a ripple of disquiet across the entire Middle East, and in retaliation, the Organization of Petroleum Exporting Countries (OPEC) imposed an oil embargo on the United States and other supporters of Israel. Imports of oil into the United States dropped off steeply, and prices more than quadrupled. This signaled that OPEC unequivocally controlled oil pricing throughout the world. Although this oil shortage was brief, it did serve to bring attention to the need for conservation and alternative fuel sources. Environmental concerns had been growing in the American consciousness since the publication of *Silent Spring* in 1962. The first Earth Day was celebrated in 1970. However, this conservationist fervor soon died down as OPEC eased off the embargo and oil prices stabilized in late 1974.

In 1976, Jimmy Carter, the former governor of Georgia, defeated Gerald Ford to become president of the United States. Carter only served one term, but it was one full of many highs and lows. Carter began the process of turning over control of the U.S.-built Panama Canal to the government of Panama. He also brokered a peace treaty between Israel and Egypt at Camp David, Maryland, in September 1978. Carter met with President Anwar Sadat of Egypt and Prime Minister Menachem Begin

> "Watergate is now an all-encompassing term used to refer to: political burglary, bribery, extortion, phone tapping, conspiracy, obstruction of justice, destruction of evidence, tax fraud, illegal use of government agencies such as the CIA and the FBI, illegal campaign contributions, use of public money for private purposes. Most of all, 'Watergate' is synonymous with abuse of power." (*Watergate.info*, http://watergate.info/background)

of Israel to broker the accord, which called for Israeli troop withdrawal from the Sinai Peninsula and the establishing of diplomatic relations between the two countries in 1979. Known as the Camp David Accords, this conference helped ease some of the rising tensions in the Middle East.

While international strife between Middle Eastern countries was being settled, no one could stop the domestic discord playing out in Iran in 1979. Shah Mohammed Reza Pahlavi was an autocratic leader who often antagonized religious leaders and was seen to be catering to the West. He was overthrown in a popular revolution, and control of the country was placed in the hands of the Shiite Ayatollah Ruhollah Khomeini. He instituted fundamentalist Islamic law across the entire nation and restricted oil sales to the United States. His acrimony toward the United States prompted his followers to take over the U.S. Embassy in the capital city of Tehran. The American hostages would be held for almost two years and be used as a political tool by the Iranians as well as both the Republicans and Democrats in the United States.

The brief oil embargo in 1974 paled in comparison to the massive oil shortages that began in 1979. The conservation and alternative fuel ideas talked about earlier in the decade had been all but forgotten in the four years of stable prices and abundant supply. The American people were caught off guard by the sudden shortfall, and gas stations were forced to close as they ran out of fuel to sell. Lines for gasoline went for blocks and lasted for hours, even days in some rare occasions. The problem was compounded by cars running out of gas while waiting in the long lines to refuel.

President Carter began his own series of "fireside chats"[1] to address the fuel crisis. Like his Depression-era predecessor Franklin D. Roosevelt, Carter used the media to make the American people feel at home with him, to give the impression that he was one of them. He dressed unassumingly in a sweater and slacks instead of a suit and sat casually in a living room instead of standing behind a podium. He spoke of the energy crisis as if it were a war to be won. Carter outlined his plans directly to the people, because the programs had gone nowhere in Congress. He urged people conserve energy in their homes and issued a presidential mandate that public buildings could not set their air-conditioner thermostats below 78 degrees in the summer or above 65 degrees in the winter. People were encouraged to dress for the season and not rely on temperature-controlled buildings. These conservation measures, coupled with a worldwide recession, helped end the oil shortage and brought prices back to a stable plateau. President Ronald Reagan removed price controls in 1981, and the goals of obtaining independence from foreign oil were abandoned as the memories of high prices and long lines for gas were quickly forgotten.

In addition to the oil crisis, the seventies was a difficult decade for many around the world. The world economy had boomed in the 1960s but was struggling in the 1970s. In the United States, inflation and unemployment were at a post-Depression high.

In the Soviet Union and Soviet-controlled Eastern Europe, there was growing dissent. The people had been promised more government support to agriculture and industry and greater accessibility to better consumer goods, but increased military actions took government attention away from the people, and crop failures gave them little to sustain themselves. Images of Russia and other Eastern Bloc countries at this time mirror those of the United States in the

1930s during the Great Depression. There were long lines for food and people living in abject poverty with hardly more in their possession than the clothes on their backs. Some of the Soviet Union's finest minds were exiled or fled the country, including writer and Nobel Prize–winner Alexander Solzhenitsyn, who left Russia in 1974. Russia also ended the decade on a sour note as it invaded Afghanistan, the start of a ten-year occupation that would further drain the country of money and the lives of its citizens in the decade to come.

Although the Soviet Union was far behind the times, across Europe and into the United States, modern life was changing, especially for women. In 1973, the U.S. Supreme Court ruled that abortion was legal under *Roe v. Wade*. Across the West, divorce rates rose and marriage rates dropped. Those who were interested in marrying often delayed the wedding for months or even years. Couples began to live together premarriage, and slowly the idea of cohabitation became more and more socially acceptable. Millions of people across the United States and Europe were living as in a married relationship, but without any legal or ecclesiastical sanctions. Because marriage was delayed, childbearing was also often delayed. With the divorce rate climbing, so did the instances of remarriages, often with children involved from the previous marriage. These blended families were made more socially acceptable with television programs like *The Brady Bunch* and became increasingly common. In many cases, divorced people, even if they remarried, did not have any more children. During the 1970s, the birthrate actually slipped below what was required to replace the population, due to the decline in marriage rates and more women entering the workforce and delaying childbearing. More access to birth control throughout the 1970s also had a profound effect on the drop in birthrate.

The 1970s saw many great strides in equality for women. In 1976, it was estimated that half of American mothers worked outside of the home. That same year, it was estimated that only 40 percent of American jobs provided enough income to support a family. This led even more women to seek paid employment outside the home. Women suffered discrimination, however, with income levels that did not equal male earnings and limited advancement opportunities. The gradual increase of women in the workplace across the United States and Europe spurred a major reallocation of fashion resources as designers rushed to take advantage of this wide, new market.

As the decade of the 1970s turned into the 1980s, many of the issues brought to the fore were still unresolved. But a new sense of modernism and internationalism would be the hallmark of the decades that closed out not only the century but also the millennium.

ART AND MEDIA

While fine art did not have the same dramatic effect on fashion in the 1970s that it had in the 1960s, there was some interplay between the two fields. In 1977, the "Treasures of King Tutankhamun" exhibit toured the United States. It had already toured Europe and other parts of the world. Along with ethnic influences from other areas of the world, especially Africa and Eastern Europe, ancient Egyptian styles were eagerly translated into popular fashion. Metallic gold, lapis blue, and rich reds, yellows, greens, and oranges were seen in jewelry and accessories. Some pieces of jewelry were made as replicas of the originals, and many others were made in Egyptian styles. Sandals, often in gold leather, were also attributed to this trend.

But the defining influence on fashion in the 1970s was movies and television. Films like *Saturday Night Fever* in 1977 and *Thank God It's Friday* in 1978 glamorized the disco styles and exposed the world to what was worn in dance clubs like Studio 54 in New York. *Annie Hall* (1977) popularized the fashion of women wearing large shirts and men's vests and the general style of combining layers of separates in a look of thrift store chic. Television shows such as *Charlie's Angels* (1976–1981) showed off glamorous frosted hair and a weekly review of what the producers thought of as sexy for Farrah Fawcett and the other Angels to wear. Thousands of young women and teenage girls planned their wardrobes accordingly. Television coverage of the Olympic Games first made fashion news in the 1960s with innovations in swimwear. During the 1976 Olympics, short haircuts like that of skating medalist Dorothy Hamill were all the rage. Television coverage of Olympic skiing also influenced what people the world over were wearing on the slopes.

Labeling and licensing were probably the most important media tie-in of the decade and set the stage for the onslaught of licensed products in the decades to come. The art and business of licensing began with the Pop art trend of the 1960s, in which cartoon and comic book characters were featured on garments. In the 1970s, popular cartoon characters began to appear on T-shirts, pajamas, undergarments, lunch boxes, sleeping bags, and breakfast cereals. One of the most iconic applications of this type of licensing was Underoos, 100 percent polyester undergarments for children developed in 1978 by Fruit of the Loom. They were made for both girls and boys and featured characters like Wonder Woman, Superman, and Batman, as well as movie characters from *Star Wars* (1977) and cartoon characters from such favorites as *Scooby-Doo* and *Josie and the Pussycats*.[2]

The practice of licensing was begun at the retail level, the lowest rung of the fashion ladder, but it did not take long for top designers in prêt-à-porter to realize the appeal. While they were not about to put their names on children's undergarments (a trend that would eventually become commonplace by the late 1990s), they sought to maximize their sales by licensing out their names and logos for mass-produced garments such as jeans, T-shirts, and other basic garments. Many designers at this time also branched out into home décor and other nonwearable fashion. These designers often partnered with retail establishments or began to move their higher-end boutiques to a mass-market level. The late 1970s would see an explosion of this trend that would increase into the 1980s, when designers would go to the next step and use costumes in film and television as commercial product placement venues.

WOMEN'S CLOTHING

The seventies ushered in an era of hyperstylization for women. The explosion of styles corresponded to the feelings of "anarchy" that defined a generation that refused to bow to the dictates of its parents. After the swell of styles and fashions that dominated the sixties, there was some backlash as young consumers turned away from commercial offerings. The world of couture continued to blossom until 1974 when the international oil crisis, brought on by OPEC, nearly crushed the industry. With increasing diversity in the fashion market, the near-magical atmosphere of the 1960s dissolved into a period restructuring and reorganizing in the fashion industry.

Major designers managed to hold onto prominence, and although the industry as a whole was losing some support, the lines of specific designers were still eagerly awaited by women the world over every season. Women of wealth vied to be the first to wear new designs before those designs were translated into the prêt-à-porter market, even though these couture garments cost at least ten times more than their ready-to-wear counterparts. There was still great status attached to fresh-from-the-runway, custom-tailored couture garments.

As the world of couture changed, major designers found that they had to change with it. Some up-and-coming designers split off from their peers and set up their houses, tailoring shops, and boutiques and storefronts in the area of Saint-Honoré in Paris, while the traditional couturiers remained in the original fashion area of Paris in the sixth *arrondissement* in the neighborhood of Saint-Germain-des-Prés. The designers taking up residence in this new fashion district had brand-new ideas to match their new address. Top designers were now creating fashion-forward maternity clothing, for example, and others were using elements of Eastern, especially Japanese, design.

With the prêt-à-porter market growing ever stronger, even some couturiers got into the act. Yves Saint-Laurent had opened Rive Gauche, his ready-to-wear boutique, in the late 1960s, and by the 1970s it was a trend leader in the prêt-à-porter market. Pierre Cardin and other major couture players followed suit with great success. In 1973, following close on the heels of a Parisian fashion industry trade union, Mode et Création was organized. It paired rising designers with houses specializing in prêt-à-porter lines. This style co-op would remain popular and powerful for decades to come. Designers were able to expand their designs and showcase new ideas using these alliances. Wearable art and retro styles were very popular among the new designers as well as the buying public.

The fashion media found that no matter what they presented to the public, the public would make its own decisions. For example, in 1970, *Women's Wear Daily* and other important fashion publications insisted that the "midi" skirt would replace the miniskirt. The midi, also called the *longuette*, was a mid-calf-length skirt. There were organized protests, rallies, and parades against the change to the midi. Retailers could not sell very many of the skirts, and it was devastating to them because they had ordered large quantities in anticipation of the large-scale changeover to the new styles. Women who decided to try the new midi length were often ridiculed. Stories circulated of women being "laughed out of the office" and of a junior high school student denied participation in commencement because she wore a long skirt.[3] A few years later, after the media had given up pushing the style, the midi took off and by 1974 became high fashion. The fashion press declared that fashion was "dead," and the power of the press was seriously undermined in the 1970s.

Pants were far more accepted in the seventies than they had been in the preceding decade, and fashion began to cater to trousers for women. Like skirts, pants were available in a variety of lengths—from long, wide-leg trousers to calf-length gaucho pants to extremely short "hot pants." Matching pants and jackets had become popular business attire in the late 1960s and far surpassed skirt suits in the 1970s. Bell-bottoms remained popular until about 1976. A few years later, the pants had widened and were worn with a gathered look at the waist and usually with the hems cuffed at the ankle.

Jeans became a very common element in wardrobe by the seventies, having broken almost entirely free of the connection to the counterculture so prevalent in the sixties. Jeans were emblazoned with labels as designers began to add the fashion staple to their ready-to-wear lines. Toward the end of the decade, girls and young women often wore extremely tight blue jeans, often requiring them to lie on the floor in order to get them zipped.

The explosion of technology and trends so prevalent in the 1960s contracted quite a bit in the 1970s. Designers went back to basics, using wool, jute, and other more traditional fabrics, but in nontraditional ways. While polyester was still extraordinarily popular, it was being supplanted by the move back to natural fibers.

There was an interest in a simpler and more innocent mood in fashion, a sense of returning to its roots. Traditional and folk costumes were disappearing around the world, and many designers sought to reclaim those designs. Looks that were derived from India, Native Americans, Eastern Europe, and Africa became extremely popular. Many of these styles were paired with a nostalgic air of Victorian or Edwardian dress. The incorporation of these retro styles in the seventies was different than their uses in the Mod and hippie fashions of the sixties, however. The seventies aimed for a more wholesome and less flamboyant look. Designers like Anne-Marie Beretta and Laura Ashley focused on natural fibers, muted colors, and elegant and simple styles. Many of these designers looked toward artwork, both contemporary and antique. Ashley was particularly interested in the Victorian-era illustrations of artist Kate Greenaway.

Women's fashion of this time period has been described as "fluid."[4] The emphasis was on casual fit and easy styling, with attention to individuality. Whereas the silhouette had been unfitted but stiff in the sixties, the mode in the seventies was softer lines and more draping fabrics that clung to the body, hugging curves. Knits in cotton, polyester, wool, and blends of natural fibers with polyester were employed in dresses and pantsuits. Neutrals and earth tones replaced the vivid and bold patterns of the previous decade, as well. Dresses used stretchy fabrics and elastic waistbands or drawstring waists for more comfortable wear.

Diane Von Furstenburg was one of the vanguards of this new styling. Her signature dress was a cotton knit wrap that tied shut with an attached belt. Swirling wrap skirts were also very popular, influenced by Von Furstenburg's designs. They were often made from cotton imported from India and printed in the traditional manner.

Early in the decade, skirts were available in a wide variety of lengths, but by the end of the 1970s, skirts were predominantly knee length, although some were longer and some were shorter, but never so short at the iconic miniskirts of the 1960s.

The popularity of discotheques was as much a part of women's fashion as it was men's. The disco became a place to show off one's most fashionable attire, but there was no formality. Women wore flirty dresses or hot pants or jeans, depending on their mood. Tall, platform-soled shoes were popular in all facets of daily wear but were especially favored at the disco. Makeup and hairdressing were also important there. Although a natural look was favored early on, larger hair and brighter makeup soon became the accepted style. Television, movies, and other media had a serious impact on how women chose to style their hair. Whether it was the short Dorothy Hamill wedge or the full, teased, and frosted hair of Farrah Fawcett, or even tight frizzled curls like Barbra Streisand's in *A Star Is Born* (1976), women increasingly looked to the media to help them decide their style.

MEN'S CLOTHING

The 1970s was a milestone decade in men's clothing design. For the first time, designers were creating and licensing exclusive fashion for men. What started with Pierre Cardin in 1957 came to be a fashion staple by the 1970s. Designer labels became more important than brand names for both women and men, but especially for men. For the first time, designer menswear was a major part of the fashion world and earned a permanent place there. Attention to fashionable color and texture that changed from year to year was a new experience for most men.

Color and Fabrics

Early in the decade, the "Peacock Revolution" was still going strong. Men wore colorful shirts and brightly printed ties. New advances in dyes and synthetic textiles were responsible for this upsurge in availability of such a variety of colors and textures. Even for business attire, the white shirt was losing some prominence in favor for muted colors such as pale pink, blue, and other soft shades. More vivid colors were worn for casual wear. Later in the decade, color could also be seen in jackets and slacks.

Sweaters

Sweaters for men rose in popularity beginning in the late sixties were very popular in the seventies, continuing the attention to color and texture. Early in the 1970s, sweaters were snugly fit and ended just below the natural waist. There was a sense of body consciousness that remained popular though the decade. Clingy stretch-knit sweaters and turtlenecks hugged the torso and showed off the physique. These tops were very popular among young men. But toward the end of the seventies, shirt and sweater silhouettes grew larger, looser, and slightly longer.

Shirts

Shirts for men remained colorful throughout the decade and offered men many options. White and understated colors were still available for business or more formal attire, but shirts for more casual occasions were created in vivid colors and bold prints as well as stripes.

Another signature shirt element of menswear in the 1970s was the western-wear influence. With the availability of and interest in clothes available in a variety of colors, prints, and decorative styling, the Western-style shirt was a popular choice. Although Lyndon Johnson was not a style leader like John F. Kennedy had been, his Texan background led to wider interest in Western wear across the United States and to a much smaller degree in England, particularly London. The most common textile used in these shirts was a cotton-polyester blend, and they were worn with colorful ties often as wide as three inches (8 cm); ties would become narrower again near the end of the decade.

A V-neck, less structured shirt was also popular. These were often made with a 100-percent polyester knit and were usually printed with vivid colors and prints. Some of these shirts were made with very wide, deep collars, and some were collarless like a tunic. These tops were usually worn tucked into slacks with a wide belt.

The Leisure Suit

The popular V-neck top and slacks combination was soon being made in matching fabrics, usually of colorful polyester. These were marketed as an alternative casual look, dubbed "leisure suits." Leisure suits were available in a staggering array of colors and patterns and were worn with the V-neck top or button-down shirt with long sleeves. The collars of these shirts were usually very large. Leisure suits were one of the defining looks for men in the 1970s, but their popularity did not last beyond the close of the decade.

Formal Dress

Another characteristic style of menswear of this time period was colorful suits and tuxedoes. The Peacock Revolution inspired more body consciousness and use of color in all facets of menswear, and even formalwear was subject to this trend. Tuxedoes were produced in a large variety of colors such as blue, green, burgundy, and brown. They were often made of polyester, and velvet was frequently used in accents on the wide collars and lapels or even as the base fabric for the entire suit. The shirts worn with these colorful tuxedoes usually matched the color, but in a paler hue. These shirts were typically ruffled down the front.

Sports Clothing

The 1972 Olympics was a large influence in men's active sportswear. Slimmer, racing-inspired swimsuits were now being sold along with the small, European-styled "slip" swimsuits. An interest in surfing that had begun in the sixties continued through the seventies and spawned its own styles of long trunks made in nylon and cotton called "jams."[5] For the first time, a swimsuit for every man's preference was available on the market, from the very tiny European styles to the longer, looser-fitting surf shorts.

Tennis was also a popular leisure activity and a professional sport that a lot of people followed all over the world. Interest in tennis was very high in the 1970s, and clothing originally designed for active wear began to be seen on the street. The most long-lasting piece of active wear that migrated into daily attire was the athletic shoe, which was commonly known as the "tennis shoe." White was the predominant color for tennis clothing through the early 1970s, but by the middle of the decade, the interest in color in other areas of fashion translated into tennis clothes. Men's and women's clothing designed for tennis was beginning to be made in colors other than white, although white would always remain an important element of the color scheme.

Hair

Long hair remained in vogue across the United States and Europe through the decade for many young men, but by the end of the 1970s, shorter styles became popular again. Although some military-inspired styles persisted, once American soldiers were officially recalled from the Vietnam War, most people wanted to forget it ever happened.

For the most part, the world over, men adopted colorful styles and longer hair that had not been seen since the eighteenth century. This interest in color and the new importance of label recognition would set the stage for the high-profile, high-fashion interest in designer clothes for men that would emerge in the decades to follow.

CHILDREN'S WEAR

Clothing for children in the 1970s did not experience much innovation. New advances in textiles rippled through the sixties into the seventies. Safety and comfort were still important concerns for construction of children's clothing. Washable, easy-care textiles introduced in the 1960s grew in usage as designers and manufacturers found clever ways to create and market children's clothing.

Although there were few changes in the design of children's clothing, what did change was the approach to marketing. Manufacturers were starting to recognize the untapped consumer base that was the children's clothing market. In 1976, the Garan Corporation developed a line of children's wear aimed at the children themselves. They were designed for small children age two and older and had colorful animal labels. Children could pick out their own ensembles by matching the "Garanimals" on the labels. This promotion was very popular with parents and children through the early 1980s.[6]

Making clothes at home for children was still fairly popular. Major pattern companies routinely produced many trendy and seasonal patterns for children's wear.

Infant and toddler wear did not develop much further than the easy-access terrycloth one-piece, although it was made available in more styles, colors, and decorative elements throughout the decade. Cotton was still the textile of choice for infant wear and for young children's clothes, but it began to be blended with polyester and other synthetic fibers. Pastel colors were easier to achieve by advancements in dyes and were readily used in clothes for infants. Embroidery and smocking continued to be popular choices for day clothes, especially those designed for the gift-giving market and aimed toward grandparents.

Clothing for toddlers was designed with child development in mind. Bright, primary colors said to appeal to a child's developing vision were used in design for toddlers. Cotton and synthetics were also employed in design for toddlers for comfort, safety, durability, and good color retention.

Young boys still wore clothing based on the styles of adult men. Sport jackets and pants, both short and long, were worn by many boys. Mod-inspired,

Edwardian-style three-piece suits were also popular for some children in the 1970s. Adult-style leisure suits with bell-bottom pants in a variety of colors, weaves, and prints were being sold for preteen and adolescent boys, as well, and were very popular.

Knit T-shirts and polo shirts soon became the mainstay of casual dressing for boys. T-shirts were available with bold graphics, often of popular cartoon characters and other images meant to appeal to boys. "Polo shirts" were made in rich colors, usually with a white collar and a horizontal stripe often in a contrasting color. T-shirts and polos were very popular casual and play clothes for boys.

Young girls in the 1970s had a very wide array of clothing from which to choose. They could wear various lengths of skirts or even pants. The maxi-length skirts were popular for dressy or party clothes. The silhouette was more fitted than it had been in the 1960s, and belts were often worn. Comfort for children became increasingly important, and this was seen in fashion for girls in the 1970s when pants began to be worn more often than skirts for everyday. At first, pants were only worn for casual wear or for play clothes, but by the middle of the decade, girls were routinely wearing pants to school.

Throughout the seventies, blue jeans were a mainstay of children's fashion for both boys and girls. They were comfortable, durable, washable, and trendy. Jeans also started to play a role in the new strength of designer labels, even for children. The power of licensing began to take shape in the late 1970s with logo T-shirts and blue jeans with prominently displayed labels, not only for adults but for children. Focusing on a children's market like this helped establish a loyal customer for life by introducing a designer's product to the young and impressionable.

STYLE TRIBES AND OTHER FASHIONS

At the opening of the 1970s, "style tribes" were still an integral part of fashion, particularly within youth subcultures. Although the term would not be applied to the phenomenon until the 1990s by Ted Polhemus,[7] the idea of style tribes defines these groups very well.

Antiwar protest and hippie fashions were the leading dress of the counterculture. But soon jeans went from a symbol of protest and youth culture to a hot trend in demand around the world. Stories circulated that in Soviet-controlled Eastern Bloc countries, blue jeans could be traded as currency, so valuable were these icons of Western culture.[8] For most youth, the 1970s was a time of paring down and adopting a simple, comfortable, and durable style.

Although it was highly protested, the Vietnam War created an interest in military styles. Some used these styles as part of their protests, drawing peace symbols on army jackets and fatigues to draw attention to their cause. Many young women used military styles, usually closely associated with masculinity, as "an aggressive demand for equal rights."[9] Across Europe and in the United States, military-influenced styles such as peacoats and items styled to look like army fatigues were remarked on by the fashion press. Some groups utilized military surplus and others started with a militaristic look and made it their own. The most popular use of this latter style was taking the camouflage pattern and producing it in unusual colors. This style would prove to be popular through the 1970s and for decades beyond, even into the new millennium.

A defining style tribe of the seventies was the Punk Rockers. Starting around the mid-1970s, fans of a genre of British music known as punk rock began to establish their own style. Leftover influence from the Rockers of the early 1960s fed into this deconstructed style. Devotees of punk music used their clothes, like most of the adolescent style tribe members, as a means of identifying themselves with the subculture and alienating themselves from the mainstream. Punk was as much a state of mind as it was a fashion statement and had as much worldwide influence on youth as the hippies and Mods had in the 1960s.

The punk movement was centered on a teenage sense of lost youth and innocence. Punks rejected the aesthetically pleasing and often took common items and used them in shocking ways. Clothing was chosen and manipulated to send specific messages. School uniform blazers were torn apart, crudely patched, held together with safety pin, worn inside out, or all of the above. Anything that they thought would be shocking to the mainstream was used with gusto in punk style: Mohawk hairstyles dyed outrageous colors, totally shaved heads, razor blades, swastikas, condoms, chains, pornography, and sexually explicit material. The entire style was aimed at being as shocking as possible.

Vivienne Westwood, the owner of a popular London boutique called Let It Rock, was instantly interested in this new, unique style. A schoolteacher by trade, Westwood was a self-taught seamstress and teamed up with Malcolm McLaren and began designing for the punk movement. Westwood's shop changed its name to Too Fast to Live, Too Young to Die in 1972; Sex in 1974; and Seditionaries in 1977.[10] Both Sex and Seditionaries are names of Westwood boutiques that are still in business in many cities around the world, including London, Paris, and New York.

Three pioneers of the punk style were Johnny Rotten and Sid Vicious, both of the punk band the Sex Pistols, and Jordan, a shop assistant at Westwood's boutique. The punk trend-setters were very high-profile throughout London, and their influence soon reached the rest of the world. Two iconic pieces of punk fashion that Westwood created were "drainpipe pants," ultra skinny-leg jeans that were a backlash against bell-bottoms, and "bondage pants," tight-fitted pants often cut from Tartan plaid with leather straps that wrapped around both legs. Although the original punk movement officially lasted only from the summer of 1975 until January 1978,[11] the fashion and the music still lives on. Nor did Westwood's success end with the punk movement. She would go on to become one of the most cutting-edge designers of the late twentieth century.

Zandra Rhodes was the only mainstream designer to incorporate the punk look into her couture lines. Designing in England, she tapped into some of the more acceptable aspects of the style: ripped black fishnets, chains, heavy black eye makeup, and hair dyed black with streaks of red, green, blue, or purple. Her clothes inspired a short-lived interest in punk styles, but she would never have the lasting consumer loyalty and popularity that Westwood took from the movement.

But possibly the most defining style tribe of the 1970s was the disco fashion. No other style is so indicative of its time than was disco. Disco was a "fashion characterized by superficiality."[12] The very mention of the word conjures up precise images of polyester suits, platform shoes, lighted dance floors, and mirror balls. Like punk, the style of the disco was a specific coded vocabulary decipherable only to those who were part of the style tribe.

Much of the disco fashion was related to the clubs themselves. The dance floors lit from below directed attention to the legs. The light displays and mirror balls created an interest in clothing that was reflective. Clothing for both men and women was very tight fitting, often with a flare at the hem. Tall shoes added to the illusion of height and long proportions. This created the impression that the dancer was "simultaneously suspended above, and rooted to, the dance floor by the weight of the shoes."[13] Shimmering fabrics like Lurex, satin, PVC, and leather were also popular; shiny, "wet look" lip gloss for the women enhanced this otherworldly effect. Metallic features in clothing and footwear were extremely popular. There was also a sense of androgyny as both men and women dressed in tight-fitting clothes, sometimes even catsuits and leotard-like bodysuits, and experimented in color, texture, and form. Like punk, disco was a short-lived phenomenon, but it left an indelible mark on fashion history.

CONCLUSION

By decade's end, fashion had become diverse and often dilute. No one designer led the way when it came to style. Consumers bought what they fancied and did not wait for trendsetters or the fashion press to tell them what was hot. World events and energy crises had a much larger impact on the fashion industry than anyone could have foreseen and proved further dissipate the influence of couture. This rise in individualism would be one of the hallmarks of the decade that would be its legacy through the years to come.

NOTES

1. The original fireside chats were a series of addresses made by President Franklin D. Roosevelt in the 1930s. "The first Presidential radio broadcast was introduced by Robert Trout of CBS, who read from a folksy script approved by FDR: 'The President wants to come into your home and sit at your fireside for a little fireside chat.' FDR brought natural talent to the role. His speaking voice was a beautiful, relaxed tenor, not the contrived basso profundo of pompous politicians" (Jonathan Alter, *The Defining Moment: FDR's Hundred Days and the Triumph of Hope* [New York: Simon & Schuster, 2006], quoted in "The Voice of Courage," *Reader's Digest*, May 2006, http://www.rd.com/content/openContent.do?contentId=26499>).

2. Sarah McNeill, "Underoos to the Rescue," *Brandchannel.com*, August 27, 2001, http://www.brandchannel.com/features_profile.asp?pr_id=32.

3. Phyllis Tortora and Keith Eubank, *Survey of Historic Costume: A History of Western Dress*, 4th ed. (New York: Fairchild, 2005), 485.

4. Tortora and Eubank, *Survey of Historic Costume*, 481.

5. Tortora and Eubank, *Survey of Historic Costume*, 489.

6. Tortora and Eubank, *Survey of Historic Costume*, 492.

7. Polhemus, Ted. *Street Style: From the Sidewalk to the Catwalk*. New York: Thames and Hudson, 1994.

8. Tortora and Eubank, *Survey of Historic Costume*, 462.

9. Gerda Buxbaum, ed., *Icons of Fashion: The 20th Century* (Munich, Germany: Prestel, 1999), 106.

10. Buxbaum, *Icons of Fashion*, 119.

11. Buxbaum, *Icons of Fashion*, 120.

12. Buxbaum, *Icons of Fashion*, 116.
13. Buxbaum, *Icons of Fashion*, 116.

FURTHER READING

Boucher, François. *20,000 Years of Fashion: The History of Costume and Personal Adornment*. New York: H. N. Abrams, 1987.

Buxbaum, Gerda, ed. *Icons of Fashion: The 20th Century*. Munich, Germany: Prestel, 1999.

Polhemus, Ted. *Street Style: From the Sidewalk to the Catwalk*. New York: Thames and Hudson, 1994.

Tortora, Phyllis, and Keith Eubank. *Survey of Historic Costume: A History of Western Dress*. 4th ed. New York: Fairchild, 2005.

MOVIES

Annie Hall (1977)
Boogie Nights (1997)
54 (1998)
Saturday Night Fever (1977)
Shaft (1971)
Shampoo (1975)
Thank God It's Friday (1978)
That 70s Show (Fox, 1998–2006)

The Eighties

Jennifer Grayer Moore

TIMELINE

1980	Hollywood actor Ronald Reagan elected president of the United States; black majority rule achieved in Zimbabwe (formerly Rhodesia)
1980–1988	Iran-Iraq War
1981	Prince Charles marries Lady Diana Spencer; Polartec invented by Malden Mills from recycled soft drink bottles
1983	Paris prêt-à-porter shows allow Japanese designers to show collections
1984	Apple personal computers become popular
1987	Christian Lacroix breathes new life into the Paris fashion scene by opening his couture house
1988	George H. W. Bush elected president of the United States

The 1980s was a decade of extremes. These extremes to a great extent can be tied to the economics of the time, with the first two-thirds of the decade characterized by an economic boom both in the United States (under the administration of Ronald Reagan and his Republican "Reaganomics") and in Europe and Asia. Economic prosperity was on the downturn worldwide by the end of the decade, however, and was definitively marked in the United States by the stock market crash of October 19, 1987.

The Cold War continued until the end of the decade, when the imminent collapse of the powerful Soviet system of government was obvious, lasting only until early in the next decade. Throughout the early eighties, though, people continued to fear nuclear war between the United States and the Soviet Union. The United States boycotted the 1980 Olympic Games in Moscow, and the Soviets did the same for the 1984 Olympics in Los Angeles. Behind the Iron Curtain, life was quite different from that in the West, and economically and socially, life was difficult. Defections were exciting news, and Russian ballet stars such as Mikhail Baryshnikov became stars in the West, showing their talents with North American dance troops.

Extreme wealth impacted fashion dramatically in the 1980s. It was a time during which haute couture was a bustling segment of the fashion industry and new couturiers came upon the scene. Wealthy clients, men and women alike, sought out designer goods as a means of conspicuous displays of prosperity, and the fashion industry stepped up to the demand by developing and expanding product lines and signature goods. There was nothing subtle about 1980s designer fashions.

At the other extreme, youth culture and pop culture were to have profound impacts upon both high style and street fashions. The products of this influence are among the most vibrant, bold, and memorable designs of the twentieth century. In the 1980s, with the expansion and improvement of media delivery systems such as cable television and VHS and Betamax video recorders, the communication of fashionable dress through movies, television series, and, perhaps most importantly, the new medium of music videos became undeniably important.

The eighties was a tumultuous time for race relations, which were exacerbated by incidents in the United States of senseless urban violence, such as Bernard Goetz's 1985 shooting of four black youths or the 1986 Howard Beach, New York, lynching of Michael Griffith by four white teens. Despite widespread racial tensions, nonwhite style became far more influential in this period. Black culture tied to break dancing and rap music penetrated mainstream media and influenced a generation of kids across cultural lines. Japanese fashions, so very different in their aesthetics and philosophies, finally infiltrated the Western imagination.

AIDS was beginning to show the dangers of the free love philosophy of the sixties and seventies, initially affecting the gay communities in bigger urban centers in the industrialized countries, having spread from across the world. Eventually this disease affected not only gay men but spread to the wider population through blood transfusions as well as sexual activity. A change in lifestyle was recommended, and vast sums of money were raised, and continue to be raised, in an effort to fight the disease worldwide.

In an era of great diversity, characterized by extremes, it is impossible to address every trend or every meritorious moment in a work of this scope. Rather, this chapter presents a foundation and context for understanding the fashions of this era and what they meant.

The decade of the 1980s is perhaps best recalled as an era of conspicuous consumption. Many of the fashions of the period speak loudly of a time of economic boom in which stocks and bonds moved the world. The character Gordon Gekko from the 1987 movie *Wall Street* is often cited as having made the clarion call of a generation when he stated, "Greed is good." Style commentator Peter York, so captivated by the ambition and accomplishment of this young generation of go-getters, was moved to coin the term *yuppies* (a play on "young urban professionals") as a catchall phrase to describe them. The children of the postwar Baby Boom enjoyed great prosperity and successful careers in urban centers. They were concerned about appearances in all aspects of life—from dress, home, and the cars they drove to the coffee they drank.

An indisputable response on the part of the fashion industry to the desire of young professionals to display their achievement through fashion was the proliferation of labeled or logo-emblazoned goods. Brands such as Chanel, Gucci, Fendi, and Versace built collections, especially of accessories, around their trademark symbols—overlapping *C*'s (Chanel), opposing *G*'s (Gucci), interlocking *F*'s (Fendi), and Versace's Medusa head insignia on everything from textile patterns to buttons and buckles to interior design elements. Brands that had long built lines of designer goods around signature patterns or branding gained even more cachet in the 1980s, for example, Louis Vuitton with its label plastered all over its traditional luggage, purses, and wallets.

In addition to expanding lines of apparel and accessories to accommodate this new taste, designers capitalized on their brand identity by expanding their licensed goods, most notably through extensive lines of fragrance and cosmetics. The rage for designer goods influenced fashion at all levels. Brands at lower prices began to produce logoed or label-centric goods as well, and although these brands may not have had any cachet and failed to make the same type of statement of exclusivity as the haute couture labels, such items sold well to those with money to spend. Common examples of label mania among mass-produced garments and accessories included the brands Benetton of Italy, Naf Naf from France, and Roots from Canada, which utilized prominent labeling on most of their goods.

Counterfeiting of designer-label goods became a problem of phenomenal proportions, with manufacturers based in Asia cashing in on the craze for nearly identical knockoffs. Goods were sold illegally in markets for a fraction of the price of the real thing, so it wasn't long before millions of women were walking around towns across the world with their "Gucci" bags. It was sometimes hard to tell the differences between the real thing and the copies, but generally the quality was very poor and the colors and designs nothing like the real thing.

Copying the Louis Vuitton signature print was especially popular among American urban blacks, who used the illegal textiles to make anything from baseball caps and bomber jackets. These styles were never produced by the real company and were clearly not the designer's goods. More problematic for the designer goods producers, however, was the reproduction of handbags, wallets, and belts that were sold as the real thing. This problem only continued to proliferate and intensify through the ensuing decades as technology for accurate reproduction became better and more readily available.

Perhaps the most important development of the 1980s was the advent of *diffusion lines*. Designers as diverse in aesthetics as Calvin Klein, Gianni Versace, Donna Karan, and Giorgio Armani, sensing that there were untapped markets for their designs, albeit at lower price points, developed diffusion lines under names such as CK Jeans, Versace Jeans Couture, DKNY, and Armani Exchange. Each of these brands offered the illustrious appeal of the designer's name, but with garments that were simpler in construction, required less in terms of detailing, and were generally made of less expensive fabrics, allowing the prices to suit more consumers' budgets.

Not all designers were so enthusiastic about the trend toward conspicuous labeling. The most prominent example of a designer opposed to this movement was the "bad boy of Italian fashion," Franco Moschino. Rather than following lockstep and capitalizing on the desires of consumers, Moschino used his clothes and accessories as commentary on the industry. His garment designs were lighthearted and often mocked what he viewed as the fashion victims of the age. A famous and poignant example of Moschino's work was a black tote bag accented in red that bore the word "LOGO" in white text in constant repetition across the entire surface of the handbag.

Conspicuous labels and logos were not the only way for a fashion aficionado to proclaim his or her devotion to designer goods and financial status. Women of means found haute couture to be a perfectly viable means communicating their status. In the 1980s, there were estimated to be close to three thousand haute couture clients worldwide. By most estimates, the average has generally hovered closer to two thousand in more recent times. The strong U.S. dollar and booming Japanese market of the time are considered the reasons for the increased clientele. To accommodate these clients, there were five dominant haute couture ateliers in the 1980s: Chanel, Dior, Ungaro, Givenchy, and Yves Saint-Laurent.

By most accounts, the majority of couture being produced by these houses could be described as "classic French design." However, this changed in some instances over the course of the decade, most notably at the House of Chanel, where in 1982 Karl Lagerfeld was tapped to take over the haute couture segment of the business. Lagerfeld, while retaining the spirit of the founding designer Gabrielle (Coco) Chanel, breathed new life and a pronounced youthfulness into the brand that had lapsed into conservative repetition of house standards ever since the death of Chanel herself in 1971. By 1983 Lagerfeld had taken over as the design consultant to the entire house, thereby influencing the ready-to-wear and accessory lines as well.

In 1987, French haute couture celebrated a new star in the witty and iconoclastic designs of Christian Lacroix. Loved by many for his opulence, color, glamour, and overall extravagance, Lacroix breathed new life, ironically by taking inspiration from the past, into the traditions that were typically explored by the other French couturiers. In fact, journalists of the period declared that Lacroix had "saved" or "revived" French haute couture. His fledgling operation, backed by LVMH (Louis Vuitton Moet Hennessy) chairman and 51-percent owner Bernard Arnault, was positioned for success and opulence. The opulence of Lacroix's designs recalled luxury not seen since eighteenth-century France with their flamboyant luxurious fabrics and staged fashion shows.

Lacroix certainly had his detractors as well. There were social commentators who, in the economic downturn of the late 1980s, remarked upon the inappropriateness of his opulent theatrical designs. Feminists formed another group of Lacroix critics. In an age in which women were entering the white-collar workforce in unprecedented numbers, his elaborate, ultrafeminine designs, replete with crinolines, were interpreted as a step backward for womankind. In an age of extremes, Lacroix was the perfect target for a social critique. Indeed the opulence of Christian Lacroix's work and the lifestyle of those who wore it was lampooned in the BBC series *Absolutely Fabulous*, in which the oft-times intoxicated, always careless, self-centered, and disgustingly rich Edina Monsoon could often be found stumbling about in ill-fitting Lacroix gowns in great profusion, looking every bit the fashion victim.

Lacroix was not the only designer of the 1980s raising ire within the elite circles of the fashion world. Jean-Paul Gaultier was every inch the rabble-rouser and gadfly. His approach to fashion can only be described as postmodern, as he sought to undermine so many of the accepted standards of design, taste, decency, gender, and even ethnicity. Gaultier is perhaps most often recalled for his bondage- or fetish-inspired conical bras that were widely publicized when first shown and were popularized when they were translated into part of the stage costume of pop icon Madonna for her 1993 "Blond Ambition" tour.

Gaultier also experimented with gender-bending aesthetics, putting female models into Dr. Martens combat boots and men into garments that looked like skirts from the front. Early on, Gaultier challenged accepted standards of beauty by using models who were old, fat, tattooed, and pierced. His ability to raise eyebrows continued into ensuing decades, perhaps most notably in his 1993 collection inspired by Hasidim.

JAPANESE INFLUENCES

European designers were not the only ones shaking up the fashion scene in the 1980s. A great part of the diversity of the decade can be attributed to the newly felt presence and appreciation of Japanese designers. Issey Miyake had been a well-established designer in Japan since the 1970s, but his innovations and the presence of other adventurous Japanese designers were not truly felt until after 1981 when they began to show their collections in Paris and thereby excited and inspired the European and American imaginations.

Miyake, renowned to the present day for his innovative textiles—which, through minimal construction techniques, hold crisp, architectural peaks and have inspired copycat versions of his permanently pleated polyester fabrics—has inspired awe and evoked critical acclaim as he has continuously sought out new and innovate silhouettes that defy or ignore the natural curves of the body, creating interesting otherworldly silhouettes. Among the other maverick Japanese designers to show their collections in Paris commencing in 1981 was Rei Kawakubo, acting as lead designer for Commes de Garçons. Kawakubo's designs turned innumerable aspects of Western fashion on their head as she explored bold and architectural silhouettes, innovative and atypical materials, and gender-bending aesthetics. Also among this first class of Japanese innovators was Yohji Yamamoto, who, in his early collections, explored the aesthetics of beggars and victims of the atomic bombs dropped on Hiroshima and Nagasaki in 1945.

In addition to the many landmark designs and collections of top designers, there were also broader movements in fashion that are noteworthy. Early in the 1980s, there was a widespread trend, especially in the United States, for all things Australian. Sturdy garments suitable for trekking in the outback were marketed as fashionable dress. The most widely recognized brand of Australian apparel, R. M. Williams, sold apparel using the slogan "the Original Bushman's Outfitters." Aussie brand hair care products with their bold purple packaging and exotic tropical scent were a must-have, despite the fact that the product lacked unique performance characteristics. Banana Republic, in its earliest incarnation, sold garments and marketed its brand identity using a single note—safari-inspired apparel. Khaki pants, jackets with patch pockets, and wide-brimmed hats were standard fare. These garments evoked the Australian outback, fresh in the imaginations of Americans thanks to the *Crocodile Dundee* movies of the mid-1980s, as much as they did an African safari or island outpost.

SLOANE RANGERS

The impact of the English aesthetic on international style cannot be attributed to a single brand, but rather to a group of women living in West London near

Sloane Square. This group of upper-middle-class women was known as the "Sloane Rangers" (or more simply as "Sloanes" or "Sloanies"), thanks in part to the Peter York book *The Official Sloane Ranger Handbook: The First Guide to What Really Matters in Life*. This group adopted a look that was instantly recognizable and emblematic of the 1980s, even though it typified conservative, traditional dress. The worldwide fascination with Lady Diana Spencer, later Diana, Princess of Wales, popularized the look, as she was a member of this social set prior to her marriage to Prince Charles.

In the same vein as the preppies in America, the Sloane Ranger look consisted of beautifully crafted, subtle pieces of utterly feminine attire as well as traditional sportswear. Impeccable pastel-colored sweaters made of cashmere, flawlessly tailored button-down shirts or ruffled blouses, and skirts in traditional florals or tartans were mainstays of the style. Traditional sporting attire, tweeds, headbands, and perhaps a status accessory such as an Hermés foulard and precious but understated jewelry such as a strand of pearls completed the look. The Sloane Ranger is often described as being purposefully deconstructed, with simply cut, shoulder-length hair held pulled into a ponytail or held with a headband. The Sloane Ranger was not a frivolous dresser and, although she might come from a family of some means, the display of wealth was encrypted in the high-quality clothing and accessories she wore.

AMERICAN STYLE

In the 1980s, American style rose to the fore of world fashion with the international influence of designers such as Calvin Klein and Donna Karan. These designers were at the vanguard of establishing a style that was distinctively American, rather than simply reinterpreting European trends. Fueled in part by the rise of women in the American corporate workplace, these fresh, new designs, characterized by their simplicity and wearability, were introduced at a time when there was an emerging market with both the need and means to purchase suitable clothes. This category of corporate consumers was only one fraction of the market that proliferated the styles of Klein and Karan, but their influence is indisputable.

Both Klein and Karan capitalized on the possibilities of creating lines of interchangeable separates. Blouses, jackets, slacks, and skirts were austere by comparison to European design and therefore were suitable to the corporate environment in which a woman was well advised to blend in with the largely male infrastructure. Simplicity of cut and color characterized this new American aesthetic and enabled a new way of dressing. The possibilities of different looks with interchangeable pieces also had the potential to allow an outfit to go from the workplace to an evening out by simply changing one part of the outfit. Karan's early designs, characterized by the use of supple jersey fabrics and monochrome, were especially popular for the urban executive. Indeed, she has proclaimed that New York City life was a great source of inspiration for the aesthetics of her brand.

A parallel phenomenon of the 1980s was the development of the "power suit." For women seeking respect and equality in a workplace dominated by men, covering up the feminine seemed essential. Working in corporate climates with regimented dress policies, suiting (with exceptionally wide shoulders) was mandatory. The power suit consisted of a mannish-style suit jacket with well-padded shoulders and a roomy cut, a pair of trousers or a skirt (long or at least to the knee), a blouse with a high neck, sometimes ruffled, and a ribbon or tie around the neck. Shoes were sensible pumps with a bit of a heel. As this uniform became well established in the corporate world, designers in both Europe and America capitalized on the need for fashionable yet, in many ways, traditional dress.

Designers such as Thierry Mugler, Giorgio Armani, and Claude Montana each interpreted the power suit in a unique way. Italian designer Armani created menswear-inspired suits for women, but with a soft, somewhat rounded drape to the shoulders and fabrics that draped softly around the body. These suits were constructed using minimal interfacings and interlinings, thus creating a new interpretation of traditional suiting forms that communicated a sophisticated and understated elegance. Montana's version of the power suit was diametrically opposed to that of Armani. While he stayed true to the menswear tradition, his highly structured, and shoulder-padded looks conveyed a monumentality and masculinity not seen in Armani's work. The shoulder pad itself became a fixture of 1980s dressing and was a mainstay of women's suiting at most price levels. Mugler's vision of the power suit was loosely based on traditional concepts of women's suiting that date back as the 1890s, but the overall aesthetic and message of Mugler's garments was sexy and bold as opposed to traditional or conservative. His garments were typically crafted in bold colors and often utilized multichrome palettes. Jackets were tailored with aggressively padded shoulder lines that were often offset with architectural, sometimes plunging necklines. The overall communication of these clothes was thoroughly modern, and the woman who donned them would have appeared vibrant and strong.

THE FITNESS CRAZE

Physical fitness was a craze in the 1980s with the advent of aerobics classes (largely inspired in America by Jane Fonda's workout); gyms and aerobics studios opened all around the world so people could get their hour of exercise every day and care for their health and body. Strength and fitness affected fashion both inside and outside the gym as the 1980s health craze defined myriad trends and fashions. Some scholars have argued that the mania for physical fitness was a backlash to the excess and debauchery of the 1970s, when substance use and abuse was rampant. Wherever the impetus for aerobics, Dancercise, and cross-training came from, it is clear that physical fitness was of great importance in this decade, and its hold over the American imagination can be recalled by referencing music (Olivia Newton John's number-one hit in 1981, "Physical") and movies (*Flashdance* was a cultural phenomenon in 1983) or by simply looking at the types of garments that were made and sold in this era.

Norma Kamali made fashion history when, in 1981, she took the fleece tracksuit from the mundane and made it high style in a collection she designed for the Jones Apparel Group. Until this time, the tracksuit had been a standard and unremarkable pairing of a simple pullover and loose pull-on pants with

Jennifer Beals (as Alex Owens) stars in Adrian Lyne's 1983 film, *Flashdance.* Courtesy of Photofest.

elasticized waistband and ankles. Kamali transformed this basic look into high fashion as she shortened the pants to knickers, put shoulder pads in the sweatshirt, and added a peplum flounce. Although gray was still the most sought-after color in this line, the suiting was also available in black, pink, and powder blue.

Designer athletic gear, whether used for sports of not, proliferated throughout the 1980s with garments available in velour, terry cloth, cotton jersey, and nylon. Versions from the last of these, known as "shell suits," were typically constructed of piecework in vivid multicolor and enjoyed great popularity among men and women. Stirrup pants, first popularized on the ski slopes, were also a sports-inspired fashion trend for women in middecade; they furnished an alternative to stretch leggings, derived from the dance studio, and created a body-conscious line, often offset by an oversized, off-the-shoulder top.

Leotards, cropped leggings, leg warmers, wrist guards, headbands, and cropped tops, all derived from dance-wear, were popular street wear in the 1980s and were often colored with bright neon colors like acid green, yellow, shocking pink, or orange. Using nylon fibers blended with spandex meant that the colors could be excessively vibrant and the fabric would maintain its color and never fade. The rise in popularity of dance-inspired fashion may be linked in part to the fascination with physical fitness and the desire to carry those habits of dress from the gym to the street, but their trendiness may also be linked to the looks presented by omnipresent pop icon Madonna, who popularized that look beginning in 1983 in music videos such as "Lucky Star."

FABRICS

The fashionable nature and suitability of athletics-related apparel as street wear can be attributed in part to the development and innovations in stretch textiles made with spandex. This fiber gave fabrics their stretchiness and recovery and had durability not offered by the other stretch alternative, rubber. Lycra, invented by the Dupont Company in the 1960s, had made inroads into fashion over the course of the ensuing fifteen years, most notably influencing the design of swimwear and hosiery. By the 1980s, however, Lycra blends had improved and the diversity of textiles had expanded. High-gloss Lycra-spandex and stretch velvet were among the most influential textiles used to make these body-conscious fashions.

Polar fleece was another invention of the 1980s, debuting in 1981. In part a response to newly found ecological concerns, polar fleece was an innovation born of the necessity to utilize the profusion of plastic soda bottles that were clogging landfills across the country. It is likely that the vogue for natural fibers and natural dyes was also, at least in part, a response to concerns about the environment. In the 1980s there was substantial, highly publicized protest against the use of natural fur. Protesters were renowned for splashing paint onto women in fur coats, thereby ruining the coat and publicly humiliating the woman. Faux furs, available since the eighteenth century, were improved and gained popularity over the course of the decade.

Cloth printed with ethnic patterns, kente cloth in particular, was yet another way in which the textile industry innovated, but it is also an indication of the increased importance of African-American culture in the fashion industry. The influence of popular culture on athletic wear–inspired attire has already been mentioned with regard to pop music and popular movies, but the proliferation and increased popularity of rap music and the visibility of its artists through the music videos streaming twenty-four hours a day on MTV also had a profound impact. Early rap artists such as Run DMC and the Beastie Boys performed and were photographed wearing logo T-shirts, sweat suits, sneakers, and sateen baseball jackets, typically those produced by the Adidas Company. Adidas, a German company that had been in business since the 1920s, had always produced reliable athletic shoes and exercise apparel but had never attempted to establish itself as a fashion brand. However, the high visibility of their branding and the cultural cachet of the artists who wore their apparel in the 1980s served to reposition the brand and altered the use of their lines of products, transforming them into fashionable street wear.

BODY-CONSCIOUS FASHIONS

The exercise obsession of the 1980s also directly related to the design of haute couture garments that fell in line with the new interest in physique. Body-conscious clothing was often the part of designer collections. Jean-Paul Gaultier offered lingerie-inspired tops with skintight leggings, while both Alexander McQueen and Issey Miyake offered bodices that both conformed to and accentuated the female body. Perhaps the most iconic designer of the period, with regard to body-conscious dressing, was Azzedine Alaïa, known as "the king of cling." Alaïa worked extensively with rayon-spandex and stretch-knit fabrics to craft garments that clung to the body. Through his use of circular or spiral seams, and careful draping, his ultrafeminine garments reached a level of symbiosis with the body not seen since the work of Madeline Vionnet. Alaïa's work can be viewed both as an aesthetic and design milestone and as a cross-section of the many currents at work on the consciousness of fashion-minded individuals in the 1980s.

MEDIA INFLUENCE OF FASHION

Music

The currents of culture in the 1980s were as diverse as they were rich, and the number and kind of ideas that were active in the Western imagination were sparked and fueled by the progressively increasing availability of media. There can be no doubt that popular music has been an important factor in the communication of style, especially in youth culture, since the 1950s when shows like *American Bandstand* first broadcast images of pop bands and carefully selected teens dressing in fashionable clothes. With the advent of MTV on August 1, 1981, the influence of popular music and youth-oriented media went into a state of overdrive that is undiminished in current times.

An effort to catalogue every trend that was set in motion by a music video would be a monumental task; however, a few remarkable and widespread examples can provide a glimpse into the powerful impact of this new medium.

The release of Michael Jackson's epic album *Thriller* in December 1982 was the start of period of Jackson mania that would continue for years to come. The garments worn by Jackson in the first few videos, among them "Billie Jean" and the title track "Thriller," spawned fads that transcended race, age, and gender. Among the most readily identified of these was the wearing of a single glove—a Michael Jackson trademark—socks that contrasted boldly with dark-colored loafers, and most importantly, leather (or "pleather") jackets accented with a riot of decorative zippers. Jackson's choice of a red jacket in this style was the touchstone for hordes of copycats.

Dress inspired by break dancing, an athletic and rhythmic style of stepping, hopping, and spinning on one's back or head, was developed in among urban black and Hispanic youths. These kids wore loose, comfortable, flexible clothes such as shell suits and sleeveless T-shirts, coupled with athletic shoes such as Converse All Stars. This can be attributed both to a need for the flexibility requirements of the dance style as well as the budgetary constraints felt by these youthful city dwellers. This dance craze and the look that accompanied it were commercialized and packaged by the Hollywood studio system in 1984 with the rapid successive releases of *Breakin'* and *Breakin' 2: Electric Boogaloo*. These films took the street look and massaged it by color-coordinating objects like socks and headbands or shirts and shoes. The color schemes were typically bright and playful, with high doses of neon green, pink, yellow, and orange. This look was consequently adopted on a wide scale by young people across the United States.

Pop superstar Madonna Louise Veronica Ciccone was and still is a cultural phenomenon that launched a thousand trends, but her ability to capture the imaginations of young girls was unprecedented in the early 1980s. The carefully crafted look that Madonna embodied included short skirts over three-quarter-length dance tights coupled with midriff tops that left her brassiere exposed. Layers of jewelry, including black rubber bracelets and crucifixes, complemented the look, while loose, tousled hair was partially captured with a floppy bow. This look, which was popularized through music videos, was mimicked by legions of girls and young women known as "Madonna wannabees." They appeared in droves at her concerts and could be spotted anywhere on the street sporting this look. The rage for adopting Madonna's style was specifically commercialized by the fashion industry in response to the 1985 movie *Desperately Seeking Susan*, in which Madonna had the title role. A pair of black, sequin-covered boots with a bold graphic lining was worn by Susan in the film and was sold at shoe retailer Bakers.

Another example of the intermingling of the worlds of fashion design and pop music is the relationship between Vivienne Westwood's "New Romanticism" and artists such as Adam Ant, Spandau Ballet, or Boy George. Westwood had begun her career closely linked to the groundbreaking punk band the Sex Pistols, but by the late 1970s her attention had turned to historical referents of the eighteenth century. Her garments embodied the symbols of power and control as she mimicked the opulent detailing of the eighteenth century and the restrictive structure of the corset. While Westwood's collections represented one current among many as she explored these looks between 1978 and 1982, the aforementioned pop stars brought this look to the forefront of the public's imagination.

Adam Ant's video for "Stand and Deliver" is perhaps the best example of this look brought to life. Its clothes, often derived in part from theatrical costumes, included elements associated with pirates and eighteenth-century gentlemen. Wigs and heavy makeup were in part historical images, but could also be regarded as a bold statement of gender, as the 1980s was a time in which homosexuals openly struggled to attain an open and equal place in society. Although the look associated with New Romanticism was not adopted by throngs of men, nor was it a fetish that crossed age boundaries, it may be argued that this moment of ostentation in men's dressing highlighted the possibilities of men's apparel and may have led to increased interest in the menswear segment of the fashion industry.

Countless pop and rock bands influenced fashions in the 1980s. "Hair bands" such as Poison who sang overtly heterosexual lyrics adopted a look that was fetishistic and gender bending. New Wave artists such as Howard Jones, the Thompson Twins, and Flock of Seagulls dressed in colorful, oversized garments and sported equally oversized and whimsical hairstyles not seen since the eighteenth century. Cyndi Lauper's thrift-store aesthetic no doubt encouraged a generation of teens to seek out the fashions of bygone eras and make them modern through whimsical combinations of color and pattern and purposeful deconstruction and distressing. So powerful were images of the icons of pop music that in 1985 the Council of Fashion Designers of America (CFDA) gave a special award to MTV for its influence on fashion.

Television

Television was equally influential but targeted an older demographic. The obsession with wealth and opulence was brought to life before millions of followers of the series *Dallas* and the similar *Dynasty*, which premiered in 1980 and 1981, respectively. Both of these series included cast members who were already fashion models in their own right, and the emphasis on beauty, glamour, and greed was everywhere in the storylines. *Lifestyles of the Rich and Famous*, which first aired in 1984, took another approach to perpetuating the national obsession with glamorous living as host Robin Leach took the viewer through the houses, yachts, and closets of the super wealthy, describing the fabulousness of each and every object, for which he gave the dollar values. These types of programs strongly influenced the way scores of average people dressed as they endeavored to emulate the ostentatious jewelry, thick and colorful makeup, carefully coiffed hair, and garments characterized by broad shoulder lines and allusions to opulence.

FASHION AS A SOCIAL STATEMENT

Not all fashion was driven by glamour and greed. In the 1980s there were a handful of trends and collections by designers who were socially aware. Perhaps the most iconic example was offered by Katherine Hamnet in 1983. Her oversized white T-shirts emblazoned with the phrase "Choose Life" were popularized by the pop band Wham! Hamnet also created garments inspired by decontamination suits and fatigues, references to the troubled political times that defined the Cold War era. Georgina Godley offered a collection in 1986 called "Lumps and Bumps," in which padded forms enlarged models' hips and posteriors, causing her form-fitting dresses to bulge in ways that were generally considered unattractive. Godley's aim was to challenge the prevailing notion of trim and toned beauty.

T-shirts purchased to support a cause were also part of fashionable casual dress, as benefits to support Amnesty International, concerts to aid famine victims in East Africa (e.g., Live Aid), or efforts such as Hands Across America, which sought to raise funds for beleaguered social programs in the United States, all offered shirts and hats as part of their fundraising efforts. The wearing of these items was essentially a badge of honor.

The issue of gender and body pervaded fashion across categories of age, gender, and sexual orientation. There can be no doubt that many women redefined their gender through clothes in the 1980s as they donned their power suits and joined the ranks dominated by men. Women such as Margaret Thatcher, who became the first female prime minister of Great Britain in 1979, helped to set the standard of powerful femininity, but it was certainly a challenge for many women to strike a reasonable balance between masculine and feminine attributes of dress and behavior.

Androgyny

Fashion design also explored notions of androgyny in the 1980s. Foremost among them was Calvin Klein, whose thoroughly minimalist designs could be considered neither truly masculine nor feminine. In 1983, however, Klein introduced a new underwear line that turned conceptions of women's lingerie on its head. Calvin Klein's boy-cut underwear was modeled on traditional men's briefs, replete with a fly front. These underpants caused a sensation and formed the backbone of a style that would find lasting favor.

Rei Kawakubo, designing for the Japanese label Comme des Garçons (meaning Like the Boys), has consistently explored ideas of sexuality, gender, and beauty. In 1983 she offered a collection of garments that was decidedly outside of the mainstream glamorous tone of the moment. The collection was wrought exclusively in black and was characterized by boxy, irregular, imperfect silhouettes that were so loose that they provided no recognizable shape. Assailed by some critics with epithets such as "the end of fashion," the loose, flowing manner of dress found favor among a large sector of fashion consumers.

Also testing the bounds of gender was the always unpredictable and frequently controversial designer Jean-Paul Gaultier. In 1985, he showed a collection called "And God Created Man," in which he showed a collection of garments that appeared to be skirts and kilts when viewed from the front, although they were bifurcated when viewed from behind. That same year, he also showed a collection called "Wardrobe for Two" in which he presented androgynous looks that explored ideas of sexuality and gender.

Underwear as Outerwear

Another way fashions of the 1980s explored notions of sex and gender was in terms of an aggressive self-identification through overtly sexual apparel. Vivienne Westwood and Gaultier led the way with high-style collections that featured underwear as outerwear. Westwood's autumn/winter 1982/83 collection featured satin bras in bright colors worn over sweatshirts, while Gaultier presented bra tops of thick, padded coils shaped into conical protrusions and dressed, and pants fashioned with details of girdles in 1987. Prior to her partnership with Gaultier for the design of her tour costumes, Madonna proclaimed an aggressive and uncompromising sexuality when she wore bras and bustiers in lieu of any other top. This aroused notable controversy when in 1985 she danced and rolled around on the stage in a "bridal costume" consisting of a white backless bustier and tulle petticoats worn over cropped tights. Issey Miyake's red molded plastic bustier made a bold statement about the female anatomy not seen since Yves Saint-Laurent molded breasts in gold, including nipples, along with a belly button and perfectly sculpted abdominals.

MEN'S CLOTHING

Menswear truly came into its own in the 1980s as a new male consumer with a heightened interest in personal appearance and the language of clothing came to the fore. The 1980s saw the birth of publications geared to this consumer. Among these periodicals were *Cosmo Man*, *GQ*, *The Face*, *Arena*, *i-D*, and English, French, and Italian editions of *Vogue*. Each of these magazines took a unique look at currents in fashions, grooming, and issues of cultural significance to men such as arts and leisure activities, automobiles, alcohol and tobacco products, and travel.

Style that was uniquely British was one facet of Western fashion. In terms of menswear, English designer Paul Smith expanded to helping proliferate the "British look." This look was based on the most basic forms of menswear such as button-down shirts, ties, and suits but was unique and noteworthy because of its bold and adventurous use of color and its unique take on the mixing of patterns. Adding to the British look, in 1986 a new company appeared on the scene with all the trappings of centuries of English heritage. Charles Tyrwhitt

Richard Gere (as Julian Kaye) stars in Paul Schrader's 1980 film, *American Gigolo*. Courtesy of Photofest.

of Jermyn Street began as a purveyor of shirts and ties in the same vein as the Paul Smith aesthetic and was also destined to blossom into an international look.

Well-established designers who had for years produced only womenswear lines moved into the realm of menswear in the 1980s. Among them were Thierry Mugler in 1980; Claude Montana in 1981; Kenzo, Byblos, and Commes des Garçons in 1984; John Galliano and Franco Moschino in 1986; and Karl Lagerfeld in 1989. Perhaps the most important story in menswear, however, was Giorgio Armani's reinvention of men's suiting whereby he softened the tailoring of traditional suit forms by abandoning padding and stiff interfacings. His use of soft fabrics and his innovations in terms of cut, including long, draping lapels, emphasized the body beneath the clothes.

The name Armani became synonymous with sex appeal in the 1980s as the Hollywood blockbuster *American Gigolo*, starring Richard Gere, featured Armani suits in numerous key scenes, including a depiction of Gere's character shopping for the suits in a luxurious retailer. The cachet of Armani suits was further bolstered when Armani designed the wardrobe for *The Untouchables*, the 1987 cinematic portrayal of the downfall of Al Capone.

Male sex appeal was the prevailing theme of Calvin Klein's marketing to men in the 1980s (and it no doubt raised the brand's identity to women in the process). In 1982, the Calvin Klein underwear division partnered with photographer Bruce Weber to created images of monumental men dressed only in a pair of briefs emblazoned with the Calvin Klein label across the waistband. These ads, which were often reproduced on a gigantic scale on billboards, advertised not only the underwear but also a bold new conception of masculine sex appeal that captivated the imaginations of both homo- and heterosexual men.

Television and movies were as influential on menswear as they were on youth culture, with blockbuster movies spawning trends for specific types of garments as well as overall looks. In 1980, John Travolta appeared in *Urban Cowboy*, creating a taste for country and Western garb. *Raiders of the Lost Ark* (1981) featured actor Harrison Ford as an adventurer and archaeologist in a distressed brown leather bomber jacket and fedora, and this image of rugged masculinity spawned legions of copycats. *Risky Business* (1983) introduced audiences to Tom

Cruise and made Ray Ban a household name as men and women sought out their simple black frames with dark black lenses. Two years later, *Top Gun* (1986) presented heartthrob Cruise as a rugged, renegade, sexually charged Navy pilot; the flight jacket he wore throughout the movie also spawned look-alike models. The 1987 film *Wall Street* depicted Michael Douglas as Gordon Gekko, a Wall Street tycoon. Gekko was typically attired in a striped shirt with white cuffs and collar, and this variation of a traditional shirt became known as a "Gekko shirt" in the late 1980s as yuppies sought to emulate this quintessential financial high-roller.

On the small screen, Miami was the hotbed of men's fashion innovation for much of the decade. *Miami Vice*, which first aired in 1984, featured characters James "Sonny" Crockett (Don Johnson) and Ricardo "Rico" Tubbs (Phillip Michael Thomas) as two young hip cops battling the seedy underbelly of Miami's drug trade. The highly stylized show featured fast cars, a slick soundtrack, and fashions that would be emulated long past the show's cancellation in 1989. Both characters wore variations of men's suiting. While Tubbs was typically attired in traditional suiting consisting of a double-breasted jacket and button-down shirt, Crockett was most often dressed in suiting of very soft structure. His jackets were typically left unbuttoned to reveal a snug T-shirt or unbuttoned dress shirt and his holstered gun. Pastel colors dominated the wardrobe of the show's characters. Both the Sonny Crockett look and the Miami-inspired color palette were dominant features of 1980s attire.

Apart from the aforementioned trends, men's style in the 1980s can be summarized in terms of relationships to women's apparel. Shoulder pads were a predominant trend in women's fashions, and the same was also true in menswear. Fashionable dress for women included both and colorful textiles, and this was especially true of men's shirts of the period, which were fairly diverse in terms of cut, with collars of various shapes and widths proliferating. Collars were also highly diverse in terms of where and how they closed, with asymmetrical plackets and zippers on diagonals being typical of casual attire. The cut of men's pant legs varied from tapered to boot cut, and there was a preference for turn-up. The front of men's pants was typically pleated in this period.

Shoes were perhaps more decorative and diverse in this period than they had been throughout most of the course of men's footwear. Thick soles, silver hardware, and colored suede were often found in men's shoe designs. Hosiery in bright colors was often purchased to match pullovers or polo shirts and was as diverse in color as the coordinating garments, with pastels and bright hues ruling the decade.

CHILDREN'S CLOTHING

The development of children's designer clothing lines is also an important innovation of the 1980s. It was in the eighties that the prosperous Baby Boomers, products of the post–World War II era, reached childbearing age. These young professional parents, so concerned with the language of fashion, desired to dress their children in the language of wealth and prestige as well. As a result, boutiques that sold only "couture" kids' clothes began to proliferate and top-name designers began to offer lines of clothing for children. Oftentimes, these kids' lines were small interpretations of the clothes that were available for adults, which is a common theme from the rest of history. The business of baby and children's clothes only grew from the 1980s on, later becoming an enormous industry within the fashion world.

CONCLUSION

The 1980s was an era of great diversity, marking the beginning of what appears to be the permanent fragmentation of the fashion industry into schools of thought or factions of trends. As such, it is a period that is both rich and poor—rich in its panoply of looks and moments of great innovation, and poor in that it is fragmented in a postmodern way. It is its division, however, that makes this decade such an interesting source from which to weave narrative threads about culture, which can often be understood through the lasting language of clothes.

FURTHER READING

Constantino, Maria. *Men's Fashion in the Twentieth Century*. New York: Costume and Fashion Press, 1997.
Steele, Valerie. *Fifty Years of Fashion: The New Look to Now*. New Haven, CT: Yale University Press, 2000.

WEB RESOURCES

www.fashionera.com
http://www.metmuseum.org/toah/splash.htm
http://www.vam.ac.uk/collections/fashion/index.html

MOVIES

American Gigolo (1980)
Flashdance (1983)
Miami Vice (NBC, 1984–1990)
Pretty in Pink (1986)
Risky Business (1983)
Sixteen Candles (1984)
Top Gun (1986)
Urban Cowboy (1980)
Valley Girl (1983)
Wall Street (1987)
The Wedding Singer (1998)
Working Girl (1988)

The Nineties

Jennifer Grayer Moore

TIMELINE

1990	East and West Berlin reunite after the fall of the Berlin Wall
1991	USSR breaks up; civil war erupts in Yugoslavia; First Gulf War
1992	Yugoslavia splits in two; Bill Clinton elected president of the United States
1993	Israeli-PLO peace talks; first terrorist attack on the World Trade Center in New York; North American Free Trade Agreement (NAFTA) signed
1994	World Trade Organization formed; ethnic genocide in Rwanda
1997	Hong Kong reverts to China after a century and a half as a British colony; economic crisis affects the Far East
1999	Macao reverts back to China from Portugal

The 1990s was a decade of drastic change. At the close of the twentieth century, the world was truly a smaller place as the flow of media reached a fever pitch, travel by air was inexpensive enough to be available to most, and the world could be reached from the comfort of one's armchair with the advent of home Internet service and increasing numbers of television sets and stations worldwide.

The late 1980s had seen an economic downturn both in the United States and in Japan. By the mid-1990s, however, under the presidency of Bill Clinton, the United States had experienced an upswing, while the Japanese economy remained in turmoil until the end of the decade. From 1991 to 1996, the New York Stock Exchange saw growth of 152 percent, a strong indicator of the amassing of wealth among Americans.

In 1991, there was a dramatic collapse of communism, and the Soviet Union broke up into its constituent republics, leaving the United States as the world's only superpower. The Russians democratically elected Boris Yeltsin in 1996. The collapse of communism in Europe also meant that East and West Germany were able to reunite as one country under a single democratic government. The social problems this caused were a challenge for both sides, as they tried to coexist after decades of polar differences in development. Russia and other formerly communist countries saw the challenges they faced as they attempted to modernize, in terms of not only technology but also government, economics, and trade. Turmoil is the best description for what followed the relief of shedding the repressive communist governments. Whole new markets opened up for Western companies, where there was a demand for fashionable goods, including clothes, electronics, and other consumer goods.

The year 1991 was a monumental one for human rights as the end of apartheid arrived in South Africa. In Europe, barriers to travel and trade were gradually being removed as the European Union took on greater power and significance. By the middle of the 1990s, there were no border barriers among the nations of Portugal, Spain, France, Belgium, Luxembourg, Germany, and the Netherlands.

Not everything was about unity, peace, and prosperity in the 1990s, of course. By the middle of the decade, the collapse of communism in the Soviet Bloc had led to power struggles, civil wars, and ethnic cleansing in the Balkan states, notably in places such as Chechnya and Bosnia-Herzegovina. Political and financial instability in the former Soviet Union led Yeltsin to step down and appoint in his stead former KGB colonel Vladimir Putin to the post of prime minister. Putin scaled back newly acquired democratic freedoms, suppressed the media, punished capitalists, and fanned the flames of civil war in the Balkans. In the Middle East, there was economic prosperity due to the ever-increasing demand for oil. However, control of oil resources contributed to political instability that ultimately led to war as the Iraqi invasion of Kuwait in turn led to an American response that culminated in the first Persian Gulf War.

On American soil, international terrorism was felt for the first time. On February 25, 1993, a bomb in the parking garage of the World Trade Center in New York City killed six people and injured more than 1,000 and caused a generation of Americans to reconsider their place in the international landscape. On April 19, 1995, the bombing of the Federal Building in Oklahoma City killed 168 people, including numerous children, and brought to light divisions within American society.

In the 1990s, the life expectancy of an American black male was less than that of males in many Third World nations. Social strife, racism, and poverty led to astronomical homicide and imprisonment rates for young African-American males, which in turn led to a social response that culminated in the Million Man March on Washington, D.C., in 1995.

In Asia, the lead-up to Britain handing back Hong Kong to communist China caused great concern over the bustling port city-state. Would a return to China mean that Hong Kong, a thriving metropolis of trade and international business, suffer economic hardships under the central Beijing government? With the uncertainty, there was a migration of moneyed and educated young people to Western nations such as the United States and Canada, as well as Australia and Europe. Fears stemming from the handover meant that financial markets were uncertain in the run-up to the change, and Western nations, used to trading and dealing with Hong Kong's British-style government, had to rethink their relationships with mainland China. In the end, the handover went smoothly and life remained, at least on the surface, stable and progressive as a special economic zone of China.

ART

By most accounts, fine art and design, including architecture and graphics, reached a peak of diversity in the late twentieth century, with no single current dominating visual language and no single ideology underpinning artists' raison d'être. While fragmentation, diversity, and dissension over what was good and important ruled the era, there were undoubtedly a few monumental moments in the arts that will likely span the test of time.

In the world of architecture, the undulating and seemingly light-as-air work of Frank Gehry captivated the imagination of the world with installations in southern California as well as at the Disney Village outside Paris (1992) and the Guggenheim Museum in Bilbao, Spain (1997). In the visual arts, British artist Damien Hirst captured headlines with his intimate exploration of death. Hirst, perhaps best known for suspending the carcasses of animals (oftentimes cut into cross-sections) in large vitrines of formaldehyde, gained international acclaim due in part to his liaison with world-famous collector Charles Saatchi.

Fine art at the end of the century was often controversial. An excellent snapshot of this is provided by referencing the "Sensation" exhibit (a group show of eighteen British artists) that was displayed in London, New York, and Berlin and cancelled in November 1999 by the National Gallery of Australia. So controversial was this body of contemporary art that it fueled protests, including rosary chanting and manure throwing. Vomit bags were also dispensed as part of the protests. The world of fine art had become intensely conceptual and not everyone agreed with the concepts in play.

THE "MILLENNIUM BUG"

The approach of the new millennium brought with it waves of excited anticipation among would-be revelers, religious sects, and the technologically minded. While parties were planned years in advance by some, others anticipated the end of the world or the day of the apocalypse. Computer programmers worried about the "Y2K" phenomenon, a problem stemming from the simplification of years to two digits within many computer programs and data banks. A worldwide crash of databases was foretold, with energy and weapons systems in danger of going offline and financial institutions left helpless without functioning databases. The crisis was averted, however, and the new millennium dawned without serious incident, but the fear created a burgeoning market for computer programmers hired to reconfigure computers to function properly after the rollover to a new century at midnight on January 1, 2000.

THE INTERNET

In 1994, the World Wide Web became widely available to the general public, and it would influence business models, the mode and speed of communications, and consumer habits. In response to the perceived viability of the Internet as an interface for two-way communication, many young and entrepreneurially minded people entered the speculative business of online commerce, including publishing, advertising, and mail-order services. These upstart businesses, many of which were run by members of "Generation X" (bright, well-educated twenty-somethings), were generally referred to as "dot-coms," a reference to the ending of the vast majority of the URLs that the Internet addresses employed. The businesses, which often eschewed tested financial models and long-held beliefs in financial planning, cast off the typical conservatism of Wall Street investing and emphasized market share over profitability. Venture capitalists eager to cash in on the promise of these new businesses, but lacking a true understanding of this nascent industry, hedged the possibility of financial failure by the sheer quantity of ventures they funded. These dot-com businesses boomed in both quantity and stock value beginning in 1995 but would ultimately burst in the spring of 2000 when the reality of short-sighted business models and failure to turn a profit brought stock investors to their senses, thereby causing them to offload their overvalued stocks.

Apart from the new financial models introduced by the dot-coms, many of these cutting-edge businesses also embodied a new idea of the business or workplace culture. The actual setting for many of these businesses was often outside of the traditional business park, but regardless of physical location, the physical plants favored minimalist, modern, and utterly casual settings—ideal for the twenty-somethings who worked there. Video games, Ping-Pong and air hockey tables, fully stocked kitchens, and loads of free branded giveaways typified the new "corporate" culture. As part of the relaxed nature of the workspace, dress codes were relaxed to the point of nonexistence. Jeans worn with T-shirts or polo shirts and casual shoes were the norm. This phenomenon of dressing down would ultimately influence corporate culture across age and industry lines.

Catering to the widespread acceptance of casual dressing for men were a panoply of companies. Notable among the leaders in preppy, relaxed apparel was J. Crew, which offered khaki pants in a variety of cuts and polo shirts in every color of the rainbow. Abercrombie and Fitch, a luxury-lifestyle brand that had been on the scene since the beginning of the twentieth century, was repositioned in the late 1980s by Limited Brands and had major cachet in the mid- to late 1990s. Its branded T-shirts and garments inspired by blue-blood sports such as lacrosse and rugby were standard fare among teens and young adults in their twenties. Garments made and sold under the brand name Gap were also synonymous with a casual chic adopted by men and women alike.

INTERNATIONAL FASHION

In the late twentieth century, it became apparent that national characteristics of dress were dissipating in favor of a far more homogenous world fashion. Whereas in decades past, one might be inclined to pinpoint a man strolling down New York's Fifth Avenue as being most assuredly from Europe, or even more specifically from Paris or Rome, such an ability to distinguish national origin based on fashion was far less assured in the 1990s. In the last two or three years of the decade, travel, communication via press or Internet, cable and satellite media, and the global diffusion of brands led to widespread availability of looks from around the world. People living in Tokyo or Moscow could readily purchase Western clothes from H&M or Nike, while fashions in New York and Paris were influenced by Japanese anime art and South American sensuality. While some regional highlights or proclivities remained, fashion had become largely a global rather than a regional phenomenon.

The fashion industry had begun a process of change in the 1980s that came to fruition in the 1990s. The fashion industry was no longer driven from the top down, that is, European and American high style no longer led the way for fashion adoption within all sectors of society. Style trends were increasingly becoming more personal and driven by sociocultural phenomena such as race, ethnicity, allegiance to a group dynamic, music, or sexual orientation, to name but a few determining factors. As a result, some fashion designers responded to the unique demands of different subsets, while others created their high-style collections based on street and popular culture. This "trickle-up" phenomenon of fashionable dress had been glimpsed briefly in the 1940s and 1950s with the zoot-suiters and beatniks and had gained momentum in the 1960s and 1970s with hippies and disco dancers, but it became a defining factor in the 1980s and 1990s fashion industry. In the nineties, the interconnection between luxury lines, mass-produced goods, and street style was not always easy to pinpoint because communication among fashion sectors and adoption leading to adaptation of trends occurred at such a rapid pace.

The way in which information about fashion was disseminated changed in the 1990s. The improved access to the World Wide Web on personal computers led fashion magazines and newspapers such as *Vogue* and *Women's Wear Daily* to create Internet portals. Brands as diverse as Gucci and the Gap put up websites that, at first, allowed customers only the ability to look at merchandise but soon allowed online purchasing of goods that were then shipped to customers. Department stores such as Saks Fifth Avenue, Macy's, and Selfridges in England also created online shopping. Toward the end of the decade, people were able to watch runway shows from Paris, Milan, or New York online as they happened in real time. As the decade progressed, even the lag time between the showing of a collection and its dissemination to the public at large shortened. Digital media such as live webcasts became widely available toward the end of the millennium.

In addition to online shopping, catalogues were an important way in which apparel companies advertised and sold their lines, and these catalogues often mirrored or complemented the selections available online. Notable names that made virtual empires out of mail-order retailing include the lingerie and apparel company Victoria's Secret, purveyor of traditional and bohemian apparel J. Peterman, and sportswear and leisure wear giant J. Crew, a popular brand that had very few "brick and mortar" retail outlets early in the decade.

The looks that existed in the 1990s represent a diversity never before seen. Trends included clothes inspired by priests' garb (1993), a look described as "power sluts" (1994), a Neo-Japonisme movement (1994), a return to the classics of the 1950s (1995), and a passion for Latin inspiration (1997). In the nineties, fashion weeks were held in the capitals of Europe, in Asia, on both coasts of the United States, and, beginning in 1994, in Australia. Despite the fact that styles in the 1990s were acutely fragmented across markets and were largely defined by lifestyle and age, and despite the rapidly swinging pendulum of taste that set the fashion cycle on a constantly accelerating course, there were among the many facets of fashion some remarkable, unusual, iconic, and long-lasting statements that are of significant importance.

HAUTE COUTURE

The economic downturn of the late 1980s impacted the world of haute couture in the 1990s. Most estimates place the number of haute couture clients at less than two thousand individuals worldwide, a reduction of several hundred from the heyday of the 1980s. If less haute couture was being bought in the 1990s, even less of it was seen, photographed, commented on, and copied, because a large portion of the purchasing body consisted of the wives of Middle Eastern oil magnates. The Middle Eastern market for luxury goods has a curious negative impact on the fashion cycle, as the garments are seldom displayed in public. Hidden beneath nondescript outer robes, the costly garments are displayed only in private circles where cameras never go, and there have been few occasions when the Western media have captured the display of these fashions. Therefore, though the haute couture market was still alive in the 1990s, it may be argued that it had little impact on mainstream attire.

Luxury, however, did still reign in certain sectors. In addition, luxury brands remained visible and relevant, especially because the nature and quantity of ready-to-wear was on the rise among these high-style designers. American designer Tom Ford was a man on a mission to change and revive a tried-and-true luxury brand, and he did just that for Gucci within the span of a decade. In 1990, just four years after graduating from the Parsons New School for Design, Ford was tapped to head up the design of women's wear at Gucci. Two years later, he became design director, and in 1994 he assumed the mighty post of creative director, where he controlled the creative direction of all product lines, as well as advertising and brand identity. If there was but one word to summarize the identity that Ford crafted for Gucci, it would have to be "sexy." Gucci in the 1990s was synonymous with sleek, chic, and sensual. In Ford's view, the fashions were about "hedonism." The fashions at Gucci in the 1990s were characterized by stretch fabrics of silk jersey, satin, and velvet. Colors were rich, often favoring the hues of gemstones. Embellishment was artful, and there was no lack of fur, sequins, rhinestones, or exotic skins. Accessories, especially sky-high stiletto heels, were emphasized in even the most casual outfits.

If Gucci clothing in the 1990s was hedonistic, then a stronger word must be sought to describe many of the advertising campaigns of the era. Skin was in, and shirts were seldom buttoned past midabdomen. Legs were emphasized, and garments were often in disarray. Models were often depicted in compromising, salacious positions that alluded to sex acts. One advertisement, perhaps the most scandalous of the lot, depicted a man on his knees, tugging at a woman's bikini bottom to reveal a Gucci G shaved into the pubic hair of the female model. These clothes and images, omnipresent in the fashion media, shaped the brand identity afresh and influenced the imaginations of a generation.

The fashions of Gianni Versace had dominated the luxury landscape in the eighties, and in the nineties Versace's work continued to be significant. His colorful, elaborate designs, rich with referents to Roman and Renaissance patterns, were instantly recognizable in a sea of fashions characterized by diversity. In

1993, Versace expanded his empire with his "Home Signature" collection that included a wide variety of home furnishings such as fine china, carpets, quilts, and upholstered products.

Versace is also widely regarded as being the creator of the supermodel phenomenon that began at the end of the previous decade but came into full bloom in the early 1990s. The Versace advertising campaigns had long featured the famous faces of the era, including Cindy Crawford, Claudia Schiffer, Linda Evangelista, Christy Turlington, and Naomi Campbell. Photographs often included numerous models grouped together in similar looks, creating a rather monumental installation of female beauty. The way in which Versace used his models as the faces of a coordinated campaign of print, runway, and entourage catapulted the women into a sphere of fame that had not been glimpsed by mannequins before them. Many of these women had brief forays into acting, but all became household names of the same rank as Hollywood celebrities simply by virtue of their work as models. The celebrity of this elite group of women benefited them by earning them celebrity pay; Linda Evangelista is quoted as infamously declaring that she would not get out of bed for less that $10,000 per day.

While many designers had diversified their ready-to-wear offerings through diffusion lines launched in the 1980s and continued to profit and diversify through both diffusion lines and licensed goods, there was one notable newcomer to this segment of the fashion industry who appeared late in the 1990s. Louis Vuitton, established as a luggage maker in the late nineteenth century, had from the very beginning been associated with luxury, namely, the luxurious lifestyle of the elite on the Grand Tour, with trunks and cases of clothes and treasures from all corners of the world in tow. Indeed, from the first years of the company's legacy, it was forced to fend off imitators and counterfeiters by constantly innovating and making its patterns more complex. In the 1990s, the cachet of Louis Vuitton was undiminished, but the leadership at the conglomerate that owned the label (Louis Vuitton Moet Hennessy, or LVMH) sought to explore the profitable arena of both ready-to-wear apparel and additional variations of tried and true themes.

In 1997, the young American designer (whom some have called a prodigy) Marc Jacobs was tapped to head up the design of the nascent line. While Jacobs is renowned for bucking the general trends of the season and for his own labels creates subtle garments inspired by traditional conceptions of femininity, the Louis Vuitton line is characterized by youthful, sexy, elegant, and powerful garments in a style that is in keeping with the general currents of fashionable dress. Catering first to the elite clientele that Louis Vuitton has always appealed to, the ready-to-wear collections initially focused on elegant street wear and eveningwear for women. Over the course of the ensuing decade, the line expanded to include resort collections, swimwear, and outerwear and diversified to include virtually all components of menswear. The Louis Vuitton label and brand identity would only continue to grow and innovate under the leadership of Jacobs, who turned the identity of the company on its ear in two ways. First, its signature logo was partially obscured by the graffiti of Stephen Sprouse (2001) and again in 2003 through the unexpected juxtaposition of the much-beloved LV insignia with the playful anime graphics of Japanese artist Takashi Murakami. Second, advertising campaigns, especially after the turn of the millennium, began to feature celebrity spokespeople from previously unexplored demographics: campaigns have included Latin pop princess Jennifer Lopez and rap/hip-hop star Pharrell Williams.

Fashionable dress in the last decades of the twentieth century is often defined by unusual juxtapositions, decontextualized historical references, and mixing of styles from cultural and social strata that do not mix in the greater scheme of society—for example, punk influences being found in the realm of pricy and elite couture clothes and worn by middle- to upper-class suburban teens.

STREET STYLE

In 1996, the Victoria and Albert Museum in London, an institution that was a forerunner in the movement to legitimize the study of fashion, held an exhibit devoted to street style. The catalogue and text that accompanied the installation brought to light a series of categories that influence how people dress. Among them were music, sports, politics, race, ethnicity, and sexual orientation. Aligning oneself with one of these elements has the effect of placing one in a "fashion segment," so the curators argued. This is a useful structure under which to operate as one tries to make sense of the diversity of fashion and even the diversity of fashion designers (many of whom cater to a specific segment) in our time. The fashion segments (what others have termed "style tribes" or "cults") that were in play in the 1990s are numerous; among the more important and widespread were Grunge, Hip-Hop, and Cyberpunk. Each of these movements began as a youth movement outside of the mainstream and found a voice in mainstream fashion.

Grunge was a movement in music and dress that began in the late 1980s in the Pacific Northwest. The music, exemplified by bands like Pearl Jam and Nirvana, was a gritty kind of rock-and-roll that often included bleak lyrics. The look embodied by the front men of these bands was equally gritty and certainly shunned the mainstream fashions of the day. The typical look included ripped, worn jeans, old Converse All Stars sneakers or Dr. Martens combat boots, and a ragged T-shirt worn beneath an unbuttoned flannel shirt. The look embodied carelessness, destitution, and, in essence, antifashion. Young people, especially in the Western world readily adopted this look, even in the absence of devotion to the music, and they were especially visible among college students.

Hollywood picked up on the grunge vibe and in 1992 produced the movie *Singles*, a film about twenty-somethings in Seattle that further perpetuated interest in the scene and the style. Fashion designers, sensing the mood and relevance of the music, sought to elevate the style to the runway, but with little success. In 1992, Marc Jacobs infamously crafted a line for Perry Ellis that led to his immediate termination from the company, while in 1994 Anna Sui also formulated a grunge collection that met with limited financial returns. Fashion magazines instructed readers to create a grunge look by mixing high and low style, such as putting a long-sleeved T-shirt under a dress, or wearing flannel over a blouse. There is no doubt that the grunge look was widespread, but it simply wasn't a look that could be produced for commercial success.

Cyberpunk refers primarily to a subgenre of science-fiction literature that explores "high-tech and low life." The name is essentially an amalgam of the words *cybernetics* and *punk*. The look, described in popular fiction, was brought to life in films such as *The Matrix* (1999) and *Blade Runner* (1982), as well as in games such as Cyberpunk 2020 and Shadowrun. The look, subsequently adopted by young fans, included elements of punk such as leather, metal studs or spikes, chains, T-shirts, and ripped clothes. The interpretation of the "cyber" or futuristic element of the genre was voiced through use of rubber, vinyl, plastic, and other industrial materials more typically found in fetishistic or industrial clothes. This look also made it to the runway in the collections of Jean-Paul Gaultier in 1992 and to a certain extent in the bondage fetish look offered by Gianni Versace in that same year.

Hip-hop and rap music, however, have perhaps had the most profound impact both on street style and high style in the last several decades. The music and the look, both of which originally began in the streets and found a widely heard voice only in the mid-1980s with the advent of black-owned labels, is at its root a very simple look. Baggy, oversized pants that allowed the waistband of the underwear to show were originally worn without a belt as a reference to prison culture (belts are one of the first personal effects taken from a person who is incarcerated). Over time, designer brands gradually inflated the size of the seat and leg while restraining the waistband. Hooded sweatshirts, called "hoodies" in the vernacular, were originally off-the-shelf versions, either no-name or brand-name such as Adidas, but over time they evolved into more elaborate affairs with slogans and logos of all kinds. Sneakers, called "kicks" on the street, or Timberland boots were the most popular forms of footwear and were available in stiletto versions for women.

By the middle of the 1990s, the look shifted somewhat as gangsta rap entered the mainstream. This subgenre of hip-hop made popular by Public Enemy, Ice-T, and Dr. Dre, among others, adopted a Mafioso or pimp aesthetic of dress to align their look with their lyrics that relied heavily on misogynistic, homophobic, and materialistic imagery. Oversized suits and fedora hats were worn, and objects of conspicuous consumption such as gold teeth, grilles, Rolexes, and diamond-encrusted jewelry completed the look. It was the hip-hop artist B.G. who popularized the widely used catch phrase "bling-bling" in a 1999 lyric. In fact, the widespread appeal of the genre came quickly as lyrics moderated somewhat and the lifestyle and look were popularized through artists like Coolio, whose 1998 hit "Gangsta's Paradise" brought the notion of a "gangsta" to middle America, Europe, and Asia.

Bling or jewelry, especially diamond and gold jewelry, remains a mainstay of the hip-hop look, as do all of the aforementioned aspects of dress, although much of the music scene has softened in terms of lyrics and public persona, with the late 1990s being dominated by artists such as Sean Combs. As numerous artists of the hip-hop movement moved into the mainstream by largely abandoning the hard-edged lyrics, young people both within and outside urban black communities followed the music and mimicked the styles.

The broad popularity of this segment of fashionable dress allowed it to burgeon into a highly profitable realm for ready-to-wear design and production. Companies such as Fubu ("For Us By Us") and Karl Kani were early success stories. Later on, many of the hip-hop brands were owned and/or designed by players on the music scene, including Phat Farm (Russell Simmons), Roca Wear (Jay-Z and Damon Dash), Shady Ltd. (Eminem), and OutKast Clothing

(OutKast). In addition, extant labels that were favored by hip-hop artists capitalized on the appeal by targeting advertising campaigns to this new demographic. When artists Coolio and Snoop Dogg became visible patrons of preppie American designer Tommy Hilfiger, the brand began producing advertisements with elements of the street aesthetic, including heavy gold jewelry and an emphasis on labels and logos.

RETRO FASHIONS

Although fashionable dress in the postmodern era is being driven by a diverse field of impulses, many of them new and innovative, the inclination toward eclectic, unpredictable historicism was also very much an aspect of late-twentieth-century fashion design. "Retro" fashions, looks that reference back in time or are retroactive, were a small facet of design as early as the eighteenth century; however, in the late twentieth century, the cycle of revivalism reached a fevered pitch, and designers were sometimes reviving trends from only a few years earlier. For example, when Rastafarianism made a splash in Western culture in the 1970s, many people adopted some of the characteristic elements of Jamaican attire, including the national colors. Less than twenty years later in 1991, Rifat Ozbek was again looking back to these influences. The House of Dior also sought inspiration in Rastafarianism for the design of its 2003 accessories collection.

The Mod look of the 1960s took roughly thirty years to be revived, but when it captured the interest of designers in 1995 and 1996, the list of designers seeking inspiration in this retro look was long and illustrious, including Marc Jacobs, Anna Sui, Helmut Lange, and Calvin Klein.

A few important designers have essentially based their body of work on the principle of using the past for inspiration and consequently creating new, often incongruous juxtapositions of silhouettes, patterns, and other design elements. John Galliano is one designer who is most renowned for this. His couture collections for the House of Dior have looked as far back as ancient Egypt but have also looked to the extravagant eighteenth century and the Belle Époque. English designer Vivienne Westwood is well known for incorporating historical elements in her eclectic designs; most notably, she revived the precise appearance of eighteenth-century stays.

While high-style designers looking to the past for inspiration influence retro trends in modern fashion, the many other sources of visual language, including movies in wide release, were also very influential. There were several big movies in the 1990s that looked back to the 1960s and 1970s, which may be held, at least in part, responsible for minor elements of revivalism. Both *Boogie Nights* (1997) and *54* (1998) looked back to the heyday of the 1970s disco scene and depicted clingy shirts left unbuttoned and trousers cut very snuggly to accentuate the backside. One need only look to the Gucci advertising campaigns of the late 1990s to find similar references.

The Austin Powers films, the first of which was released in 1997, were immensely popular. *Austin Powers: International Man of Mystery* comically depicted the style of the great peacocks of the 1960s. Platform shoes, psychedelic colors and patterns, ruffled collars, and sequins were just a few elements amid the cacophony of design that characterized this look. Its sequels similarly highlighted the 1970s and 1980s.

Many high-style collections of the late 1990s, including Dolce e Gabbana and Prada, also embodied these references. How people chose to dress in the late 1990s may have had something to do with the movies they were watching and what designers were designing, but it is impossible to know exactly how and why many of the retro trends occurred, because the great variety of influences cannot always be channeled into causal relationships.

TEXTILES

Innovations in textiles also strongly impacted the types of clothes being made. High-tech textiles that had the ability to repel water, heat the body, cool the body, or wick away perspiration strongly influenced sportswear and adventure gear. Sympatex and Gore-Tex were high-tech laminates that were introduced early in the decade. When adhered to another textile, these ultrathin products had the ability to repel water and insulate the body. Polartec was a type of fleece that was designed to be wind-resistant. Micro-fiber blends of nylon and polyester were engineered to be lightweight, pliable, and soft. Textiles could also be treated with a silicone finish to make them water-repellent, or engineered with Kevlar, a substance used most frequently by soldiers and firefighters for safety garments. Public awareness of these amazing new products became widespread due in part to highly publicized high-tech sporting apparel that was worn by swimmers and track and field athletes at the 1992 Olympics in Barcelona.

Japanese fashion designers in the nineties were also renowned for experimenting with synthetic textiles, but for aesthetic reasons. Rei Kawakubo began in 1990 to experiment with synthetics, including nonwoven nylon-urethane and acrylic. Yohji Yamamoto worked with a polyester textile that had plastic in the weave; this addition permitted him to create architectural, undulating volume. Hiroshigi Maki founded a company in the 1990s known as Gomme, referring to the rubber that was feature in the garments. Prada, for its autumn/winter 1998/99 collection, joined the ranks of the avant-garde and created garments of plastic and other nonwoven synthetics.

Textiles also began to look different as textile designers and fashion designers alike experimented with newly available printing and screening techniques, many of which developed as computer technology became more sophisticated. Issey Miyake's 1998 collections were early examples of garments that were screened with photographic prints.

Denim, an important category in fashion design since the 1970s, flourished in the 1990s due in part to innovations in textile treatments. Perhaps the innovation with the greatest longevity was the blending of denim with spandex, which allowed for better and snugger-fitting jeans that also provided greater comfort.

Distressed denim was trendy for several years in the mid-1990s. Jeans would be sold in the washed-out shades of blue that were traditionally obtained only after years of wear and washing. These subtle colors were attained through new rinse-washing techniques and through sandblasting. Rips, tears, and wear spots were also introduced; these finishes were highly sought after and often commanded high prices. Acid wash, a treatment that leaves the background a dark shade of blue while bringing a rippled foreground close to white, was popular at the beginning of the decade but became much maligned as time went by and was out of fashion long before the new millennium.

General trends in textile manufacture and treatment found specific applications in many high-style collections of the decade. The worn, weathered, vintage look was embodied in gray wool dresses offered by Kawakubo in autumn/winter 1994/95. These garments came replete with wear marks and permanent wrinkles. Even Gucci embraced this trend with skirts in denim and leather offered in 1999. Interest in technology, and indeed inspiration in technology, is easily found in the work of Turkish Cypriot fashion innovator Hussein Chalayan, whose garments frequently employ building materials such as nuts, bolts, and screws. Chalayan's innovative body of work has often been favored by fashion editors and received critical acclaim ever since his debut in 1994.

SPORTSWEAR

Innovations in textiles and interest in sports, especially the new "extreme sports," collided to produced some new innovations in active wear. The new lightweight micro-fiber textiles, many of which were superinsulating or water-repellent, could be crafted into new, sleek silhouettes that revealed the body and allowed for greater mobility. For sports, there were new styles for activities such as cycling, skiing, snowboarding, rock climbing, and hiking. These garments were in turn translated into street wear. Close-fitting "warm-up" jackets, cargo pants, fleece pullovers, and snug-fitting turtlenecks were among the garments that translated from mountain path or slope to street. Ralph Lauren launched his Polo Sport line in 1993 in response to the emphasis on outdoor activities that was a burgeoning part of culture, especially among men. The garments produced under this label draw from the language of functional sports apparel but also employ a decidedly aesthetic component. The garments often emphasize a nautical theme and are frequently overtly patriotic, with American flags and nautical flags operating as common motifs.

Athletic Shoes

Athletic shoes also developed in response to the emphasis on sports in the 1990s. Specialized sneakers marketed with a specific sport or activity in mind were a new phenomenon. No longer was it the norm to purchase a single pair of athletic shoes; on the contrary, one purchased running shoes, walking shoes, hiking shoes, cross-training shoes, or any of numerous other options, depending on the specific activity to be undertaken. Athletic shoes were marketed as fashionable items, with color schemes changing periodically and a diversity of styles proliferating.

Athletic shoes were strongly bound to celebrity athletes through endorsements and branding. When Air Jordans, a sneaker made by Nike and endorsed by Chicago Bulls superstar Michael Jordan came to the market, they caused a sensation and produced long lines as young men clamored for a pair.

The Reebok pump, first marketed in 1989, was extremely popular in the early 1990s. The shoe featured a pump that activated an internal mechanism designed to inflate the shoe to attain maximum comfort and precision fit. Throughout the early years of the 1990s, the Reebok pump, first offered only as a basketball shoe, became available in models for football, track, and tennis.

Athletic shoes as fashionable apparel or status apparel was a phenomenon that developed in urban centers among young men as early as the 1980s. By the 1990s, the fashionable nature of athletic shoes had reached a much broader audience. While athletic shoe designers made offerings more diverse in order to expedite the fashion cycle and whet appetites for purchasing, designers unknown to the sports segment of the fashion industry also got on board with shoes as well as apparel. Designer sneakers were offered by companies such as Ralph Lauren. Gucci, Prada, and Coach. Although these shoes were not necessarily designed for rigorous athletics, the shoes emphasized comfort and were crafted with a profile that mirrored true athletic shoes. Often these designer versions were heavily branded or logoed in keeping with the notion of athletic shoes as status apparel.

Street Fashion

The influence of athletic apparel on street wear was far reaching in the 1990s and touched women's apparel almost as much as it did men's. In 1994, Donna Karan's DKNY label offered dresses that were inspired by baseball shirts. The jersey dress featured three-quarter-length sleeves in a color contrasting the body of the dress. A large number was emblazoned across the chest of the zip-front dress, which was modeled with training shoes on the runway.

In 1996, Jean-Paul Gaultier offered a spandex hooded body suit covered in an Op-art pattern reminiscent of 1960s Victor Vasarely paintings. This skintight form had been introduced just four years earlier at the 1992 Olympics by track and field marvel Linford Christie.

Backpacks, long the hand luggage choice of schoolchildren and athletes alike, were shrunk to a diminutive size in the 1990s and became a popular handbag style. Likewise, fanny packs, small zipper-closed pouches attached to a belt, began their lives as a sensible carryalls for runners and cyclists. Throughout much of the decade, they were street wear, worn either around the waist or over the shoulder. Even Chanel designed a fanny pack. Late in the decade, fashion commentators came to their senses and lambasted the object as unattractive, relegating it back to the track.

BUSINESS CLOTHING

Apparel suitable for the corporate workplace typically does not walk lockstep with the currents of fashion because there are, generally speaking, codes of dress and conservative or traditional views about corporate attire, often enforced by company dress codes. In the 1990s, however, many companies, especially in the United States, began to implement dress-down policies. In some cases, Fridays were designated as "casual Fridays," whereas in locales such as Silicon Valley in California, where start-up technology companies and dot-com businesses flourished, dressing down was the norm.

While this new corporate culture had a negative impact on segments of the fashion industry that catered to the corporate look, such as hosiery makers and necktie designers, other types of clothes proliferated. Polo shirts were especially popular in the 1990s for men and women alike, while khaki pants were particularly favored in the casual man's wardrobe. Sweater sets consisting of a crewneck, short-sleeved sweater, and cardigan were a mainstay of women's apparel, as were capri pants. While companies typically retained some restrictions on dress, such as skirt-length minimums and prohibitions on bare midriffs, overall a new, casual attitude reigned.

UNDERGARMENTS

Along with the emphatic interest in physical fitness that was so much a part of 1990s lifestyle and fashion came new ideas for decorating and presenting the body. While underwear as outerwear had come upon the scene in the 1980s thanks to Madonna and Jean-Paul Gaultier, this trend continued in the 1990s, with typically conservative designers such as Calvin Klein entering the fray. Whereas showing one's underwear had often been an aspect of women's dress to this point, in the 1990s as a result of the trend for baggy jeans, coupled with the new vogue for men's designer underwear, showing the labeled brand of one's underwear was a trend. Leading the way in the exploitation of this trend were the brands Calvin Klein and Joe Boxer.

Women's underwear got a boost in 1994 with the launch of the Wonderbra. This trademarked brassiere was shaped and padded to provide maximum décolletage. The Wonderbra was a buzzword for a year and spawned numerous imitators. Underpants designed to boost the shape and size of one's posterior were also a fad of the mid-1990s and were brought to the mainstream under the brand names Rear-Riser and Butt-Booster. Although padded posteriors had long been a facet of biking shorts and fetish apparel, their presence in the mainstream was quite remarkable.

BODY ART

Tattooing and body piercing are traditions that have existed longer than fashion itself, and they are elements of personal style that have often been restricted by the mainstream, or viewed as avant-garde or fetishistic. In the 1990s, piercing was a fad. Multiple earrings had come into use in the 1980s, but in the 1990s eyebrows and noses were frequently adorned, while piercing the belly button was extremely popular. The vogue for midriff shirts no doubt related to this fashion. Tattooing was also common across age, gender, and ethnicity groups. While hip-hop fans and gangsta rappers opted for simple black ink tattoos or "tats," young white women selected elaborate, feminine, colorful designs such as scrolling vines. Ankle tattoos were especially trendy as several fashion models of the period boasted them.

HEROIN CHIC

Body image in the 1990s was in flux. While interest in physical fitness lasted the duration of the decade, fashion advertising and modeling went a different direction. Whereas the decade began with supermodels such as Cindy Crawford and Naomi Campbell who were tall, voluptuous, healthy, and typically styled with flowing hair and makeup that enhanced a healthy glow and color, the tide began to turn after 1993. In 1993, Kate Moss was introduced to the fashion media, and her look was to launch both a firestorm of criticism as well as a decade of copycats.

Moss, who was discovered in a London airport and who quickly became the face of Calvin Klein and arguably the face of the 1990s, epitomized the "waif look." Moss was petite by supermodel standards, fine boned, and very thin. Her slender appearance was manipulated by fashion photographers to create images that recalled prepubescence and drug addiction. This consequently became a trend in modeling with the faces of fashion becoming progressively thinner as the decade wore on. There was a trend in the mid-1990s to style models with ratty, apparently dirty hair, and heavy, smudged makeup. This look, applied to the waif-like women, spawned the sobriquet "heroin chic" in 1995.

PLUS SIZES

While the face of fashion thinned, the average person in both Europe and America got progressively heavier. With obesity rates skyrocketing in the last decades of the century, the fashion industry was forced to respond to the clothing needs of this growing category of consumers. Increased body size led to several phenomena.

Vanity sizing, whereby a lower size number is applied to a garment, bearing no relation to standard dress-form sizes, became apparent in the 1990s and fluctuated downward: What had been a size 8 was vanity sized down to a 6 and then to a 4. While vanity sizing was a secret that individual companies kept, to some it became apparent that size mattered but that the size on a garment tag was becoming meaningless beyond personal vanity.

Meanwhile, "plus-size" or "women's-size" clothing became an increasingly important category for the fashion industry. Designers such as Anne Klein, Donna Karan, Marina Rinaldi, and Gianfranco Ferre began to create fashions over size 14. Department stores such as Saks Fifth Avenue devoted retail space especially designed and artfully marketed to this emerging demographic.

CHILDREN'S CLOTHING

The category of children's apparel grew in the last decade of the twentieth century. Many companies that had previously dealt only with adult apparel made the leap into children's garments. The Gap, which had begun its Gap Kids line in 1986, forayed into infant and toddler apparel in 1990 with the launch of Baby Gap. Retailer the Children's Place, which specializes in apparel for children ages 0–10, became publicly traded in 1997, leading to a proliferation of stores across the United States. Department stores around the globe expanded and revised their youth departments offering apparel and amenities for the increasingly fashion-conscious young consumer.

"Tweens" became a new market, with girls especially demanding fashionable clothing choices in the years between early childhood and the teenage years. Girls-only stores cropped up in the late 1990s for these girls and offered anything a girl could ever want, including clothing and accessories and even cosmetics geared to the young set.

The teen market was mixed in with adult clothing in some cases and was again simply miniaturized versions of the adult styles, with some details pertaining to the age of the buyer.

CONCLUSION

The disconnect between the images that the fashion industry set forth and the state of affairs among the majority of modern women is yet another layer in the dizzying diversity of the modern fashion universe. In fact, the many layers of disconnection between what fashion designers and fashion media offer and what people actually look like and wear have led many a fashion commentator to declare the death of the fashion industry.

Fashion design at the end of the twentieth century was most certainly not dead, nor even defunct, but it had changed into an industry that would be virtually unrecognizable to traditional designers such as Christian Dior and Cristobal Balenciaga, or even early style mavericks like Paul Poiret or Mariano Fortuny. The power and influence of an individual fashion designer had become diminished and fleeting, and the type of person entering the fray of design was diverse in terms of age and ethnicity. Consumers had become diverse and fickle, easily distracted by the barrage of influences operating on their senses. A sure and steady sense of direction was essentially unattainable.

The uncertainty of modern fashion is not, however, the death of fashion. On the contrary, the uncertainty is one of the many factors that has enticed designers to dream, innovate, and experiment. The fast-paced nature of modern fashion has the benefit of allowing mistakes, misjudgments, and missteps to fall by the wayside or be picked up later and reworked. The impermanence of modern design is precisely the thing that makes it so rich, interesting, and completely alive and vibrant.

FURTHER READING

English, Bonnie. *A Cultural History of Fashion in the Twentieth Century*. Oxford, UK: Berg Publishers, 2007.
Steele, Valerie. *Fifty Years of Fashion: The New Look to Now*. New Haven, CT: Yale University Press, 2000.

WEB RESOURCES

www.fashionera.com
http://www.metmuseum.org/toah/splash.htm
http://www.vam.ac.uk/collections/fashion/index.html

MOVIES

Election (1999)
First Wives Club (1996)
Four Weddings and a Funeral (1994)
Notting Hill (1999)
Primary Colors (1998)
Runaway Bride (1999)
Singles (1992)
Sliding Doors (1998)

2000–Present

Jennifer Grayer Moore

TIMELINE

2000   New Millenium
             George H. W. Bush elected
2001   Terrorist attacks on World Trade Center and Pentagon,
              September 11
2002   War in Iraq and Afghanistan

RECENT HISTORY

The new millennium dawned in the Western world for a population that was eager to enjoy the many fruits of an increasingly international, technological, and prosperous society. Cities such as London, Paris, and New York rang in New Year's Day 2000 with great fanfare and great expense. In the United States, the dollar was strong but a financial downturn was imminent with the dot-com bubble about to burst in February. In the European Union, the introduction of the euro as the common currency was just two years off, set for January 1, 2002. These impending changes of monumental proportions brought with them a panoply of economic forecasts, both enthusiastic and sober. While the day-to-day life of the average citizen of the Western world had been largely characterized by peace and prosperity in the preceding decades, the new millennium would bring with it both a sense of international freedom and a sense of insecurity as the world became a smaller place, open to infiltration by disgruntled sects.

Terrorism touched every corner of the world in the early years of the new millennium. The terrorist bombing of the USS *Cole* in Yemen in October 2000 marked an undermining of U.S. security, but it was overshadowed by the attacks of September 11, 2001, that killed nearly three thousand at the World Trade Center in New York and the Pentagon in Washington, D.C. While the fallout of terrorist attacks against the United States would lead to military conflicts in Afghanistan and Iraq and the destabilization of the Middle East at large, terrorist bombings were hardly limited to a single region, nor were they levied against a single people. Between 2001 and 2006, extremists seeking international attention spilled blood with bombings and mass shootings in Indonesia, Saudi Arabia, Spain, England, India, Turkey, and Chechnya.

Global unrest also came in the form of political upheaval. The conflict between Israel and Palestine raged on with little respite while tensions also mounted and subsided in Northern Ireland. Political instability was rife in the former Soviet Union. Haiti ousted its president Jean-Bertrand Aristide in February 2004. Religious and ethnic conflict led to bloodshed in Macedonia with the persecution of ethnic Albanians, in India where Hindus and Muslims clashed with bloody results, and in Darfur, where the massacres defied quantification.

Even in places where cultural and religious disparity did not lead to bloodshed, it nevertheless sparked heated debate in the media and dominated current events. The viability of "intelligent design," rather than evolution, as a model for the teaching of science dominated scholarly debate among scientists and educators in both Europe and America, with the papacy registering its viewpoint as well. Same-sex union, also known as gay marriage, was hotly debated in the United States and was legalized in many places throughout the world, including South Africa. Both the right to life and the right to die were hotly argued by scientific, religious, and political entities throughout the world.

It seemed in the first years of the new millennium that with every triumph, there came a defeat. While in April 2001 the first space tourist, Dennis Tito, was launched into orbit, the *Columbia* spacecraft explosion of January 2003 brought the space industry to its knees. While stock markets around the world flourished, corporate fraud reached extraordinary levels, especially in the United States, rocking consumer confidence and investors' bottom line. While the building industry flourished worldwide, straining the supply of steel I-beams, nature—perhaps off kilter due to human impact on the environment— unleashed devastation upon Asia with the December 26, 2004, tsunami and on the United States with devastating hurricanes in 2005, especially Katrina, which all but obliterated the historic city of New Orleans. If highs and lows, triumphs and defeats, defined the world climate in general, it may be argued that disparity and polarity defined fashions as well.

FASHION IN THE TWENTY-FIRST CENTURY

Fashionable trends in modern times are set in a myriad of ways. Haute couture continues to have a trickle-down effect into mainstream Western ready-to-wear for adult women and, to a lesser extent, youth apparel. High-style runway shows in the Western world similarly have a trickle-down effect to the ready-to-wear racks at all price points. While runway shows are now taking place in Australia, India, and South America, to name just a few outposts beyond Paris, Milan, and New York, the impact of these designer lines is far less apparent, because reporting and publication of these collections is minimal and sporadic in the international press. Hollywood movies, music videos, and celebrities strongly influence fads and preferences, with celebrity endorsements playing an additional role in influencing public tastes. The phenomenon of popular culture influencing fashion can be analyzed in subsets, with urban, youth, and adult media as relevant categories.

The profusion and proliferation of Western goods and media has, it seems, caused some homogenization in terms of international style. No longer is it the case that national dress is pure and utterly unique. Dissemination of trends through media is indisputable throughout most of the world. Western brands reach many outposts in South America, Africa, and Asia. Western companies sell products online that can be shipped to customers anywhere. While elements of regional dress are maintained in Africa, Asia, South America, and the Pacific Rim, the regional style is less certain. The transmission of style from non-Western lands to the West is less prolific, steady, and certain. The occasional designer from Africa, Asia, or South America may be singled out by the Western press, but for the most part, collections shown outside of Europe and America are not acknowledged. When they are, it is the exception to the rule. Influence from non-Western designers is often transmitted via celebrities or other influential patrons who bring the work to light or who entice mimicry by virtue of their role in the public eye.

Although fashion is arguably dominated by the West, it has failed in the first years of the millennium to be dominated by any single mood or theme. Ideas about fashion seem to be at the whim of the individual designer, the fashion editor, and the consumer. All of these entities mix, match, co-opt, revive, and reinterpret at will. Attitudes are utterly postmodern, with inexplicable juxtapositions both within and among collections seeming to be the best way to summarize the content in the cacophony.

Women's Clothing

Women's apparel in the 2000s has continued many of the same trends that were apparent at the end of the 1990s. Garments are being made for all levels of comfort and sophistication and are available for a multitude of lifestyles. Fashion designers are tapping into the wide variety of fashion segments, from couture to sportswear, and are making their respective categories sought after on a seasonal basis as they have become part of the overall fashion scene. In fact, although there exists a diversity of fashion categories, fashion editors and the general public alike take great joy and creative license in mixing high and low style, street and runway, sportswear and formal attire. Some designer collections go as far as to reinvent and transport fashions from one segment of fashion culture to another.

Shoes and accessories for women are as diversified as apparel in the new millennium, with shoes and handbags, hats, scarves, and gloves being designed for a wide variety of tastes, age groups, and price levels. Sources of inspiration and aesthetic sensibilities are as varied as the purchasing populace. Mainstream lines have a strong tendency to diffuse European and American runway fashions. Lines for younger clients have a strong tendency to tap into ideas that are a part of the broader cultural milieu.

Men's Clothing

Menswear, like women's apparel, is varied in terms of its aesthetics, with garments being designed for all walks of life, age groups, and orientations. European and American designer lines have a pronounced effect on mainstream ready-to-wear collections at all price points, while urban influences are equally

The cast of Bravo's *Queer Eye for the Straight Guy,* from left, Carson Kressley, Jai Rodriguez, Thom Filicia, Ted Allen, and Kyan Douglas arrive at the fifteenth Annual GLAAD Media Awards in New York, 2004. © AP Photo / Diane Bondareff.

relevant. Trends in men's dressing can be traced to people in the media as well as to the increasing influence and proliferation of men's fashion and lifestyle magazines and websites. While the inclination to dress down in the workplace is still an idea with great currency in a variety of industries, the notion of a man with a finely tuned sense of fashion and a meticulous flair for dressing has also gained notoriety and widespread adoption. These men, referred to as metrosexuals (due to the fact that many reside in metropolitan areas and adopt a refined fashion sense, which is often regarded as a homosexual characteristic), typically adopt European suiting as a staple of their wardrobe, but many adopt a wide variety of clean, neat, elegant apparel. Men's suiting across age and cultural subsets remains traditional and tends to be either streamlined and modern or a straightforward revival. These men are also renowned for meticulous grooming, an interest in beauty products, and careful accessorizing.

Men's accessories lines, while less diversified than women's, offer a wider variety of options than has previously been made available. Shoes, bags, belts, hats, and multimedia accessories are produced by designers catering to conservative, casual, urban, and sports-minded consumers. While men continue, on the whole, to be less experimental with their manner of dressing—for example, less mixing of styles and categories is evident in men's fashion and lifestyle publications—the average man in the new millennium is likely to own a more diversified wardrobe than in previous eras.

Children's Clothing

Children's apparel in the new millennium constitutes a category of unprecedented diversity and visibility. Designers as disparate in terms of aesthetics and cost as the Gap, Enyce, and Ralph Lauren have offered and aggressively advertised their children's apparel lines, resulting in excellent commercial success. Both large department stores and stand-alone boutiques offer garments to an increasingly savvy parent and young consumer. Clothes for infants, toddlers, children, tweens (pre-teens), and teens have become more diversified in the new millennium with as many looks for the young as there are for adults. Clothing lines at all prices interpret adult styles as disparate as the hip-hop aesthetic and conservative tweeds and polo shirts.

Clothing for tweens and teenagers became a more visible and inherently fashionable category late in the 1990s with the launch of teen versions of *Vogue* and *Cosmopolitan*, filled with ideas about fashion in the tradition of their adult counterparts. In addition, media such as movies, music videos, and other programs related to popular culture further disseminate ideas about fashionable dress. Numerous teens, such as Mary Kate and Ashley Olsen, Mandy Moore, and Avril Lavigne were hot celebrities in the early years of the millennium and thereby provided models for mimicry and set standards for aesthetics.

STYLES AND DESIGNERS

Writing the history of the last six years is a challenge that is daunting to a historian of any subject but is perhaps especially challenging to a fashion historian, because fashion, by its very nature, is ephemeral, momentary, and fleeting. In the twenty-first century, the quantity and diversity of fashions is also unprecedented and presents a vast body of work for consideration. A historian must look at the evidence and not only report it but also evaluate the evidence and seek out themes of greater significance. This is difficult when so little time has passed and there is so little distance from which to step back and consider.

Contemporary fashion is as diverse as the populations of the world. Fashions can be categorized for both males and females under headings such as premiere designer, urban, sportswear, teen, tween, and children. Within many of these categories, during the last six years, there has been great polarity in terms of styles. Each season has shown a marked division among designers, with some opting for tradition and revivalism while others push their design forward with innovative and ultramodern aesthetics. It is impossible to explain and analyze every remarkable designer's style for every season over the past six years, as each has such a distinct, trademark look. Furthermore, in a culture that celebrates change and innovation, each season requires something completely different in order to keep sales steady. The fashion cycle in the new millennium turns at a dizzying pace. In order to try and put clothing into some context, it is best to analyze the broader trends and significant moments of the past six years.

The world at the beginning of the twenty-first century can best be described as factionalized. There were increasingly greater and conflicting points of view on matters of religion, finance, and politics in the world, and the strain of relations between countries was a cause of great concern. It is therefore no surprise that the visual language of the times—whether it was fine art, political cartoons, cinema, or fashion—is also equally factionalized and thoroughly diverse. In light of this diversity, however, there are some observable trends and important events that stand out above all others within the short span of the first six years of the twenty-first century.

Despite political upheaval, war, fear of terrorism, and financial ups and downs, consumption of designer goods has blossomed in the new millennium. Fashion commentators have voiced their awe at the inability of designers such as Michael Kors to maintain a healthy supply of coats costing five figures on the racks of boutiques and department stores. For a substantial subset of fashion consumers, price has become of only marginal importance and designers have stepped up the level of luxury available in their lines. Use of luxury skins and furs has been evident in lines of high-style accessories from companies such as Louis Vuitton, Fendi, and Christian Dior. Designers, both veterans and newcomers, have included extensive handwork in ready-to-wear garments, causing the price of off-the-rack attire to reach previously unattained heights.

The line between ready-to-wear and haute couture has in fact been blurred by the introduction of lines that are referred to as *demi-couture*. These garments are purchased off the rack but have a pedigree consisting of hundreds of hours of handwork, such as embroidery, hand stitching, and beading—and they demand a price to match the labor. A garment costing more than $100,000 may now be found hanging on the ready-to-wear racks of both European and American designers.

While women's apparel and accessories typically encourage the greatest expenditures and the most lavish materials and construction techniques, men's apparel and accessories have also experienced a renewed interest in luxury, with increased demand for both garments and services. Customers can be pampered while consuming their fashions at haute couture ateliers in Paris, but they can also make exclusive appointments to have their running shoes custom made to their exact specifications in Manhattan's fashionable Nolita neighborhood where the Nike ID Design Studio is positioned to make bespoke sneakers.

On the other hand, while designers have encouraged conspicuous consumption among clientele with lots of money to spend, there has also been a recent surge in the number of designers creating diffusion lines at markedly lower price points for large European and American retailers. For example, Target, a Midwestern U.S. mass retailer, has established a solid relationship with Isaac Mizrahi, who designs clothing aimed at the shopper with considerably less money, who shops for fashion alongside housewares, hardware, and detergents rather than a designer studio. This has proven to be a huge hit with consumers, who can feel they possess a little of the fashion exclusivity held by those with means to buy high-style fashions. They get good design and do not have to pay high prices. Traditional, elegant forms derived in great part from classic American and European design define this highly successful line of women's wear and accessories. The line avoids trendiness and offers tasteful and fashionable clothes to a public clamoring for good design but without the means to buy the high-priced couture. The use of inexpensive fabrics and offshore production with lower labor costs has allowed the label to keep prices low. Italian designer Mossimo and designer Behnaz Sarafpour have followed suit with agreements with Target.

Swedish retailer H&M, a worldwide retailer offering high-fashion, trendy clothes for men, women, and children has also formed alliances for special limited editions of designer lines of clothing with the likes of Karl Lagerfeld and

Viktor & Rolf. These diffusion lines have so far been offered for a limited time and have typically caused young women and men in New York, London, Berlin, and Beijing to line up for hours waiting for the stores to open, with a frenzy of buying ensuing. It has been typical for these lines of clothes to sell out immediately.

Footwear and other accessory lines have also been developed by designers and made available in department stores around the world. Mass-produced footwear has been designed by Vivienne Westwood for American footwear chain Nine West, and British designer Alexander McQueen designed sneakers for sportswear-maker Puma.

High-end designers have also searched for broader market share with diffusions lines that maintain the high-quality fabrics and standards of construction, but frequently have more modern, simpler lines. Valentino, who is known for elaborate, romantic designs, began to offer a collection called Valentino Red in 2005. This line, priced considerably lower than his boutique collection, is offered in department stores such as Saks Fifth Avenue in the United States. Its target market is a younger client with a simpler sensibility who still enjoys the romance of his timeless designs. Valentino made headlines with the launch of this collection, but he is in good company with designers such as Roberto Cavalli, whose Just Cavalli lower-priced line has been available for years.

Designers and celebrities have been marketing fashion for causes such as AIDS and cancer to make a statement about their social concern, making a difference in the fight against these two deadly diseases. Wearing pink, for example, signifies support of the breast cancer cause, and red has been associated with AIDS research. In 2004, American cyclist Lance Armstrong's foundation began selling yellow rubber Livestrong bracelets as a fundraiser for cancer research. This developed into a fad, where people of all ages and classes started wearing them. Rubber bracelets in a myriad of other colors soon surfaced, indicating support for other causes. Fashion for a cause, especially in the United States, has indicated a concern for social and health issues permeating society.

The counterfeiting of fashionable goods goes back to antiquity, at least as far as when dyestuffs derived from precious sources were faked and sold in the Roman marketplace. Ever since the 1980s boom in popularity of designer goods, and especially of logo-emblazoned goods, there has been increased presence of designer counterfeits. Their production is notoriously linked to organized crime, and the goods, produced largely in China, are sold all over the world in illegal street markets and on the Internet. Policing counterfeit sales is more successful in some countries than others, but law enforcement is dedicated to eradicating the trade of counterfeit fashion goods. After the terrorist attacks of 2001, the general public has increasingly been made aware of the illegality of counterfeit goods, some of which may generate funds that support terrorists. Mainstream publications such as *Harper's Bazaar* and *Vogue* have made a consistent effort to educate the public about the negative impact of purchasing these. The fashion industry has also stepped up its efforts to curtail counterfeiting by waging costly wars in the courts, while industry leaders also seek to tighten controls on intellectual property.

Celebrities have become synonymous with fashion in the twenty-first century, and it seems as though everyone wants to be a designer. The number of celebrity designers has grown from a small handful to several dozen. In the United States, pop stars such as Jennifer Lopez, Jessica Simpson, Hilary Duff, Sean "Diddy" Combs, the Olsen twins, Gwen Stefani, and Beyoncé, among many others, have presented lines of fashion for mass consumption to the young and hip consumer. Australian supermodel Elle Macpherson has also stepped into the realm of design with well-received lingerie lines. Essentially, the celebrities are marketing their own look so that the mainstream consumer can emulate their favorite celebrity, much as they have done since the golden age of Hollywood in the 1930s and 1940s.

Trends in fashion continue to come from movies and television. Fashion trends are communicated worldwide as American shows made in Hollywood are bought and shown on European, Middle Eastern, and Asian networks. The Internet, faster than ever and more prevalent for mass use, has been an increasingly important method of spreading fashion ideas around the world. Technology has become more trendy, and the cell phone has become an accessory in the same way people wear earrings or hats. Fashion designers create cell phone holders emblazoned with their logos. The iPod's trademark white earbuds (earphones) mark the wearer as trendy and aware of good design and technology. Designers have improved upon earbuds, cell phones, and Bluetooth devices by encrusting them with Swarovski crystals. Some designers have even embraced the design and decoration of the cell phones themselves.

Designer denim, an important category for the fashion industry since the 1970s, saw a surge of new designers offering products for both men and women. Jeans, worn for all occasions, both for casual and dressy, became more of staple fashion must-have for everyone, and designers, even the most costly, all had some kind of denim product available for their customers. The prices of jeans ranged greatly, with chic designs available at all price levels from under twenty (U.S.) dollars to three hundred or more. Among the successful brands were Seven for All Mankind, which offered both men's and ladies apparel, and which notably partnered with top young American designer Zac Posen. Citizens for Humanity, Lucky Brand, and Miss Sixty were also among the brands offering well-cut denim at high prices.

Many of these companies made their products objects of desire through careful cut and good fit, but innovations in denim textiles have also been part of the story, with Lycra blends and new washes providing diversity among the products. Detailing of denim also made the story of blue jeans more interesting at the beginning of the twenty-first century. Both men's and women's apparel was frequently embroidered, patched, distressed, and decorated with grommets, crystals, or lace. Designers such as Cavalli and Dolce & Gabbana are among the top designers who contributed to this current in fashion.

Haute couture, much like in the 1990s, is still making an impact on the world, largely as entertainment and inspiration for fashion ideas. Designers are admired by members of the fashion press who look at collections each season and spot the prevalent themes, colors, and fads. Designers are celebrities in the world of fashion and are household names for many. They have made names for themselves working for established design houses in Paris, London, and Milan, creating lines but not starting their own houses. American Tom Ford is famous for his work in the house of Yves Saint-Laurent Rive Gauche, and his move to Italian Gucci, which is a massive fashion company with great influence in European fashion. Some young designers are making headlines with their own lines, such as Posen, Doo Ri, and the duo Proenza Schouler.

The beginning of the twenty-first century has also seen the rise of a few new promising stars. Among them is the youthful and handsome Hollywood darling Posen. His business, started in 2001, received critical acclaim from the very beginning as he offered up timeless and nostalgic garments that were neither too trendy nor too staid. In 2004, he won the Council of Fashion Designers of America (CFDA) Swarovski-Perry Ellis Award for Ready-to-Wear. His fashions are popular among the red carpet set and also find strong retail results.

In addition to the rise of a handful of promising young, new designers, the first years of this decade have seen a great deal of revivalism as well—rebirth of defunct designer labels, of landmark designs of years gone by, and of the essence of decades as a whole. From 2000 to 2006, fashionable dress has vividly revived the 1960s, the 1970s, and the 1980s, to a great extent in chronological order.

First, fashion saw the revival of the sixties with what fashion editors referred to as "boho-chic." Designers in all sectors of the fashion industry offered up tunics, ponchos, and caftans. Trouser legs were markedly flared, textiles playful and brightly colored, and beads, tassels, and fringe abounded everywhere. Sandals and hand luggage followed lockstep with the apparel designers, creating an overall aesthetic that was decisively reminiscent of the 1960s but was sharper, cleaner, and more sophisticated and coordinated than the bohemian original. As with most fashion revivals, the trend lasted a short time and the bohemian duds were relegated to the closet in anticipation of the next revival.

Seventies styles also resurfaced, although perhaps more subtly. Pop icon Madonna, a fashion maverick since the 1980s, may have played a part in the revived interest in the sleek and utterly casual aesthetic as she starred in numerous music videos that capture the spirit of the time, including "Music" and "Hung Up." Designers such as Donatella Versace produced sleek suiting for women inspired by the leisure suits of the seventies, while platform shoes not seen since disco was king also made a strong reappearance that extended into the 2007 summer season. Fashion stylists revisited the flyaway bangs recalling Farrah Fawcett and *Charlie's Angels*.

Eighties revivalism was on the fashion radar by 2005 and many of the icons of that era were brought back in full force. The eighties look, with leg warmers, tights, big slouchy sweaters, and ankle booties, was found in runway presentations, photo shoots, and music videos by such artists as Jennifer Lopez. Heavy, colorful makeup was promoted by stylists and cosmetics companies but translated only loosely into the streets. There was even a half-hearted attempt to revive neon clothes and accessories toward the end of 2005, but the success of that ill-conceived restoration was hardly a prominent trend. Eighties-era designs were on offer at the lowest prices still in 2007.

In the new millennium, fashion brands that seemed defunct found new life. Among the notable examples are Jordache and Gloria Vanderbilt jeans, both of which had been mainstays of the fashion scene in the 1970s and 1980s. Aggressive marketing, improved manufacturing techniques, and retailing through such glamorous outposts as Barney's New York lent new cachet to these once-forgotten brands.

The Pucci label, a virtual unknown in the United States in the 1980s and 1990s took on new life once it was purchased by LVMH (the Louis Vuitton Moet Hennessey Group), and in the first years of this century, the once-dated graphic patterns found new devotees. Patterns, both archival and new, have been screened onto hip and current forms such as makeup cases, handbags, shoes, scarves, and dresses. A boutique nestled among the other major players of European fashion on New York City's Fifth Avenue is a strong indication of the strength of the brand's newly regained identity.

Signature garments and collections have also found new lives in recent fashion. A fine example of this is the 2006 collection offered by Norma Kamali through Nordstrom department stores. Through a partnership with the athletic apparel giant Everlast, Kamali has created a line of designer sportswear; however, this line falls out of step with the standard fare of the age, which is sleek and tailored. Instead Kamali has revisited her collections of the early 1980s and has created peplum flounces and puffed sleeves on women's sweat suits.

The House of Balenciaga, under the direction of Nicolas Ghesquiere, has also delved into the archives for inspiration. Ghesquiere's 2005 and 2006 collections directly borrowed from archival designs that were revitalized with a modern aesthetic to great critical and commercial acclaim. At the House of Dior, John Galliano also reworked garments of the house's namesake in jacket markets as the new New Look.

One cannot discuss fashions of the early twenty-first century without referencing street, urban, hip-hop, and black fashions. In 2006 the Museum of the City of New York held an exhibition comprised of garments, photographs, and other historical memorabilia that documented the impact of African Americans on the fashion industry. In addition to highlighting the names of black designers of the early twentieth century that are seldom mentioned in surveys of American fashion, the exhibit cast a special light on the rise and importance of fashions related to the urban and hip-hop aesthetic.

Like so many fashions of the twentieth century, the black urban and hip-hop-inspired aesthetic began in the streets on a limited budget and was an expression of personal style and a reaction to both the media mainstream and socioeconomic constraints. Airbrushed jackets, T-shirts, and hats, once the product of neighborhood artists, were mass-produced and sold at major retailers by 2000. Baggy jeans, oversized jerseys, and customized sneakers reached a wide market through mainstream retailers. The power and influence of the hip-hop music scene and its exposure through music videos is undeniable and far reaching. What may still be referred to as "black style" is far reaching and crosses lines of race or color, as youths in all sectors of society aim to live the aesthetic that the garments proclaim.

Commercialization of the black aesthetic is widespread, but the presence of powerhouse labels is also noteworthy. Among them are brands such as FUBU (For Us, By Us), Phat Farm, Baby Phat, and Enyce. So popular are many of these brands that they have been touched by the evil reach of the counterfeiting industry, which was a celebrated aspect of black style in the 1980s at the advent of logo and designer mania.

The impact of black style and the hip-hop aesthetic may also be considered in light of the sportswear and fan-wear industry. Because many looks include team jerseys and team hats, makers of these goods, not typically considered part of the fashion sector, have expanded their lines to include greater diversity of color, cut, and logo typeface or insignia. A passion for retro team apparel is a trend of the early twenty-first century that crosses racial and cultural lines.

CONCLUSION

The story of the past few years of fashion is one that is rich, colorful, and varied. In this highly industrialized, media-driven, culturally diverse, short-attention-span society, trends pass quickly and the word *ephemeral* takes on new intensity as the speed with which things come and go is oftentimes dizzying. In ten or twenty years' time, it may become clear that trends or styles not mentioned here have become important to designers perhaps not yet known and, by virtue of their reference through revival, will take on new significance. In addition, as fashion editors in seasons to come look back on the trends now passed, they will instruct their reading public as to what should be kept for wear in years to come. Our individual archives of fashions will also determine what will be considered important in the annals of history.

Lastly, in a landscape of design that is so thoroughly diverse, the scope and understanding of a historian so close to the moment in question will always be nearsighted. It remains for the reader to continue to look carefully and critically at the world of fashion that is alive, vibrant, and constantly changing all around us. The nature and meaning of fashion are continually evolving and are rich with meaning. Fashion functions as a current of dialogue that we all may understand if we stop to listen and that we participate in whether we mean to or not.

FURTHER READING

Jones, Terry, and Susie Rushton, eds. *Fashion Now*. Cologne, Germany: Taschen, 2006.
All the current fashion periodicals are useful guides to current fashion and style. These include *Vogue, Elle, Harper's Bazaar, Glamour, Marie Claire, Fashion Planet, Flare, GQ,* and *InStyle*

WEB RESOURCES

www.fashion-planet.com
www.flare.com

Glossary

à la jardinière
A dress with one or more frills on the shoulder, and a wristband, ruching, or plaiting at the hand, with the fullness caught at the shoulder and/or wrist with gathering or pleating.

acetate
Generic term for a manufactured fiber composed of acetylated cellulose used since the 1950s.

acid dyes
Class of dyes used primarily for protein and nylon fibers.

aiglet
Decorative metal tip applied to ribbons and other ties used to fasten clothing.

alpaca
Long, fine, natural protein hair fiber obtained from the domesticated South American alpaca, a member of the camel family; a wool variant.

altobasso
Velvets characterized by a sculpted effect given by the juxtaposition of two (or more) heights of the velvet pile cut with velvet irons in Renaissance clothing.

anaxyrides or braka
Pants, which were rare in Byzantium. *Braka* is a German term for pants. Many images in Byzantine art show the Persian's wearing pants, but they do not seem to be a part of Byzantine dress until the 12th century. The exception may be the pants (or stockings) shown throughout the Menologian of Basil II, worn by soldiers.

angora
Goat native to Turkey from which the natural protein fiber, mohair, is obtained; a wool variant.

animal fiber
General term for natural protein fiber of animal origin, such as wool (sheep) or silk (silkworm).

apoptygma
Overfold of the peplos, formed by folding the top part of the fabric over and below the shoulders. It could be unbelted, or belted, either under or over the overfold; the excess of the *apoptygma* pulled over the belt created a pouch of fabric known as a *kolpos*.

Ara Pacis
The marble *Ara Pacis Augustae*, "Altar of Augustan Peace (13 BCE), celebrated the peace established in the Empire after

Augustus's victories in Gaul and Spain. Its elaborate relief decoration represented the actual procession that took place on the occasion of the triumph, with the realistic portraits of the priests, attendants, and members of the family of Augustus, dressed in their official costumes.

armcye   The part of the shirt or sleeved jacket where the top of the sleeve is sewn or attached.

attifet   A heart-shaped wired headdress that sat atop the hair that was brushed aside into two rolls and sat with its point just touching the forehead.

baion   A scepter held by a Byzantine empress.

baltadin   A belt with precious stones, insignia for certain offices in the Ninth–Tenth centuries.

Banyan   Eighteenth-century long robe worn as outerwear by men.

barathea   Twill variation with a broken rib weave on one side and a pebbly texture on the other.

bark cloth   A roughly woven drapery fabric with a bark-like texture, or a nonwoven material made from soaked and beaten inner bark of tropical trees such as tapa.

bast fibers   Woody fibers from the stems of plants such as flax, jute, and hemp.

batik   Resist print in which wax is drawn or blocked onto a fabric before dyeing so the color does not penetrate in the waxed area.

batiste   Fine, sheer, plain-woven cloth of combed and carded long-staple cotton.

bavolet   A loose fitting cap with a flap on the nape of the neck worn primarily by French peasant women. A large ruffle around the band helped keep sun off the face and neck.

beater   Movable frame on a loom that holds the reed and packs the filling yarns into place.

bias   Invisible diagonal line at a 45-degree angle to the grain of a fabric, popular in the 1930s.

binyeo   Long bobbin-headed hair pin.

bionda   A homemade bleaching mixture composed mostly of lemon juice, ammonia, and urine: the combined effect of the *bionda* and of the sun exposure bleached the hair to the signature Venetian blonde in the Italian Renaissance.

blackwork (or Spanish work)   A type of embroidery that creates geometric, lace-like patterns in black silk thread worked on white linen or silk, usually seen on cuffs, collars, and sleeves of shirts and chemises.

blanket   A textile sample showing a series of patterns or colors all on the same warp.

bleaching   Basic finishing process to whiten untreated fabrics (greige goods).

bleeding	A fault in which dye runs from one pattern area into another.
blend	Yarn of two or more staple fiber types spun together, or fabric containing blended yarns in the warp and filling directions.
block printing	General term for a hand-printing process using wood or other solid material blocks into which patterns have been cut.
blotch printing	Open-screen roller-printing process by which the plain background of a printed fabric can be colored.
bobbin lace	Single-element construction, originally handmade on a pillow with numerous threads.
bodice	A close-fitting woman's garment worn over the stays (later, corsets), sometimes with detachable sleeves. The bodice also describes the upper part of a one-piece gown.
bolt	An entire length of fabric, usually rolled full-width on a tube; sometimes folded before rolling.
bombasina	Cotton fabric in the Italian Renaissance.
bombazine	A mixture of silk and wool.
borzacchini	Leather ankle boots worn by people in the Italian Renaissance.
brache	Italian Renaissance trousers.
braghetta	Italian renaissance codpiece. A fabric triangle, originally created to cover the male groin area.
braid	Flat or round, woven or plaited fabric used for trimming.
breeches (or Upper Stocks)	Men's short (usually knee-length) trousers. The style of these changed drastically from period to period and were either close-fitted hose or very elaborately puffed, slashed, and structured.
broadcloth	Tightly woven, lustrous cotton fabric in a plain weave with a fine crosswise rib, or wool fabric with a close twill weave, brushed and sheared to give a uniform, slightly felted, smooth appearance. Originally describes a finely woven wool cloth used for better grades of clothing. At 29-inches wide, it was broader than most woven fabrics of the early American Colonial era.
brocade	Jacquard-woven fabric with a supplementary warp and/or filling which creates an all-over design: background is satin or twill weave.
brushing	Finishing process in which fibers are raised to obscure the construction of the fabric.
buckram	Plain-woven cotton fabric stiffened with sizing.
bulla	An amulet worn by Etruscan children as a good-luck charm, by young men on bracelets on their upper arms, and on horse trappings; or the locket worn by Roman male children as the sign of their free-born status. They were made of leather, bronze, silver, or gold, and were dedicated to the gods when the boys put on the *toga virilis*, or man's toga, around the age of fifteen, signifying the end of their childhood.

burlap	Plain-woven cloth of retted, single-ply jute.
busk	A piece of wood, metal, or bone that slid into the center front of the female dress bodice to provide stiffness and structure.
busun	Padded/quilted sock, made from specially shaped forms with a heal, thick ankle and pointy curled-up toe.
calashes	Very large hoods worn in eighteenth-century France and the colonies to fit over the large piled hairstyles. These were pulled over the towering hairstyles with specially made devices that the woman could manipulate to reach high enough to come over the hair.
calcagnini	Typically Venetian footwear that could reach the height of 50 centimeters. Fashionable in the late fifteenth–early sixteenth century in Italy.
calcei	The high-topped, laced boots that a Roman citizen wore with the toga in public; indoors he wore sandals. A patrician's calcei were dark red (mullei), the Senator's calcei had black laces and a buckle. Their basic form derived from the laced, pointed shoes represented on Etruscan monuments of the Archaic period, though the Roman calcei were not pointed.
calendering	Standard finishing process in which cloth is pressed heavily and/or repeatedly under steel rollers to produce a polished surface also used to emboss fabrics.
calico	Ancient, basic woven cotton cloth.
calze solate (or calzebraghe)	Tight-fitting footed hoses made in wool cloth with a central seam in the back. Used in the fifteenth and early sixteenth centuries in Italy.
camel hair	Natural protein fiber obtained from the undercoat of the Asiatic camel.
camise (or camicia)	Shirts, sometimes ruffled at the cuffs and neck, in which the ruffles were gathered in a short collar decorated with embroidery worn during the Renaissance period.
cammellotti (or ciambellotti, zambellotti)	Very warm wool cloth used for winter clothing in Renaissance Italy. Originally, probably made with camel hair, hence the name.
cammino	A textile pattern characterized by a horizontal sequence of lobed Italian Renaissance motifs framing the "Italian artichoke," a pomegranate, or a pinecone.
camora	A petticoat skirt worn as a feminine gown in the Renaissance. It was known in Italy under various names, according to different regions: *gamurra* or *camurra* in Florence; *camora, socha,* or *zupa* in northern Italy; and *Gonna, gonnella,* or *sottana* in the south.
candys	A long under-tunic thought to be the precursor to the caftan, developed from the Sumerian shawl.
canion	Men's leggings worn over hose and attached to the culots. Very short breeches were laced to the culots and usually came to just below the knee. They were a close fit, but not tight.

capelet	Upper part of the Greek female dress of Daedalic figures; a tightly fitting tubular dress cinched in tightly at the waist.
capigliara	Elaborate hairstyle fashionable in sixteenth century Italy that mixed the hair with postiches, ribbons, bows, jewels, and pearls.
carded yarn	Yarn spun from a carded sliver of fibers.
carding process	Used for all natural fibers, in which they are separated and brought into general alignment prior to spinning.
carrick	A long coat usually of wool broadcloth with buttons down the front and a many-tiered capelet topped by a conventional collar.
cashmere	Fine, extremely soft natural protein fiber obtained from the undercoat of the Himalayan Kashmir goat.
casque à la Minerve	A small, plumed hat styled to look like the one worn by the Roman goddess of wisdom.
casso, busto	Corset, often made with wood or metal busks in Renaissance clothing.
cassock	Long, front-buttoning gowns worn by various clergy.
caul	Hairstyle tied up in a netted *caul* and topped with a flat, very wide-brimmed hat.
ceinture fleshée	Multicolored woven belt worn by the coureurs des bois in Canada.
cellulose	Organic fibrous substance found in all vegetation that is the basic constituent of both natural and manufactured fabrics such as cotton.
cellulosic fibers	Such as cotton, linen, jute, and rayon.
chōnin	The townsmen and merchants, the lowest class in Japan's inflexible class system and the fashion leaders of the urban, cash-based society of Edo Japan.
ch'ma	High-waisted full skirt worn in Korea, with narrow shoulder straps that wrapped to overlap in the back and flowed in slight pleats to the ankles.
ch'ma-chogori	Top and bottom of Korean hanbok.
chang-ot	Outercloak/veil in Korean dress.
chatelaine	A heavy hook with a collection of small thimbles, scissors, needle-cases, scent cases, seals, patch-boxes, toothpick cases, keys, and watches.
cheesecloth	Cotton in loose, plain weave with a very low thread count, originally used to wrap cheese.
chemise dress	A simple straight shift dress made of cotton or light silk, sashed at the waist and adorned at the neckline and hem with a deep ruffle.
chemisette	An underlayer of sheer white fabric made into a sleeveless tunic; the lace decoration around the neckline was often worn to peak over the neckline of the main gown.

chiffon	Sheer fabric, made usually of silk.
chinoiserie	Objects made in Europe in imitation of Chinese styles.
chintz	A plain woven fabric, usually made of cotton, printed with colorful lively patterns such as flowers.
chiton	A Greek rectangular garment used as a basic shirt by both men and women in all periods, made from a single piece of cloth, uncut and unfitted, woven to order, straight from the loom. Its length varied. A long chiton was worn by women, old men, charioteers, and musicians. Active men wore a short or three-quarter length chiton. Also, a tunic worn by middle-rank courtiers in the early Byzantine period. Biblical figures are illustrated wearing the *chiton* throughout the history of the Byzantine empire.
chlamys	A short or long cloak fastened over the right shoulder with a *fibula* (pin). When worn for military purposes the chlamys was left plain and was usually made of felt. The civilian chlamys is decorated with a *tablion*, a trapezoidal or rectangular embroidered panel sewn onto the front and back, along the side of its opening in the knee area. By the sixth century the chlamys became part of the dress for the emperor and began to slowly lose its military connotation. It could be made out of luxury fabrics like silk or wool with embroidered decoration of high quality. By the sixth century, the empress also wore the chlamys.
chogori	Top jacket or blouse with long curved sleeves, *sohme*, that evolved to a short bolero length for women that is overlapped to close right of center front and ties above the bust line with two long sashes, *korum*, in a large loop. Men's chogori length has remained more static overtime, reaching to just below the waist.
choli	Indian woman's short, tight-fitting blouse.
city-states	Athens, Sparta, Corinth, and others, were independent Greek cities, each with its surrounding territory, characterized by different political systems, social customs, and artistic specialties but bound together by language and religion.
clavus (i)	Vertical stripes of embroidery on a tunic, usually two stripes (clavi).
cleaning	**Dry**: immersion of fabric in petroleum or synthetic solvents to remove oil or grease. **Wet**: removal of waterborne soil or stains by a soap or detergent and water process, done usually on a flat surface with a brush, not to be confused with laundering by immersion.
cloth count	*See* thread count.
cloth	General term used for any pliable material whether woven, knitted, felted, knotted, or extruded.
coazzone	Typically fifteenth-century northern Italian ponytail wrapped in ribbons and trimmed with jewels.
codpiece	A man's accessory used to connect the two legs of the breeches and cover the opening at the center front. Codpieces could be a

plain patch of cloth or very decorative, stuffed, and ornamental, often considered risqué.

coir	Coarse and extremely durable fiber obtained from the outer husks of coconuts.
colobium	A sleeveless or short-sleeved tunic.
color	A hue, as contrasted with white, black, or gray.
color abrasion	Loss of color, particularly in pigment prints or from poor dye penetration.
colorfast	Term applied to fabrics colored in such a way as to prevent color fading from light or cleaning.
combing	The process of making carded fibers parallel and removing impurities and short fibers before spinning.
corsaletti	Upper body armor made of steel plates, worn in the Renaissance.
cotton	Natural vegetable fiber from the cotton plant, grown in the southern United States, Egypt, Russia, and China.
coureurs des bois (or Voyageurs)	French fur trappers of the seventeenth and eighteenth century who traveled and hunted with Native American groups in the Great Lakes and Hudson Bay area of North America. They often trapped the beaver used for fashionable hats in the seventeenth century.
courtesans	Prostitutes.
courtiers	The privileged who frequently attended the royal courts of Europe.
couturiers	High-fashion designers.
cravat	A scarf or band of fabric worn by men around the neck as a tie.
crease	A line in a fabric caused by a fold, usually along the front of trouser legs.
crêpe	Yarn that is overtwisted to create a crinkled profile and stretchy resilience; fabric woven of crepe yarn, which has a matte surface texture and slight stretch.
crewel	A hand embroidery technique from Kashmir in which fine, loosely twisted two-ply yarn is stitched onto a cotton base.
cuirasse	Named after the ancient piece of armor formed of leather that protected the upper torso. These long, figure-hugging bodices emphasized a woman's hourglass figure, created by the very heavily boned corsets of the day. By 1878 the cuirasse bodices had reached the thighs. The cuirasse bodice was corset-like-and dipped even deeper in both front and back, extending well down the hips creating the look of a body encased in armor.
culots	Very short breeches often worn with canions, but could be worn only with hose. Culots were so short that they appear in contemporary images as just a band of puffed fabric around the hips.

cuoietto, coletto Upper body garment worn in the Renaissance made of leather, hence the name.

daedalic style An artistic style typical of the seventh-century Orientalizing period in Greece, featuring a frontal stance, flat surfaces, a triangular face with triangular, almond-shaped eyes, and a wig-like, layered hairstyle.

daimyo The top class in Japan's strict four class system. This military class included the elite military leaders and *samurai.*

dalmatic A wide short or long-sleeved unbelted robe or tunic, with sleeves usually cut on a diagonal and decorated with clavi (lengthwise stripes). This is an older Roman term which may have gone out of use, but this is unclear.

damask Woven pattern based upon contrasting warp-face and filling-face cloths.

darbar Term referring to the Mughal court. Paintings of *darbar* scenes are major records of clothing worn at the Mughal court.

ddidon Fastener for precious metal pendants to the top of an outfit or at the waist or belt section, then a *juche* or knot, and finished with one tassel *yuso,* or three.

decating (decatizing) Basic finishing process that includes light scouring and single calendering.

degumming Removal of natural gums from silk yarn or fabric by boiling in a mild alkaline solution.

denim Yarn-dyed cotton cloth woven in a warp-faced twill, usually with a dyed warp and a natural filling.

density The measure of the set of a cloth—the total number of ends and picks.

deshabille A type of "undress" for both men and women such as a dressing gown with often quite extravagant decoration worn among the upper classes in the eighteenth century.

Dionysos God of wine and drama: in the fifth century Greek drama was presented at Athens at his festivals. As god of the wild, he had a retinue of maenads and ithyphallic satyrs.

direct printing General term for a process in which color is applied directly onto the fabric.

discharge printing Process in which pattern is obtained by bleaching portions of already dyed cloth. It may be left white or dyed another color.

disperse dyeing Process for coloring acetate, acrylic, nylon, and polyester in which a slightly water-soluble dye is dispersed in the fiber solution. Sometimes subject to fume-fading and sublimation.

divetesion A ceremonial, long, silk tunic usually worn in the Byzantine era over another tunic and belted. The emperor wore this tunic under a *chlamys, loros,* or *sagion,* depending on the time period.

dopo dooroomakee	Korean overcoat that had wider sleeves and collar than chogori, and were generally considered as more formal; the *dopo's* tie position was adjusted above that of the *chogori's* in order that the two ties would not overlap on a man's chest.
double cloth	Compound cloth based on two sets each of warp or filling yarns held together at regular intervals by a warp or filling thread passing from one fabric to the other.
double crown	Emblematic of both upper and lower Egypt (the red and white crowns are combined) with the white crown (symbolizing upper Egypt) set in the red crown (symbolizing lower Egypt) called the pschent ( ).
double knit	Knitted fabric made with a double set of needles to produce a double thickness of fabric which is consequently denser and has greater stability than a single knit. Popular in the 1970s.
double weave	Fabric woven with two sets of warp and filling yarns, with an extra yarn to loosely hold the two cloths together. The connecting yarn is cut, leaving two cut-pile fabrics.
doublet	In each era a doublet has slightly different characteristics. It is generally a man's close fitting buttoned jacket, sometimes short and padded with broad shoulders and tight waist, usually with sleeves and flared at the hips. Worn from the fifteenth to the seventeenth centuries.
dye house	Facility where greige goods are dyed or printed.
dyeing	The process of applying color to fiber, yarn, or fabric with natural or synthetic coloring agents.
Egyptian cotton	Fine grade of cotton known for its long staple fibers that create a smooth cotton fabric.
elasticity	Ability of a stretched material to recover its original size and shape.
elastomer	Elastic synthetic fiber with the physical properties and strength of natural rubber such as Spandex.
embades	High boots represented on Greek hunters, for example Artemis, the huntress, or other active figures, usually with shortened chiton, folded about the waist to get it out of the way.
embroidery	Basic cloth embellished with ornamental needlework.
Empire dress	Essentially a tube dress with one drawstring at a round neck and another at a high waistline. The neckline was low, the sleeves short, and the waistline high, located just under the bust. Skirts were very narrow, and because of this comparatively form-fitting silhouette, a reduction of underpinnings was necessary.
ephebe	A member of an adolescent age group or a social status, the age of young men of training age. At a certain point an official institution (*ephebia*) saw to building them into citizens, especially training them as soldiers, as part of the militia of citizens.

fabric	General term for any woven, knitted, knotted, felted, or otherwise constructed material made from fibers or yarns. Cloth, carpet, and matting are all defined as fabric.
fabric width	Crosswise measurement of cloth.
face	The side on which a fabric is finished.
fading	Color loss due to light, pollutants, cleaning, etc.
faldia, faldiglia, verducato	Farthingale or early hoop dress worn (origins in Spain) in Italian Renaissance.
falling band	A large, square, turned-down collar that rested on the shoulders.
farsetto, giubbetto, zuparello	Characteristically short upper body garment. Used in fifteenth and early sixteenth century Italian Renaissance clothing.
farthingale	A round bell-shaped hoop skirt of Spanish origin; a roll of padding, sometimes called a hoop, worn around the hips or waist extending the width of a skirt.
felt	Nonwoven fabric made of fibers joined through the application of heat, agitation, and moisture, or by mechanical treatment; woven fabric that has been treated with heat, moisture, and pressure to achieve greater strength and fullness.
fiber	The basic element of yarn and cloth. Any tough, hair-like substance, natural or manufactured, that can be spun or thrown to form yarn, or felted or otherwise joined into a fabric.
fibula	A brooch like a large safety pin used to fasten a variety of Roman garments. Like many devices meant to fasten or bind—the bride's belt, for example—it could have a symbolic meaning. So the mantle of the *flamen*, a priest, had to be *infibulatus*, fastened with a fibula in back. The bride's wedding dress was tied with a square knot, the Hercules knot. (*See* Herakles knot.)
filament fiber	Of indefinite length, either natural (silk) or manufactured. Silk filament is the actual thread of a silkworm's cocoon; manufactured filaments are produced by forcing a solution through a spinneret.
Filling yarn (or weft or woof)	In weaving, the crosswise yarn or yarns that interlace at right angles with the lengthwise warp.
filling faced	A term used to describe fabrics in which the filling picks predominate over the warp ends. The filling may conceal the warp completely.
finish	Any treatment given to a fiber, yarn, or fabric to alter its original or greige goods state.
flamen (plural flamines)	The highest rank of Roman priesthoods, at one point including four priests dedicated to the cult of particular divinities. Their costume is best represented on the Ara Pacis, where they wear the *laena, galerus* hat with *apex,* and *calcei.*
flannel	Medium weight, slightly napped plain or twill-woven cloth, most often of wool or cotton.

flapper	A flighty young girl of questionable morals in the 1920s who danced the Charleston and wore straight, uneven hemmed dresses that swung around while she danced—originated from a British word for a kind of fish that thrashed about when thrown into a hot pan.
flax plant	Plant from which linen is produced.
fleece	The woolly coat of a sheep, usually clipped in one large piece; fabric with a deep soft woolly pile.
float	Portion of warp or filling yarns covering two or more adjacent yarns to form a design or satin surface.
fontange	A tall headdress created by counting elaborate bits of lace and ribbons onto tall wires and placing it at the front and center on a woman's head.
frenello	Big jewel made with a central stone surrounded by pearls or diamonds; usually worn on the top of the head in Renaissance clothing.
frieze	A coarse, woolly woven cloth used for outerwear.
fringe	A kind of braid or tassel attached at each shoulder of a female figure's chiton in the fourth century BC was a sign of status, often marking her as a priestess or divinity.
frogging	Ornamental closures made of braid or cording.
fulling	A finishing operation dependent on the felting properties of wool that shrinks the fabric to make it heavier and thicker.
furisode kosode	Style for young Japanese women featuring long, swinging sleeves.
gabardine	Fabric of fine worsted yarns closely woven in a diagonal twill and finished with a high sheen.
galerus	The characteristic hat of the flamen, a helmet-like leather head covering, topped by a spike, the *apex*.
garibaldi	Renaissance style of shirt with a full-sleeve. Sometimes made in red or black lightweight wool, or flannel, but more often in white cotton, with the full front gathered or pleated at the neckline.
garters	Before the invention of elastic, garters were generally silk bands tied around the leg to hold up hose. Worn by both men and women, though rarely visible under the latter's dresses.
gat	Nobleman's hat; stacked onto a headband, *mangeon*, and high cap, *tanggeoun*, fastened to the head with a tie around the chin; the wide brim was positioned carefully to sit lower in the front.
gauze	Openly constructed sheer cloth of any fiber.
Geometric Period	The period of Greek art characterized by vases decorated with geometric patterns.
gilet corsage	A woman's garment made in imitation of a man's waistcoat, and front-buttoning jackets with short *basques* that extended below the waistline could all be softened by wearing underneath a

chemisette usually in white muslin or cambric with frills showing at the neckline and cuffs.

gin (cotton gin)   A machine used to separate seeds and impurities from raw cotton fibers.

giornea   A sort of cloak opened at the sides, with a scooped neck in the back. Worn by both men and by women in fifteenth century Italy.

gokkal   Peaked hat, worn by women in warm weather made of paper or cloth that is folded repeatedly and fixed to the hair.

gorgiera   A ruff made either of thickly pleated linen trimmed with lace or linen worn in the Renaissance.

grain   The alignment of vertical (lengthwise) and horizontal (crosswise) elements in a fabric to form a right-angle relationship.

grass fibers   General class of fibers that includes abaca, sea grass, grain straw, bamboo, rattan, and cane.

grey goods (or greige goods)   Woven fabric as it comes from the loom: unbleached, not dyed or printed, unfinished.

griccia   Vertical arrangement of vegetable motifs on fabric, many of which were inspired by Persian, Chinese, and Indian patterns and used in Renaissance clothing.

grosgrain   Heavy, corded ribbon or cloth; large-scale frieze cloth with a heavy, regular warp pile.

grottesche   Composite pattern (architectural details mixed with medallions, cartouches, festoons, mermaids, sphinxes, fountains, and other heterogeneous motifs) used especially in sixteenth-century lace and inspired by the rediscovery of the frescoed decorations of Nero's Domus Aurea, in Rome.

gulle   A bonnet style embroidered hat worn by children, with a number of dangling tassels and ribbons.

hackling   Combing process as it applies to flax.

hair fibers   Animal fibers that lack the crimp and resilience of wool, such as rabbit hair and fur fibers.

hakama   Trousers worn by both men and women in Japan.

hanbok   Traditonal Korean costume bodice, made up of the ch'ma and the chogori.

hand   The tactile quality of fabric.

hand-spun yarn   Yarn spun by hand on a spinning wheel.

handwoven fabric   Cloth woven on a hand or foot-powered loom, or woven by hand without a loom.

harness   Rectangular frame on a loom that holds the heddles through which the warp yarns pass. The harnesses raise and lower the heddles in predetermined patterns so that the filling yarns can be inserted through the shed to produce the desired weave pattern.

headrail (also *conch* or *whisk*)	A wired veil worn by women that stood up from the back of the shoulders and created a heart-shaped silhouette behind the head and shoulders.
heather	Mixture of yarn composed of fibers dyed in different colors.
heddles	Needlelike wires on a loom through which the warp yarns are threaded. They are mounted in the harness, which is raised and lowered during weaving.
Hellenistic Period	Period after the death of Alexander in 323 BC and before the rule of Augustus as the first Roman emperor.
hemp	Coarse natural cellulose fiber.
Herakles knot	A strong knot created by two intertwined ribbons, used in ancient Greece and Rome as a protective amulet, for both men and women, with a variety of symbolic meanings.
hetaira	Professional female entertainer, musician, or prostitute, slave or foreign, non-citizen, hired to work at an all-male Greek drinking party, the symposium. Similar to a Japanese *geisha*.
himation	A square, large woolen mantle worn by both men and women over the chiton, draped in a variety of ways. Both men and women pulled it over the head in a mourning gesture. Typical of a bride was the gesture of holding it out as if to cover her head. In Roman times, Greek men wore the square himation with sandals, in contrast with the costume of the Roman citizen, the toga and calcei.
hinagata-bon Kosode	Design books published in Japan between 1666 and about 1820.
Homeric Greece	The early period of Greek history, when the Greek cities were ruled by the feudal monarchies described by the poet, Homer, in the *Iliad* and the *Odyssey*.
homespun	Originally, a plain-woven, fabric from hand-spun yarns; currently, a machine-woven fabric with irregular yarns to simulate the original textures.
hongnyong-po	King's robes of Choson or official costume; a long, wide sleeved, red, blue, or yellow robe decorated with large elaborate golden crests on the front chest, back, and two shoulders with the royal motif of a dragon with five claws.
hoplites	Greek foot soldiers, infantrymen, fighting in formation, in contrast to the earlier system of hand-to-hand single combat.
hopsacking	Coarse basket-weave fabric of jute, hemp, or cotton.
houndstooth	Variation of a twill weave, with a broken check pattern.
hue	Color, shade, or tint of a color.
hwanwonsam	Outer ceremonial jacket worn by the Korean queens of the Choson period; covering several layered embellished garments.
ikat	Fabric woven with tie-dyed yarns.

Incroyables	Young and fashionable French men and women born into well-to-do families who, after the end of Robespierre's bloody dictatorship, blossomed into a subculture boldly dressing in eccentric and expensive clothing proclaiming a return of individual freedom after the revolutionary terror ended. This included both ancient regime elements with revolutionary elements blending to provoke the singularity of the sans-culottes who also elevated politics above fashion.
indigo	Natural vegetable dye from the indigo plant used to color fabric deep blue or purple.
interlining	A layer of fabric between the outer, decorative fabric and the lining.
jacket bodice	Developed during the 1840s as an alternative style for day wear. It had a loose straight fit that was more masculine than the traditional fitted bodice.
jacquard	Loom attachment that uses a punched card system to raise and lower single heddles. It permits the weaving of fabrics with complex patterns such as tapestry and brocade.
jama	Generic name for a coat or outer garment worn at the Mughal Indian court.
jangot	Woman's hooded cloak, originating from the men's style of overcoat.
Japonism	Japanese-inspired styles of art and design.
jean	Sturdy cotton twill fabric (also called denim).
jeanette	Was a necklace made of a narrow braid of hair or velvet with a cross or heart charm that was worn around the neck in the later 1830s.
jegwan	Confucian horse hair hat worn by men, architecturally tiered upwards from the crown of the head in geometrical shapes and points.
jeongjagwan	Confucian hat worn by some kings.
jerkin	Short close-fitting sleeveless vest worn over the doublet by young men.
jokdur	Women's crown or headdress, small jewelled, round corner cube or architectural shape, sits forward on the head with dangling ornaments and tassels draping down the side and forehead.
juche	Knot used on Korean clothing.
justaucorps	Knee length, elegant, close-fitting men's coat usually made of rich fabrics such as velvet or brocade and decorated with cords, often with a long slightly flared skirt. Worn in the Renaissance and rococo periods.
jute	Coarse natural cellulose fiber, used primarily in burlap.
kabbadion	A Byzantine caftan or robe with an opening in the front. In the ninth century it is noted as the costume of the *ethnikoi*, probably

referring to the fact that this was a common garment in Islam. By the fourteenth century according to Pseudo-Kodinos, it is typical for many courtiers to wear a *kabbadion*. It seems that aristocrats who were influenced by Islamic culture may have been wearing these as early as the tenth century. This is also the word for knee-length quilted coats.

kalisaris	Worn by ancient Egyptian women and men. A richly ornamented narrow shell with straps. Also worn as a shift in transparent finely pleated fabric.
kamellaukia	Felt caps worn by the infantry in the tenth century.
kanoko shibori	"Fawn spot" shibori dyeing technique in which a pattern of tiny round or square dots of undyed fabric forms a design on fabric.
kapok	Natural cellulose fiber.
katabira	Summer *kosode* worn by members of the samurai class in Edo Japan.
kerchief	A large square cloth, which when folded diagonally, was worn as a head or neck covering.
khat headdress	The Egyptian king wore head-cloths arranged in two different ways; the *nemes*-headdress and the *khat*-headdress or *bag wig*. Both were made by securing a rectangular piece of cloth with a band stretching over the brow and above the ears in the manner of a kercheif. The *khat*-headdress was generally plain, with the pieces of cloth tucked up under the band instead of hanging lose around the face as on the nemes.
kil	Main body of the Korean garment.
kit	Collar of Korean dress.
knickerbockers	Pants gathered or tied at the knee known as knickers for short in the 1860s and 1870s.
knit fabric	Textile produced by continuous interlooping of one or more yarns.
kore	A type of monumental life-size stone statue representing a standing youthful woman, beautifully dressed, presented as a gift to the gods. The best known are the sixth-century Archaic korai from the Akropolis at Athens.
korum	Long sash on the chogori top in Korean women's dress.
koshimaki	Formal summer robes made of crisp fabric worn in Edo period Japan.
kouros	A type of monumental, life-size or bigger, stone statue representing a standing youthful nude male figure, which started to be made in different Greek cities in the seventh century BCE. Emphasis was placed on their nudity. They were used as votive gifts to the gods, representations of Apollo, or funerary markers.
kranea or kassidia	Iron helmets.

lace	A decorative trim created by manipulating a fine yarn or thread into a two-dimensional fabric with an open structure, often with floral or geometric patterns.
lacis (also filet)	An Italian style of cutwork where a fine piece of netting is embroidered and cut out to form a decorative trim. It is a precursor to lace.
laena	The Roman rounded garment worn by the flamines; it was draped back to front, forming a semicircle in front, and fastened with a fibula in back.
lambswool	First fleece sheared from a young sheep. The previously unclipped fiber ends are tapered, producing a very soft texture.
lappets	Flat lace caps with tapered ends that extended into long tails or *lappets* at the sides. Worn into the 1860s, this headdress was placed far back on the head.
lattughini	Small ruffles at the cuffs and neckline worn in Renaissance clothing.
lawn	Lightweight, sheer, fine cotton or linen fabric.
leading strings	Used in the walking and crawling stage, toddlers often wore sturdy ribbons, called *leading strings*, attached to the shoulders of their clothing. These kept adventurous children from wandering too far away, and helped a bodice-bound mother pick them up when the nursemaid wasn't around.
lenza	Thin silk cordonnet that crossed the forehead and from which dangled jewels or other decorations; used in the Italian Renaissance.
line	Long linen fibers that have great luster and strength.
linen	Natural cellulose yarn made from flax fibers, noted for strength, cool hand, and luster; low resilience fabric woven from linen yarn.
lining	Material attached under the principal material of a cloth or piece of clothing to protect the outer fabric and sometimes to help give stability and shape to a garment.
livery	Comes from the Old French term *livrer,* which indicates the feeding and clothing of servants provided by the employer.
llama	South American animal of the camel family whose fleece is produced in a variety of colors.
long back braid	The typical hairstyle for women in the seventh and eighth centuries BCE.
loom	Machine that produces woven textiles by interlacing warp and filling yarns at right angles to each other.
loroi	A lighter scarf used in insignia, especially for the eparch.
loros	A heavy stole worn by both the emperor and empress as much as five meters long, often studded with precious stones. Originally this formed an X over the body, coming over the

shoulders from behind, which evolved out of the *trabea trium-phalis*, the toga of the Roman consuls. During the tenth and eleventh centuries the *loros* gained a slit so that it could be pulled over the head. The empress's *loros* wrapped around the body differently and was once thought to be a different garment called a *thorakion*.

luster The gloss or sheen on the surface of a fiber, yarn or fabric.

Lycra® Trade name of a spandex fiber.

maitress en titre A royal mistress.

mandyas In Roman times, this was a light cloak, resembling the *chlamys*. The *mandyas* came to be known as the long, dark, undecorated cloak worn by both monastic men and women. The *mandyas* was knee length and slit up the front with drawstrings at the neck and waist for closure. The Bishop wore this garment over his *omophorion* when celebrating the liturgy. The emperor wore a gold *mandyas* during coronation by the fourteenth century.

mangeon Headband that the gat was stacked on top of in Korean men's adornment.

maniakion A torque, or collar, worn by barbarians and sometimes associated with soldiers. In *listes de preseances* this is the word they use for collars of insignia for certain soldiers.

manikelia Padded wool arm guards sometimes covered with mail or wood and worn by both infantrymen and cavalry.

mantle A loose cloak or wrap, usually sleeveless.

mantua A gown heavily gathered at the back and often open at the front bodice and skirts to reveal a matching or contrasting stomacher and petticoat underneath.

manufactured fiber Inclusive term for manufactured fibers of natural or synthetic origin.

maphorion A hood that covered the neck and shoulders dating back to the fourth century. Sometimes this term is used to describe the hooded part of male and female monastic garb. By the middle Byzantine era, *maphorion* were also associated with the dress of noble women. The Virgin Mary is always shown wearing a *maphorion*. The occasional man is described as wearing a *mapho-rion* as well. In *The Book of Ceremonies*, a member of the Senate wears a *maphorion* that covers his entire body.

maspilli Precious buttons used in Renaissance clothing.

mauveine William Perkin discovered mauveine, a bright purple dye synthe-sized under laboratory conditions in 1856.

mazzocchio The typical Florentine headwear worn with the long scarf called *becchetto* in Renaissance clothing.

mercerization Caustic soda treatment for cotton and linen, which makes the yarn or cloth stronger and increases luster and dye affinity.

merino	Breed of sheep yielding a high grade wool used for fine woolen and worsted cloth.
microfiber	Extremely fine fibers of one denier or less. Fibers are often spun in bicomponent form and excess material is dissolved, leaving fine, strong fibers.
mineral fiber	Natural or manufactured fiber derived from a mineral, such as asbestos or fiberglass.
Minoan	Name used by archaeologists to refer to the civilization the pre-Greek Myceneans found on Crete. The name refers to the mythological king of Crete, Minos, son of Europa and father of the Minotaur.
mitra	A gold, embroidered kerchief-like headdress or veil worn by the patriarch of Constantinople in fourteenth century Byzantium.
moccasin	Native American soft leather shoes or boots, often fur lined and decorated with intricate quill and beadwork. Worn by native Americans and settlers in the colonies of North America.
modiste	Seamstress, needlewoman, or someone who made and repaired dresses.
mohair	Processed fiber of the long, silky hair of the Angora goat.
monk's cloth	Basket-woven cotton fabric.
monmouth cap	A knitted cap, with a rounded crown and small band. Worn primarily by sailors and soldiers originally but later widely adopted.
monofilament	Single synthesized filament; fishing line is one example.
mordant	A metallic salt used to fix dyes.
motif	A pattern unit, usually repeated.
multifilament yarn	Composed of several, or hundreds, of extruded filament fibers.
muslin	Plain-woven, uncombed cotton fabric, ranging from sheer to coarse.
Mycenean	Name used by archaeologists to refer to the civilization the pre-Greek invaders brought to the Greek mainland. The name refers to the city of Mycenae in the Peloponnesus.
Nambawi	Dark fur and silk-detailed hat worn by fashionable women and offered warmth in the winter.
natural fiber	Any textile fiber obtained from an animal, vegetable, or mineral source, such as wool, cotton, or asbestos.
Nemes **headdress**	The king wore head-cloths arranged in two different ways called the *nemes*-headdress and the *khat*-headdress or *bag wig*. Both were made by securing a rectangular piece of cloth with a band stretching over the brow and above the ears in the manner of a kerchief. The *nemes*-headdress was generally made with striped fabric, and the excess fabric was left hanging at the back in a kind of tail. At the sides, two strands or lappets hung down beside the face.

new chevron	A zigzag band applied around the hem dress.
Nuishime	Japanese *shibori*-dyeing technique in which a running stitch creates lines of resist pattern.
nylon	Generic term for synthetic polyamide fiber; nylon 6,6 has 6 carbon atoms.
obi sash	Wrapped around the waist of the Japanese *kosode* and *kimono*.
off-grain	Finishing fault in which the horizontal structure is not at right angles to the vertical.
organdy	Sheer, plain-woven cotton cloth with a crisp hand.
organza	Similar to organdy but made of silk, rayon, or nylon.
ormesini	Silk fabric originally coming from Ormuz, an island in the Persian Gulf.
paenula	A short, hooded cloak worn by farmers, shepherds, and other lower-income people in late antiquity and as the cloak of a shepherd until the fifteenth century. The *chasuble*, worn by the Pope, stems from the *paenula*.
paijama	Trousers worn in South Asia. During the Mughal period the *paijama* typically was cut full through the waist, hips, and thighs and snug fitting from knee to ankle.
pajama	A loose-fitting garment consisting of trousers and a jacket, worn for sleeping or lounging; Loose-fitting trousers worn in the Far East by men and women.
paji-chogori	*Hanbok* for Korean men includes the wide-leg trouser *paji* and an earlier longer version of the chogori.
paletot	A heavy knee-length coat with three, layered capes and slit armholes; worn by young women of the 1820s.
palla	The Roman word for the square Greek *himation* worn by women over their tunics and stolas.
pallium	The Roman word for the square Greek *himation*, worn by men, usually without a tunic, when they were not dressed in the formal attire of the Roman citizen.
paludamentum	A short cloak worn by soldiers, hunters and riders. This is a Roman term and was used in late antiquity but was replaced by the term *chlamys*.
panier	Eighteenth century hoop skirts, typically very wide at the sides but flattened in the front and back.
pantalettes	Women wore long under drawers, called *pantalettes*, with lace, ruffles, or pleats at the edges that showed at the hem of dresses.
pantaloons	Very tight-fitting ankle trousers usually made from knitted jersey.
pantofle	Shoes with cork soles the name of which is derived from the Greek word *pantophellos*, meaning "cork."

parthenon	Temple of the Greek goddess Athena Parthenos, "the virgin," built on the hill of the Acropolis of Athens in the fifth century BCE (447–432), when the Athenian empire was at its height, and the goal of the Panathenaic procession. The gold and ivory statue of the goddess in the temple, and the relief frieze of a procession outside the temple, are high points of Greek art.
paternostr	Precious belts composed of large gold beads inside which are aromatic pastes and holding the hanging *pomanders*—gold or silver filigree spheres containing sponges imbued with perfumes or scented pastes—worn in Renaissance Italy.
patka	Sash from the Mughal period in India.
pattern	The arrangement of form, design, or decoration in a fabric; guide for cutting fabric.
peascod belly	The stuffing of the belly of a man's doublet. Said to derive from the shape of plate armor.
Peisistratus	Ruled as tyrant at Athens at various times (not elected), with his sons, the Peisistratids, from c. 560 to 510 BCE. He beautified the Akropolis, encouraged the Panathenaic Festival and the city's Dionysiac festival, and brought Athens to cultural prominence among the Greek city-states.
pellanda, cioppa	In Bologna called *sacco*, elsewhere *veste* or *vestito*; a corruption of the North European name of *houppelande*, indicating a garment similarly characterized by magniloquent lines, long, trailing sleeves, and decorated with precious trimmings.
pelisse	A cape-like garment with arm slits, sometimes made with a hood and worn over dresses.
peplos	Female garment, characteristic costume of Athena, and the typical dress of the Early Classical female period, though it was worn and represented in Roman times. It was made from a rectangular piece of woolen fabric draped around the body and pinned at the shoulder, usually not sewn together at the side; its simple shape contrasted with the flowing lines of the earlier fine linen Ionian chiton.
pereline	A deep cape that covered the arms to the elbows with long, broad front lappets worn over a belt.
Pericles	Political elected leader and general at Athens, active from c. 460–430 BCE, under whom Athens had its years of greatest power and influence, including the building of the Parthenon and other buildings on the Akropolis.
perizoma	Short pants worn by active males to avoid complete nudity. They are represented in Greek art, and no doubt worn in Greece before the innovation of public nudity for males, as well as elsewhere, in areas where this innovation was never accepted in real life, and only partially in art.
peruke	A wig, especially one worn by men in the seventeenth and eighteenth centuries; a periwig. French *perruque*, from Old French, head of hair, from Old Italian *perrucca*.

petticoat
An ankle- or shin-length skirt that tied around the waist or a woman's underskirt, sometimes exposed by an open-fronted robe.

pharos
A wide mantle, used as a mantle by day and a blanket by night, mentioned by Homer.

pianelle
Slippers that do not cover the heels and are characterized by a very tall wedge obtained by overlapping layers of cork covered in leather, worn in the Italian Renaissance.

picadil
A decorative trim made from a loop of fabric that was added to the hem and/or shoulder of a doublet or bodice.

pick
In weaving, a single passage of filling yarn through the warp shed.

piece dying
Dyeing of cloth after construction.

pigment
Insoluble powdered coloring agent carried in a liquid binder and printed or padded onto the surface of a cloth.

pile weave
Construction in which cut or uncut loops protrude from the ground cloth; loops may be warp or filling yarns and be produced by a double weave or with wires. The wire method uses round-tipped, removable wires to raise loops for uncut pile, and sharp-edged cut wires for cut pile such as velvet.

pinafore apron
A type of apron worn by women. It originates from "pin afore," reflecting that the bib part of an apron was earlier often secured to the chest using pins.

plaid
Pattern of unevenly spaced repeated stripes crossing at right angles.

plain weave
Simplest method of interlacing warp and weft yarns to make cloth. Each filling (weft) passes alternately under and over the warp yarns to produce a balanced construction. It is strong, inexpensive to produce, and the best ground cloth for printing; the thread count determines the fabric's strength.

plied yarn
Yarn formed by twisting together two or more single strands.

plus fours
Full knickerbockers worn by men in the 1920s and 1930s.

ply
A single strand of yarn that is twisted with one or more strands of yarn together.

points
Ribbons with metal tips that could be threaded through sleeves and attached to jackets, or could be used to lace trunkhose to doublets.

polos hat
A tall, tubular hat worn in the Orientalizing and Archaic periods in Greece by images of goddesses.

polyester
Generic term for a manufactured fiber in which the fiber-forming substance is a long-chain synthetic polymer composed on a complex ester, popular in the 1970s.

poplin
Plain-woven, warp-faced fabric with a fine crosswise rib.

posta	Silk sash worn in the Italian Renaissance.
printing	Application of color designs to the surface of cloth.
protein fiber	Natural fiber originating from an animal such as a sheep (wool) or silkworm (silk).
pteryges or kremasmata	An apron-like covering for mid-section, sometimes known as a "fighting skirt." It was generally suspended over the shoulders with leather straps and tied around the waist.
pudding cap	A padded cap, sometimes made of crossed bands, worn by toddlers to protect their heads from injury.
quilting	Compound fabric construction of two layers of cloth with a layer of padding (batting) between, stitched through all three layers.
ramie	Fine, oriental bast fiber.
raw fiber	Textile fiber in its most natural state, for example, cotton before ginning, wool before scouring.
raw silk	Silk that is not fully degummed. It is stiff, tacky, and caramel in color.
rayon	Generic term for a manufactured fiber derived from regenerated cellulose.
red crown	The royal headdress symbolizing lower Egypt called the *deshret* (𓋔), this was probably made of metal.
reed	Comb-like device on a loom through which the warp ends pass.
reed mark	Vertical streak in woven fabric caused by a bent wire in the reed.
reeled silk	Continuous filament silk as it is reeled off the softened cocoon of the cultivated silkworm.
repeat	The amount of surface a single pattern covers on a fabric that is repeated over and over.
resist printing	General term for printing processes in which the motif or the ground is treated with a dye-resistant substance before dyeing the fabric.
restello	An elaborate, carved, painted, and gilded shelf that could be completed with a glass mirror and pegs used during the Italian Renaissance.
reticule	Small bags used to keep small necessary objects close at hand.
retting	Soaking of bast fiber plants to permit bacterial or chemical breakdown of the outer bark, in order to loosen the fibers.
rib	Raised ridge running lengthwise, crosswise, or diagonally on a fabric, usually formed by the insertion of a heavy thread; also formed by embossing with heated rollers.
rib weave	Modification of plain weave in which fine warp ends are closely set and two picks (or one heavier pick) interlace as one; any woven fabric construction with a horizontal rib or cord.

roba, robone	Imposing knee-length coat made of velvet or wool, completely open at the front with wide *revers* or lapels, that showed the precious furs or silk linings, worn by both men and women during the Italian Renaissance.
robe à l'anglaise	In the imported French fashion magazines this new form kept the open-fronted skirts and pointed bodice of earlier 1700s, but the waistline was higher, and the long drape formerly falling from the shoulders was drawn back into the waistline, allowing the fullness of the back draping to emphasize the rear end; often long sleeved.
roller printing	Mechanical printing of fabric with engraved rollers.
ropa (also Spanish surcote)	A long outer gown that fastened up the center front from neck to hem and could be worn open or closed. It had a high neckline and was worn unbelted in an A-line silhouette over a gown.
rotary-screen printing	A fast and accurate printing process in which the cloth moves under a series of large, patterned cylinders.
rotella	Round shield used in the Italian Renaissance.
round gown	Gowns like the Empire style dress in France, had an unstructured bodice; the shaping was provided by a drawstring around the neck opening, or by lining flaps pinned together under an apron front. The neckline shape was most often rounded, rather than wide or square. The waistline was raised to just under the bust and was formed like the neckline, by a drawstring. To support the bosom two gussets were inserted underneath the bust line at either side.
roving	Bundle of fibers that are carded and combed and arranged in parallel alignment before spinning.
ruff	A rounded, densely ruffled collar popular in the late sixteenth and early seventeenth centuries. It required extensive pleating and starching to maintain its stiff appearance. Thin strips of starched or stiffened fabric were accordion-folded or folded in a figure-eight and tacked to a band that closed at the front or the back with a hidden fastening. Ruffs were worn by men and women at the neck and wrists. Large ruffs required a *supportase* to keep them from collapsing.
sacque gown or robe à la francaise	A voluminous gown fitted tightly at the front and box-pleated at the back of the shoulders to fall in an elegant drape at the back all the way to the floor.
Sagion	A term for several types of Byzantine cloaks. Like the *chlamys*, it had a military use in its early history (sixth century are earliest mentions). But it appears to be heavier than a *chlamys* because soldiers could use it as a blanket or tent. In the middle Byzantine period it is associated with the costumes of several courtiers, such as *protospatharioi*. Monks and hermits are noted as wearing *sagia* in the twelfth century.
saio, saione	Occasionally worn by Italian women around 1520; it could have short sleeves that let the *giubbone* sleeve show. It could be made with two or more different fabrics.

sakkos	A tunic that replaced the *divetesion* for Byzantine imperial dress in Paleologan times. The origins of this garment are in the sackcloth, worn by ascetics. In the thirteenth century it had some ecclesiastical use.
samhoejang	Chogori worn by Korean noble women on special occasions.
samjak norigai	A triple-tasselled pendant for women.
samo or coronet	Hat worn by a male public official; woven with side wings out of bamboo or horsehair. Royal men wore tall silk black cylindrical versions.
samurai	Warriors of Japan's military class who were reduced to membership in a highly controlled urban feudal aristocracy during the Edo period.
sans culottes	Men who wore full-length trousers instead of knee-length breeches in revolutionary France. The term referred to the ill-clad and ill-equipped volunteers of the Revolutionary army during the early years of the war.
sarabula, intercula	Briefs worn during the Italian Renaissance.
sateen	Filling-faced satin-woven fabric with horizontal rather than vertical floats.
satin weave	Basic weave in which the fabric face is composed almost entirely of warp or filling floats, producing a smooth, lustrous surface.
sbernie	Mantles that leave one arm free.
scarpette	Shoes that were used throughout Italy under different names; *zibre* or *zibrette* in Milan, *cibre* in other cities in North Italy, *tapine* in the South.
scarsella	A small pouch that substituted for the missing pockets in Renaissance garments.
scouring	Washing of fiber, yarn, or fabric to remove grease, dirt, sizing, or color.
screen printing	Hand- or machine- printing process in which a pattern-making stencil or screen held in a frame is positioned on the cloth and coloring agent applied.
segmenta	Gold patches or embroidery used to decorate a *sakkos* or other tunic.
selvage	Reinforced edge on either side of a woven or flat-knitted cloth, finished to prevent raveling.
serge	Smooth-finished fabric in a balanced twill weave, identical on face and back.
sericin	Gummy substance that holds silk fibers together as they are spun (in pairs) from the silkworm; removed from silk before spinning.
sericulture	Raising of silkworms and production of silk.
sex crines hairstyle	This special hairstyle, worn by brides and priestesses, the Vestal Virgins, was based on the Archaic Etruscan *tutulus* hairstyle,

which consisted of a high bun formed by separate strands or braids of hair. The ritual dressing of the Roman bride's hair included parting the strands with a spear, which were twisted on top of her head to form a kind of bun made up of six braids or coils.

shantung silk   Dense, plain-woven silk cloth with a slightly irregular surface due to uneven, slubbed filling yarns.

shaube   A sleeveless robe with a large shawl collar became a popular garment with mayors, sheriffs, and other men of rank.

shed   The space formed as the harnesses of a loom raise some warp yarns and lower others, through which the shuttle passes to lay in the filling.

sheer   Very thin, transparent, or semi-opaque fabric.

shenti   Hip skirt or loin cloth with pleats and decorations worn by Egyptian men.

shibori   General name for the Japanese resist dye technique often translated as "tie-dye." Shibori includes various resist techniques including clamping, stitching, and tying.

shift   The universal undergarment for women, rich or poor, was a smock-like low-necked shirt. Called a "shift" or later a "chemise," this long garment functioned as both blouse and slip.

shogun   Literally "the general who quells barbarians;" the head of the military bureaucracy that controlled Japan during the Edo period.

shuttle   Device on a loom to carry the filling yarn through the shed to interlace it with the warp.

silk   Natural protein fiber unwound from the cocoon of the silkworm.

siren suits   Suits that could be zipped into quickly for lightning-fast escapes to underground shelters in wartime London, 1940s.

sisal   Strong natural cellulose fiber used in making cord and matting.

sizing   Starch applied to warp threads to strengthen them for the weaving process, usually removed by scouring during finishing; starch applied to cotton or linen cloth that is removed when the fabric is washed.

skaranikon   A word mentioned in a twelfth century poem and Pseudo-Kodinos, according to the Oxford Dictionary of Byzantium. It is unclear whether this is a cloak or a hat similar to the *skiadion*.

skeleton suit   A young boy's outfit consisting of long trousers attached by buttons at the waist to a long-sleeved, short-waisted jacket, worn by eighteenth-century boys.

skiadion   A squarish hat worn by courtiers and sometimes the emperor in Paleologan times.

sliver   Continuous ropelike strand of loosely assembled fibers before twisting into yarns.

slub	Lump or knot in a yarn; may be a defect or purposely spun to produce a textured surface in cloth.
smock	Loose-fitting knee-length over-blouses worn by the working class for centuries. They were also a very practical fashion for children.
Socrates	Athenian philosopher (449–399 BCE) during the Golden Age of Athens, teacher of Plato, developed the Socratic method of question and answer, focusing on ethical problems, in contrast to the relativism of the sophistic philosophers.
sohme	Long curved sleeves on the Korean chogori.
soprarizzo, cesellato	Rich fabrics with textured appearance that was obtained with the alternation of cut and looped velvet. It was often brocaded with gold threads, and the details of the pattern could be highlighted with the *allucciolature*, very thin gold or silver plate loops threaded through the fabric, and variously twisted in order to achieve the desired decorative effect. Used in Renaissance clothing.
spandex	Generic term for synthetic elastic fibers composed of segmented polyurethane made popular during the 1980s fitness craze.
spencer	By 1804–5, a long sleeved, short-waisted, fitted jacket called the *Spencer* became very fashionable for women.
spinneret	Metal disc with numerous fine holes through which a chemical solution is extruded to produce synthetic fibers.
spinning	Drawing out and twisting fiber into yarn or thread; extruding manufactured filaments through a spinneret.
spoon bonnet	A hat with a narrow brim close to the ears, rising vertically above the forehead in a spoon shaped curve and sloping down behind to a very small crown.
spun yarn	Yarn spun from staple-length fiber, either natural or cut synthetic filaments.
staple	Natural or manufactured fiber that has a relatively short length.
stays	An early term for corset. A stiff undergarment tied or fastened around the torso to give a desired shape to a gown's silhouette.
stemma	A Greek crown that replaced the late antique *diadem*, or headband, for imperial head-gear. A crown is made of precious metals and gemstones, and sometimes has enameling or other luxury arts techniques used in its construction. *Perpendulia*, or simply, *pendulia*, are strings of pearls that hang from the stemma at the temples.
stola	The stola was a long garment worn by respectable upper-class Roman married women (*matronae*) over the tunic and under the palla; it can be recognized on portraits by the thin straps coming down from the shoulders.
stomacher	Stiff, triangular garment that attached to the front of a dress bodice. Sometimes embroidered or adorned with ribbons and bows.

Stratagliati, accoltellati	Fabrics, mostly simple silk satins, but also damasks and velvets, slashed and cut following specific decorative patterns such as little flowers, zigzag motifs, and crosses. Fashionable in the second half of the sixteenth century in Italy.
stretch fabrics	Constructed of stretch yarns to have much greater than normal stretch and recovery characteristics. "Comfort stretch" is a designation for fabrics with up to 30 percent stretch and recovery; "power or action stretch" describes fabrics with 30–50 percent stretch and recovery. These became popular in the 1980s.
stretch yarn	Yarn with a durable, springy elongation and exceptional recovery.
stripe	Narrow section of a fabric differing in color or texture from the adjoining area.
sugacapi	Hair towels used during the Italian Renaissance.
sugar loaf hat	A conical hat, rounded at the top with a broad brim. Similar in shape to the form in which bulk sugar was purchased in the seventeenth and eighteenth centuries. Later became identified with classic Puritan costume.
sulphur dye	Dye that produces heavy shades of black or brown in cellulosic fabrics.
sumptuary laws	Laws that governed how people of all classes were allowed to dress. Versions of these laws appear in most periods in history and most regions up until modern times. Purple, for example, has often be restricted by sumptuary law to be worn only by royalty.
sun rot	Deterioration caused by sun or light.
superhumeral	A collar with a mock turtleneck that extended out to the shoulders and down to the chest, usually decorated with gem stones and metallic threads, worn over a tunic. Worn by Byzantine aristocratic men, including the emperor in the eleventh century and beyond.
supportase (also underpropper)	A wired structure worn by both men and women that served to hold up the elaborate ruffs; wide ruffled bands worn at the neck.
synthetic fiber	Textile fiber made from a petrochemical rather than a natural base. All synthetic fibers are manufactured, but not all manufactured fibers are synthetic, e. g., rayon.
tabì, tabin, tabinetto, tabinazzo	Sometimes defined as a fabric similar to damask or as thick taffetas; characterized by a "wave" effect. Seen in the Italian Renaissance.
taffeta	Crisp, plain-woven fabric in which the filling is heavier than the warp, producing a fine, lustrous rib.
tainia	A purple headband worn by Byzantine children in the palace in the Palaeologan period. It was also acceptable for children to go without any hat.
Tanaquil	Etruscan queen, wife of the first Tarquin, legendary figure in Roman tradition. Her story is told by the first-century Roman historian, Livy.

tanggeoun   High cap onto which the gat was placed in Korean men's clothing.

tapestry   Jacquard-woven fabric with supplementary multicolored yarns that form an intricate design or scene. The finished products were often used to cover walls in cold castles in Europe.

tarquins   Etruscan dynasty who ruled at Rome in the sixth century BCE, whose fall brought about the Roman Republic. The last Tarquin especially, Tarquinius Superbus, brought to Rome many elements of Etruscan culture, including the Temple of Jupiter Capitoline, most aspects of the Roman triumph, music, and theater. Such important Roman symbols as the curved priestly *lituus*, the *fasces* and the axe of the lictor hark back to Etruscan models, and in dress, the toga, decorative purple borders, the *laena, calcei, sex crines*, and *galerus* with *apex*.

tea-gown   An unboned, loose-fitting afternoon gown, often with *watteau* style backs, that fell in folds from the neck to the hem.

tebenna   The rounded mantle worn by the Veii Apollo and other male figures from mid-sixth century Rome, the ancestor of the Roman toga.

terrycloth   Uncut warp-pile fabric, plain or jacquard; woven of cotton, linen, or rayon.

textile   Orginally, a general term for any woven cloth; now, a general term for any fabric made from fibers or yarns, natural or manufactured made into any fabric structure such as woven, knits, nonwoven etc.

thorax   From the sixth through tenth centuries cavalrymen wore this body armor made of chain mail, a shirt, with or without sleeves, made of metal links which sometimes was mounted on leather, or lamellar, small plates of iron or leather laced together or attached to a leather backing. These varied in length from ankles to waist.

thread   A strand of plied and twisted yarn with a smooth finish that is used in sewing and stitching.

thread count   The number of warp and filling yarns per square measure (inch or centimeter).

throwing   Slight twisting of filament yarns.

tippets   A short shoulder cape with a longer hanging front worn over dresses by women.

toga   The rounded mantle clearly distinguished a Roman from a Greek, who wore the rectangular himation mantle. The Romans' were by definition the *gens togata,* (Vergil, *Aeneid*). Different colors and decorations distinguished the various kinds of togas, all of them deeply symbolic of age, rank, status or office. The purple borders of the *toga praetexta*, for example, characterized the costume of the higher levels of office, the curule magistracies; it was also the dress of boys, who wore it until they discarded it for the *toga virilis*, the normal plain woolen toga of adult men. A bright white *toga candida* marked the wearer as a candidate for office, a dark *toga pulla*, a mourner. Most prestigious was the *toga triumphalis*, worn by the victorious general when he celebrated a triumph.

toile	Plain, coarse twill-woven fabric, often in linen. Most noteworthy were the toiles de Jouy; eighteenth-century French fabrics printed with scenes of one color on pale cotton, linen, or silk.
tondo	The circular area in the center of a Greek vase.
tongjong	A thin, replaceable outer layer on the neckline of the Korean chogori; white woven hemp, cotton, or ramie protected the garment from wearing at the neck.
tow	Short or broken fibers of flax, hemp, or synthetic materials used for yarn, twine, or stuffing; thick bundle of continuous filaments assembled without twisting into a loose ropy strand for cutting into staple length.
trade name	Name given by manufacturer to distinguish a product produced and sold by that manufacturer, for example, Lycra.
trademark	Word, letter, or symbol used in connection with a specific product originating and owned by a particular manufacturer.
treadle	Lever or pedal on a loom that activates the lowering or raising of a harness.
Trojan War	Mythological story, the subject of Homer's *Iliad*, of the siege of the city of Troy, by the united force of the Greeks, in 1200 BC.
trunk hose	Short, puffy breeches, bound above the knee by a ribbon or garter to hold up the stockings. Worn from the sixteenth to the seventeenth centuries.
tsujigahana	Complex Japanese technique using *shibori*, painting, metallic leaf, and embroidery techniques to pattern fabric for *kosode*.
tti	Additional tie belt, fastened around the outside of jacket layers in Korean dress.
tunic	Tunics are the main piece of the Byzantine wardrobe. The T-shaped garment could be long or short, with various length sleeves. They were worn as an undergarment (this is the closest item to Byzantine underwear) and as a regular garment; typically more than one tunic was worn at one time. Or, tunic is the Roman word for the shirt or chiton worn under the mantle. The vertical purple stripes that decorated it were either broad or narrow, indicating the wearer's status.
turban	Called *phakeolis* or *phakiolion*. Worn by both Byzantine men and women by the tenth century according to evidence found on Cappadocian frescoes.
turumagi	Additional layered long overcoat in Korean dress.
tussah	Brownish silk fabric from uncultivated silkworms.

tweed	Medium-weight, rough woolen fabric, usually twill woven. Named tweeds such as Donegal, Connemara, Harris, and Galashiels are produced in Ireland and Scotland.
twill	Basic weave that produces a surface of diagonal lines by passing filling threads over two or more ends in a regular progression. Denim is a common modern example of a twill weave.
twist	The tightness and direction of the twist spun into a yarn. *S* twist is a clockwise twist and is the most common; *Z* twist is a counterclockwise twist.
twistless yarn	Yarns formed by combining fibers by means other than twisting.
uccelletti di Cipro	"Cyprus birds," solid perfumes kept in small leather cases in the shape of tiny birds, used by Italian women during the Italian Renaissance.
uchikake	Formal, outer *kosode*, worn unbelted.
ukiyo	Literally the "floating world," the pleasure quarter of Edo period Japan where prominence was determined by one's taste and ability to pay, not by position in the period's inflexible class system.
underpropper (supportase)	At the height of their fashion and their width, ruffs needed more than starch to stay rigid and were worn with this wire understructure.
ungarina	Bell-shaped Renaissance dress made from precious fabrics. The gown reached the ankles and closed in the front with frogs. Usually worn by boys aged between two and four. The name refers to the heavy braiding decorations, very common in clothing of Eastern European countries, such as Hungary.
vegetable fibers	Natural textile fibers of plant origin, such as cotton, flax, or hemp.
velour	Cut warp-pile fabric, usually of cotton or wool, with higher, less dense pile than velvet.
velvet	Close-cropped, warp-pile fabric with a smooth, rich surface, produced by double weaving or with wires. Originally woven in silk, now made with cotton or synthetic fibers as well.
velveteen	Single-woven weft pile fabric with a dense-cut surface.
vicuna	Small, wild Andean animal of the camel family, from the undercoat of which is derived a fine, lustrous fiber.
vinyl	Nonwoven fabric made from a petrochemical solution; thick or thin, it is usually soft and pliable.
virgin wool	New wool; not reused, reprocessed, or respun.
viscose rayon	The most common rayon, formed by converting cellulose into a soluble form and regenerating it into a synthetic fiber.
voile	Soft, sheer cloth, plain-woven of fine crepe (overtwisted) yarns.
waistcoat	Also called a vest. A front-buttoning, sleeveless garment worn usually by men under a jacket or coat. Occasionally had detachable sleeves.

wale	A horizontal, vertical, or diagonal rib in a fabric; the vertical rib on the face of a knitted fabric.
warp	Lengthwise yarns in a fabric, running vertically through the loom, parallel to the selvages.
weave	Structural pattern in which yarns are interlaced to produce fabric.
weaving	Process of making a fabric on a loom by interlacing horizontal yarns (weft) at right angles with vertical yarns (warp).
weft	Horizontal or crosswise element of a woven cloth.
weighted silk	Silk treated with metallic salts to increase the weight and apparent value, strictly controlled and now virtually obsolete. Historic textiles treated with this finish deteriorate quickly and damage the silk fibers.
whisk	A large unstarched falling collar, often with a deep lace trim that reaches past the shoulders.
white crown	Emblematic of Lower Egypt and probably made of metal; the white crown is also known by many names, including *hedjet* (⚪).
Windsor knot	A knot for a man's necktie named for and popularized by the Duke of Windsor in the early twentieth century.
wisk	Deep linen lace collars.
woolen	Fuzzy, loosely twisted yarn spun from carded short wool fibers. Woolen cloths are generally simple weaves and show coarser finishes than wools.
worsted	Smooth, compact yarns spun from carded and combed long wool fibers. Worsted cloths are more closely constructed and have smoother finishes than woolens.
yangban	Male aristocrats in the Korean Choson Dynasty (1392–1910).
yarn	Any form of spun, twisted or extruded fibers, natural or manufactured, that can be used in weaving, knitting, or other fabric construction.
yarn dyeing	Dyeing at the yarn stage of production, as opposed to solution, stock, or piece dyeing.
yeomnang or gangnang	Small pouches used in place of garment pockets in Korean dress.
zanana	The women's quarters at the court of Mughal India.
zebellino da mane	Fur stole worn on the shoulders during the Italian Renaissance.
zetanini avvellutati	Silk velvets originally made in the Chinese city of Zayton, worn during the Italian Renaissance.
zimarra	A Turkish-inspired overcoat, similar to a kaftan. Usually made with very expensive and showy fabrics and suitable to be worn inside the house in the Italian Renaissance.
zovi	A general word for belt, girdle or sash.

List of Museums

CLOTHING COLLECTIONS

Clothing artifacts are housed in a number of different museums around the world. In fact, most museums, from large metropolitan collections to local museums, will house at least some items of textiles and clothing in their collections even if it is not devoted to the study of clothing and costume. The staffs of dedicated employees at these museums are trained in the conservation and preservation of the textile artifacts. Specific technical skills are needed to allow costume resources to survive through time, and if only these techniques had been known long ago, there would be many more examples for study today. However, at this time in history, it is well known that climate and humidity affect textiles to a great extent and need to be controlled or the textiles will rot, fade, and disappear.

Certain types of fibers are more durable and will last longer than others. Silk is a valuable fiber that has been known to shatter rather dramatically into dust if not kept at the right temperature and moisture level. Many of the most beautiful beaded and embellished silk gowns are in desperate shape because of the fragile nature of the fabric. Often, because silk was sold by weight—and to allow the fabric to drape well—it was weighted with metals that over time have meant that the fiber has deteriorated. Hanging a heavily embellished garment can cause undue stress of the shoulder seams and rip the garment.

These garments and fabrics are sometimes hung up but more often stored in acid-free tissue paper in boxes and placed in climate-controlled rooms until they are displayed or used for research purposes to make sure there is no further degradation of the fibers. In some cases, they are never displayed for fear that they may completely fall apart. Lighting of displays is usually kept at a very low level so as not to disturb the textiles and harm them while on show for people to learn from and admire. Hats, purses, parasols, and shoes are all fitted with special supports to make sure they are not crushed further in the storage and display process.

Sometimes garments that have great historical value but are not in very good condition are received by museums. After a *condition report* is written, a plan is made to try to either restore the artifact or stabilize it so it does not decay any further. Painstaking hours are spent on single portions of garments to make sure they are saved for further study in the years to come. A single cuff may need the attention of a conservator for weeks or even months. The job of the conservator is often at odds with that of the curator, who is concerned with creating the displays and educating the public about the clothes in the collection. It is a sad day when a piece of clothing is too weak to display, especially when that item has exquisite detailing that should be seen by the museum-going public. There are thousands of historical garments stored away safely in museums around the world, many waiting to be studied.

Local museum collections will have items of interest to the history of the region, exemplifying what life was like throughout time in the community. Large urban museums will collect and house textiles and clothing from all over the world to give an idea of many different cultures and their ideas on dress and adornment.

The most famous museums with excellent costume collections include the Victoria and Albert Museum in London and the Costume Institute at the Metropolitan Museum of Art in New York. These two outstanding museums house excellent collections of all kinds of costumes from all over the world. They also have extensive study rooms with information on clothing and textile history. There are many other museums devoted to clothing artifacts, though, ranging from the purely civilian dress of the fashionable people to military uniforms.

The following is a list of collections with excellent resources that might be helpful to a student of clothing and history (websites and mailing addresses are included where available). This list by no means represents even a fraction of the many collections of costume, but it is meant to give the student of costume an idea of where to look for costume resources.

The Bata Shoe Museum
327 Bloor St. West
Toronto, ONT, Canada M5S 1W7
Phone: (416) 979-7799
www.batashoemuseum.ca

Bernberg Museum of Costume
Corner Duncombe Rd and Jan Smuts Ave
Forest Town, Johannesburg
Phone: (011) 646-0416
http://www.places.co.za/html/bernberg.html

Colonial Williamsburg
The Museums of Colonial Williamsburg
P.O. Box 1776
Williamsburg, VA 23187-1776
Phone: (757) 229-1000
http://www.history.org

Costume Museum of Canada
109 Pacific Ave
Winnipeg, MB, Canada R3B0M1
Phone: 204-999-0072
www.costumemuseum.com

Fashion and Textile Museum
83 Bermondsey Street
London SE1 3XF
http://www.ftmlondon.org/

Fashion Museum
Assembly Rooms
Bennett Street
Bath
Avon BA1 2QH
http://www.fashionmuseum.co.uk/

Fortress of Louisbourg, National Historic Site of Canada
259 Park Service Road
Louisbourg, NS, Canada B1C 2L2
Phone: (902) 733-2280
http://www.pc.gc.ca/

Gallery of Costume
Platt Hall
Rusholme
Manchester M14 5LL
http://www.manchestergalleries.org/our-other-venues/platt-hall-gallery-of-costume/

London Sewing Machine Museum
292-312 Balham High Road
Tooting Bec
London SW17 7AA
http://www.sewantique.com/

McCord Museum of Canadian History
690 Sherbrooke Street West
Montreal, QUE, Canada H3A 1E9
Phone: (514) 398-7100
http://www.mccord-museum.qc.ca/en/

The Metropolitan Museum of Art
1000 Fifth Avenue
New York, NY 10028-0198
Phone: (212) 535-7710
http://www.metmuseum.org/visitor/index.asp

Musee Carnavalet—Histoire de Paris
23 rue de Sévigné
75003 Paris
http://www.paris.fr/portail/Culture/Portal.lut?page_id=6468

Museo del Tessuto
Via Santa Chiara 24
59100 Prato (PO), Italia
Phone: +39 0574 611503
http://www.museodeltessuto.it

Museo Rubelli
Venice
Phone: +39 041-2417329
e-mail: museo@rubelli.com

Museo Stibbert
Via Stibbert 26
50134 Firenze
info@museostibbert.it

Museum of Greek Costume
7, Dimokritou Street
Kolonaki
Athens
http://www.athensinfoguide.com/wtsmuseums/greekcostume.htm

Pitti Palace Costume Collection
Florence
www.polomuseale.firenze.it

Royal Ceremonial Dress Collection
Kensington Palace
London W8 4PX
Phone: +44 (0)207 937 956
http://www.hrp.org.uk/

Royal Ontario Museum
100 Queen's Park
Toronto, ONT, Canada
M5S 2C6
Canada
www.rom.on.ca

The Shoe Museum
C&J Clark Ltd.
40 High Street
Somerset BA16 0YA

The Textile Museum
2320 S Street, NW
Washington, DC 20008-4088
Phone: (202) 667-0441
Fax: (202) 483-0994
http://www.textilemuseum.org/

Textile Museum of Canada
55 Centre Ave.
Toronto, ONT, Canada M5G 2H5
Phone: (416) 599-5321
info@textilemuseum.ca

Totnes Costume Museum
Bogan House
43 High Street
Totnes

SPECIALIZED COSTUME LIBRARIES

Centro Studi del Tessuto e del Costume di Palazzo Mocenigo, Venice: seven thousand volumes focusing on textile and costume history and textile collections from the sixteenth to twentieth centuries. http://www.museiciviciveneziani.it.

Metropolitan Museum of Art, New York, Antonio Ratti Textile Center and Reference Library: The reference library of the Textile Center contains approximately 3,400 books and journals related to the historical, technical, and cultural study of textiles. http://www.metmuseum.org/research.

Metropolitan Museum of Art, New York, Irene Lewisohn Costume Reference Library: One of the most important fashion libraries in the world, with 30,000 items related to clothing history. http://www.metmuseum.org/research.

Textile Museum, Arthur D. Jenkins Library of Textile Arts, Washington, D.C.: The materials preserved in the library's holdings, such as books, periodicals, and slides, cover every aspect related to textile and costume history, textile structures and techniques, and textile conservation. http://www.textilemuseum.org/library.htm.

COSTUME HISTORY SOCIETIES

There are a number of historical societies devoted to the study of costume history. In the United States, the Costume Society of America has a worldwide membership that represents interests in historical as well as historical theatrical costumes. This group meets every year for a national symposium that allows its members to share in the exciting developments in the areas of clothing history. Lectures and working sessions make the event highly worthwhile. The periodical *Dress* is a publication of the society. A similar organization in the United Kingdom is the British Costume Association, which also produces a journal, *Costume*, and has numerous events throughout the year for those interested in the study of clothing history.

About the Editor and Contributors

Jill Condra has taught clothing and textile history at the University of British Columbia, the University of Prince Edward Island, and the University of Manitoba. Her costume research has been largely based on using material history models to look at clothing in historical context, which has allowed her to do research at the most exciting costume collections around the world. Condra has also co-written a book on textiles called *Guide to Textiles for Interiors*, Third Edition. She is currently an independent scholar living in Minneapolis, MN, and Winnipeg, Canada.

Sara M. Harvey holds a master's degree in costume studies from New York University and currently teaches fashion design at the International Academy of Art and Technology in Nashville, Tennessee. She is also freelance costume designer and a novelist.

Ellen Hymowitz is a New York–based freelance researcher in fashion and art. She has degrees from Princeton University (A.B., English) and the Fashion Institute of Technology (M.A., Museum Studies).

Jennifer Grayer Moore is an art historian with special interests in the history and iconography of dress. She resides in Manhattan, where she teaches art history and the history of fashion at the Art Institute of New York City.

Index